Examining Japan's Lost Decades

This book examines five features of Japan's "lost decades": the speed of the economic decline in Japan compared to Japan's earlier global prowess, a rapidly declining population, considerable political instability and failed reform attempts, shifting balances of power in the region and changing relations with Asian neighboring nations, and the lingering legacy of World War II. Addressing the question of why the decades were lost, this book offers 15 new perspectives ranging from economics to ideology and beyond. Investigating problems such as the risk-averse behavior of Japan's bureaucracy and the absence of strong political leadership, the authors analyze how the delay of "loss-cutting policies" led to the 1997 financial crisis and a state of political gridlock, in which policymakers could not decide on firm strategies that would benefit national interests.

To discuss the rebuilding of Japan, the authors argue that it is first essential to critically examine Japan's lost decades, and this book offers a comprehensive overview of Japan's recent twenty years of crisis. The book reveals that the problem of the lost decades is not an issue unique to the Japanese context but has global relevance, and its study can provide important insights into challenges being faced in other mature economies. With chapters written by some of the world's leading Japan specialists and focusing on a variety of disciplines, this book will be of interest to students and scholars in the areas of Japan studies, politics, international relations, security studies, government policy, and history.

Yoichi Funabashi is Chairman of the Rebuild Japan Initiative Foundation and a former editor-in-chief for the *Asahi Shimbun*.

Barak Kushner is Senior Lecturer at the University of Cambridge, UK.

Routledge Contemporary Japan Series

The world is still trying to understand what went on in Japan's "Lost Decades", a topic that has become all the more relevant as much of the west succumbs to Japan-style problems of deflation and low growth. This collection of essays by experts in their field will help the reader pick through this important subject. For readers seeking to understand Japan and for ones wondering whether "Japanization" is coming to a country near them, this should prove a fascinating read.

David Pilling, *Financial Times*

This book contains a superb and timely collection of essays on the troubles Japan has been having, economically and politically, since the 1990s. The period coincides with the ending of the Cold War and the acceleration of economic globalization. The studies show how a nation that seemed to fare so well during the Cold War has stagnated in a globalizing world. As the editors note, Japan's example could be followed by other countries and deserves serious attention.

Akira Iriye, *Harvard University, USA*

Examining Japan's Lost Decades

Edited by Yoichi Funabashi and Barak Kushner

Routledge
Taylor & Francis Group

LONDON AND NEW YORK

First published 2015
by Routledge
2 Park Square, Milton Park, Abingdon, Oxon OX14 4RN

and by Routledge
711 Third Avenue, New York, NY 10017

*Routledge is an imprint of the Taylor & Francis Group,
an informa business*

British Library Cataloguing in Publication Data
A catalogue record for this book is available from the British Library

Library of Congress Cataloging-in-Publication Data
A catalog record for this book has been requested

ISBN: 978-1-138-88575-2 (hbk)
ISBN: 978-1-138-88580-6 (pbk)
ISBN: 978-1-315-71522-3 (ebk)

Typeset in Times New Roman
by Apex CoVantage, LLC

Printed and bound in Great Britain by
CPI Group (UK) Ltd, Croydon, CR0 4YY

Contents

Figures

Tables

Preface

The Rebuild Japan Initiative Foundation (RJIF) is an independent think tank that was established in September 2011. On March 11 of the same year, Japan confronted a major national crisis caused by the earthquake and tsunami in the northeast region of the country. These natural disasters led to a further catastrophe with the Fukushima nuclear power plant accident and meltdown. Back then I strongly felt that Japan's "lost decades," which plagued the country since the 1990s, had bottomed out. I believed that Japan's institutional culture and its social systems harbored serious problems across many sectors – including risk management, governance, and leadership.

I opted to christen the think tank with the word "Rebuild" because Japan suffered a major loss due to its lumbering efforts to respond to the accident. Japan was, in a sense, beset by both the natural causes and social structures that, in part, led to the accident. At that moment, I understood Japan as nothing less, consequently, than a defeated country. The only way to start afresh was to rebuild.

The think tank's first task was to probe the causes of the Fukushima nuclear accident, to investigate the social and structural causes that were responsible for the accident, and to examine the state of Japan's crisis management plans in light of how it responded to the situation. On the basis of these analyses, we carved out lessons and offered proposals concerning new safety regulations. We were able to quickly publish our results in February 2012, first in Japanese and later in English in 2014, as *The Fukushima Daiichi Nuclear Power Station Disaster: Investigating the Myth and Reality*. Upon completing the final report of our Independent Investigation Commission on the Fukushima Nuclear Accident, I strongly felt the necessity for a thorough study of Japan's lost decades. This need arose because the more we explored the causes and background behind the Fukushima nuclear accident, the more they seemed to overlap – seemingly from their very genesis to their conclusion – with the underlying causes of Japan's lost decades.

The lost decades project began in the spring of 2013. I imposed several important conditions upon setting up the research team and framing the investigation and surveys. First, I opted for authors who are considered prominent specialists in their respective fields. Second, I included both Japanese and non-Japanese authors. Third, with a global audience in mind, I thought that results had to be published in English first. Fourth, I also asked a top-class English-language editor to assist in the production. Fifth and finally, I set up a working group made up of leading young researchers, who assisted the authors in organizing their arguments, gathering research material, and conducting interviews. I was pleased that the project proceeded along the goals I set and satisfied my ambition. All of the authors are incredibly busy and as many as three of them also work as university deans. I would like to express my sincere appreciation to everyone for their participation while they simultaneously grappled with their own strenuous work schedules.

Having Dr. Barak Kushner, a historian specializing in the history of modern Japan and a senior lecturer at the University of Cambridge, was a piece of unexpected good fortune. As the project's deputy editor, Dr. Kushner repeatedly flew to Japan in 2013 to assist. He not only assisted in running our May 2013 international conference with the authors, but also during the duration of the project kept up a continual exchange of ideas with the authors and the working group members concerning the content and scope of the project, striving to arrive at a shared consensus over the issues at hand. This book would have not been possible without Dr. Kushner's selfless contribution and for this I would like to offer my deepest thanks.

Members of the working group debated the issues at hand for so many hours at RJIF headquarters that it became like a second home. They also submitted detailed reports and were in constant contact with the Foundation. I gratefully acknowledge their labor and participation. The members of the working group are: Dr. Aizawa Nobuhiro, Dr. Ken Hijino, Horio Kenta, Igata Akira, Dr. Murai Tetsuya, Nikkuni Shinichi, Dr. Shimoda Hiraku, Uchiyama Hiroyuki, and Jan Zelezny. In addition, journalist Nishizaki Kaoru, Senior Global Correspondent at the *Asahi Newspaper*, served as an advisor to the working group and deftly added to our debates and discussion. I offer my heartfelt thanks for his support.

The lost decades project's staff director, RJIF fellow Kitazawa Kay, also headed our project on the Fukushima nuclear accident. Her professional attitude, as one who always kept her poise in the midst of whatever hardship, has once again seamlessly brought the work to completion. Researcher Takezawa Rie skillfully assisted the English manuscripts and gave much of her time.

RJIF's financial support is entirely dependent on private companies and I would like to once again express my deep gratitude to the companies that support us. We have also twice received generous grants from the U.S.-Japan Foundation to whom we need to offer thanks.

In conclusion, on September 26, 2014, I was sadly informed that one of our authors, Dr. Kitazawa Koichi, President of Tokyo Metropolitan University, had unfortunately passed away. Dr. Kitazawa had taken the reigns of our civilian research team committee, which examined the causes behind the Fukushima nuclear power plant accident. The fact that our final investigative report on the accident became known throughout the world was due to Dr. Kitazawa's unrelenting efforts. It fills me with a great sadness that I will no longer be able to see his warm and almost fatherly reflection. I would like to use this opportunity to express my deepest condolences.

Funabashi Yoichi
October 1, 2014
Chairman, Rebuild Japan Initiative Foundation

Contributors

AKIYAMA Nobumasa is a Professor of International Politics at the Graduate School of Law and School of International and Public Policy at Hitotsubashi University, Tokyo. Dr. Akiyama is also an Adjunct Fellow of the Japan Institute of International Affairs.

Shiro Armstrong is Co-director of the Australia-Japan Research Centre and Director of the East Asian Bureau of Economic Research at the Crawford School of Public Policy at the Australian National University. He specializes in East Asian economic integration and the East Asian economies. He is Editor of the *East Asia Forum* and *East Asia Forum Quarterly*.

Peter Drysdale is Emeritus Professor of Economics, Head of the East Asia Bureau of Economic Research, and Co-editor of *East Asian Forum* in the Crawford School of Public Policy in the College of Asia and the Pacific at the Australian National University.

FUNABASHI Yoichi is the Chairman of the Rebuild Japan Initiative Foundation and former editor-in-chief and columnist for the *Asahi Shimbun*. He is also a contributing editor of *Foreign Policy*. In 1985 he received the Vaughn-Ueda Prize for his reporting on international affairs. He won the Japan Press Award, Japan's "Pulitzer Prize," in 1994 for his columns on foreign policy, and his articles in *Foreign Affairs* and *Foreign Policy* won the Ishibashi Tanzan Prize in 1992. He is the author of several award-winning books including *Alliance Adrift* (Council on Foreign Relations Press, 1998, winner of the Shincho Arts and Sciences Award), *Asia-Pacific Fusion: Japan's Role in APEC* (Institute for International Economics, 1995, winner of the Mainichi Shimbun Asia Pacific Grand Prix Award), and others.

Andrew Gordon is the Lee and Juliet Folger Fund Professor of History at Harvard University. He works on the history of modern Japan, and is currently working on a study of the postwar transformations that culminated in the period described as lost decades.

Michael J. Green is Senior Vice President for Asia/Japan Chair at the Center for Strategic & International Studies and Associate Professor in the Edmund A. Walsh School of Foreign Service at Georgetown University. His current research and writing is focused on Asian regional architecture, Japanese politics, U.S. foreign policy history, the Korean peninsula, Tibet, Burma, and U.S.-India relations.

G. John Ikenberry is the Albert G. Milbank Professor of Politics and International Affairs at Princeton University in the Department of Politics and the Woodrow Wilson School of Public and International Affairs. He serves as Co-director of Princeton's Center for International Security Studies. Ikenberry is the author of seven books, including *Liberal Leviathan: The Origins, Crisis, and Transformation of the American System* (Princeton, 2011); *After Victory: Institutions, Strategic Restraint, and the Rebuilding of Order after Major Wars* (Princeton, 2001); and *Crisis of American Foreign Policy: Wilsonianism in the 21st Century* (Princeton, 2009). His most recent book is *The Rise of Korean Leadership: Emerging Powers and the Liberal International Order* (Palgrave, 2013).

IWAISAKO Tokuo is a Professor at the Institute of Economic Research, Hitotsubashi University. He also teaches finance and macroeconomics in the Department of Economics and at Hitotsubashi's Business School (*Graduate School of International Corporate Strategy*). He held the position of Principal Economist at the Institute of Policy Research, Ministry of Finance, Japan, from April 2009 to March 2011. Professor Iwaisako earned his Ph.D. in economics from Harvard University in 1997.

KARIYA Takehiko is a Professor in the Sociology of Japanese Society at Oxford University and a Fellow of St. Antony's College. He has conducted sociological studies of education, social stratification and social mobility, school-to-work transition, and the social influence of education policies in Japan. He recently published *Education Reform and Social Class in Japan* (Routledge, 2013).

KITAZAWA Koichi was President of Tokyo City University and the former president of the Japan Science and Technology Agency. He served as chairman of the Independent Investigation Commission on the Nuclear Accident of the Tokyo Electric Daiichi Nuclear Power Station founded by the Japan Rebuild Initiative Foundation.

KOBAYASHI Keiichiro is Professor in the Faculty of Economics at Keio University. He received a Ph.D. in economics from the University of Chicago in 1998. He researches macroeconomic theory. He currently works on theoretical models of financial crises and monetary theory. He joined the Ministry of International Trade and Industry of Japan in 1991, and from 2013 he has been a Professor at Keio University.

Kenneth Kuttner is the Robert F. White Class of 1952 Professor of Economics at Williams College, in Williamstown, Massachusetts. His research has addressed a range of monetary policy issues, such as the impact of interest rates on financial markets, policy implementation and transmission, and inflation targeting.

MACHIDORI Satoshi is Professor of Political Science in the Graduate School of Law at Kyoto University. He obtained his Ph.D. in law from Kyoto University in 2003 and he has taught there since 2007, focusing on comparative political institutions. His publications include *Shusho Seiji no Seido Bunseki* [The Japanese Premiership: An Institutional Analysis of the Power Relations] in Japanese, which was awarded the Suntory Prize in 2012.

Adam Posen is President of the Peterson Institute for International Economics, the world's leading independent think tank on economics and globalization. He received his Ph.D. from Harvard University and is a member of the Council on Foreign Relations, of the Trilateral Commission, and of the faculty of the World Economic Forum. The author and editor of five books, he has been the recipient of major grants and research fellowships from the American Academy in Berlin, the Bank of England, the Brookings Institution, the European Commission, the Ford Foundation, the Sloan Foundation, and the U.S. National Science Foundation.

SEIKE Atsushi is President of Keio University, Tokyo. He obtained his Ph.D. in business and commerce from Keio in 1993 and became a Professor in Keio's Faculty of Business and Commerce in 1992, serving as Dean from 2007 to 2009. He is a specialist in labor economics and the author of numerous books. He has received a number of academic prizes including a Commendation of Excellent Labor Related Publications Prize and the Yomiuri Shimbun Prize in 1994. Currently, he is also a member of the Labor Policy Council and Chairman of the Policy Studies Group for the Aged Society.

SHIRAISHI Takashi is President of the National Graduate Institute for Policy Studies (GRIPS) and President of the JETRO Institute of Developing Economies. He has taught at the University of Tokyo, Cornell University, and Kyoto University. He served as a standing executive member for the Council for Science and Technology Policy, a Japanese cabinet office.

Sheila A. Smith is the Senior Fellow for Japan Studies at the Council on Foreign Relations (CFR). Based in Washington, DC. She is an expert on Japanese politics and foreign policy, and she is the author of *Intimate Rivals: Japanese Domestic Politics and a Rising China* (Columbia University Press, 2015).

TOGO Kazuhiko is Professor and Director of the Institute for World Affairs, Kyoto Sangyo University and the author of numerous books in Japanese and English. He served in the Japanese Foreign Ministry and devoted half of his career to Russian affairs. After his retirement in 2002, he works mainly on Japan's foreign policy, territorial and historical memory issues, and conflict in East Asia.

TOYAMA Kazuhiko is CEO and Representative Director of Industrial Growth Platform, Inc. With a background in business and a reputation as an innovator, he founded this company in 2007 and has seen it thrive by providing management support services to struggling companies and offering strategies for long-term, sustainable business operations. He is a member of Japan's Council on Economic Fiscal Policy and the Council for Science and Technology's Basic Plan Special Committee.

Researchers and project office

AIZAWA Nobuhiro
Researcher, JETRO Institute of Developing Economies

Ken Leonard Victor HIJINO
Associate Professor, Graduate School of System, Design and Management, Keio University

HORIO Kenta
Ph.D candidate, Department of Nuclear Engineering and Management School of Engineering, the University of Tokyo

IGATA Akira
Doctoral student, the Department of Law, Keio University

IWAISAKO Tokuo
Professor, Institute of Economic Research, Hitotsubashi University

KITAZAWA Kay (Staff Director)
Senior Fellow, Rebuild Japan Initiative Foundation

MURAI Tetsuya
Part-time Lecturer, the School of Law, Meiji University

NIKKUNI Shinichi
Manager, Industrial Growth Platform, Inc. (IGPI)

Andrea Ryoko NINOMIYA
Research assistant, Rebuild Japan Initiative Foundation

NISHIZAKI Kaoru (Advisor)
Senior Global Correspondent, the *Asahi Shimbun*

OZEKI Hiromi
Assistant, Rebuild Japan Initiative Foundation

Giulio Pugliese
Editorial Assistant, Rebuild Japan Initiative Foundation

SHIMODA Hiraku
Associate Professor, Faculty of Law, Waseda University

SHIOMI Yoko
Editorial Assistant, Rebuild Japan Initiative Foundation

TAKEZAWA Rie
Researcher, Rebuild Japan Initiative Foundation

TANAKA Akiko
Editorial Assistant, Rebuild Japan Initiative Foundation

TSUCHIYA Emi
Assistant, Rebuild Japan Initiative Foundation

UCHIYAMA Hiroyuki
Professor, Faculty of Social Work, Japan College of Social Work

Jan ZELEZNY
Manager, Industrial Growth Platform, Inc. (IGPI)

Introduction

The start of Japan's lost decades coincided almost exactly with the death of Emperor Hirohito in 1989 – and thus the dawn of a new era, that of his son, Emperor Akihito. This is perhaps one of the great ironies of history. Hirohito's long reign, marked by Japan's Fifteen Years War (1931–1945) and its complicated legacy, had finally ended. A new emperor, appropriate for the new Constitution of Japan, had ascended the throne. Moreover, the Cold War was just coming to an end. Throughout the world, people eagerly anticipated a new world order that would pay a "peace dividend." Who would have thought that Hirohito's death would actually be followed by an era pregnant with both economic stagnation and political instability?

Needless to say, Japan did not plunge directly into a deep economic recession at the end of the 1980s, nor did the bursting of its economic "bubble" mean that recession was inevitable. As Kuttner, Iwaisako, and Posen underscore in Chapter 2, Japan's Great Recession of 1990–2003 and the subsequent fifteen years of deflation since 1998 were avoidable. Looking at the lost decades shows us that few of the turn of events that occurred during the post-bubble era were preordained by fate, though they may seem so in retrospect. In fact, at various times a multitude of policy options were available that could have led to a variety of different outcomes.

Sadly, the first lost decade in the 1990s was followed by yet another lost decade in the twenty-first century. On the heels of this long downturn, the March 11, 2011, disaster occurred. A powerful earthquake in northeastern Japan, followed by a massive tsunami, which caused a meltdown at the Fukushima nuclear power plant, plunged Japan into its worst crisis since the end of World War II. China's rise to great power status and its aggressive diplomatic posture, along with the territorial disputes over the Senkaku Islands in 2010 and 2012, also shook Japan. The situation appeared dire just when the Japanese people had become keenly aware that they seemed to be drifting without any sense of direction. Many feared that this situation might continue forever. To some, the disasters and the tense political environment only sharpened their sense of the urgent need to bring Japan's lost decades to an end. For others, the events aggravated an even deeper sense of resignation.

How should Japanese policymakers have reacted – have they made any significant efforts to revitalize Japan or have they just accepted a gentle national decline? The inauguration of Prime Minister Abe Shinzo's second administration in December 2012 and the adoption of the economic measures known collectively as "Abenomics" were the result of a general sense that Japan had arrived at a critical juncture in its history. The campaign slogan for the Liberal Democratic Party (LDP) in the general elections of 2012 was "Take Back Japan!" and voters gave the LDP a landslide victory. This slogan was used during the Upper House election in July 2013, and again the LDP won a large number of seats. But what was it that was to be "taken back"? Was it nostalgia for the "good old years" of the postwar period, when the Japanese economy had been expanding, leading the country toward prosperity? Or was it traditional Japanese culture and customs, which had supposedly disappeared during the postwar decades? Or was it, in fact, Japan's power and national pride, which had been restrained during Japan's long postwar era? The aim and content of the slogan remained ambiguous, but it resounded throughout Abe's campaign, an appeal that unmistakably epitomized Japan's lost decades. As is now clear, the Abe administration immediately got to grips with the ramifications of the lost decades, implementing antideflationary policies and adopting a strong posture toward Japan's neighbors, including China and South Korea. Abe's policies may succeed in bringing Japan's "losses" or "lost decades" to an end. At this time, however, it is not clear how these policies will affect the status quo, and Japan's lost decades do not appear to have concluded.

The lost decades: Truth or illusion?

When visiting Japan, many foreigners are puzzled: despite all the stories, the economy seems on an even keel. Visitors scratch their heads in surprise: is the narrative of the lost decades true? The relative calmness and apparent social stability in Japan, even after such a long recession, is indeed remarkable. Japanese society is resilient. Asia correspondent for the *Financial Times*, David Pilling, recently wrote a book on Japan's lost decades with a rather upbeat title: *Bending Adversity – Japan and the Art of Survival*. The author quotes Japanese novelist Murakami Haruki: "We are lost and we don't know which way we should go. But this is a very natural thing, a very healthy thing."[1] In other words, the postwar Japanese social model was an old, dysfunctional model, and so it was only natural that such a model should be lost. Such loss should, in Murakami's view, be welcomed.

However, during the 1990s and 2000s no one was the wiser that Japan's models might be old and outdated and such thinking had no part in political thinking in Japan. If it had, such ideas might have served as a wellspring for possible alternatives for policy choices. Why were alternative models not given more serious consideration, and why did they not ripen into practical plans? Such questions go to the very heart of Japan's lost decades. In Chapter 8, Machidori Satoshi looks on the political side at some of these reforms and what happened. The essays in this book were all written in an effort to put the concept of the lost decades under a critical microscope and to try to elucidate answers to these questions. The Japanese people already perceive the term "lost decades" as the best way to describe these past two decades in Japanese history, as vividly demonstrated by a 2009 *Asahi Newspaper* public opinion poll. When asked about their images of prewar, postwar, and present (post-1989) Japan, respondents stated that they had the most positive view of the postwar period (1945–1989) until Emperor Hirohito's death, which was regarded as "vibrant" and "progressive." By contrast, the images they had of the prewar period (1926–1945) were "conservative" and "dark." Most remarkably, the "stagnant" and "dark" images that respondents associated with post-1989 Japan (Japan after Emperor Hirohito died) surpassed those of prewar era. In other words, life in contemporary Japan is perceived as harsher than that of the prewar period, characterized as it was by fascism and a military ideology.[2]

As Japan's recession has continued, other countries have become increasingly conscious that Japan had lost its way. Since the second half of the 1990s, perhaps as successive Japanese governments proved themselves unable to deal with nonperforming loans (NPLs) and as deflation became ever more severe, interest in Japan's lost decades has deepened. In April 2002, on the eve of Prime Minister Koizumi Junichiro's state visit to China, Chinese Premier Zhu Rongji was reported to have said: "Whoever manages to put the Japanese economy back on track, will certainly win the Nobel Prize."[3] Under Koizumi, Japan finally dealt with its NPLs and resumed economic growth. Unfortunately, Koizumi's reforms did not take root. The Koizumi years were characterized by an increase in the number of nonregular workers and layoffs, as summarized by some who defined its economy as "growth without employment." As a consequence, the Japanese people were unable to feel the benefits of economic growth. Kobayashi Keiichiro examines such issues on the macroeconomic level in Chapter 3, while Toyama Kazuhiko analyzes the situation at the micro level in Chapter 4.

In the United States and Europe, especially after the Lehman Shock, the expression "turning Japanese" was used with increasing frequency, and in a cautionary sense – as something that Western countries should avoid. That is to say, they had to avoid following in the footsteps of Japan and letting their economies plunge into decades of stagnation. In October 2008, after the collapse of Lehmann Brothers, a meeting of the Federal Reserve's Federal Open Market Committee (FOMC) was convened and president and CEO of the Federal Reserve Bank of San Francisco, Janet Yellen, called for a more aggressive policy of monetary relaxation: "Historical precedents," she said, "such as the case of Japan, teach us that it is a mistake to act cautiously as the economy unravels."[4] In 2010, economist Paul Krugman wrote in the *New York Times*, in a column with the title "Lost Decade Looming?": "Despite a chorus of voices claiming otherwise, we (i.e., the developed economies) aren't Greece. We are, however, looking more and more like Japan."[5] A July 2011 issue of the *Economist* also produced a special issue that carried representations of U.S. President Barack Obama and German Chancellor Angela Merkel wearing traditional Japanese clothes on its cover, followed by the title: "Turning Japanese."[6] Prime Minister Noda Yoshihiko would later recall how shocked he had been by that title.[7] Similarly, Fareed Zakaria has expressed the following caution over the deepening crisis in Western democracies, which face the challenges of "budgetary pressures, political paralysis, and demographic stress."

> There once was an advanced industrial democracy that could not reform. It went from dominating the world economy to growing for two decades at the anemic average rate of just 0.8 percent. Many members of its aging, well-educated population continued to live pleasant lives, but they left an increasingly barren legacy for future generations. Its debt burden is now staggering, and its per capita income has dropped to 24th in the world and is falling. If the Americans and the Europeans fail to get their acts together, their future will be easy to see. All they have to do is look at Japan.[8]

As these examples suggest, "turning Japanese" described the situation of countries that were in their own turn starting to face the very same issues that had plagued Japan – including an ageing population, NPLs, rising public debt and deflation, an inability to deal with the impact of globalization on employment, income gaps, and a growing share of public debt placed on the shoulders of younger generations. As China's high-growth era shows signs of reaching an impasse, there are fears that it too might suffer lost decades similar to Japan, and some have now also begun to issue cautions to China about "turning Japanese." Reuters columnist, Andy Mukherjee, in a column titled "The Lessons for China from Japan's Lost Decade," described China's situation as follows: "[The Chinese] economy today has three big similarities with Japan in the late 1980s: High and rising debt, diminishing export competitiveness and an ageing society. China can avoid slipping into Japan's deflationary hole, but only if it learns from Tokyo's failure to cleanse its banking system."[9] Japan's fate now appears to be held up as a negative role model for a number of other countries.

A great many attempts were taken to analyze the many facets of Japan's lost decades and to offer policy remedies. This period in fact saw a succession of reforms. Nonetheless, no real effort was made to understand Japan's lost decades holistically, not only from the perspective of demographics, fiscal and monetary policies, and management, but from all sides, including politics, foreign policy and security, ideas, and ideology. In Japan, reviews of government and legislators' public policy failures by committees made up of third party specialists, and attempts to extract lessons, tend to be unsatisfactory. This is partly due to weak government oversight functions held by the Diet.

The Fukushima nuclear accident in March 2011 changed all this. Following the accident, three investigative commissions were set up by the Cabinet, by the Diet, and by an independent body. All three commissions attempted to analyze and shed light on the underlying and structural causes that led to the accident. Among the three, the Diet investigation commission holds investigative powers and it is in fact the first time the Diet's government oversight function has been exercised in this fashion. Ahead of the Diet commission was the independent investigation commission, which was managed by the Rebuild Japan Initiative

Foundation (RJIF).[10] We are proud that the commission's independent investigation contributed to an increased interest concerning the need to probe Japan's public policies. RJIF's project on Japan's lost decades is similarly centered on public policy evaluation.

During the lost decades, the governments of Japan changed at a bewildering speed. It was not rare for newly installed administrations to resign before they even had a chance to implement the new policy plans they had formulated. Neither the government nor the Diet confronted the effects, or lack thereof, of the various policies taken under different administrations. No progress was made in policy research either. Such failures represent the breakdown of policy think tanks as well. In addition to providing information on Japan's case, and offering examples to other countries around the globe, many of whom are now going through a version of their own lost decades, concerning what to avoid, we wanted to make sure to analyze the issues in their original context. We wanted to ask ourselves what were the issues that Japan was grappling with during this period, perhaps for the first time in its history. What did not work? And why? What should we call into question?

On the basis of these sorts of queries, in 2012 the Rebuild Japan Initiative Foundation assembled a team of researchers from around the world and conducted long discussions that resulted in this book. Japan's lost decades coincided with the end of the Cold War and the start of the "post–Cold War era" and "post–Cold War world." In December 1990, the value of shares on the Tokyo Stock Exchange plunged, and this marked the beginning of the collapse of the bubble economy. In Japan, these years closely overlapped with the beginning of Japan after the death of Emperor Hirohito, but most Japanese people did not notice that this new era differed in nature from the postwar era. In fact, the Japanese people probably began to feel that the "long postwar" had undergone radical changes only by the fiftieth anniversary of the end of World War II, in 1995. In the same year Japan was hit by the Kobe earthquake and the Tokyo subway sarin gas terrorist attack; on both occasions the government was extremely slow to respond. In the January 1995 Kobe earthquake, it was reported that the first group to distribute water, food, and blankets were the *yakuza*, or organized crime syndicates (sometimes dubbed the "Japanese mafia"), and there is a general sense that volunteer efforts far surpassed those of the government. The earthquake exposed the complete lack of crisis management capabilities – the negligence – on the part of Japanese authorities. In 1995 the term "lost decade" had yet to be coined, but these events radically shook trust in the government. The March 1995 Aum Shinrikyo sarin gas attack deepened the nation's mistrust of feckless political leaders unable to defend the people, bringing the degraded state of the nation and of society to the forefront of people's consciousness and tearing down Japan's myth of domestic safety. The fanatical behavior of Aum Shinrikyo believers exposed the fact that some people despise the world so much they feel impelled to destroy it. The sarin gas attack offered a glimpse of the social and psychological dislocation of some of Japan's younger generation. And as Robert Jay Lifton notes, people's "diffuse Aum-related anxiety now became part of a larger constellation of fears about earthquakes, economic recession or depression, weakening family ties, and increasing domestic and social violence."[11]

The next major watershed moment came around 1998, when the financial crisis grew more severe. In the years following 1998, deflation in Japan turned chronic – in other words, deflation became structural. Despite some years during the Koizumi administration when there was economic recovery, economic stagnation basically continued for more than twenty years. As pointed out by Kuttner, Iwaisako, and Posen in Chapter 2, macroeconomic policy failures from 1999 to 2012 resulted from fundamental governance problems in Japan. Another key moment came in 2011 with the earthquake in northeastern Japan, the tsunami, and the resulting Fukushima nuclear power plant disasters. The latter in particular exposed the myth of absolute nuclear safety that had been advanced by Japan's "nuclear village," a cozy collection of politicians, bureaucrats, businessmen, and scholars who advocated nuclear energy. The Fukushima nuclear disaster revealed the deficiencies of Japanese institutions in risk preparedness and the problems in governance and overall leadership, as well as the closed-minded and insular institutional culture prevalent in Japan, often referred to as the "Galapagos syndrome." It became clear to everyone that the "Japanese model" lacked the capacity to deal with national emergencies, because Japan had never directly confronted them in the postwar period. As Shirai Satoshi noted, decades after the end of the war, the tragic state of things in 2011 gave people a feeling of desperation, which we have to say is epitomized by the word "defeat."[12]

To summarize: The seeds of the lost decades were sown in 1989 and 1990, just after the death of Emperor Hirohito and just before the collapse of the bubble economy. The loss of confidence began with the shock to the national psyche following the 1995 Kobe earthquake and the Tokyo subway sarin gas attack, intensified during the 1997–98 financial crisis, and became absolutely entrenched after the 2011 earthquake and the ensuing Fukushima nuclear accident. In the end, all these events led people to seriously question whether Japan could ever break away from the morass of its lost decades – or whether it would simply sink even deeper. The often-heard definition of Abenomics as Japan's "last chance" reflects the expectations and insecurities stemming from this feeling that Japan has almost completely lost its way.

When discussing the lost decades, we need to define what was "lost." First, we can say that substance was lost. There are two kinds of such losses: absolute losses, or numerical and quantitative losses in absolute terms; and relative loss, or decline, due to the rise of the rest of the world while Japan stagnated. A classic example of loss in absolute terms is the drop in birthrate and Japan's overall population decline, as Seike Atsushi describes in Chapter 1. The fertility rate continued to decrease throughout the 1990s and has dropped to the 1.2 level. The working-age population started to decline after peaking in 1995 (87.17 million people). Japan's total population also started to decline after peaking in 2008 (128.08 million people). One could say that the clearest indicator and also, perhaps, perpetrator, of the lost decades was demographic decline. Along with demographic decline, there was the loss of economic growth. The loss of the value of stocks and property following the collapse of the bubble was as high as 2.9 times Japan's gross domestic product (GDP), a loss in asset value that was greater than during America's Great Depression that followed "Black Thursday" in 1929.[13] During this period, Japan suffered long-term deflation that had no previous equivalent in the world. The average yearly economic growth from 1992 to 2001 in Japan amounted to just 0.8 percent. By the end of October 1997, the yield to maturity on five-year interest bonds dropped to 1.11 percent, breaking the all-time global record low.

On February 12, 1999, following eight full hours of discussion over a Monetary Policy Meeting, the Bank of Japan (BoJ) decided to adopt a zero interest-rate policy (ZIRP), the first such decision by a central bank. However, loans to Japanese firms did not increase as intended, and for ten years since 1995 the total value of bank loans dropped to 30 percent. Banks hoarded government bonds rather than making loans, and during this period the ratio of loans to deposits in so-called city banks – Japan's large commercial banks – dropped from roughly 80 percent during the pre-2000 years, to 60 percent in 2010.[14] The government implemented numerous fiscal stimulus packages but gained limited results. In the meantime, social security spending increased, adding to government deficits and the public debt. The public debt to GDP ratio leaped from 71 percent in 1992 to 230 percent in 2011, a threefold increase. Nonetheless, the government continued issuing bonds. During this period, and for over ten years, the Japanese government was able to float bonds that had interest rates lower than 1 percent. According to financial analyst Peter Tasker, Japan's prolonged public financing at such low interest rates was the first case since ancient Babylonia.[15] The collapse of Japan's economic bubble generated a massive amount of nonperforming loans (NPLs) that weighed down the Japanese economy. Yet, from 1992 to 1997 the disposal of NPLs continued to be postponed and only the failure of major financial institutions in 1997 and 1998 forced a change. From the end of the 1990s, deflation had turned into chronic deflation. From 1999 to 2012, consumer prices fell by 0.3 percent every year.

At the start of the twenty-first century, depopulation and deflation started to draw dividends on Japan's economic malaise. During this period, Japan's declining population and deflationary economy had the heaviest impact on the countryside. A strong yen led to manufacturing offshoring, a drop in public works resulted in a sharp decrease in construction projects, and Japan's shrinking population caused sluggish consumption. All of the above weakened the economic and labor market foundations of Japan's rural areas. This phenomenon was the flipside to the overconcentration of people in Tokyo that has become especially marked since 2000. Overconcentration in Tokyo is evident from the large number of enterprises listed on the Tokyo Exchange Market, the total amount of bank deposits and loans, sales in information and advertising industries, and the number of university students. There has been a population shift, made up especially of young people, moving from the countryside to big urban centers, Tokyo in particular.

What about employment?

Japanese companies embarked on full-scale restructuring of their businesses in 1998. The aim was to deal with the three excesses of "employment, debt, and equipment," with particular emphasis on the reduction of personnel costs through adjustments in the employment system. Regular employment, which supported Japan's prosperity in the postwar years, was reduced and irregular employment increased. While the irregular-to-regular employment ratio was 20.2 percent (8.81 million people) of the total workforce in 1990, this ratio increased to 35.1 percent (18.11 million people) in 2011.[16] Corporate activities also lost their former momentum as a result of population decline, deflation, market contraction, increasing social security expenses, yen appreciation, and other factors. Japan's international competitiveness and return on equity also declined. In 1990, Japan was the world leader in international competitiveness. In 2011, Japan had dropped sharply to twenty-sixth place in the world.[17] These losses could also be seen in the field of education, with a decrease in the quality of education and an increase in the significance of economic disparity, as investigated by Kariya Takehiko in Chapter 6. The number of Japanese universities that are considered to rank among the world's top 400 universities (in results that have been published since the early 2000s), decreased from twenty-seven in 2005 to sixteen in 2010. The rank of the University of Tokyo dropped from sixteenth in 2005 to thirtieth in 2012. Beginning in the early 2000s, there was a noticeable decrease in the number of Japanese students studying overseas: from 83,000 students in 2004 to 58,000 in 2011. The drop was particularly pronounced in the number of Japanese students studying in the United States, from 46,000 students in 2001 to 19,966 students in 2011, a reduction of over 50 percent.

The opportunity gap linked to economic disparity that has emerged is particularly serious. A growing inequality was evident in children's academic performance, motivation for learning, and learning behavior, respectively. An exceptionally dismal piece of data from the lost decades is the increase in suicides, which rose steeply from 1998 onward. Before 1998, the number of suicides was between 22,000 and 23,000, but that year it suddenly jumped to 32,000. According to the 2013 Cabinet Office's *White Paper on Suicide Prevention*, there is a strong correlation between the suicide rate and the unemployment rate.[18] During the next fourteen consecutive years, from 1998 to 2011, the annual number of suicides exceeded 30,000. In 2000, author Murakami Ryu wrote his Japanese novel *Exodus from the Land of Hope* and later commented that "This country has everything. You can find whatever you want here. The only thing you can't find is hope."[19] These words epitomized a sentiment that became increasingly widespread during Japan's lost period.

On the other hand, Japan also experienced relative losses, meaning that even if Japan did not decline in some sectors, it stagnated while other nations advanced, and so its decline is relative in that sense. In 2010 China overtook Japan as the world's second biggest economy, an event which probably sounded like a death knell and reminded Japan of its lost decades woes. However, as highlighted by Shiraishi Takashi in Chapter 11, the other side of Japan's decline is Asia's prosperity, the most dramatic example being China's massive economic growth. In the context of the so-called rise of the rest, apart from Japan, other mature economies are also losing their relative economic standing in several types of global rankings. We need to understand Japanese losses through this particular prism. During this period, overall Japan's per capita GDP fell from eighth place in 1991 to twenty-fourth place in 2012 in the world rankings. However, this drop is relative because Japan's GDP per capita actually increased from US $20,465 to US $36,265 over these two decades. Similarly, in the world's container port ranking, Yokohama and Kobe both fell from thirteenth place and fourth place in 1991 to fortieth place and forty-ninth place in 2012, as a result of the "rise of the rest." With regard to the number of Nobel prizes in the field of natural sciences during the 2000s, Japan rose to second place (9) after the United States (47). According to these figures, the past two decades were not lost decades at all – if anything they were fruitful decades. But if we look at the number of citations from natural science articles produced in Japan, while there was an increase in 2009–11 relative to the 1999–2001 period, Japan's overall world ranking dropped in relative terms due to the rise of contributions in other nations, including China. Japan, in fact, dropped from fourth place to seventh place in the top 10 percent of most cited articles, and from fifth place to eighth place in the top 1 percent of most cited works. By contrast, China rose from thirteenth place to fourth place in both categories.[20]

What about Japan's "lost opportunities"? Following the bursting of the bubble economy, the amount of NPLs began to swell. If the government had opted for capital injections by resolutely using public funds and had responded more adroitly to the situation, the ensuing financial crisis would have not become so grave and deflation would not have become endemic. However, LDP administrations delayed NPL disposal fearing popular opposition, and in the end ten years were needed to resolve this problem. This was the first and biggest lost opportunity of Japan's lost decades. In the end, leaders were timid in their development of new policies. Japan seemed to lack the strength and the focus necessary to forcefully advance international initiatives. The failure of the Japanese proposal for an Asian Monetary Fund (AMF) in 1997–98 to respond to the Asian Financial Crisis is a representative case. In addition, Japan continued to hesitate in its trade liberalization, and this lack of progress in market liberalization further obstructed domestic structural reforms. The fundamental cause behind Japan's botched response to the Asian Financial Crisis lay in a lack of political willingness to link structural reforms with market liberalization. Peter Drysdale and Shiro Armstrong in Chapter 10 highlight Japan's failure in trade policies and economic diplomacy as a means to achieve structural reforms. Shiraishi Takashi, too, speaks of lost opportunities with regard to Japan's role in managing regional cooperation in East Asia. It would have been much more effective to back Japan's trade policy with an economic partnership agreement (EPA), leading to increased imports from Japan.

Japan also had several lost opportunities regarding the history issue and how the population deals with war memory and responsibility. John Ikenberry, partly in Chapter 15, asks what would have happened if Japan had solved its history problems at the beginning of the 1990s, when both Japan's economy and its international standing were strong and China was in a weaker position. Looking back, he says, the lost opportunity to settle the history issues might have been in the early 1990s when Japan was at the high tide of its economic growth and international prestige. Somehow, Japanese leaders might have found a way to settle these issues, and would have done so from a position of strength. Today, growing nationalism in Japan coincides with anxiety about Japan's geopolitical decline, and this combination make gestures of historical reconciliation very difficult.

Lastly, Japan seemingly lost its principles and vision of the future, which at one time were highly praised due to the strength of Japan's socioeconomic foundations and its internationalization. This may qualify as a "lost dream." The notion of a society that was once almost completely middle class illustrates this absence. In fact, a substantial middle class, together with a small disparity between rich and poor, constituted the foundation of Japan's postwar growth and stability and formed the core of Japan's success story. In 1979, Ezra Vogel wrote in *Japan as Number One* that the gap between the rich and poor in Japan was "one of the world's narrowest."[21] In the past twenty years, this core value of the postwar model has begun to disappear. The income gap between the wealthiest 10 percent and poorest 10 percent of Japanese society consisted of a eightfold difference, but by 2006 this gap had increased to a twentyfold disparity.[22] Japan's income gap is still small compared to that of the United States, Britain, and many developing nations, and it did not increase as much as many people believed during the lost decades. However, when the notion or myth of Japanese society as almost completely middle class was shaken, the result was palpable. The society that emerged at this time – characterized by a growing number of nonregular employees, gaps in income and education (which were often related), and a widening disparity in wealth amongst the elderly population, as well as a sudden increase of households on public benefits – deeply shocked many. The dramatic increase of nonregular employees meant that a large number of young people became commodities in the labor market and produced a dual labor market with major differences in salary and employment security. The fragility of Japan's employment system became apparent following the 2008 Lehman Shock, with most of the negative outcomes hitting nonregular employees largely made up of young people.[23]

Those who probably lost the most during the lost decades were those who belong to Japan's "lost generation." Such an understanding was reinforced in 2006 when Japan's public television station, NHK, broadcasted a defining two-part documentary titled, "The Working Poor."[24] This documentary delved into the situation of people who work full time but earn less than they would on welfare. The year 2006 was also when the newly coined term "herbivore men" began to appear in the Japanese media. This term is a half-serious reference to young men who lack aspiration, either for a career or in terms of interest in the opposite sex. Numerous polls targeted at young men reveal that a large percentage consider themselves to be "herbivores."[25] At the beginning of 2007, the *Asahi Newspaper* ran a series of articles on the lost generation by adopting a Japanese abbreviation of the phrase (*rosu gene*). This moment was when the term "lost generation" came into the popular lexicon. This new vocabulary reflected the life modes of those aged twenty-five to thirty-five years, who had become adults in the aftermath of the collapse of the economic bubble. The media shed light on a generation of younger people who are variously described as "freeters" (underemployed part-time workers), NEETs ("Not in Education, Employment, or Training"), and social recluses (*hikikomori*), as well as on a plethora of nonregular, temporary workers who are dispatched from agencies and full-time employed regular workers.

The intensification of globalization and market competition, the effects of long-term economic stagnation and business restructuring, and, finally, a declining, ageing society coupled with seemingly ever-expanding government debt, greatly undermined the long-held popular belief that Japan was a safe and secure country. Yet, the more such difficulties beset Japan the more the government tried to reassure people that Japanese society was as safe as it ever had been. Former Prime Minister Aso Taro asserted as much when he said that the administration policies attempted to maintain a "society which provides peace of mind to its members."[26]

The Fukushima nuclear disaster further shattered people's trust in politicians. As Kitazawa Koichi discusses in Chapter 7, this accident represented Japan's most serious crisis since the end of World War II. Notwithstanding the multiple warnings the International Atomic Energy Agency (IAEA) had issued to Japan about fundamental issues regarding its nuclear safety regulations, Japanese nuclear operators, regulators, government officials, and academics were so completely cocooned in their myth of "nuclear safety" that they continued to ignore the IAEA's caution and the need for preparedness. This insularity should qualify as a "lost opportunity," a lost chance to mitigate a potential disaster. The myth of nuclear safety depended on a kind of state paternalism that had always acted as the guarantor of safety and reassurance and dismissed the possibility of the potential of severe accidents such as Fukushima due to the dogmatic believe in Japanese infallibility. Inertia characterized regulatory governance, which was both complex and ambiguous. Those who managed the regulations, that is to say the government, were completely enthralled by their cozy relations to political power and avowed know-how of those who were supposed to be regulated, the electric power companies.

Other areas we need to consider are the effects and side effects of such losses. These are problems that arose from policy failures, or so-called lost policies, and their shape varies depending on the case. Does the trauma resulting from a loss lead to new innovations or developments? For instance, the 1990–91 Gulf War severely shook Japan's long-held belief of its insular pacifism, which was limited to maintaining peace on its own archipelago. This political shock paved the way for Japan's later participation in peacekeeping operations (PKO), and it is possible to say that such a change constitutes an example of a loss that Japan successfully transformed into a longer-term lesson concerning how to manage its security policy. In Chapter 9, Michael Green and Igata Akira have described such traumas as "teachable moments" for Japan, in an attempt to be positive and forward looking. In fact, during this period Cold War ideological and partisan cleavages in Japanese foreign and security policy issues grew less pronounced, and a kind of national consensus matured out of, for instance, greater faith in the Japanese Self-Defense Forces and the Japan-U.S. alliance. It is thus not possible to make sweeping statements and dismiss the period as totally lost.

By contrast, in the field of foreign and security policy, no consensus has been found between Japan, the United States, and Okinawa concerning the issue of U.S. military bases in Okinawa. Sheila Smith, in Chapter 12, outlines the inadequacies in the strategic coordination within the U.S.-Japan alliance. Neither country can sufficiently come to grips with scenarios that engage the possibility of the North Korea nuclear threat and the rise of China. Unfortunately, the Japan-China dispute over the Senkaku Islands raised the issue even further. As Smith enunciates, for the first time the two allies confronted the prospect of a direct use of force against Japan. Strategic issues involving the realignment of U.S. military forces stationed in Japan and the composition and capability of such forces continue to go unanswered, while the issue of the bases remains overall unresolved.

In 1995, under the Murayama administration, Japan moved toward acknowledging aspects of its war responsibility and expressed contrition. The Prime Ministerial address, known as the Murayama Statement, was an attempt to come to terms with and overcome the issue of Japan's history in Asia following the end of the Cold War. However, the statement then provoked a backlash from revisionist forces within the LDP. This would later lead to visits by Prime Ministers Koizumi Junichiro and Abe Shinzo to the Yasukuni Shrine and to a deleterious diplomatic environment that Togo Kazuhiko describes in Chapter 13. The history issue continues to create friction with neighboring Asian countries and the United States. As Akiyama Nobumasa suggests in Chapter 14, the Koizumi government's 2005 campaign to secure a permanent seat on the UN Security Council ended in failure. China, which holds a permanent seat with veto power, opposed Japan's bid and pressured other countries, especially in Asia, not to support Japan's efforts. In the end, Japan was able to secure only three votes from Asian countries. A former diplomat, who was involved in Japan's campaign for a seat, recalls proposing a review in the Ministry of Foreign Affairs "to look into the causes behind Japan's failure, in order to extrapolate lessons." The proposal however, was ignored.[27] With such failures in mind, it is imperative that we coolly and calmly analyze what was "lost" within diplomatic, security, and crisis management circles.

Prolonged deflation, increases in irregular employment, stagnant wages, and uncertain future prospects could very well discourage people's aspirations; stifle their optimism, energy, and willingness to take risks; crush entrepreneurship; dull the luster of marriage; limit the desire to go abroad to study or work; and drive society toward narrow-minded nationalism. Despite these examples, it is difficult to say with pinpoint accuracy what Japan lost and what the country gained. Losses for some may also be gains for others. The optimal solution for one community can often be a suboptimal solution for the group as a whole. In employment, for instance, the flexibility longed for by employers is usually understood by employees as insecurity.

As Andrew Gordon writes in Chapter 5, there are many instances where one's solution is another's problem. The only way to judge whether something is actually a problem is to determine whether the result was positive or negative with respect to the general long-term interests of the nation as a whole. It can be deemed "lost" if it has a negative effect on the overall and long-term interests of the nation. Assessing the full value of the reforms that were designed to address the fundamental causes of the lost decades remains a very difficult proposition and is one of the key aims of this book.

Japan's lost decades were not simply the result of the government's inaction. Countless plans for reform were proposed and some specific ones actually drawn up, as Machidori Satoshi makes clear in Chapter 8. Some plans became policies and some materialized in new regulations, including the lifting and relaxation of previous controls. Nevertheless, these reforms were mostly ineffective. Partial effects notwithstanding, the overall impact was negative. At the same time, however, it is too simple to dismiss the reforms as lost. We can go further and analyze why these reforms did not perform as intended, question what the essence of failure was, and ask if policymakers have learned any lessons from their failures. It is only by taking stock of the situation now that we will be able to say whether or not the decades were truly lost and how extensive the losses were. The problems that have beset Japan's lost decades are challenges that other countries too are facing. It is true that the assets, opportunities, and perceptions that Japan lost during this time are rooted in the structural factors stemming from Japan's institutional culture. However, such losses are not actually cultural phenomena unique to Japan.

In the 1990s many economists, including Ben Bernanke, former head of the U.S. Federal Reserve, criticized the Bank of Japan's monetary policy – its timid quantitative easing, for example. Much of the criticism was appropriate. In the stagnation that affected their countries in the wake of the 2008 credit crunch, however, many of these economists experienced the same problems that economists had encountered in Japan – political opposition to the disposal of NPLs and wariness of long-term risk that came with bold quantitative easing. Bernanke later let it be known that privately "he regret[ted] the tone of those attacks (directed toward Japan)," suggesting that his direct experience now gave him a different perspective.[28] In this sense, Adam Posen has suggested that we should stop thinking of "turning Japanese" in the context of the lost decades "as a syndrome specific to Japan." "While our economies in Europe and the United States may not ever 'turn Japanese,'" Posen continues, "we all share some risks and problems in common with Japan circa 1995 . . . Japan's economic experience is similarly of universal relevance, offering parallels to today, but not some alternative state of the world."[29]

The thrust of this book is to present an intellectual framework that shows how Japan during the lost decades performed precisely as Posen suggests and that offers parallels to present-day issues that other countries now face.

Notes

1 David Pilling, *Bending Adversity: Japan and the Art of Survival* (New York, Penguin Press, 2014), p. xvi.
2 The poll sample was of 3,000 respondents nationwide and the response rate was 79 percent. Asahi Shimbun, *"Kenshō, shōwa hōdō shuzaihan"* ["Inspection of Reporting During Shōwa Japan," Reporting Group], in *Shimbun to shōwa* [Newspapers and Shōwa Japan] (Tokyo: Asahi Shimbun Shuppan, 2010), p. 486.

3 Yomiuri Shimbun, *Henshū techō* [Editor's Agenda], July 10, 2002.
4 Nathaniel Popper, "As Crisis Loomed, Yellen Made Wry Calls for Action," *New York Times*, February 21, 2014.
5 Paul Krugman, "Lost Decade Looming?" *New York Times*, May 20, 2010.
6 "Turning Japanese," *Economist*, July 30, 2011.
7 NHK, *Kenryoku no kōbō – jimin ichi kyō* [The Rise and Fall of Power, the Primacy of the LDP], December 22, 2013.
8 The subheading of the essay was "Turning Japanese." Fareed Zakaria, "Can America Be Fixed?" *Foreign Affairs*, January/February 2013.
9 Andy Mukherjee, "The Lessons for China from Japan's Lost Decade," *Reuters*, September 3, 2013.
10 Rebuild Japan Initiative Foundation, *The Fukushima Daiichi Nuclear Power Station Disaster: Investigating the Myth and Reality* (Oxford: Routledge, 2014).
11 Robert Jay Lifton, *Destroying the World to Save It – Aum Shinrikyo, Apocalyptic Violence, and the New Global Terrorism* (New York: Metropolitan Books, 1999), pp. 10, 236.
12 Satoshi Shirai, *Eizoku haisenron: Sengo nihon no kakushin* [Permanent Defeat: The Nucleus of Post-war Japan] (Tokyo: Ota Shuppan, 2013), and Funabashi Yoichi, *Genpatsu haisen – kiki no rīdāshippu* [Nuclear Defeat, Crisis Leadership] (Tokyo: Bungei Shinsho, 2014).
13 Martin Wolf, "Unreformed, But Japan is Back," *Financial Times*, March 7, 2006.
14 Cabinet Office, Government of Japan, *Nenji keizai zaisei hōkoku* [Annual Report on the Japanese Economy and Public Finance], 2013, http://www5.cao.go.jp/j-j/wp/wp-je13/index_pdf.html, accessed October 6, 2014.
15 Peter Tasker, "How to Make Monkeys Out of the Rating Agencies," *Financial Times*, August 11, 2011.
16 Ministry of Health, Labor and Welfare, *"Hiseiki koyō" no genjō to kadai* [The Present Situation and Challenges of "Non-regular Employment"], http://www.mhlw.go.jp/stf/seisakunitsuite/bunya/0000046231.html.
17 Japan ranked twenty-sixth in the Swiss IMD Business School's *World Competitiveness Ranking 2011*, http://www.mri.co.jp/NEWS/report/economy/__icsFiles/afieldfile/2011/05/18/dep20110518–01.pdf. However, Japan ranked sixth according to the World Economic Forum's *Global Competitiveness Report 2010–2011*, http://www3.weforum.org/docs/WEF_GlobalCompetitivenessReport_2010–11.pdf.
18 Cabinet Office, Government of Japan, *"Tokushū: Jisatsu tōkei no bunseki"* ["Special Feature: Analysis of Suicide Statistics"], in *Jisatsu taisaku hakusho* [White Paper on Suicide Prevention], 2013.
19 Ryu Murakami, "Amid Shortages, a Surplus of Hope," *New York Times*, March 16, 2011.
20 Ministry of Education, Culture, Sports, Science and Technology, *Kagaku gijutsu hakusho* [White Paper on Science and Technology], 2013, pp. 47–48.
21 Ezra F. Vogel, *Japan as Number One: Lessons for America* (Cambridge, MA: Harvard University Press, 1979), p. 120.
22 Organization for Economic Co-operation and Development, *Divided We Stand: Why Inequality Keeps Rising* (Paris: OECD, 2011).
23 Chad Steinberg and Masato Nakane, "To Fire or to Hoard? Explaining Japan's Labor Market Response in the Great Recession," *IMF Working Paper*, January 2011, and Shinichirō and Miki Ohata, *"Rīman shokkugo ni koyō jōsei ha dō henbō shita noka"* ["How Has Japan's Employment Situation Changed since the Lehman Shock?"], *Rikan seisaku keiei kenkyū*, Vol. 2 (Mitsubishi UFJ Research & Consulting, 2010).
24 NHK Special, two-part documentary from 2006, *Wāking pua, hataraite mo hataraite mo yutaka ni narenai* [Working Poor: Unable to Become Affluent No Matter How Hard One Works], and *Wāking pua, doryoku sureba nukedasemasu ka* [Working Poor: Can Effort Free One from Poverty?].

25 See for example a survey in 2010 by Japanese dating agency, Partner Agent, where 39 percent of male respondents considered themselves to be "herbivores." Partner Agent, *Press Information: We Asked Unmarried Men and Women in Their Thirties, A Survey on "Herbivore Men" and "Carnivore Women,"* March 3, 2010, www.p-a.jp/company/pdf/release_20100303.pdf.
26 Office of the Prime Minister, *Asō naikaku sōri daijin kōen: "watashi no mezasu anshin shakai"* [Speech by Prime Minister Asō Tarō: "Society Providing Peace of Mind which I Seek to Achieve"], June 25, 2009, http://www.kantei.go.jp/jp/asospeech/2009/06/25 speech.html.
27 The author's interview with a retired diplomat, December 27, 2013.
28 Jon Hilsenrath, "Fed Chief Gets Set to Apply Lessons from Japan's History," *Wall Street Journal*, October 12, 2010.
29 Adam S. Posen, *The Realities and Relevance of Japan's Great Recession: Neither Ran nor Rashomon*, The Suntory and Toyota International Centres for Economics and Related Disciplines (STICERD) Public Lecture at the London School of Economics, May 24, 2010.

1   Japan's demographic collapse

Seike Atsushi

Japan's population is ageing at an unprecedented rate, both in terms of scale and speed. Around 25 percent of the population is made up of those who are sixty-five years or older, meaning that a staggering one in four are of retirement age. When we consider that in the early 1990s this figure was only one in ten, the nature of this issue comes sharply into focus. The change in demographics is perhaps best appreciated in the remarkable swiftness of the transition. The proportion rose from 7 percent of the population in 1970 to a total of 14 percent in 1994, an increase of 7 percent in just twenty-four years. This is a fraction of the time of comparable transformations in countries such as France, which experienced a similar leap over a period of more than one hundred years. The proportion of elderly people has continued to rise in Japan, from 14 percent in 1994 to 21 percent in 2007 – a further rise of 7 percent but even more quickly, in less than thirteen years. The graying of Japan's population looks as if it knows no limits.

One major factor behind this phenomenon is the remarkable improvement in life expectancy. Simply put, many more people are living longer. At the end of World War II the average life expectancy in Japan was fifty years for men and fifty-four for women. In a few short decades Japan's average life expectancy has risen to rank among the highest in the world, eighty and eighty-six years for men and women respectively. This rise of course stems from the combination of better nutrition, better health care, and a safer and for most people less physically demanding working life. These developments are due in no small part to Japan's remarkable postwar economic progress, and more particularly the increase in per capita gross domestic product (GDP).

The other factor supporting the graying of Japan's population is the decline in the birthrate. A country's birthrate decreases when it transitions from being a developing nation, which usually means that it has a high poverty rate and high infant mortality and birth rates, to being a developed nation with low infant mortality, birth, and overall mortality rates. The decline is usually associated with economic growth. This was precisely the course that Japan followed. Immediately after World War II, Japan's fertility rate, previously at 4.5 births per woman, declined rapidly. In the 1960s and 1970s, after a period of unprecedented high growth, Japan joined the ranks of developed nations and the birth rate fell to just above two births per woman. This level is known as the replacement rate, which is needed to maintain population equilibrium.

The problem was that this trend went too far – the fertility rate did not stop decreasing. From the mid-1970s onward, when Japan's economy was entering its phase of greatest expansion, the fertility rate decreased to below two births per woman, which meant that Japan's population was on track to decrease with each succeeding generation. This downturn in the fertility rate has been put down to the fact that while wages grew in line with the nation's economic growth, the financial burden on families of having and raising children – even though the Japanese economy was on the rise – was just too great, particularly in the cities. At the end of the 1980s, Japan's fertility rate dropped to a low of 1.57 births per woman, a figure that dipped below the sharp and temporary drop to 1.58 in 1966, a year which according to traditional beliefs and the Chinese zodiac was the "Year of the Fiery Horse."[1] This decrease in the fertility rate continued with the collapse of the bubble economy in the early 1990s. After reaching an astounding nadir of 1.26 births per woman in 2005, it has since recovered slightly. Japan's Ministry of Health, Labor and Welfare has reported that the rate for 2013 was at 1.43, up from 1.41 in 2012.[2]

Japan's rapidly aging population is a phenomenon that is unmatched in other countries in the world and the birth rate has reached an all-time low. How could this have been allowed to happen? A nation's population is its most fundamental base and the possibility of its collapse should be a key focus of concern for politicians and other leaders of society. When Japan's fertility rate first dipped below two births per woman in the mid-1970s and clear predictions were made that the

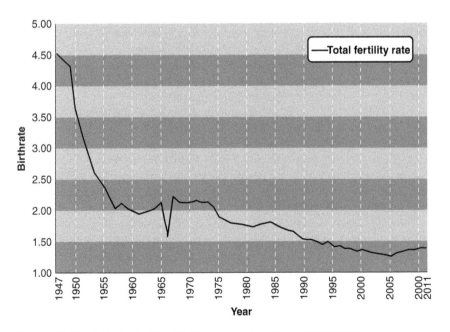

Figure 1.1 Trends in the fertility (birth) rate in postwar Japan (1947–2011)

Source: Based on data from the *Demographic Statistics Data Book* (2013), National Institute of Population and Social Security Research.

population would start to decline in one generation's time, plans to counter this trend ought to have been at the forefront of social and political discussion. However, as I show below, no sense of urgency seemed to ignite political concern, with the consequence that countermeasures, when they came, were addressing a situation that had already occurred.

Many people in Japan now fear that the downward trend in the population and the seemingly unstoppable overall ageing of the population will have deep and costly negative effects on the economy. It will cause a shrunken labor force that will limit production and will produce a smaller consumer market less able to stimulate demand. Of course, if per capita productivity and the consumption rate grow sufficiently to compensate for the population decline, the effects on the economy might not be so damaging. There is no guarantee, however, that such a scenario will be possible. A decline in population not only affects the economy but also leads to a decrease in the human resources that sustain society, such as public services and education. In short, the consequences could be considerable.

The shape of provincial Japan in the future: The Masuda Report

What shape will Japan be in demographically in thirty – or fifty – years' time? In recent years, as the population decline has finally begun to become a matter of public debate, this is a question that increasingly preoccupies a number of population specialists, politicians, and business leaders.

The December 2013 issue of *Chuo Koron*, a special edition on "Disappearing Regional Cities," carried an essay by the demography researcher Masuda Hiroya entitled "Regional Cities Will Disappear by 2040: A Polarized Society Will Emerge."[3] The author, a former governor of Iwate Prefecture for twelve years, writes with concern about the demographic crisis now confronting Japan, and particularly on how the decline of the population will affect Japan's provincial areas. Based on his experiences of dealing with depopulation in Iwate Prefecture, in northeastern Japan, Masuda argues that Japan now faces the prospect of more and more marginalized settlements all over the country, with myriads of villages and hamlets suffering depopulation and becoming "hollowed out."[4]

Masuda bases his analyses on reports and statistics compiled by the National Institute of Population and Social Security Research (NIPSSR), Japan's Ministry of Health, Labor and Welfare think tank. NIPSSR publishes a report every five years, entitled *Population Projection for Japan*. It also publishes a more detailed report entitled *Regional Population Projections for Japan*, which tabulates statistics and trends for towns and villages outside the larger cities.

The *Regional Population Projections for Japan: 2010–2040*, compiled in March 2013, calculates that if the current situation prevails, Japan's population of roughly 128 million in 2010 will fall to around 107 million in 2040.[5] Long-range estimates tabulated in January 2012 project a further decline to 86 million in 2060, and roughly 42 million in 2110. The proportion of the elderly population (aged sixty-five and above) will be 36.1 percent in 2040, and 39.9 percent in 2060.[6]

It is worth noting that these median fertility scenario projections are based on several assumptions: that the proportion of people born in 1995 and now graduating from high school and who will remain unmarried has peaked; that the proportion of those who will remain single all their lives – "lifelong singles" (it is assumed that this segment will not have children) – will stay unchanged; and that the number of children born to married couples will not drop any further. Forecasts predict that Japan's fertility rate will fall to 1.39 in 2014, then decrease further to 1.33 in 2024, and increase slightly to 1.35 by 2060.[7] While such assumptions may hold for now, they are not necessarily applicable to those aged eighteen years or older (born in 1995 and after) and the possibility that the figures will decline, which may stimulate a further drop in the population figures, remains real.

Based on the figures gathered by NIPSSR, Masuda predicts that the changes in Japanese demography will affect different segments of the population in different ways. Dividing the period he analyzes into three stages: 2010–2040, 2040–2060, and 2060–2090, he predicts that the proportion of young people (those below fifteen years old) and the proportion of working-age population (from fifteen to sixty-five years of age), will continue to decline more or less steadily from 2010 to 2090. The proportion of the elderly population (sixty-five and above), however, will increase until 2040, and then will remain almost unchanged for the following two decades. It will eventually start to decline in 2060. As a result, Japan's total population will decline at only a moderate rate until approximately 2040, but after that it will begin to fall rapidly.[8]

The rate of depopulation, a result of the combination of an ageing population combined with a declining birthrate, will be considerably higher in outlying regions than in the cities and also in Japan as a whole. In Iwate Prefecture, in the northeast of Japan's main island, the population will shrink 30 percent by 2040. Projections are that the population of Wakayama Prefecture in western Japan and Kochi Prefecture in southern Shikoku island will also contract by roughly 30 percent, while that of Akita Prefecture in northeastern Japan will contract by 35 percent. The rate of depopulation will be much higher in remote towns and villages (the "marginalized settlements") and somewhat less in towns and cities, especially those that are prefectural capitals.[9]

The potential crisis facing Japan as a result of this demographic contraction will have significant consequences. Of particular interest are the different ways that population decline may affect the different regions, and also the ways this will impact the cities. Among other things, Masuda predicts that a clear divide will appear between urban and rural areas. There will be a "polarization" between the big cities (Tokyo, Osaka, and Nagoya) and the provincial regions in Japan, with the latter marked by a disproportionate population of elderly people and extremely limited employment opportunities, if any. These areas will gradually empty out, as more and more young people migrate to a few large cities. The disappearance of young women in rural areas will only exacerbate the population decline in these places – so these regions will in the end become unsustainable and thus probably disappear. At the same time, as the growing populations in the urban areas gradually grow older, the proportion of the elderly living in the cities will increase, leading to a shortage of labor – which will only exacerbate further "population migration." In time, the cities will become subject to a "population black hole." This is a phenomenon where the increase in people migrating to the cities finds little support for childbirth and childcare either from families or the local community, and thus will cause an inevitable decrease in the birthrate, which will lead to a sort of collapse. All of this will only add to the overall and increasing rate of Japan's population decline, as the population continues to plummet and one community after another becomes unsustainable. In addition, the overconcentration of people in the large cities, Masuda argues, will make the country much more vulnerable to the effects of disasters, both economic and natural.[10]

Masuda is particularly anxious about the loss of communities in outlying regions, as population decline makes them unsustainable. If the decline in population proceeds at the current rate, not only will regional communities cease to function properly as communities, but services indispensable to daily life, such as medical and educational services and disaster prevention, will also become impossible to maintain. This, Masuda argues, is a reality that provincial areas will confront twenty years in advance of Japan's major metropolitan areas – indeed it is a process that is already underway in towns and villages in outlying regions. What is required, he argues, are visionary policies that are tailored to particular local circumstances, that focus on each regional area with a view to coordinated, comprehensive but localized regeneration (both economic and demographic) rather than focusing on fostering the economy, or GDP, of the nation as a whole.[11]

In a similar vein, a 2013 study published by the Rebuild Japan Initiative Foundation titled, *Japan's Worst-case Senarios: The Nine Blind Spots*, identifies nine potential crisis-management blind spots that Japan might well have to face in the near future, one of which is demographic collapse. The case study on demographics (translated in the English version as "Weakened population: 2050, the day youths become terrorists") offered a hypothetical scenario for risk management in which population decline in Japan has led to a general sense of despair, which has overcome the nation in just a few decades. In this case study, the argument is made that "in order to avert such a scenario, we must be prepared to relinquish the traditional Japanese views on society, family, and marriage."[12]

Can Japan afford to remain calm based on these dire forecasts and predictions? What countermeasures have been taken to avert the looming population crisis? As I discuss in the following sections, policymakers have shown remarkably little vision in tackling Japan's demographic problem.

Japan's ageing population: Problems and countermeasures

While the graying of a nation and the decline of its population are significant events, it is the precise shape and timing of the demographic shift that determines if a society can weather the decline. Japan is not the only country to confront a shrinking and ageing population – many European countries anticipate similar population declines. The greatest problem of an ageing society is the dependency ratio – the proportion of people who are economically dependent and the proportion of people who are economically active – and the risk that it poses to the viability of the social security system. An ageing population increases the amount that has to be paid out as social security benefits, placing a heavy burden on the working age population who will have to fund these increases with their taxes. In Japan, the budget for state pensions, medical and long-term care, and social security benefits, which are claimed by elderly people, more than doubled between the years 1990 to 2012, from roughly 50 trillion yen (approx. US $457 billion at the 2014 exchange rate) to over 100 trillion yen (approx. US $914 billion at the 2014 exchange rate). This budget increase occurred partly because the population of people over sixty-five years of age doubled, from roughly fifteen million to thirty million over the same time period.[13] The rapid upsurge in budget demands to cope with this shift is one reason why Japan now has massive public debt worth more than double its national GDP. Japan's working-age population, that is to say the proportion of people from fifteen to sixty-five years of age, decreased by roughly six million people in 2010. To put it differently, the working-age population lost the equivalent of the population of six cities.[14] The result was a reduction of economic growth on both the supply side and demand side.

In the early 1990s, Japan faced a dramatic stock market collapse (the bursting of its "bubble economy") followed by a slump that lasted the entire decade. This was followed by what is now referred to as the "dotcom downturn" in 2001, and the global financial crisis, referred to in Japan as the "Lehman Shock," of 2008. It is arguable whether such crises were predictable, but there is no doubt that population change *is* one of the most predictable of all economic variables. It was quite clear by the early 1990s that Japan's population would age and that the proportion of the working-age population would decrease. Swift countermeasures should have been discussed and put into place at this time.

The countermeasures for population ageing broadly divide into two categories, aimed at an increase in life expectancy on the one hand and stemming the declining birthrate on the other. With regard to life expectancy, by "countermeasures" I refer to interventions aimed at accommodating the overall effects of population ageing. Such countermeasures cover efforts to maintain and even increase numbers in the work force, that is to say the economically active (wage-earning and tax-paying) population. Efforts to reform the social security system are also required so that payments for the support of those who are economically dependent become less burdensome. The other category of countermeasures involves curtailing population decline by increasing the birth rate. This necessitates taking fundamental measures to make it easier for people to have families – providing child-bearing incentives and offering social structures, child care provisions for example, to render the "life-work balance" easier.

What countermeasures for population ageing did the Japanese government pursue after 1992? Below, I will provide a brief overview, first of the measures that were taken to increase the numbers of the elderly in the workforce and to reform the social security system, and then of the measures to counter the decline in the birthrate.

Japan's working elderly: A success story

It is now quite clear that Japan's population will not increase for the foreseeable future. Even if fertility rates were to recover, it would be another twenty years before the effects would be seen. What is required are policies to strengthen the labor force participation rates even as the proportion of "working-age" people

Table 1.1 Labor force participation rate of older people in developed nations (2009).

	Japan	*United States*	*Germany*	*France*	*Korea*
Males aged 60–64	76.3	60.9	50.8	20.3	68.8
Females aged 60–64	44.6	49.9	32.9	15.9	42.0
Males aged 65 and above	29.4	21.9	5.9	2.7	41.5
Females aged 65 and above	13.1	13.6	2.7	1.0	22.2

Note: Units are percentages.

Source: Based on data from the *Ageing Society Statistics Data Book* (2011), Japan Organization for Employment of the Elderly, Persons with Disabilities and Job Seekers.

(those aged from fifteen to sixty-five years) declines, and more particularly the participation rate of certain population segments: women and older people.

Policies regarding labor force participation by middle-aged and elderly people in Japan appear to have been relatively successful. As Table 1.1 shows, the labor force participation rate among the elderly in Japan, along with Korea, is remarkably high in comparison with other Organisation for Economic Co-operation and Development (OECD) countries.

This is due to a number of factors. Japan has been fairly consistent in promoting work and employment of older people since the 1980s.[15] By contrast, from the late 1970s to the early 1990s, many countries in Europe and elsewhere adopted policies to encourage early retirement to alleviate unemployment levels among younger people. Subsequently, in the 1990s, the governments of these countries had to reverse these plans and introduce measures to promote hiring older people. As a result, the labor force participation rate of the elderly population in these countries remains low, or at least behind that of Japan.

One of the most important measures that the Japanese government took in response to the problem of the ageing population was the revision of the Act on Stabilization of Employment of Elderly Persons in 2004. Measures in this act were designed to ensure employment opportunities until sixty-five years of age, legally obliging employers to institute systems to continue employment of regular employees up to pension eligibility age, to promote re-employment for the middle-aged and the older working population, and to promote diverse employment and social participation for elderly persons who wish to do temporary or short-term or other light jobs after their retirement. In 2006, the employment ratio rate among people in their early sixties showed a distinct rise, of around 3 percent.[16] An amendment to the law, which reinforced the legal obligation for continuous employment, was passed in 2013. Of course, even with these policies to increase the labor force participation rate, Japan will not be able to avoid some sort of decrease in its overall labor force.

The social security system: Incomplete reform

In the postwar period, Japan built up a generous social security pension program. However, due to the growing stress on financing social security arrangements caused by both demographic and economic factors, since 1980 Japan has been carrying out repeated pension reforms every five years. The pension benefits have been gradually reduced, along with an increase in the retirement age from sixty to sixty-five. In addition, the contribution rate has gradually been raised. However, pension provisions still remain generous, and the growing proportion of elderly people in the population who will need to receive pensions, medical care, and long-term nursing care mean that the system will continue to face financial difficulties in the future.

The Pension Reform of 2004 made a substantial stab at balancing pension benefits and contributions over the next century, and it is generally considered to be one of the most successful areas of social security reform. The law provided for public pension contributions to be raised by 0.354 percent annually; from 2017 they were to be fixed at 18.3 percent of the annual wage income (a feature that was dubbed "fixed contribution") – setting a ceiling on contributions, already quite burdensome on those who paid them. Secondly, the reform incorporated the automatic adjustment of pension benefit levels ("macroeconomic indexation"). This effectively introduced restrictions on the amount of benefits paid out, which enabled the pension program to adjust flexibly to social and economic changes, and thus helped minimize the need for further reforms and adjustments by law.[17]

The 2004 reform to the pension system looks as if it has successfully addressed certain problems in the sustainability of pension financing. There remain questions surrounding the macroeconomic indexation of pension benefits in times of deflation, however, and adjustments should be made in the system accordingly – presumably negative consumer price indexation can be carried out and a recalculation of benefits made accordingly. In addition, more research needs to be done into the possibilities of raising consumption tax as a means of funding basic pension benefits.

In comparison with financing pensions, the problem of financing medical and long-term care for the elderly is a much more complex matter. The matter of pensions is a linear problem since these benefits will simply increase proportionally in line with the rise in the number of the elderly. In contrast, medical, elderly, and long-term care benefits, which will increase rapidly with population ageing, are nonlinear issues. Unlike pensions, the amount paid out as medical and elderly care insurance is increasing at a higher pace than the rate of increase in the elderly population, in a nonlinear pattern – due to the increase in the number of people aged seventy-five or over, improvements in medical technology, and other factors. The amount of benefits paid out to people aged seventy-five or older, the segment of the population who receive the greatest portion of benefits, is due to increase substantially. Whereas the problems surrounding pensions can be said to be an exclusively financial issue of collecting pension premiums and tax to fund the paying out of monetary benefits, issues concerning medical and elderly care benefits involve the additional cost of paying for professionals who take on the medical and long-term care and others who provide these services.

The main focus of the political debate on financing Japan's social security system has tended to be on pensions, an issue that was solved in 2004 as far as fiscal sustainability is concerned. The government has hesitated both to raise the rate of consumption tax and to tackle the low percentage of medical care costs that elderly people have to pay themselves. This reflects the tendency to prioritize the interests of the current electorate at the expense of future generations who will bear the ever-increasing burden of the costs for social welfare and pensions. This trend will only worsen as the proportion of elderly people who occupy the electorate rises.

Birthrate countermeasures: Childcare support and pronatal policy interventions

In June 1990, the total fertility rate of the nation dropped to its lowest value ever: 1.57 births per woman. This number drew considerable attention since the figure was lower than the fertility rate of 1.58 that had been registered in 1966 (the above-mentioned "Year of the Fiery Horse"). The term "1.57 shock" consequently found currency in the national media. Japan's fertility rate had in fact fallen below the level needed to maintain the current population level a good fifteen years before this time, in 1974. However, during the 1970s the issue that most concerned people was *overpopulation* – especially in developing countries. A 1974 *White Paper on Health and Welfare* expressed satisfaction at Japan's fertility rate, and emphasized the need to maintain equilibrium. The report referred to the negative effects that could be anticipated in a population with fewer young people, but fell short of analyzing the results of an overall demographic shrinkage.[18] A subsequent *White Paper on Health and Welfare* in 1979 mentioned the fact that the fertility rate had fallen below the population replacement level, and for the first time referred to the risks which came with a shrinking population. However, there was no discussion of any countermeasures to tackle the declining birthrate. Instead, the focus was on measures for raising individual productivity as the way to sustain a society with a reduced working population.[19]

In 1980, a *Special Report by Council Members*, compiled by the Council on Population Problems – an advisory committee to the Ministry of Health, Labor, and Welfare – stated plainly that Japan would soon have a shrinking population.[20] This was still ten years ahead of the 1.57 shock in 1990, and debates should have started within public policy circles to prevent population decline at this time. The report mentioned the fact that fertility rates were insufficient for population replacement in the following manner:

> It is possible that the crude fertility rate and the age-specific fertility rate will decrease, but no great change will occur to the potential level of fertility judging from the figure for births per couple, which will remain constant. At the same time [. . .] we do need to acknowledge that the current rate of births per married couple, 2.0, is not sufficient for population regeneration.[21]

No real sense of urgency was noted in media reports either. In 1980 the *Asahi Newspaper* stated: "There will not be a severe population decline," and again simply said "Ageing will not speed up."[22] In other words, at this point the fact that

Japan's population was decreasing was not seen as a problem of concern that required immediate attention. It is a great pity that no one had any greater vision and thought to inquire about the consequences of a drop in fertility rates. At this point there might still have been time to reverse the decline. The government's reticence about taking more proactive action was due partly to the legacy of pre-war and wartime policy when citizens of Japan were subjected to intensive prona-talist propaganda to "bear children and multiply," and officials made five children per woman a national goal, bestowing awards on women who bore ten offspring. However, the conflicting demands of modern life now require the government to support couples that wish to have families, not out of a wish to provide children for the nation but out of personal desire.

After the 1.57 shock in 1990, the Japanese government finally turned its attention to the problem and began assembling countermeasures and making policy interventions. Starting in the 1990s, slowly at first and then with increasing frequency in the 2000s, the government passed acts and laws designed to tackle the problem. Most of the actions were centered on encouraging the provision and facilitation of childcare. Steps taken included the provision of economic incentives (e.g., child allowances and tax incentives), laws that facilitate childcare leave for working parents (allowing for paid leave and setting limits on working hours and overtime), the encouragement and development of childcare facilities, and attempts to help working couples improve their work-life balance.

In 2003, the Japanese government enacted the Act on Advancement of Measures to Support Raising Next-Generation Children. At this time, the fertility rate was on the brink of dipping below the 1.2 level, and time was of the essence. The measure required local authorities and corporations to devise action plans for childcare support policies and more importantly to create improved conditions that would allow parents to balance raising children with their work life. However, it only required corporations and other organizations to establish childcare support policies "to the extent possible," and few corporations took measures. A temporary improvement in the fertility rate was seen after 2006, which may have been related to a sense of optimism connected to the passing of the law.

One of the major problems has been a simple lack of childcare facilities. Eliminating childcare waiting lists thus became a central pillar of countermeasures pitted against a declining birthrate. The 2013 Plan to Accelerate the Elimination of Childcare Waiting Lists finally acknowledged that it was unacceptable – it made no sense – for children to be placed on waiting lists to receive childcare. The way was in fact led by the city of Yokohama, which in May 2013 announced that it no longer had any children waiting on its lists for daycare centers in any of its eighteen wards.[23] This was a remarkable achievement, which had been implemented by the tireless efforts of city officials, who had worked for over three years with private enterprises to secure spaces – almost any space at all – to build daycare centers. This innovative way of dealing with the problem forced the central government to recognize that it was indeed possible to reach these goals.

Looking at all the countermeasures attempted since the 1.57 shock gives one the impression that such policies were mostly reactive rather than proactive. Every five years the government produced a five-year plan to set new goals or to resolve new problems. There was the 1994 Angel Plan (a five-year plan from 1995 to 1999 designed to increase the number of childcare placements); the 1999 New Angel Plan (a five-year plan from 2000 to 2004); the 2002 Plus One Plan to End the Declining Birthrate; the 2004 Child and Child-Rearing Support Plan (a five-year plan from 2005 to 2009); the 2009 Vision for Children and Childcare (a five-year plan from 2010 to 2014); and then the 2013 Plan to Accelerate the Elimination of Childcare Waiting Lists.[24]

The government's involvement in pronatalist measures also got off to a shaky start. In May 2013, the Task Force for Overcoming the Declining Birthrate Crisis set out a proposal involving a number of aid programs aimed at promoting marriage, pregnancy, and childcare. During the task force's deliberations, a proposal was made for a "Handbook on Life and Women."[25] A number of nongovernmental organizations (NGOs) and women's groups voiced concerns that the state was interfering in citizens' private affairs, making fertility and population solely a women's problem and propagating the idea that women's value lay only in their ability to provide children. They also accused that the government's interference in women's lives was incoherent.[26] The idea of the handbook was eventually discarded, even though its proponents felt that it only sought to disseminate knowledge about ovarian age and fertility, making it possible for women to design their lives.

In addition, it is impossible to avoid the impression that the countermeasures aimed at the declining birthrate have tended to focus on families that have two parents, who are both married and working – this is the emphasis on the development of childcare facilities and the fostering of a new work-life balance for working couples. But one of the major factors behind Japan's declining birthrate is the growing proportion of people (especially women) who marry late and those who do not want to get married at all ("lifelong singles"). The fertility rate for such people is low. The emergence of such demographic groups is common knowledge to population specialists, but policymakers still devote the bulk of their attention to measures aimed at married couples.

Despite government efforts, the various schemes have not met with success. No matter how much effort is expended on the provision of childcare facilities and disseminating knowledge about the relationship between age and fertility, no improvements will be possible without addressing the problem of the numbers of people who opt for later marriage and the growing number of single-person households.

Immigration policy: Where does Japan stand?

As Japanese political leaders have awoken to the dire predictions about Japan's population, various suggestions have been made that Japan might become more open to immigrants. The argument is now often made that Japan will need large-scale labor immigration in order to maintain a workforce level that can ensure the functionality of the state.

In October 2008, the Japanese Business Federation (Keidanren) carried out a survey of Japanese-style immigration policies in a report titled *An Economy and Society That Responds to the Challenges of a Declining Population*. Against the backdrop of stronger competition for talent at the global level, the study called for measures oriented at the development of a legislative framework that would allow for the active and wider acceptance of foreign skilled workers on the basis of permanent residency; wider acceptance of foreign students, who are likely to become future highly qualified professionals; support for companies employing foreign students; and the acceptance of average-qualified people with specific expertise and skills.[27] This recognition was also made at the governmental level. The 2005 *White Paper on International Trade*, compiled by the Ministry of Economy, Trade, and Industry, mentioned that "on the basis of a rough calculation we will need to add about 18 million workers to maintain the workforce population to present-day's levels."[28]

In February 2012, the DPJ Minister Responsible for Declining Population, Nakagawa Masaharu, demonstrated interest in expanding the scope of foreign workers including immigrants, stating, "The Japanese people need to think of the shape of the country by taking into consideration these issues [of immigration], and have a public debate similar to the public debates on immigration policy undertaken in Northern Europe and in the United States."[29] Even within the Liberal Democratic Party (LDP), retired Secretary General Nakagawa Hidenao proposed to accept ten million immigrants in line with DPJ Diet members.[30]

More recently, during the tenth meeting of the Industrial Competitiveness Council, held on May 29, 2013, former Minister of State for Economic and Fiscal Policies Takenaka Heizo announced: "All ministries should create a venue to discuss ways for securing global talent, necessary for economic growth."[31] Minister of Justice Tanigaki Sadakazu responded:

I am thankful for the proposals in favor of surveys on immigration policies. With regard to methods pertaining to immigration, we need to study the matter from a broad and diversified perspective that takes into consideration the people's will concerning the consequences of immigration to Japan's business, public security, and labor market – all issues that pertain to the people's lives.[32]

The debates surrounding the issue of immigration are roughly in keeping with the implications of Tanigaki's statement above. The key points of contention in the debate seem to stem from two issues: ambivalence about whether Japan can bear the costs of an all-out positive immigration policy, which would be a huge and complex undertaking; and anxiety and fears within the Japanese populace. There is a fear of the loss of social stability and the deterioration of public security, of the effects on salaries of Japanese workers, of the creation of closed ethnic groups within larger Japanese society, and of the disappearance of Japanese culture.

If Japan is going to pursue a positive immigration policy, it is essential that policymakers have a clear picture of what kind of skills Japan will need and how to proactively target people with those skills, as well as the kind of arrangements that will be needed to provide for them in the long term. The aforementioned Keidanren report makes a specific reference to a need for skill mix, making a division between high, mid, low, and no skills at all.[33] Such divisions are based on the demands of the labor market for skills possessed by talented people. Although logically speaking the intake of highly qualified people (those, for instance, whose yearly income surpasses ten million yen – around US $92,000) would seem to be highly desirable, we perhaps ought to consider how many such people are actually needed in today's Japan.

In recent years, business leaders have argued for focusing less on people of exceptionally high skills and more on allowing those with mid-level skills to enter Japan. Such people would include health care staff who would play a useful role in caring for Japan's ever-increasing elderly population. Thanks to economic partnership agreements (EPA) between Japan and various other countries such as the Philippines and Indonesia, more nurses and caretakers from these countries are employed in Japan. Nonetheless, given the hurdle of the national nursing and care worker examinations, only a relatively small number of these ultimately succeed in establishing themselves in Japan. If we want to allow substantial numbers of nurses and caretakers into Japan, we need to have a thoroughgoing debate on this particular issue and what needs to be done to enable it to happen.

We also need to look at the long term in the immigration debates. Again, we can take the case of mid-level talent such as nurses and caretakers, which the Keidanren among others argue should be allowed to enter the country in greater numbers. At present within the current EPA frameworks, the people who come to Japan to work as caretakers are mostly in their twenties, and they are satisfied to work as low-level caretakers. However, after thirty years living in Japan, they will want and expect to be promoted and become head nurses/caretakers. Serious consideration needs to be given to the provision of training and promotion for foreign caretakers, as well as looking into how this will affect employment prospects for Japanese workers. It is of course essential that we avoid a dual structure in the labor market and society as a whole by ensuring that there is complete equality between Japanese people and immigrants in terms of labor standards and social security.

If immigration policies are to be pursued, realistic attention will also have to be paid to the preparation and associated costs. It is possible that huge numbers of nonskilled workers will be required. Costs would have to include some guarantee of housing, the provision of life counseling and the diffusion of information aimed at these people, the strengthening of their education in the Japanese language, the development of systems that assist their integration into the local community, and the application of a social safety net system that would cover pensions, medical expenses, and welfare in general. According to the Keidanren report mentioned above, some localities that have in the past accepted a large influx of foreigners, including second-generation Japanese, have reported that they have experienced problems, mostly relating to the lack of Japanese language proficiency, which lessened their prospects in training and work. There were also doubts about how the children of these migrants would be able to fare within the parameters of the compulsory national education system.[34]

Conclusion

During the lost decades, Japan has experienced population ageing that was globally unprecedented in its swiftness. The graying of Japanese society is in many ways a mark of the growth and success of Japan's postwar economy. However, the threat of swift population decline now threatens the sustainability of Japanese society itself. Measured responses to these issues are essential. Policies must include strategies for tackling the fertility rate, increasing the labor force participation rate of women and elderly people, and altering the social security system. These strategies all need to involve fundamental reform and to be implemented promptly.

In the case of the dwindling fertility rate, radical strategies needed to be carried out within a few years of the 1.57 shock in 1990, or at the latest within the first half of the 1990s. The policies that were drawn up in the early 2000s, when the fertility rate dropped to near 1.2, aimed to encourage corporations and organizations to improve childcare support and did contribute to a limited recovery in the birthrate in the later part of the decade, but they were not sufficient to bring about a turnaround to the general decline. The policies for increasing the labor participation rate among women overlapped with policies to encourage a recovery in the birthrate, but these too were insufficient. In order to significantly enhance these policies, it is necessary to improve the provision of support for people to balance their work and family lives, and to achieve this a dramatic increase in the provision of public childcare services is in order.

The one area where government policies can be said to have been successful is in the area of efforts to increase the labor force participation rate of older people. In this respect, the situation in Japan is demonstrably better than that of many other countries, particularly in Europe. However, the delay in social security system reforms during the lost decades was a serious issue.

As Japan continues to experience extreme rates of population ageing, it finds itself entering uncharted territory, encountering new social pressures and political challenges. Japan is often seen as a trailblazer in tackling global challenges, and there is an opportunity here to be a role model for the rest of the world. The important element is speed. Countermeasures must be put in place swiftly. The costs of policies for resolving population ageing will only continue to grow. The dwindling birthrate and other factors makes the possibility of population rate recovery seem increasingly impossible. Even so, it is important to take action sooner rather than later to minimize the effects. Implementing measures to provide robust support for people who wish to have and raise children will allow us to decrease, even if only slightly, the burden on future generations.

Notes

1 According to long-established beliefs that relate to the Chinese zodiac, children born during this particular year – when the Year of the Horse coincided with a year when the "fire" element was in the ascendancy – have volatile, willful temperaments. This is seen as particularly deleterious for women of marriageable age.
2 Kōseirōdōshō, *Heisei 25 nen jinkō dōtai tōkei (kakutei sū) no gaikyō* [Ministry of Health, Labor and Welfare, Summary Report of Vital Statistics of Japan (final data)], 2013. http://www.mhlw.go.jp/toukei/saikin/hw/jinkou/kakutei13/dl/00_all.pdf.
3 Masuda Hiroya, "2040 nen, chihō shōmetsu. Kyokuten shakai ga tōrai suru" ["Regional Cities Will Disappear by 2040: A Polarized Society Will Emerge"], *Chūō kōron*, December 2013. The issue contains articles by other researchers in the *Jinkō Genshō Mondai Kenkyūkai* [Declining Population Issue Study Group]. (The Japan

Policy Forum published an English translation of Masuda Hiroya's article: http://www.japanpolicyforum.jp/en/pdf/2014/vol18/DJweb_18_pol_01.pdf.)

4 Masuda uses the term *genkai shūraku*, originally coined by the sociologist Ōno Akira. The term "shūraku" refers to hamlets or villages – "settlements" of people. Source: German Institute for Japanese Studies, DIJ Newsletter, No. 39, March 2010, p. 2. http://www.dijtokyo.org/publications/DIJ-NL39_english.pdf. *Genkai shūraku* refers to such settlements being at the limit, on the margins – nearing extinction because of ageing and population decline.

5 National Institute of Population and Social Security Research, *Nihon no chiiki betsu shōrai suikei jinkō: 2010–2040* [Regional Population Projections for Japan: 2010–2040]. March 2013, p. 6. http://www.ipss.go.jp/pp-shicyoson/j/shicyoson13/1kouhyo/gaiyo.pdf.

6 National Institute of Population and Social Security Research, *Nihon no shōrai suikei jinkō: 2011–2060. Sankō suikei: 2061–2110* [Population Projections for Japan: 2011–2060. Auxiliary Projections 2061–2110], January 2012.http://www.ipss.go.jp/syoushika/tohkei/newest04/gh2401.pdf; http://www.ipss.go.jp/site-ad/index_english/esuikei/ppfj2012.pdf (English translation).

7 Ibid., pp. 7–8.

8 Masuda, "*2040 nen, chihō shōmetsu. Kyokuten shakai ga tōrai suru,*" p. 20.

9 National Institute of Population and Social Security Research, *Nihon no chiiki betsu shōrai suikei jinkō*, March 2013.

10 Masuda, "*2040 nen, chihō shōmetsu. Kyokuten shakai ga tōrai suru,*" pp. 23–28.

11 Ibid., pp. 28–31.

12 Rebuild Japan Initiative Foundation, *Japan in Peril? 9 crisis scenarios* (Hong Kong: CLSA Books, 2014). Quote taken from the synopsis of this publication, which is available at http://rebuildjpn.org/wp/wp-content/uploads/2012/11/crisisManagement_20130318.pdf.

13 Ministry of Finance Japan, Budget Bureau, "*Shakai hoshō yosan (iryō, kaigo nado)*" ["Expenditure for Social Security (Medical Services, Care, etc.)"], October 2012, p. 4, https://www.mof.go.jp/about_mof/councils/fiscal_system_council/sub-of_fiscal_system/proceedings/material/zaiseia241015/01.pdf; Ministry of Internal Affairs and Communications, Statistics Bureau, "*Kōreisha no jinkō*" ["The Elderly Population"], in *Tōkei kara mita waga kuni no kōreisha (65 ijō) –"Keirō no hi ni chinande"* [A Statistical Look at Our Country's Elderly (the Over 65), – In Tribute to "Respect for the Aged Day"], in *Kōreisha no jinkō*, No. 72 (September 15, 2013), http://www.stat.go.jp/data/topics/topi721.htm.

14 Assuming that "cities" are agglomerations of one million inhabitants or more.

15 Employment policies for older workers in Japan go back to 1976, when a statutory employment rate of 6 percent was established and firms in the private sector were obliged to make efforts to attain it. The first Elderly Persons Employment Security Act dates from this time. This policy was not successful. Other policies were put into place, with revisions of the Act, over the 1980s, 1990s, and 2000s. These mostly involved raising the mandatory retirement age and ensuring elderly employment up to retirement age.

16 Ministry of Internal Affairs and Communications, Statistics Bureau, "*Takamaru kōreisha no shūgyō ritsu*" ["The Rising Employment Rate of the Elderly"], in *Tōkei Today*, No. 74 (March 2014). http://www.stat.go.jp/info/today/074.htm.

17 For details on the Pension Reform of 2004, see Ministry of Health, Labor and Welfare, *Nenkin seido kaisei no pointo* [Key Points of the Pension Reform], 2004, http://www.mhlw.go.jp/topics/bukyoku/nenkin/nenkin/kaisei-h16-point.html.

18 Ministry of Health, Labor and Welfare, *Kōsei hakusho (Shōwa 49 nen ban)* [1974 White Paper on Health and Welfare], 1974, http://www.mhlw.go.jp/toukei_hakusho/hakusho/kousei/1974/.

19 Ministry of Health, Labor and Welfare, *Kōsei hakusho (Shōwa 54 nen ban)* [1979 White Paper on Health and Welfare], 1979, http://www.mhlw.go.jp/toukei_hakusho/hakusho/kousei/1979/.

20 *Shusshōryoku dōkō ni kansuru tokubetsu iinnkai hōkoku* [Special Report by Council Members on Fertility Trends], Compiled by the Council on Population Problems, an Advisory Committee to the Ministry of Health, Labor and Welfare, August 7, 1980.
21 Ibid.
22 *Asahi Shimbun*, "*Shusshōryoku teika ha ichijiteki, shinkoku na jinkō heranai, kōreika wa tomaru*" [The Decline in the Level of Fertility Is Temporary, There Will Not Be a Severe Population Decline, Ageing Will Speed Up], *Morning Edition*, August 8, 1980.
23 Yokohama City, "*Heisei 25 nen 4 gatsu 1 nichi, genzai no hoikusho taiki jidō sū ni tsuite*" ["Regarding the Current Number of Those on the Kindergarten Waiting List, April 1, 2013"], in *Yokohamashi kisha happyō shiryō* [Yokohama City Press Report], May 1, 2014, http://www.city.yokohama.lg.jp/kodomo/kinkyu/file/250520–250401taikijidousuu.pdf.
24 See: 1994 Angel Plan: http://www.mhlw.go.jp/bunya/kodomo/angelplan.html; 1999 New Angel Plan: http://www1.mhlw.go.jp/topics/syousika/tp0816–3_18.html; 2002 Plus One Plan to End the Declining Birth Rate: http://www.mhlw.go.jp/houdou/2002/09/dl/h0920–1a.pdf; 2004 Children and Childcare Support Plan: http://www.mhlw.go.jp/houdou/2004/12/h1224–4.html; 2009 Children and Childcare Vision: http://www.mhlw.go.jp/bunya/kodomo/pdf/vision-zenbun.pdf; 2013 Plan to Accelerate the Elimination of Childcare Waiting Lists: http://www.mhlw.go.jp/bunya/kodomo/pdf/taikijidokaisho_01.pdf.
25 The proposal was for a handbook that would be titled *Inochi to josei no techō* [A Handbook on Life and Women]. The idea was that the publication would be distributed to teenage girls starting in fiscal year 2014, with the idea of sparking interest in having children.
26 For examples see: All Japan Obachan Party, a civic women's group formed on Facebook and headed by Professor Taniguchi Mayumi, "The Abe administration's policies on women are entirely incoherent." The pamphlet gives the impression that women are primarily responsible for the nation's sagging birthrate. John Hofilena, "Japanese Gov't–Proposed Handbook on Pregnancy, Childbirth Criticized by Women's Groups," *Japan Daily Press* (May 8, 2013), http://japandailypress.com/japanese-govt-proposed-handbook-on-pregnancy-childbirth-criticized-by-womens-groups-0828487/. Objections also came from Soshiren, a broad coalition of over 70 women's groups. Soshiren stated that "The handbook violates women's right to make their own decisions." Soshiren, *Josei techō no sakusei, haifu ni kansuru ikensho* [An Opinion Brief on the Handbook for Women], May 19, 2013, http://www.soshiren.org/data/kougibun0519.pdf.
27 Keidanren, *Jinkō genshō ni taiō shita keizai shakai no arikata* [The Shape of Economic Society in the Face of a Decreasing Population], October 14, 2010.
28 Ministry of Economy, Trade and Industry, "*Dai 3 shō, waga kuni no shōshi kōreika*" ["Chapter 3: Japan's Ageing and the Decline in the Number of Children"], in *Tsūshō hakusho 2005 nen ban* [2005 White Paper on International Trade], http://www.meti.go.jp/report/tsuhaku2005/2005honbun/html/H3233000.html.
29 "*Nakagawa shōshikashō: Imin seisaku kentō no jiki*" ["Minister Responsible for Declining Population, Nakagawa: The time for thinking of immigration policies"], *Nikkei Shimbun*, February 23, 2012, http://www.nikkei.com/article/DGXNASFS2301T_T20C12A2PE8000/.
30 "*Jimintō 'Imin 1000 man nin ukeire' no jitsugensei*" ["LDP: The feasibility of accepting 10 million immigrants"], *Nikkei Business*, June 19, 2008, http://business.nikkeibp.co.jp/article/topics/20080617/162440/.
31 Cabinet Office, *Dai 10 kai sangyō kyōsōryoku kaigi giji yōshi* [A Summary of the Tenth Meeting of Industrial Competitiveness], May 29, 2013, pp. 7–8, http://www.kantei.go.jp/jp/singi/keizaisaisei/skkkaigi/dai10/gijiyousi.pdf.
32 Cabinet Office, *Dai 4 kai sangyō kyōsōryoku kaigi giji yōshi* [A Summary of the Fourth Meeting of Industrial Competitiveness], March 15, 2013, p. 6.
33 Keidanren, *Jinkō genshō ni taiō shita keizai shakai no arikata*.
34 Ibid.

2 Monetary and fiscal policies during the lost decades

Kenneth Kuttner, Iwaisako Tokuo, and Adam Posen

Japan's two-decade-long slump was avoidable. While some slowdown in growth following the "bubble years" in Japan was inevitable, the depth and duration of the downturn from 1995 onward was largely due to the monetary and fiscal policies pursued. Demographics and banking problems contributed to Japan's poor growth, but their role should not be exaggerated. Two facts strongly indicate that the primary cause of Japan's lost decades was depressed demand, not structural decline: the first is that deflation accompanied economic stagnation; and the second is that productivity growth returned to a relatively high rate after 2002. Demand remained depressed because monetary and fiscal policies were consistently inadequate and at times counterproductive. Recently, a third fact has driven home this reality: the coordinated fiscal and monetary policies of Prime Minister Abe, dubbed "Abenomics," since December 2012 have increased growth and inflation.

The macroeconomic policy failures of 1995–2012 resulted from fundamental governance problems in Japan, not unlike those associated with the management of the Fukushima disaster and the other policy mistakes discussed in this book. Several factors account for the errors that were committed by the Ministry of Finance (MoF) and the Bank of Japan (BoJ). One is that they viewed each other as rivals and threats, rather than as partners constructively coordinating policies. Another is that they clung to existing policies in spite of bad results and external advice. In addition, they insisted that Japan's problems were due to forces beyond their control, rather than accepting responsibility and taking action. Further, the MoF and BoJ were able to persist in making bad decisions because they were not held accountable to the public by politicians.

This chapter will make three arguments. First, we will establish the failure to exercise standard macroeconomic stabilization polices in Japan over the last twenty years and look at why this happened. To some extent, the failure can be blamed on poor implementation by the Japanese monetary and fiscal authorities – the policies were insufficiently aggressive and poorly coordinated. Apologists repeatedly claim that these policies have also been constrained by other impediments, but these constraining factors are exaggerated. It is true that the zero lower bound (ZLB) on the nominal interest rate, for example, removed the primary policy tool from the BoJ's arsenal by 1995 and that the bad loan problem reduced the effectiveness of monetary policy from 1998–2002. Yet, monetary policy can be pursued through quantitative easing effectively to go around damaged banking systems, as subsequently demonstrated by the Bank of England, the European Central Bank, and the Federal Reserve after 2009.

Similarly, a rapidly rising public debt-to-GDP ratio, largely driven by population ageing and an arguably unsustainable level of social security and medical expenditures, has constrained the Japanese government's open-ended use of expansionary fiscal policy. But that long-run constraint on government debt was not a true limit on stabilization policy. Instead, it was used counterproductively as an excuse for cutting public investment, thus squandering the opportunity for stimulus when Japan did have room to borrow. Again, the United States, United Kingdom, and France demonstrated the potential alternative of temporary fiscal stabilization in 2008–2010, as has the Abe government in 2013.

The chapter's second argument charts a future course for fiscal and monetary policy in Japan, based on a reasonable degree of BoJ and MoF coordination and sounder policy approaches in line with international norms. On the fiscal policy side, a significant consolidation is clearly necessary to stabilize the country's debt burden. But the MoF and the Japanese government need to make the budgeting process more transparent in order to build a consensus for the necessary reforms and to rationalize the allocation of scarce fiscal resources. The economic capacity is there to significantly increase taxes such as VAT to above 20 percent. The issue is sequencing the adjustment and committing to it over a multi-year period.

With respect to monetary policy, the BoJ's forceful (and long overdue) commitment since April 2013 to aggressively combat deflation is laudable. The adoption of an explicit inflation target of 2 percent is an important step forward, as is the Bank's embrace of qualitative and quantitative easing (QQE). Finally, the recent Joint Statement by the BoJ and MoF outlining the two institutions' shared macroeconomic objectives marks the beginning of a period of constructive policy coordination, signaling an end, we hope, to the conflicts that characterized fiscal and monetary policy during much of the two "lost decades."

Our third argument is for institutional reform and change in bureaucratic culture to limit the potential for a repeat of macroeconomic policies to go astray for long periods. Japan's lost decades were accompanied by recurring bad ideas and the ducking of responsibility by macroeconomic policymakers. The structural excuses offered by key officials for poor economic performance contributed to the self-reinforcing cycle of defeatism and inaction in Japan, prolonging the malaise. As with the BoJ's new 2 percent inflation target, macroeconomic officials have to be held accountable to international standards of performance more generally. It can be that such standards provide positive hope for Japan's economy, as a legitimate spur to action, and do not simply represent self-interested foreign criticism.

Monetary policy

The BoJ has deservedly been a lightning rod for criticism since the slump began in the early 1990s. Many economists and commentators, both inside and outside the country, have criticized the Bank for being slow to react to the initial downturn in the early 1990s, for being timid in the use of unconventional policy tools, and for accepting if not welcoming deflation. The BoJ is not the only central bank to refrain from activism, despite having the legal mandate and operational capacity to do more. The U.S. Federal Reserve's infamous tightening in 1933, the Bank of England's return to the gold standard in 1923, and the European Central Bank's allowing panic in 2010–12 until the announcement of its outright monetary transactions policy were all deflationary mistakes. Yet, in each of these cases, the mistaken policies were reversed within two to three years when the costly errors became apparent. Even the independent Federal Reserve and European Central Bank were held accountable for results, but the BoJ somehow eluded that responsibility for nearly twenty years. This section examines the BoJ's policies over the past two decades and draws lessons from that experience for the conduct of monetary policy going forward.

Too little, too late

If one were to date the beginning of the period now known as the "lost decades," it would be with the collapse of the stock market in 1990 and the real estate market in 1991. The BoJ had been tightening monetary policy since early 1989 to try to pop the bubble. The actual lasting decline in real estate prices, however, only came with an increase in regulation on collateral in 1991. In the subsequent years, the Nikkei lost approximately half its value and land prices fell by more than 30 percent. The drop in asset prices damaged firms' and households' balance sheets and crippled the banking system. Gross domestic product (GDP) decelerated at about the same time.[1] The BoJ responded with a series of cuts in the call rate (the BoJ's policy instrument) beginning in July 1991. From a level of 8 percent in early 1991, the rate had fallen to half a percent by mid-1995.

On the face of it, the policy rate reductions would appear to have been a forceful response to deteriorating economic conditions, comparable only to the cuts in the interest rate in the mid-1970s. The cuts were spread out over four years, however, and inflation fell by more than a percentage point over the same period. The reduction in the real, inflation-adjusted call rate was therefore gradual and relatively modest. Two years into the recession the real rate had only declined to 2 percent, a level consistent with little or no monetary stimulus. The sluggishness of the BoJ's response did not go unrecognized by Japanese observers. Kuroda Haruhiko, later to become governor of the BoJ, wrote in 2005 that "The [BoJ's] conduct of monetary policy had always been behind the curve in this period and could not stop the aggravation of recession and deflation."[2]

Faced with falling inflation and near-zero real economic growth, most central banks would have eased much more aggressively than the BoJ. The Federal Reserve, for example, reacted quite forcefully to the two most recent recessions in the United States. Its rapid rate cuts in 2001 led to a near-zero real rate by the end of the year, and the rate remained there for the following three years. The Federal Reserve's response is especially striking given the fact while the U.S. economy experienced a slow period of growth from 2002 through 2003, the 2000–01 recession was itself quite mild, not unlike Japan's initial 1991 downturn.[3] The Federal Reserve's rate cuts in 2007–09 were even more drastic, and the real rate reached zero within a year of the business cycle peak.

Despite being described repeatedly by the BoJ as "radical," the BoJ's implementation of unconventional monetary policy during the 1990s also was unduly cautious. The first significant expansion of the Bank's balance sheet did not occur until the failures of Yamaichi Securities and The Hokkaido Takushoku Bank in 1997, and even that was a relatively modest increase in level from ¥60 to ¥80 trillion. And although the BoJ gradually increased its use of short-term liquidity provision throughout the 1990s, nothing resembling the Federal Reserve's quantitative easing (QE) policies began until the stepped-up purchases of Japanese government bonds (JGBs) in 2001. Instead, the BoJ's emphasis throughout the 1990s was on short-term liquidity provision and the expansion of current account balances, rather than on bringing down long-term interest rates.[4]

This is reflected in the fact that the BoJ's purchases were largely at the short end of the yield curve. In fact, the average maturity of the Bank's portfolio of government bonds fell from nearly six years in 2001 to less than four years in 2005.[5] Simply replacing liquid, risk-free short-term government bonds with cash (or equivalently current account balances) is unlikely to affect financial markets and the economy. Quantitative easing would have been more effective had it replaced illiquid, risky assets with cash, inducing investors to invest in higher-yielding assets, such as corporate bonds, thus driving down their returns and reducing borrowing costs.

In the United States, on the other hand, QE policies were implemented within a year and a half of the business cycle peak. After short-term liquidity provision in the wake of the 2008 Lehman failure, Federal Reserve purchases of privately issued mortgage-backed securities commenced in earnest in February 2009 with QE1. QE2, which involved large-scale purchases of U.S. government bonds, followed in 2010. "Operation Twist," which lengthened the average maturity of the Federal Reserve's portfolio, and QE3, which established a program of purchasing $40 billion a month in mortgage-backed securities and $45 billion per month of long-term treasuries, were both launched in 2012.[6] Unlike the BoJ's policies, which emphasized the level of current account balances, the Federal Reserve's measures were explicitly designed either to reduce long-term interest rates or to provide credit directly to the private sector (specifically, the housing market). Given the Federal Reserve's goal of putting downward pressure on bond yields, it is not surprising that long rates fell more quickly in the United States in the six years following the crisis than they did in Japan over a comparable period.

A decisive shift in BoJ policy finally came on January 22, 2013, more than two decades after Japan's economy slid into recession. Under pressure from the newly elected Abe government, the Bank finally announced an explicit inflation target of 2 percent and committed to open-ended monetary easing.[7]

Three months later, the Bank released further details of what it referred to as a policy of Quantitative and Qualitative Monetary Easing. One element of the policy is to set a time horizon of two years for the achievement of the target announced in January. A second element is a much more rapid expansion of the monetary base, at a pace of ¥60 to 70 trillion per year. A third element is that rather than limit JGB purchases to the short end of the yield curve, the Bank extended the maturity of the bonds purchased, its first explicit effort to bring down long-term interest rates.[8] The policy also entails purchases of ETFs (Exchange-traded funds) and J-REITs (Japanese Real Estate Investment Trust), but the quantities involved (¥1 trillion and ¥30 billion, respectively) are comparable to those of the Comprehensive Monetary Easing policy under Shirakawa, and remain quite small relative to the size of the Bank's balance sheet.

The BoJ's balance sheet has grown spectacularly since the adoption of the policy. The Bank's total assets have grown from ¥163 trillion in February 2013 to ¥225 trillion as of early 2014. Most of this growth has come through increases in the purchases of long-dated JGBs, and the average maturity of the Bank's portfolio of government securities has risen from less than three years to more than seven.

Just as importantly, the Bank's communication changed dramatically with the appointment of Kuroda Haruhiko as governor. In his public statements, BoJ Governor Kuroda has reiterated the seriousness of the Bank's commitment by downplaying the risk of inflation getting out of control and by pledging to use any tools necessary to achieve the inflation target. In fact, the April 2013 announcement stated explicitly that one of the BoJ's goals was to "drastically change the expectations of markets and economic entities."

Kuroda's rhetoric makes a stark contrast with that of his three predecessors, which often emphasized the risks associated with expansionary policy and lamented the lack of effective tools for combating deflation. Taken together, these policies are a sharp break from previous BoJ policy. Prime Minister Abe Shinzo was not exaggerating when he hailed the move as a "regime change" in monetary policy.

Explaining the BoJ's conservatism

The fundamental lesson from Japan's experience of the past twenty years and the 2007–09 global financial crisis is that periods of severe economic and financial stress call for extraordinary monetary policy measures. Why, then, did the BoJ act so deliberately even as the economy slid into deflation?

One hypothesis is that members of the policy board simply were not attuned to the risks posed by the extraordinary shocks the economy experienced in the 1990s. One such shock was the sharp decline in asset prices, and the financial stress caused by the resultant balance sheet effects. Subsequent research has shown (or reminded us) that recessions precipitated by financial crises call for policies that are considerably more interventionist than in normal times.

In extreme cases, it may be appropriate for the central bank to temporarily resuscitate significant parts of the financial system through the direct provision of credit. This is essentially what the Federal Reserve did with its support of the commercial paper and mortgage-backed securities markets, where the buy side of the market simply evaporated. Referring to this form of support as "credit easing," Bernanke drew a distinction between this set of tools and conventional monetary policy and traditional liquidity provision as part of the central bank's lender of last resort function.[9]

Another aspect of the first hypothesis is that the BoJ was slow to recognize the possibility of deflation and the constraints on policy imposed by the ZLB on nominal interest rates. These issues were relevant to the 1930s, of course, but by the early 1990s these were viewed as curiosities and relegated to the footnotes in macroeconomics textbooks. It took Paul Krugman's 1998 paper to bring the ZLB issue back into policymakers' consciousness. In the absence of a sharp contraction (year-over-year real GDP growth never fell below 1 percent during the 1990–93 recession), it is perhaps understandable that BoJ policymakers would not have taken the ZLB possibility into account. The BoJ was not alone in that regard, as the consensus among economists (including those at the Federal Reserve) in the 1990s was that in practice the deleterious effects of the ZLB were relatively modest.

The 2007–09 global financial crisis forcefully demonstrated that ZLB was a far more serious problem than either the BoJ or the Federal Reserve realized in the 1990s, and that it was not an idiosyncratic Japan-specific phenomenon. Subsequent research (not to mention actual experience) has shown that the relatively sanguine view of the ZLB may have been unduly influenced by the absence of large adverse shocks during the "great moderation" period in the United States. If nothing else, the post-2007 experience shows that policy needs to be more aggressive when there is a risk of hitting the ZLB. Blanchard suggested that the ZLB threat may justify an inflation target in excess of the 2 percent adopted by most advanced-economy central banks.[10]

A second hypothesis is that the BoJ leadership clung to erroneous beliefs about ideas about the causes and risks of inflation. As discussed in Bernanke,[11] Blanchard,[12] and Posen,[13] there seems to have been a self-induced paralysis at the BoJ and at times a mistaken belief in the real benefits of tighter credit conditions.

A 2000 speech by then-Governor Hayami Masaru epitomized this mindset. Raising the specter of an inflationary spiral, he hypothesized that any increase in the target inflation rate would destabilize inflation expectations. He said:

> Inflation is most likely uncontrollable once triggered. [. . .] Some argue that since the Bank of Japan is an independent central bank, it can raise the inflation rate to 2 to 3% and then contain it around that level even if there exists further upward pressure. However, if we tried to contain inflation after it had gained momentum, we would need very strong monetary tightening, which might result in a substantial deterioration of economic activity and a steep climb in unemployment.

This view flies in the face of the experience of other industrialized countries, most of which had successfully targeted and maintained inflation rates of roughly 2 percent.

In addition to exaggerating the risk of inflation instability, BoJ officials apparently failed to recognize the potential benefits of a positive inflation target. In the same 2000 speech, Hayami asserted that because increasing inflation would have not stimulative effects, it was not a solution to Japan's economic problems. In fact, there seems to have been sympathy for the view that in the case of Japan falling prices were a manifestation of "good deflation."

These concerns receded over time, with BoJ officials recognizing that the rapid increase in current account balances posed no risk of inflation. In a 2011 interview, then-Governor Shirakawa Masaaki conceded that the proposition that "inflation is always and everywhere a monetary phenomenon" had been proven wrong by Japan's experience.[14]

A third hypothesis is that the BoJ's aversion to aggressive action had its roots in political considerations. One aspect of this centered on the fiscal implications of purchases of private-sector securities, such as asset-backed securities, which were purchased in only very small amounts. As then-Deputy Governor Yamaguchi Yutaka put it in 2001,

> The basic rule in a democratic society is that fiscal policy using taxpayers' money needs to be approved as part of a budget by a parliament composed of members elected by the people. [A policy of purchasing private-sector assets] should be discussed publicly in the context of governance in a democratic society.

Ueda Kazuo raised similar concerns, arguing that capital losses – and *in extremis* insolvency – would undermine the Bank's independence.[15] The BoJ would have been especially sensitive to this issue, having been subordinate to the Ministry of Finance until the passage of the New Bank of Japan Law in 1997. Consequently, the BoJ was eager to establish its reputation as a fully independent central bank. Cargill referred to this as an "independence gap" that led the bank to resist external advice, particularly that coming from the finance ministry.[16] This, in turn, inhibited the adoption of more innovative and aggressive policies and precluded any substantive cooperation with the MoF or the government.

Related to the independence issue, a fourth hypothesis is that underlying conflicts between the objectives of the BoJ and the MoF prevented coordination, and that this may have led the BoJ to refrain from implementing expansionary policies. The coordination problem is discussed in greater detail later in the section on policy coordination.

Fiscal policy

At the peak of Japan's prosperity in the late 1980s, the fiscal situation was sound and improving substantially. The ratio of gross government debt to GDP fell from 70 percent in 1988 to 67 percent in 1989, the first decline in ten years, thanks to the strong economy and increased tax revenue. However, the situation began to deteriorate after the real estate and stock market bubbles burst and the economy began to worsen in the early 1990s.

The economy's deceleration was initially thought to be a temporary slowdown, a hangover after the financial euphoria in late 1980s. The Japanese government undertook only half-hearted stop-start fiscal stimulus in mid-1990s, as Posen argued.[17] Later, based on the incorrect presumption that the Japanese economy was soon reversing to its previous trend, the Japanese government raised the consumption tax rate in April 1997 from 3 percent to 5 percent. Then everything went wrong for the Japanese economy for the rest of the 1990s. The Asian currency crisis started during the summer of 1997. In the fall of the same year, the domestic banking crisis hit the Japanese economy, revealing the seriousness of the non-performing loan problem. In 1998 and 1999, Japan experienced its worst recession since the first oil crisis in the early 1970s. To combat this sharp economic downturn, the government implemented a series of large fiscal stimulus packages. However, all were smaller than advertised, were less than fully implemented, and allowed cuts in public investment.[18]

Even this fiscal expansion came to an end as the economy started to improve and Koizumi Junichiro became the prime minister in 2001. Though Koizumi successfully brought the nonperforming loan problem to an end in the first half of the 2000s, the debt-to-GDP ratio continued to creep up throughout the 2000s. To cope with the 2011 earthquake and its aftermath, the Japanese government increased its spending once again for 2009 to 2012, which caused a further deterioration of Japan's fiscal situation. According to the International Monetary Fund, Japan's gross government debt-to-GDP ratio was only 12 percent in 1970. Twenty years later, in 1990, it had increased to 67 percent. The ratio more than tripled in the subsequent two decades, reaching 215 percent in 2010.[19]

Japan's fiscal erosion is most alarming when set in the context of international comparison. As shown in Figure 2.1, the gross debt-to-GDP ratio has risen much more rapidly than elsewhere –including even the troubled countries on the periphery of the Euro area. If we consider net debt-to-GDP ratios rather than gross ratios, subtracting government assets from debt outstanding, the difference between Japan and other developed economies is significantly smaller. Japan's fiscal situation becomes barely comparable with Portugal and Italy and significantly better than Greece. Even so, population ageing will continue to worsen Japan's fiscal situation, so that its net debt-to-GDP ratio will surpass Greece's by 2020.[20]

Fiscal sustainability

Exceptionally high relative to the peacetime experience of other developed countries, Japan's debt-to-GDP ratio has now reached a point that has often been associated with the onset of fiscal crises. However, unlike that of some European countries, the Japanese economy has yet to feel the threat of a fiscal crisis in the form of high interest rates on government bonds. This reflects some of Japan's fundamental attributes, including high private-sector savings, and high risk-aversion and home bias by Japanese savers, which have so far contributed to strong domestic demand for Japanese government bonds.

It can be argued that Japan should have increased the consumption tax rate much earlier than it did. Given Japan's demographics, even if the government and central bank had avoided all the macroeconomic policy mistakes since 1990,

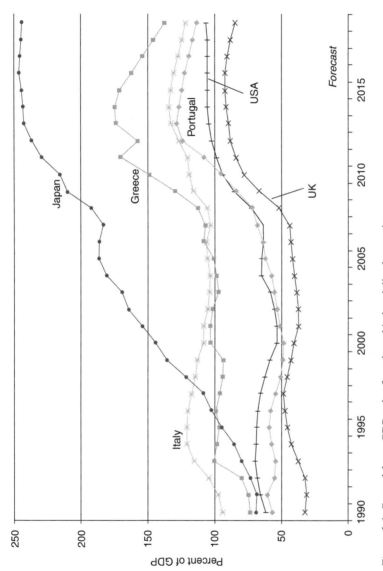

Figure 2.1 Gross debt-to-GDP ratios for selected industrialized countries

Source: IMF World Economic Outlook, October 2013.

the fiscal situation would not be significantly better than it is today. However, tax increases alone will not solve the problem. Simulation results reported by Fukao Mitsuhiro,[21] Anton Braun and Douglas Joines,[22] and by Hoshi Takeo and Ito Takatoshi[23] suggest that an increase in the consumption tax rate to over 20 percent, which would be comparable to that of Scandinavian countries, would not halt the further increase of Japan's debt-to-GDP ratio. The recently implemented consumption tax rate hike from 5 percent to 8 percent (with a further increase to 10 percent planned for October 2015) will buy time, but stabilizing and reducing Japan's debt-to-GDP ratio will eventually require major social security reforms, including significant reductions in public pension payments and medical expenditures, as well.[24]

The rapid ageing of society discussed in Seike Atsushi's Chapter 1 is closely related to the reason why Japan's long-term interest rate has remained at its current low level. While European countries presently suffering from overt fiscal crises had been running current account deficits, Japan has run current account surpluses for more than thirty years, and has, as of 2012, accumulated over ¥600 trillion in foreign assets and a net international investment position of nearly ¥300 trillion. In addition, with 90–95 percent of JGBs held by domestic investors, pressure from foreign creditors has been minimal.

But as the ageing process continues, the Japanese household sector will eventually start to dissave, and at some point the current account surplus will turn into a deficit.[25] When that happens, the Japanese government will have to start borrowing from foreign lenders at a potentially higher interest rate. Another possible scenario is that private savers will decide that the Japanese government has lost control of the debt problem, so that they start to move savings into foreign assets and to sell domestic government bonds at the same time. This could trigger a sell-off of JGBs, exacerbating the fiscal problems and increasing the risk of a financial crisis.

However, a drop in the value of JGBs would also have positive effects. It would almost certainly cause the Japanese yen to depreciate, boosting exports and increasing both GDP and tax revenues. This would ameliorate the fiscal situation, offsetting the increased debt burden caused by the rise in interest rates.[26] Of course, there might be some serious side effects. A large depreciation of local currency can create inflationary pressure above the preferred level, causing a significant increase in domestic prices of raw materials and energy prices.

Discretionary fiscal policy during the lost decades

Why has fiscal stimulus become ineffective?

Despite the multiple fiscal stimulus packages during the 1990s and 2000s, the efficacy of fiscal policy in boosting Japanese economic growth has been hotly debated. While Kuttner and Posen[27] found strong positive effects of (correctly measured) fiscal stimulus, work by Ihori Toshihiro[28] and Ito Arata[29] indicate that Japan's fiscal multiplier has declined in recent years. There are two reasons why it has been hard to discern the effects of Japanese fiscal policy.

First, as pointed out by Posen[30] and to some extent acknowledged by Ihori and others,[31] the total amounts of fiscal expenditures have been exaggerated and true numbers were much lower. The MoF had used various accounting maneuvers and rhetoric to inflate the "headline" numbers. Second, some economists argue that Japanese households became conservative and precautionary, causing them to spend less of the money they received from fiscal stimulus or tax reduction. Also, because of ongoing globalization, Japanese households spend more money on imports, with the result that some of the stimulus leaked abroad. The share of international trade, measured by the sum of export and import as a percentage of GDP, has continued to increase for the last twenty years.[32]

Another contributing factor to the perceived ineffectiveness of fiscal stimulus is the nature and timing of Japanese fiscal policy. The delay in decision making and the policy lag undermine the effectiveness of fiscal expenditure. As argued by Robert Hall,[33] Alan Auerbach[34] and Yuriy Gorodnichenko,[35] fiscal policy in the United States has tended to be more effective during times of crisis. However, the response time of fiscal expenditure tends to be longer than that of monetary policy, especially at the time of crises, such as the domestic banking crisis in 1997–98, the post-Lehman recession in 2008–09, and the Tohoku earthquake in 2011. This was relevant to the fiscal expansion that was undertaken under the Obuchi administration, and especially during the Mori administration at the beginning of 2000s. Such ill-timed policies led to further increases in the debt-to-GDP ratio while having little stimulative effect. Another important aspect about the timing issue of fiscal stimulus is the coordination with monetary policy, an issue to be discussed further later in the section on policy coordination.

Has the productivity of public investment declined?

In addition to the explanations mentioned in the previous section, many empirical analyses, such as those of Asako Kazumi and Sakamoto Kazunori[36] as well as Mitsui Kiyoshi and Inoue Jun,[37] suggest that the beneficial supply-side effects of public investment declined in recent years. These studies argue that Japan's physical infrastructure had already reached close to saturation level, so that positive productivity spillovers to private-sector investment and productivity diminished. While there is some truth to that characterization, such studies also identify at least two other problems that have undermined the effectiveness of public investment in the past two decades. First, due to a combination of privatization and fiscal decentralization, local governments in Japan started to invest and manage local transportation systems (railroads and buses), tourism, and other regional enterprises that previously were owned or at least heavily subsidized by the central government. Most of such semi-privatized or "corporatized" public enterprises suffered substantial losses, and local governments eventually had to pay for those losses.

Second, public investments by the central government increasingly favored road construction over more productive infrastructure. Most of the road construction budget was spent on roads in rural areas, with no serious assessment of the economic benefits. The main purpose of the so-called investment was in fact to redistribute income from urban areas, such as Tokyo, to rural areas that were experiencing rapid population ageing and decline. Such road construction projects helped many local Japanese cities and villages provide enough employment opportunities for their working-age populations. The evidence presented by Mitsui Kiyoshi[38] suggests that the marginal productivity of public investments in rural areas is much lower than in urban areas. Hoshi and Kashyap[39] also argue, based on Doi Takero and Ihori Toshihiro's calculation of category-wise productivity, that the share of public investments to the categories with lowest marginal productivity has significantly increased during the two lost decades.[40]

Lessons from the 1997 consumption tax hike

The arguments presented so far seem to suggest that Japan should have started fiscal restructuring much earlier than it did. However, it is not that simple. The causes of rises in the debt-to-GDP ratio derive both from increased government debt and the slowing of GDP growth. In particular, recent experiences in the Eurozone crisis strongly suggest that ill-timed and aggressive austerity does not work as it hurts growth and tax receipts, as well as growth potential for the long term. Misguided austerity can drive up net public debt as a result, and so the needed rise in consumption taxes discussed above must be spread over several years and take into account the short- and long-term impact on growth.

From this perspective, the 1997 consumption tax hike was a mistake – especially given the coincidence with the Asian financial crisis and the emergence of problems in the banking system. The tax rate hike was in fact part of a policy package, a structural reform of Japanese tax system, that had been initiated in the early 1990s.[41] The income tax rate had been cut over the 1993–95 period in a rather complicated process that included both permanent and temporary reductions. The recession after the collapse of the asset bubble in the early 1990s had necessitated a delay in the consumption tax hike that had been scheduled at that time.

Even so, the Japanese government's decision to increase the tax rate in April 1997 was questionable. According to the BoJ's Short-Term Economic Survey of Enterprises (Tankan) data, overall business conditions of Japanese firms in 1996 had bounced back to their 1992 level. However, the 1996 recovery was mainly due to the improvement of external economic conditions. At its peak in the summer of 1995, the yen had strengthened by 40 percent relative to 1990. It began to reverse in 1996, helping to restore the profitability of Japan's export sector. On the other hand, domestic business conditions had deteriorated more sharply than overall conditions following the 1990 collapse of the asset price bubbles and did not experience a comparable rebound. Business conditions remained depressed due to the serious nonperforming loan problem of the Japanese banking sector. Given the pessimistic outlook for businesses, the government should have postponed the tax hike for at least another year.

Policy coordination

Conventional wisdom is that the central bank should adjust policy in response to the fiscal stance, but should make no effort to articulate and pursue jointly specified objectives. Central bank independence has become the sacred cow of monetary policy. Any kind of coordination is taboo.[42]

Japan's experience has shown the conventional wisdom to be incorrect. No effort was made to coordinate monetary fiscal policies during the lost decades – indeed, at times the MoF and BoJ appeared to be pursuing completely different objectives. The result was that monetary and fiscal policies often worked at cross-purposes, with expansionary monetary policy offset by tight fiscal policy and vice versa. The unfortunate result was intermittent and inadequate macroeconomic stimulus.

A history of non-cooperation

Figure 2.2 illustrates graphically the lack of coordination between monetary and fiscal policies during the lost decades. One line (almost uniformly trending downward) represents the central government's fiscal balance as a share of GDP, a rough indicator of its stance on fiscal policy. The time line at the top of the figure depicts the BoJ's major policy shifts.

The figure shows that the four years spanning 1993 through 1996 were characterized by expansionary fiscal policy (a rapidly expanding deficit) and insufficient monetary stimulus (discussed earlier in the section titled "Too little, too late"). BoJ Governor Kuroda, when he was the governor of the Asian Development Bank, described the situation as one in which "monetary easing did not keep the pace with fiscal expansion, thereby leading to a rise in the value of the yen. The appreciation of the yen in this period is one of the main causes that started the prolonged deflation process, which still continues today."[43]

There was a fleeting period at the end of the 1990s during which monetary and fiscal policies were both expansionary. Responding to the severe recession triggered by the domestic banking crisis that started in late 1997, the Liberal Democratic Party government led first by Prime Minister Obuchi Keizo and later by Prime Minister Mori Yoshiro undertook a significant fiscal expansion beginning in 1998. The BoJ implemented a zero interest rate policy (ZIRP) shortly thereafter, in February 1999. This alignment of policies, however, ended with the BoJ's suspension of ZIRP six months later.

The BoJ reverted to an expansionary policy with its reinstatement of ZIRP and large-scale purchases of JGBs in early 2001. However, the policy coincided with sharp cuts in government expenditures under Prime Minister Koizumi. The result was a period of relatively easy monetary policy and a tight fiscal stance.

The case for coordination

There are a number of compelling reasons for policy coordination. At the very least, the fiscal and monetary authorities should agree on the overall goals of macroeconomic policy. In the context of inflation targeting, Bernanke and others

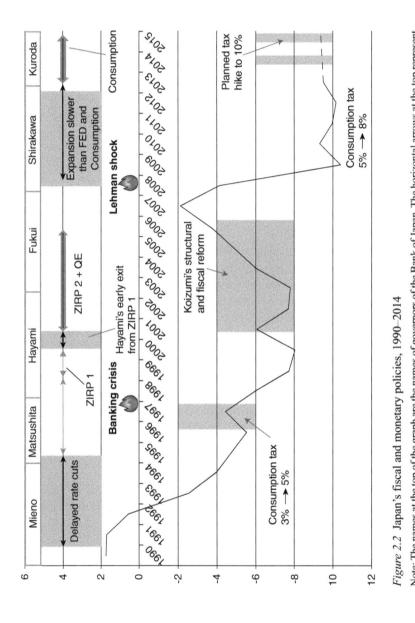

Figure 2.2 Japan's fiscal and monetary policies, 1990–2014

Note: The names at the top of the graph are the names of governors of the Bank of Japan. The horizontal arrows at the top represent monetary policy stance: the black arrows correspond to the periods of relatively tighter monetary policy stance, while the gray arrows correspond to the periods of monetary expansion (the line widths represent the "intensity" of the expansion). The kinked line shows the central government's budget balance as the share of GDP. Shaded areas represent periods in which either monetary or fiscal policy was relatively tightened.

argue that government involvement is beneficial on the grounds that it would "maximize central bank accountability while still leaving the ultimate goals of policy to be determined at least in part by democratic processes. . . . This strategy calls for the inflation targets themselves to be set by a political process in which the central bankers consult with the appropriate legislators or ministers."[44]

More fundamentally, situations can arise in which conflicts between monetary and fiscal authorities result in suboptimal policy. The solution to this problem is to coordinate policies, which necessarily involves agreeing on a common set of objectives. Often, the conflicts are such that they lead to excess inflation, as pointed out in Nordhaus[45] and Dixit and Lambertini.[46] Japan's case is different, however, as policy disagreements may have created a *de*flationary bias.

Hoshi Takeo argued that the BoJ's reluctance to continue ZIRP policy in the early 2000s resulted from concerns that doing so would reduce the pressure for financial restructuring.[47] Underlying this view is the assumption that aggressive monetary policy, in the form of very low interest rates or direct credit extensions, would allow insolvent ("zombie") firms to survive. Since the survival of firms would reduce the efficacy of monetary policy, the central bank would like the financial supervisor to close or restructure the zombies – but this is costly for the regulator. Hoshi shows how the central bank and the regulatory agency can fall into a trap with insufficient restructuring and an overly contractionary monetary policy. Posen identified this belief on the part of Japanese macroeconomic policymakers early in the Great Recession and summarized the evidence against monetary tightness causing the right firms to close.[48]

In a similar vein, Eggertsson argued that in a liquidity trap, independent, discretionary monetary policy creates a deflationary bias, preventing or at least delaying an escape from the trap.[49] The problem stems from the central bank's preference for low inflation. The central bank may *say* that it intends to target a higher rate of inflation in the future, thus bringing down the real (inflation-adjusted) interest rate and pushing the economy out of the trap. But once the economy escapes the trap, the central bank will renege on its pledge and keep inflation low. Recognizing this, the public will not believe the central bank and the deflationary mindset will remain. Coordinating with the fiscal authority can help in this situation. In theory, finance ministries like inflation, as it brings in seigniorage revenue and lowers the existing debt burden. By allowing fiscal considerations to affect monetary policy, policy coordination (or simply putting the MoF in charge of monetary policy) would make the promise of higher inflation more credible. Normally a vice, in Japan's case the use of seigniorage would have been a virtue.

Conclusions and recommendations

In retrospect, it is clear that bad luck is partly to blame for the lost decades. Japan was the first major industrialized country in recent history to experience widespread financial distress brought on by the collapse of an asset price bubble. Although the United States and many European countries were also hit hard by the collapse of the housing market in the late 2000s, most responded decisively, partly because policymakers in those countries were determined not to repeat Japan's experience in the 1990s.

Adverse, demographically driven fiscal trends are another source of bad luck. Driven largely by a plummeting fertility rate, Japan's population is shrinking and rapidly ageing. Tax hikes by themselves cannot stop the relentless rise of the debt-to-GDP ratio. The only way to do so is through a major reform of the country's pension system, which faces large (but hopefully not insurmountable) political obstacles.

Bad luck, however, is not entirely to blame for the lost decades. The Japanese government, and monetary and fiscal authorities in particular, made crucial mistakes that contributed to the initial slowdown and the subsequent stagnation. Policymakers repeatedly failed to admit previous mistakes and change course, even after the problems of chronic recession and deflation became obvious.

One reason for the inadequacy of the policy responses is that policymakers were trapped by the legacy of their own success and failed to recognize the seriousness of the economy's deterioration. Consequently, they relied on the prescriptions that had worked in the past and avoided drastic policy changes. The BoJ clung to its old monetary policy regime and was slow to adopt bold, unconventional measures as the economy slid into deflation. Similarly, failing to recognize the deceleration in trend output growth in the mid-1990s, the MoF pushed to increase the consumption tax in 1997, sending the economy into recession while exacerbating an already deteriorating fiscal situation.

At the same time, institutional inertia led policymakers to persist with bad policies, even after they had been recognized as inappropriate. While common to all bureaucracies, the aversion to changing course is particularly strong in Japan, where there is a substantial reluctance to overturning predecessors' decisions. The lack of information sharing and coordination among policymakers has also hindered effective policy making. In particular, the rocky relationship between Japanese monetary and fiscal authorities often led to perverse policy outcomes.

Going forward, four lessons can be learned from Japan's experience during the lost decades. The first is that central banks should expand the set of monetary policy tools used to revive the economy. The projected adverse side effects that inhibited the BoJ from taking strong action during the lost decades have failed to materialize. Debt management – changes in the maturity distribution of central banks' portfolio of government securities – is a potentially useful tool, one that was largely neglected by the BoJ until the recent implementation of QQE.[50] In addition, purchases of securities other than government debt have proven to be effective in reducing private-sector interest rates, and are in fact necessary to stimulate credit in a damaged financial system.

The second lesson is that communication matters. Under QQE, a public commitment by the central bank to "do what it takes" to end deflation, supported by transparent communication and positive rhetoric, has become a central element of monetary policy. While hard to measure with any precision, the impact on expectations should not be discounted.

Third, it would be an error to ignore the contractionary impact of fiscal consolidation. Although additional revenues were needed to counter ominous budgetary
trends, it was a mistake to implement a consumption tax in 1997 when the economy was already weak. Any future tax hikes should balance the need to stabilize
the debt-to-GDP ratio against the imperative to keep the economy growing. With
an expansionary monetary policy in place and a stable world economy, there is
currently a window of opportunity to take incremental steps to strengthen Japan's
finances. Flexibility must exist, however, to postpone consumption tax increases
should economic conditions soften. Regardless, expenditures should be reallo-
cated away from rural construction and towards more productive uses.

The fourth point is that coordinated fiscal–monetary stimulus is desirable,
especially in response to dire economic situations. Central bank independence is
important, but not sacrosanct. As Posen argued in 2010, government oversight of
central bank goals over a multiyear period, and voluntary policy cooperation by
the central bank in pursuit of those goals, do not harm and indeed can enhance
monetary credibility.[51] The April 2013 replacement of Governor Shirakawa
Masaaki by Kuroda Haruhiko was therefore not a blow to the BoJ's independence, as some have warned. Instead, it was a long-overdue step towards meaningful policy coordination.

There are no easy solutions to Japan's economic problems. However, the policies that have been recently implemented by Prime Minister Abe and BoJ Governor Kuroda are steps in the right direction. The BoJ's strong commitment to
end deflation and the aggressive deployment of its balance sheet to that end are
a long-overdue regime shift in monetary policy. At the same time, there appears
to be a willingness to coordinate monetary and fiscal policies. The most difficult
task ahead is to solve the country's long-term fiscal problem without jeopardizing
economic recovery.

Notes

1 The absence of a sharp drop in output makes it hard to assign a precise date to the
   beginning of the contraction. The OECD dates the peak as having occurred in August
   1990.
2 Kuroda Haruhiko, *Zaisei-kinyu seisaku no seiko to shippai* [Successes and Failures of
   Monetary and Fiscal Policy] (Tokyo: Nihon hyōronsha, 2005), p. 100.
3 For a more detailed description of the BoJ's policy during this period and a comparison
   with the Federal Reserve, see James Harrigan and Kenneth N. Kuttner, "Lost Decade
   in Translation: Did the United States Learn from Japan's Post-bubble Mistakes?" in
   Reviving Japan's Economy: Problems and Prescriptions, Takatoshi Ito et al., eds.
   (Cambridge, MA: MIT Press, 2005), pp. 79–106.
4 For a more complete chronology and comparison to the Federal Reserve, see Kenneth
   N. Kuttner, "The Fed's Response to the Financial Crisis: Pages from the BoJ Playbook,
   or a Whole New Ball Game?" *Public Policy Review* 6 (2010), pp. 407–30. (Also published in Japanese.)
5 Robert McCauley and Kazuo Ueda, "Government Debt Management at Low Interest
   Rates," *BIS Quarterly Review* (2009), pp. 35–51, documented the maturity distribution
   of the BoJ's portfolio over this period.
6 http://www.federalreserve.gov/newsevents/press/monetary/20120913a.htm.

7 Prior to the announcement, the BoJ framed its intention in terms of its "understanding of medium- to long-term price stability," as defined by the individual policy board members. The midpoint of the board members' "understanding" was a 1 percent annual rate of inflation.

8 The maturity extension required the suspension of the so-called banknote principle, which limited the purchase of long-term securities to the amount of currency in circulation.

9 Ben S. Bernanke, *The Crisis and the Policy Response*. Speech delivered at the Stamp Lecture, London School of Economics, January 13, 2009.

10 Olivier Blanchard et al., "Rethinking Macroeconomic Policy," *Journal of Money, Credit and Banking* 42 (2010), pp. 199–215.

11 Ben S. Bernanke, "Japanese Monetary Policy: A Case of Self-Induced Paralysis?" in Ryoichi Mikitani and Adam S. Posen, eds., *Japan's Financial Crisis and Its Parallels to U.S. Experience* (Washington, DC: Peterson Institute for International Economics, 2000), pp. 149–166.

12 Olivier Blanchard, "Bubbles, Liquidity Traps, and Monetary Policy," in Mikitani and Posen, *Japan's Financial Crisis*, pp. 85–193.

13 Adam S. Posen, "The Political Economy of Deflationary Monetary Policy," in Mikitani and Posen, *Japan's Financial Crisis*, pp. 194–208.

14 Apparently oblivious to the Japanese experience, some prominent economists, including Allan Meltzer and Martin Feldstein, have warned about the threat of inflation in the United States created by the expansion of the Fed's balance sheet.

15 Ueda Kazuo, *The Role of Capital for Central Banks*. Speech delivered at the Fall meeting of the Japan Society of Monetary Economics, October 25, 2003.

16 Thomas F. Cargill, et al., *Financial Policy and Central Banking in Japan* (Cambridge, MA: MIT Press, 2001).

17 Adam S. Posen, *Restoring Japan's Economic Growth* (Washington, DC: Peterson Institute for International Economics, 1998).

18 This was documented in Posen, *Restoring Japan's Economic Growth*, and Ishii Hiroko and Erika Wada, "Local Government Spending: Solving the Mystery of Japanese Fiscal Packages, *PIIE Working Paper No. 98-5*, 1998.

19 We refer to gross debt/GDP ratios rather than net ratios here, since they are readily available for international comparison. Christian Broda and David E. Weinstein, "Happy News from the Dismal Science: Reassessing Japanese Fiscal Policy and Sustainability," in Takatoshi Ito, Hugh Patrick and David E. Weinstein, eds., *Reviving Japan's Economy: Problems and Prescriptions* (Cambridge, MA: MIT Press, 2005), pp. 39–78, however, argue that the gross debt ratios significantly overstate the size of Japan's net debt burden. The true number is probably close to 150 percent of GDP, still higher than any developed economy except Greece.

20 According to Fukao Mitsuhiro, "The Sustainability of Budget Deficit in Japan" (RIETI discussion paper 2012), 12-J-018, http://www.rieti.go.jp/en/publications/summary/12060006.html, Japan's net debt-to-GDP ratio was 131 percent in 2011, which was lower than Greece at 153 percent, but still higher than any other developed economies mentioned above. Net debt-to-GDP ratio will increase to 200 percent in 2020 and to 300 percent in 2038, with the current government plan being to increase consumption tax rate to 10 percent in the near future and without any further measure/restructuring. Similarly, in a 2012 working paper, "The Implications of a Greying Japan for Public Policy," Anton R. Braun and Douglas Joines report that net debt/GDP ratio was 150 percent in 2012 and will increase to 350 percent in 2038.

21 Fukao Mitsuhiro, "The Sustainability of Budget Deficit in Japan," RIETI discussion paper.

22 Anton R. Braun and Douglas Joines, "The Implications of a Greying Japan for Public Policy," 2012 working paper.

23 Hoshi Takeo and Takatoshi Ito, "Is the Sky the Limit? Can Japanese Government Bonds Continue to Defy Gravity?" *Asian Economic Policy Review* 8, no. 2 (2013), pp. 218–47; and Hoshi Takeo and Ito Takatoshi, "Defying Gravity: Can Japanese Sovereign Debt Continue to Increase without a Crisis?" *Economic Policy* 77 (January 2014), pp. 5–44.

24 In "The Sustainability of Budget Deficit in Japan," a RIETI discussion paper, Fukao Mitsuhiro suggested that consumption tax rate has to be increased up to 25 percent to stabilize debt/GDP ratio in the near future. According to Braun and Joines' 2012 working paper, "The Implications of a Greying Japan for Public Policy," the consumption tax rate must increase to 53 percent toward the second half of the twenty-first century in order to stabilize net debt/GDP ratio, if it is the only policy tool that can be used.

25 Household saving rate or household saving as a share of GDP significantly declined in 2000s. However, as described in Iwaisako Tokuo and Okada Keiko, "Understanding the Decline in Japan's Saving Rate in the New Millennium," *Japan and the World Economy* 24, no. 3 (2012), pp. 163–73, since the late 1990s, Japan's private-sector saving measured as the share of GDP has remained relatively constant, while the increase in corporate saving offset the decline of household saving.

26 Among developed countries with flexible exchange rates, defaults on government debt denominated in the local currency are exceedingly rare. See Carmen Reinhart and Kenneth Rogoff, "Forgotten History of Domestic Debt," *National Bureau of Asian Economic Research*, Working Paper #13946, April 2008, for a comprehensive analysis of sovereign defaults on domestic debt.

27 Kenneth N. Kuttner and Adam S. Posen, "Fiscal Policy Effectiveness in Japan," *Journal of the Japanese and International Economies* 16 (2002), pp. 536–58.

28 Ihori Toshihiro, Nakazato Toru, and Kawade Masumi, "Japan's Fiscal Policies in the 1990s," *World Economy* 26 (2003), pp. 325–38.

29 Ito Arata, Watanabe Tsutomu, and Yabu Tomoyoshi, "*Seido joho wo mocha-ita zaiseijyo-su no keisoku*" ["Estimation of fiscal multiplier using institutional information"], Cabinet Office Research Institute ed., *Japanese Economy and Economic Policy in the Period of Bubble and Deflation* (Tokyo: Keio University Press, 2010), vol. 5.

30 As detailed in Posen, *Restoring Japan's Economic Growth.*

31 Ihori, Nakazato, and Kawade, "Japan's Fiscal Policies in the 1990s," pp. 325–38.

32 The share of imports in GDP was 9.2 percent in 1990, 9.7 percent in 2000, and 16.4 percent in 2007. It had declined during the global recession subsequent to the Lehman bankruptcy, but bounced back to 17.1 percent in 2012.

33 Robert E. Hall, "By How Much Does GDP Rise if the Government Buys More Output?" *Brookings Papers on Economic Activity* 2009, no. 2, pp. 183–231.

34 Alan Auerbach and Yuriy Gorodnichenko, "Measuring the Output Responses to Fiscal Policy," *American Economic Journal: Economic Policy* 4, no. 2 (May), pp. 1–27.

35 Alan Auerbach and Yuriy Gorodnichenko, "Fiscal Multipliers in Recession and Expansion," in Alberto Alesina and Francesco Giavazzi, eds., *Fiscal Policy after the Financial Crisis* (Chicago: University of Chicago Press, 2013).

36 Asako Kazumi and Sakamoto Kazunori, "The Productive Effect of Public Capital," *Financial Review* 26 (1993), pp. 97–102 (in Japanese).

37 Mitsui Kiyoshi and Inoue Jun, "Productivity Effect of Infrastructure," in Mitsui Kiyoshi and Ohta Kiyoshi, eds., *Productivity of Infrastructure and Public Finance* (Tokyo: Nihon-Hyoronsha, 1995), chap. 3 (in Japanese).

38 Mitsui Kiyoshi, "*Shakai shihon no e no juten teki seibi no hyouka: kouritsu sei no kanten kara*" ["An Analysis of Social Capital in Focused Regional Development: From a Perspective of Efficiency], in Iwata Kikuo and Miyagawa Tsutomu, eds., *Economics Series: What Are Real Factors in the Lost Decade in Japan?* (Tokyo: Toyo Keizai Inc., 2003).

39 Hoshi Takeo and Anil Kashyap, "Will the U.S. and Europe Avoid a Lost Decade? Lessons from Japan's Post Crisis Experience," presented at the IMF 14th Jacques Polak

Annual Research Conference, November 7–8, 2013, http://www.imf.org/external/np/res/seminars/2013/arc/pdf/hoshi.pdf.

40 Doi Takero and Toshihiro Ihori, *The Public Sector in Japan: Past Developments and Future Prospects* (Cheltenham: Edward Elgar, 2009).

41 For a more concrete description of the Japanese tax system reform in this period, see Iwaisako Tokuo, *"Ushinawareta nijunen no nihon no zaseiseisaku to zeisei"* ["The Lost Twenty Years of Japan's Financial Policy and Tax System"], *Hitsubashi Daigaku Keizai Kenkyujo* (Hitotsubashi University Institute of Economics), working paper, Vol. 65, No. 3, 2014, pp. 238–49.

42 William D. Nordhaus, "Policy Games: Coordination and Independence in Monetary and Fiscal Policies," *Brookings Papers on Economic Activity* 2 (1994), pp. 139–99, writes: "No one would dream of designing the human anatomy by disconnecting the controls of the left and right sides of the body. Yet, for the most important economic controls in a modern economy, monetary and fiscal policy, economists today generally endorse the separation of powers as a way of optimizing non-inflationary growth."

43 Kuroda, *"Zaisei-Kinyu Seisaku no Seiko to Shippai,"* p. 109.

44 Ben S. Bernanke, Thomas Laubach, Frederic S. Mishkin, and Adam S. Posen, *Inflation Targeting: Lessons from the International Experience* (Princeton: Princeton University Press, 1999), p. 38.

45 Nordhaus, "Policy Games," pp. 139–99.

46 Avinash Dixit and Luisa Lambertini, "Interactions of Commitment and Discretion in Monetary and Fiscal Policies," *American Economic Review* 93 (2000), pp. 1522–42.

47 Hoshi Takeo, "Role of Central Banks in Financial Stability: Lessons from the Experience of the Bank of Japan," in Douglas D. Evanoff, ed., *The Role of Central Banks in Financial Stability: How Has It Changed?* (New York: World Scientific Studies in International Economics, 2014), pp. 83–104.

48 Posen, *Restoring Japan's Economic Growth.*

49 Gauti Eggertsson and Michael Woodford, "The Zero Lower Bound on Interest Rates and Optimal Monetary Policy," *Brookings Papers on Economic Activity* 2003, no. 1, pp. 139–211.

50 To be fair, the prevailing wisdom was that debt management was ineffective, a conclusion that was based largely on the small "operation twist" experiment from the 1960s in the United States. More recent research, including Ben S. Bernanke Reinhart R. Vincent, and Brian P. Sack, "Monetary Policy Alternatives at the Zero Bound: An Empirical Assessment," *Brookings Papers on Economic Activity* 2004, no. 2, pp. 1–78, as well as Kenneth N. Kuttner, "Can Central Banks Target Bond Prices?" *National Bureau of Economic Research*, Working Paper 12454, 2006, indicates that debt management could in fact affect the term structure of interest rates, and the Federal Reserve's own "Operation Twist" in 2011 demonstrated this effectiveness on a large scale.

51 Adam S. Posen, *When Central Banks Buy Bonds: Independence and the Power to Say No*. Speech delivered at Barclays Capital 14th Annual Global Inflation-Linked Conference, June 14, 2010.

3 The two "lost decades" and macroeconomics

Changing economic policies

Kobayashi Keiichiro

Introduction

The expression "lost decades" is nowadays used to refer to the economic and market decline and broad political and social conditions in Japan in the last decade of the twentieth and the first decade of the twenty-first century. As Andrew Gordon points out in Chapter 5, the term gained currency in the media, first foreign, then Japanese, in the second half of the 1990s. At the time, the phrase was used to refer to the long-term decline in Japan's growth rate that had started at the beginning of the 1990s, in contrast to the remarkable economic growth shown in the decades after World War II, especially from the 1960s onwards.

Japan's growth rate plummeted in the 1990s, and it remained low in the early years of the twenty-first century. In terms of GDP growth, it is indeed appropriate to say that these two decades were lost. However, the demographic shifts that Seike Atsushi discusses in Chapter 1, including the population decline and changes in the working-age population since 1995, give rise to a slightly different picture. As Figure 3.1 shows, during the 2000s the working-age population's per capita GDP growth rate in Japan actually outshone that of the United States. It may not be so simple therefore to describe the past twenty years as completely "lost." The evidence suggests that the situation is slightly more nuanced, and varying opinions among economists demonstrate something far from a consensus.

This chapter adds an additional perspective to the study of the lost decades. It does so in two ways: first by investigating the macroeconomic policies that were taken at the time and second by elucidating the opportunities that were gained and lost during the two lost decades. In this way, lessons can be learned for present-day Japan and advanced Western countries.

The origins of nonperforming loans (NPLs) in the 1980s

The nature of the Japanese economy changed considerably between the 1970s and the 1980s, and in fact the origins of Japan's two lost decades can be traced back to this era.

On the domestic level, high economic growth, averaging 10 percent annual GDP, came to an end in the 1970s due to a demographic labor shift from the agricultural to the industrial sector. Japan completed its "catch-up" with other

Real GDP growth (2000 USD held constant)	Mid Growth Period 1980-1990	Two "lost decades" - first ten years 1990-2000	Two "lost decades" - latter ten years 2000-2010
Japan	4.6%	1.1%	0.3%
United States	3.2%	3.4%	1.4%
Germany	2.3%	1.9%	0.6%

Real per capita GDP growth (2000 USD held constant)	Mid Growth Period 1980-1990	Two "lost decades" - first ten years 1990-2000	Two "lost decades" - latter ten years 2000-2010
Japan	4.0%	0.9%	0.3%
United States	2.3%	2.2%	0.5%
Germany	2.2%	1.6%	0.7%

Real GDP per workforce (age 15-64) growth (2000 USD held constant)	Mid Growth Period 1980-1990	Two "lost decades" - first ten years 1990-2000	Two "lost decades" - latter ten years 2000-2010
Japan	3.7%	1.1%	0.9%
United States	2.3%	2.1%	0.3%
Germany	1.7%	1.8%	1.0%

Figure 3.1 GDP growth (Japan, Germany, and the United States)

Source: The World Bank Group. "Data | The World Bank." http://data.worldbank.org/.

advanced economies and began a mid-growth period, averaging 4 percent annual GDP. Industries in the manufacturing sector began to take advantage of a structural capital surplus in the 1980s, departing from former practice where banks kept a short "leash" on firms. Under previous practice, when capital markets faced a chronic shortage of funds, the banking industry's discipline of firms had worked effectively. However, the capital surplus that developed in the 1980s loosened the leash by banks, a change that became the underlying cause for the ensuing bubble economy, as well as a source of major inefficiencies in the Japanese economy.

On the international level, the yen appreciated considerably during the 1980s, especially after the 1985 Plaza Accord between G5 nations regarding the depreciation of the U.S. dollar. Persistent yen appreciation generated a huge perception gap in Japan and abroad on the effective solidity of the Japanese economy. The value of yen-denominated Japanese exports appeared to contract. However, when calculated in dollar-based accounting, they in fact rose. The recognition abroad of strengthened Japanese competitiveness notwithstanding, domestically a sense of crisis grew, causing many to believe that Japan would confront an imminent recession due to export contraction. This fear invited an overly expansionist monetary policy in the latter part of the 1980s – yet another factor behind the birth of the asset bubble.

With hindsight, what shape should Japan's economic policies in the 1980s have taken? On the one hand, Japan had completed playing catch-up with its international competitors, and its manufacturing industry had matured. On the other, as Seike Atsushi shows in Chapter 1, it became clear that the problem of an ageing society with a low birth rate was about to take center stage. It might therefore have been appropriate at this time to push forward the service sector – for example, financial, communications, medical, or health care businesses – in lieu of the manufacturing sector as a potential new driver of the Japanese economy. Unfortunately, the service sector in Japan was strongly regulated and characterized by a lack of free competition. It was thus very arduous to organize it as the economy's driving force.

In short, at the end of the 1980s the bubble in real estate and stock markets originated both from domestic structural changes (the progressive inefficiency of corporate management due the weakening of bank-led governance) and from changes in the macro and international environments (yen appreciation and monetary expansion).

Until the 1980s, banks lent capital to firms on a long-term basis, as if they were quasi-shareholders. This meant that a *main bank system* that enhanced corporate discipline was in place, but due to capital surplus in financial markets it gradually became less effective. As loans to existing companies decreased, banks had to cultivate new clients and, as a result, they shifted from lending to big manufacturing companies to lending to small and medium enterprises in nonmanufacturing sectors. Moreover, due to the fact that land prices in Japan had never once decreased throughout the forty-five years following the end of World War II, a myth of ever-increasing land prices gained prominence. Accordingly, land-backed loans were believed to be safe. For these reasons, bank loans continued to rely on real estate

as collateral. Because the Ministry of Finance (MoF) regulated bank management, the major financial institutions did not fear bankruptcy. These factors lay
behind another, secondary myth that the banks were indestructible – that major
banks could never go bankrupt. Such features lessened the vigilance over economic fundamentals, with the twin myths of ever-increasing land prices and indestructible banks causing a rapid increase of land-related financing through banks.
These were the factors that lay behind the formation of the economic bubble.

Why was it that the financial authorities and business circles in the 1980s
were not more wary of a bubble forming? A look at financial crises around the
world shows us that banking crises were not unknown in economically advanced
countries in the interwar years – the Great Depression of the 1930s is a notable
example. However, the Bretton Woods system that had been inaugurated in the
wake of World War II led many people to believe that financial crises in advanced
countries were almost impossible. With the collapse of this system in the 1970s,
banking crises started to occur again with alarming frequency, both in Europe (for
example, Spain) and in Latin American countries. But in Japan it was thought that
such crises could never happen, due to differences in Japan's economic structure.
At the end of the 1980s, when the U.S. savings and loan crisis occurred and there
was a marked accumulated debt problem in Latin America, no sense of crisis
whatsoever was felt in Japan.

In a 2009 interview, Nakai Sei, deputy director general of the MoF's Banking
Bureau (BB) from 1995 to 1998, summarized the rationale behind Japan's monetary policy at the time in this way:

> The Savings and Loans crisis [in the 1980s and 1990s in the United States]
> was a terrible thing – it was as if people had been defrauded of their money.
> We never imagined that something similar might take place in Japan. At the
> time [Japan's] international balance of payment imbalances, starting with
> the Japan-U.S. trade surplus, was the major problem. We considered that the
> appropriate way to deal with this for a creditor country such as Japan was
> simply to have a very low interest rate policy.[1]

As is evident from Nakai's statement, policymakers at this time were less concerned with preparing for or managing a possible financial crisis induced by a
bubble economy than with maintaining an expansionary monetary policy to alleviate the noxious effects of yen appreciation on exports.

1990s policy responses

The early 1990s saw the collapse of Japan's asset bubble. The rapid slowdown
of the economy notwithstanding, accounts were still in the black and the yen's
value remained high – until the late 1990s. The reasons behind a persistently
high yen remain a mystery. But the fact that Japan was an international creditor state that kept producing chronic current account surpluses meant that it
was insufficiently responsive to foreign investors' pressure to force its banks to

properly dispose of their nonperforming loans (NPLs) in the 1990s. As noted by Peter Drysdale and Shiro Armstrong in Chapter 10, after the collapse of multilateral trade negotiations to open its domestic market, in the early 2000s Japan finally signed free trade agreements (FTAs) and economic partnership agreements (EPAs), which opened up opportunities for such foreign investor pressure. The delay in disposing appropriately of NPLs meant that there was limited pressure from foreign direct investment (FDI) during the 1990s. Ironically, if Japan had been a debtor nation plagued by account deficits, foreign investors would have made stern demands for an overhaul of banking, and the implementation of drastic and swift reforms would have been unavoidable. It is possible that the subsequent banking crises and simultaneous yen depreciation could have been offset by exports, which might have led to a speedy economic recovery.

In actuality, since little effect could be exerted by foreign pressure, reforms were slow to arrive and NPLs proliferated. As land and stock prices dropped, the harmful effects on banks' balance sheets increased. Yet, in the first half of the 1990s, due to strong expectations of resurging land and stock prices, the MoF's Banking Bureau and financial institutions continued to postpone drastic measures for NPL disposal.

There were two reasons behind this postponement. First, the dominant understanding in Japan in the early 1990s was that the collapse of the real estate bubble had created these NPLs and that they would not really have any damaging effect on the economy. There was a widely held belief that the disposal of NPLs was not a public policy issue but rather a private matter between banks and their debtors, which led to a delay in NPL disposal measures. Second, dealing with NPLs was predicated on either the collapse of banks or capital injections into banks through public funds. The former would have assigned the loss to depositors, while the latter would have met with strong political opposition by taxpayers. The political cost of either of these two options was far too high to contemplate at this time; the only other option was the postponement of NPL disposal.

As the authorities decided to postpone resolution of the problem, land values continued to decrease, exposing the emptiness of the myth of increasing land prices that had propped up the system for so long. As shown in Figure 3.2, land prices in the commercial districts of Japan's six major cities reached a peak in 1990 and bottomed out in 2004, falling to the same level of land prices in 1975.

In 2010, Teramura Nobuyuki, former general director of the MoF's Banking Bureau between 1992 and 1994, gave an indication of the main factor behind the persistent decline in land prices:

> As various postwar regulations that curbed housing land were progressively relaxed, market mechanisms began to come into play and prices have eventually converged on the calculated returns to investment.[2]

However, the lag in disposing of NPLs continued to plague the Japanese economy, a fact that financial authorities and economic scholars failed to notice.

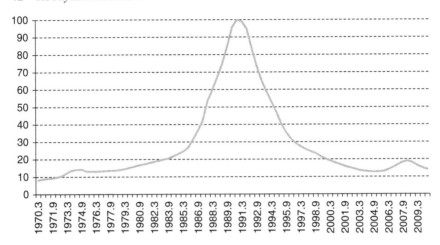

Figure 3.2 Indicator for land prices in the commercial districts of six cities

Note: Figures for September 1990 indexed as 100.

Source: Adapted from Matsushima and Takenaka, 2011.[3]

Postponement of dealing with NPLs

The view on NPLs significantly changed over the decades. Until the early 1990s, the standard view among economists was that flow variables (such as GDP growth, Indices of Industrial Production, and the unemployment rate) alone would indicate fluctuations in the economic climate.[4] Stock variables, such as the price of assets and the quantity of NPLs, were merely a *result* of economic fluctuations, not a *cause*. This was the representative line of thinking on the economy. Yet, along with economic stagnation in Japan during the 1990s, economic paradigms also changed. Recent economic theory developed in the late 1990s holds that stock variables, such as balance sheet variables, can also be a cause: they can be responsible for worsening the economy.[5] On this basis, we can say that the postponement of dealing with the NPLs (the stock variable) caused the significant increase of NPLs on the bank balance sheets, further exacerbating the economic downturn and making the pain last even longer.

What should have been done, then, in the first half of the 1990s? First, policymakers should have resolved the NPL issue to sanitize banks' balance sheets. Second, they should have contained the financial shocks by injecting public funds into banks at an earlier stage. Third, debt restructuring of NPLs should also have been considered at an earlier stage to revitalize indebted companies. Few if any such measures were enforced throughout the 1990s, however, with nothing happening but the passing of time. Following great political turmoil in 1995, 680 billion yen worth of taxes was injected into house loan corporations (*jusen*, the Japanese equivalent of American savings and loan associations) for their liquidation. This money amounted to 10 percent of the public funds eventually needed for capital injections into banks.

These capital injections gained momentum only in 1998 when several major banks went bankrupt. Between 1991 and 1997, Japanese policymakers continued to postpone the restructuring of NPLs. Individual banks kept tackling the problem on their own initiative, but the speed and scale of their efforts was suboptimal from the vantage point of society as a whole.

The peculiarities of 1990s economic policies – the taboo of NPLs

Most of the Japanese establishment assumed that NPLs evolved as a result, not as a cause, of the recession and that they were a private issue among banks and their debtors rather than a public policy affair. Moreover, banking prudential policies were consistently micro oriented, rather than macro oriented. As evident in the words of MoF Banking Bureau General Director Nishimura Yoshimasa:

> [the Banking Bureau] aimed to avoid the instability of the overall system by maintaining the solidity of individual financial institutions," and "there was no notion of handling the NPL issue through a macro approach.[6]

At the same time, there were several incidents relating to NPLs in the early 1990s pointing to murky relationships between banks and gangster organizations: these included the 1994 execution-style killing of the manager of Sumitomo Bank's Nagoya branch and the 1993 killing of the vice-president of the small Hanwa Bank Ltd. Such incidents were one reason why bank managers and economic policymakers tended to view the NPL problem as a taboo. The peculiar structure of banking regulation and supervision centered on a closed financial community that included MoF's Banking Bureau and large private banks. The coziness of the relations in this community reinforced the thinking behind the now-famous "convoy" system of Japan's banking, in which all the main banks were helped by the government to move forward together, none were allowed to lag behind (or go bankrupt), and external actors had hardly any say. The system helped prevent the tardiness of dealing with NPLs from exposure to outside criticism, a situation that persisted due to an unspoken set of agreements between MoF's Banking Bureau and the financial world.

Parallel with the postponement of the NPL disposal, policymakers undertook annual measures to boost the economy, especially fiscal stimulus packages. Throughout the 1990s, the multiplier effect – a proportional factor that measures how much an output variable (e.g., GDP) changes in response to a change in input variables (e.g., government spending) – of expansionary fiscal policies gradually decreased. Since fiscal stimulus was better than nothing, however, the government repeatedly kept at it. The Japanese government also continued to issue orders for public works projects in an effort to help the construction industry, which was already groaning under excessive debt.

The Japanese financial system faced systemic risks due the collapse of the economic bubble. Nonetheless, the Bank of Japan's response was sluggish, monetary policy had little effect in terms of the scale of interest rate cuts, and its efforts were too late. Kuttner, Iwaisako, and Posen investigate Japan's monetary policy in detail in Chapter 2.

My own question is: Why were monetary and fiscal policy used in such small doses to alleviate the worsening situation? The answer may be twofold. First, in the 1990s both economists and government officials developed a peculiar fixation with flow variables (e.g., unemployment), which informed their economic policy decisions. Many policymakers did not take into appropriate consideration the influence of balance sheet variables, such as the fall of asset prices and the NPL issue. Since the change in flow variables was in the end not significant, many officials ended up underestimating the depth of the recession.

Second, there was a general understanding that land prices would eventually stop falling. Comments by Teramura Nobuyuki in 2010 are indicative of this perception:

> It would have been possible to adequately confront the subsequent problems if land prices had stopped at the level prior to the burst of the bubble . . . if we had told people in 1994 that prices would fall by 80 percent, they simply would have not believed us.[7]

In fact, far from simply falling to pre-bubble levels, land prices continued to fall, right down to the level of the 1970s. A drop of asset prices of this magnitude was beyond anyone's expectations, and the failure to grasp just how large and long-standing the drop would be led to an extreme tardiness in policy countermeasures.

Structural reforms

Since Keynesian policies were not effective in reviving the economy, supply-side structural issues came under great scrutiny among the economists and policy-makers as the prime cause of Japan's economic stagnation. To break away from recession, the momentum did finally grow to solve, once and for all, the long-standing structural problems. However, arguments in favor of structural reforms also became a further excuse for Japanese leaders to continue to avoid dealing with NPLs. The ineffectiveness of Keynesian countermeasures led many people to believe that a fall in the demand side was not the only cause behind economic stagnation, and supply-side structural reforms also became the target of policy debates within the Japanese establishment. In effect the NPL problem, the principal cause of Japan's economic problems, was once again ignored.

Arguments in favor of structural reforms followed the several paths. In 1993, an economic reform study group (ERSG) was established as a private advisory board to Prime Minister Hosokawa Morihiro. It was chaired by the head of the Japan Federation of Economic Organizations (the current Japan Business Federation) Hiraiwa Gaishi. The ERSG submitted a mid-term report in November 1993 entitled *On Deregulation*, also known as the Hiraiwa Report, as well as a final report in December 1993 entitled *On Economic Reforms*. The report cited "five main economic reforms," of which deregulation was one.[8]

Following this report, in 1995 the Cabinet Office approved a three-year "Plan for Promoting Deregulation." In 1998 a new "Three Year Plan for Promoting Deregulation" was compiled, and a Deregulation Committee was established within the Cabinet Office's Administrative Reforms Promotion Headquarters. This committee would later be renamed the Regulatory Reform Committee.

Around this time, economists centered on Mizuno Kazuo and others pointed to the low profitability of companies as the reason behind sluggish growth. The 1999 *White Paper on the Economy* also mentioned the structural problem constituted by the "three excesses": excessive debt, excessive equipment, and excessive employment. "The recent economic downturn has not simply originated from poor demand," the *White Paper* stated, "The larger cause stems from traditional company management practices that have prized market share expansion over operational efficiency, from the high-growth era up to the bubble period."[9] The three excesses, cited as the principal cause behind worsening profitability, became the target of structural reforms.

Until 1998, Japanese companies refrained from drastically reorganizing their business practices: they did not trim their staff and continued to pay back debts by taking advantage of profits from assets, that is to say their stocks and land. Following the Asian financial crisis in 1998, drastic cuts started to take place in employment – the hiring of nonregular employees increased and companies adopted a merit-based pay system. As a consequence, traditional Japanese-style employment practices were shaken. Andrew Gordon explores the specifics of the major transformations of Japanese-style employment in Chapter 5, and Toyama Kazuhiko provides more detail in Chapter 4.

Piecemeal responses to the 1997–99 financial crisis

The default of Sanyo Securities in November 1997 initiated a chain reaction in the interbank market that then triggered the wave of bankruptcies in the Japanese financial industry: the voluntary closure of Yamaichi Securities (YS) and the bankruptcies of Hokkaido Takushoku Bank (HTB), Nippon Credit Bank (NCB) and the Long-Term Credit Bank of Japan (LTCB). The government continued to make huge capital injections and subsidies of public funds, totaling approximately 38 trillion yen. The capital injection peaked in 2000, as the government set up a framework of public funding worth 70 trillion yen to save financial institutions. Such public money included:

- Money grants to collapsed financial institutions totaling 18.6 trillion yen: some of these were grants worth 3.2 trillion yen to LTCB, 3.1 trillion to NCB, 1.7 trillion to HTB, etc. Asset purchase of the same financial institutions totaled 6.3 trillion yen: 1.6 trillion yen went to HTB, 0.79 trillion to LTCB, and 0.38 trillion yen to NCB.
- Capital injections totaling 1.8 trillion yen went to 21 big banks in March 1998, under the provisions of the old Economic Stabilization Law.
- Capital injections totaling 8.6 trillion yen sent to 32 big banks between March 1999 and March 2002, under provisions of the Early Strengthening of Financial Functions Law.

- Capital injection of 1.9 trillion yen given to Resona Bank, one of the large banks in Japan, in May 2003, under the provisions of the Deposit Insurance Law.

In the early 2000s, the banking sector gradually accelerated the write-offs of their NPLs, and in 2002 the Koizumi government took a number of measures to further hasten this process. Market sentiments improved markedly after the rescue of Resona Bank thanks to capital injection of public funds in May 2003. At the same time, the yen started depreciating, thus leading to an appreciation of stock prices and economic growth. Macroeconomic data shows that the recovery phase of the business cycle began in February 2002, and in April 2005 the full implementation of measures to deal with the NPLs was officially announced.

Incomplete economic policies at the height of the NPL problem

The main agents behind counter-cyclical economic policies were the Ministry of Finance, the Ministry of International Trade and Industry (MITI; later renamed the Ministry of Economy, Trade and Industry, METI); and the Economic Planning Agency (EPA). Financial regulation and supervision was under the MoF's secrecy umbrella and is firmly hidden from the open debates on broader economic policies among MoF, MITI, and EPA. Consequently, banking regulation and supervision were excluded from the scope of policies directed toward economic recovery. The NPL problem is illustrative of this. Throughout the 1990s, the need to deal with the NPL problem was not considered a national problem from any general economic perspective – it was instead treated as a matter between banks and debtors, at most as a problem of the banking community. Thus it was that micro- and macroeconomic policies kept sidelining the most important factor behind Japan's economic downturn.

Against this backdrop, the economic policies that were put together and promoted by the MoF, MITI, and EPA were for the most part Keynesian expansionary policies, deregulatory policies, and institutional reforms, such as those pertaining to corporate legislation. Since Japan's essential economic problems were in the financial sector, a successful economic policy necessarily entailed tackling that sector. This was also true of government intervention in individual industries, since they all basically required getting rid of NPLs. Nevertheless, economic policies, in particular industrial policies, did not touch upon the NPL problem, and they all ended up being ineffective. In the 1990s, mainstream thinking at MITI also shifted toward economic neoliberalism, characterized by free trade, deregulation, and nonintervention, as the ministry experienced the obvious ineffectiveness of government intervention.

This was one of the main reasons behind the proliferation of voices, especially from MITI, calling for structural reforms and deregulation throughout the 1990s.

Corporate legislation reforms

From the second half of the 1990s to the 2000s, corporate legislation reforms progressed rapidly because low corporate profitability was understood as one of the main factors behind the economic slowdown. In particular, corporate governance qualified as a structural problem that needed to be improved through reform of underlying inefficient corporate legislation. From the standpoint of debtors, writing off NPLs meant the disposal of excessive debt. As a result, the lack of progress on the NPL issue was also understood as originating with inefficient corporate governance. In hindsight, reforms in both areas – writing off NPLs and adjusting corporate governance – were necessary in order to revitalize Japan's economy.

Return on equity (ROE) is one of the indicators that show Japanese companies' marginal productivity of capital (MPK). Up until the 1980s, the ROE of Japanese and American companies was roughly at the same level. Since the 1980s, however, Japanese companies' ROE has continued to fall. It is now between 6 and 9 percent, less than half the U.S. level. Figure 3.3 shows the ROE for both Japanese and American companies, according to statistics compiled by Japan's System of National Accounts.[10] These statistics show that the gap is even greater than the one derived from company-based data.

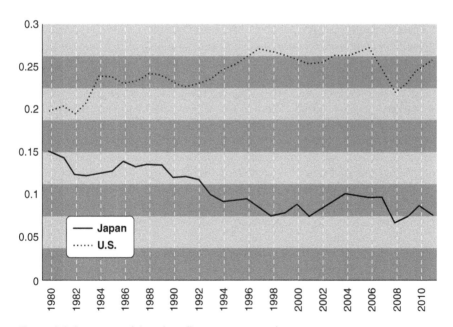

Figure 3.3 Japanese and American firms return on equity

Note: Return on Capital = Net Operating Surplus / Net Capital Stock

Source: Japan's Cabinet Office; U.S. Bureau of Economic Analysis[11]

This drop in ROE reveals that a major structural problem exists within Japanese corporate governance. It means that for twenty years since the 1990s, despite the reforms of corporate legislation that have been enacted to make Japanese corporate governance more efficient, little change resulted.

The main legislative reforms have been:

- The May 1997 introduction of stock option schemes through amendments to the Commercial Code.
- The December 1997 lift of the ban on pure holding companies through amendments to the Anti-Monopoly Law.
- The 2000 Civil Rehabilitation Law and the abolishment of the Composition Law.
- The 2002 Commercial Code amendment that allowed for share warrant and considerably relaxed limitations on class shares.
- The 2003 enactment of general revisions of the Corporate Reorganization Law.
- The 2003 introduction of companies with a committee government structure through the revision of the Commercial Code.
- The 2005 New Company Law that allowed flexibility to companies with a committee government structure and the ulterior expansion of class shares' liberty.

The above reforms were not able to bear results, however, and Japanese companies' MPK and ROE remains low. This problem also derives from problematic asset holders and entrusted asset managing companies. Examples of asset holders are life insurance companies and the Government Pension Investment Fund (GPIF), which manages and invests the reserve funds of pension insurance and the national pension. In the 1980s, Japanese banks no longer had the ability to discipline companies properly, and this meant that the so-called main bank system stopped functioning. As a consequence, institutional investors were expected to monitor and discipline the companies. Yet, Japanese institutional investors have consistently invested passively, something that is thought to occur due to major distortions in their incentives structure – for example, compensation is linked to the size of managed assets rather than performance of investment made. The above-listed corporate governance reforms were centered on a legislative overhaul of companies that attracted investment, but it was necessary to reform the system behind institutional investors as well. To date, this issue remains unresolved.[12]

Another reason behind the unsatisfactory outcome of corporate governance reforms has been the lack of clear goals. As Toyama Kazuhiko also points out in Chapter 4, governance in the 1980s rested upon a main banking system that progressively became less effective. However, policymakers at the time did not clearly envision alternative institutions for monitoring and disciplining firms. Policymakers aimed at a major change from a bank-centered to a market incentive–centered monitoring system, but what constituted the "market?" Was it shareholders or creditors (that is to say bondholders) – or both? During the 1990s and the 2000s, there was in fact no consensus among Japanese policymakers concerning shareholder-led governance and its possible reinforcement.

For this reason, the understanding that governance of institutional investors needed to undergo reform was very slow in coming. Instead, the reform of investee companies was prioritized. As a result, institutional investors remained passive shareholders and said nothing to the managements of the investee firms. Again, this has possibly been one of the main reasons behind the failure of Japanese corporate governance reform in the past twenty years.

The emergence of "activist investors," such as the entrepreneur and founder of the Livedoor website portal Horie Takafumi and fund manager and founder of M&A Consulting Murakami Yoshiaki, who was also associated with Livedoor, created a short-lived momentum in the mid-2000s for shareholder-led corporate governance, but the rapid demise of their ventures meant that the momentum was quickly lost. These investors aggressively – too aggressively, in fact – pushed for an overhaul of business management, with the aim of short-term profits for short-term shareholders. Their investments were not oriented at increasing corporate value over the long run. In the end, their behavior simply helped the cause of traditional business managers, individuals who loathed change and opposed strengthening shareholder rights over corporate governance. The establishment in Japan, particularly in the business, governmental, and judiciary sectors, has always deeply opposed active investors. METI, too, was concerned about the possible collapse of the long-term value of firms if activist investors, who aimed at short-term profits, increased their controlling rights. METI did all that it could to sabotage the activities of activist investors, reinforcing antitakeover measures. METI's intentions were to some extent appropriate, since the aim was also to build rules of conduct for takeovers that were in line with other countries. As a former METI chief made clear:

> [METI aimed at creating] an extremely just mechanism that allowed shareholders to decide whether a company's management should be assigned to existing management or new management proposed by new investors who are interested in taking over the shares and control of the company.[13]

The adoption of such defensive anti-takeover measures would perhaps have been less problematic had shareholder-led discipline over firms functioned properly. In actuality, however, the main shareholders, that is to say the institutional investors, did not have any say over corporate discipline. The division between them reinforced companies' traditional management styles and inhibited the creation of a more positively balanced shareholder-management tension.

Were there any measures that could have been taken to avoid the formation of a managerial clique other than shareholder discipline? The practice of appointing external directors to the board was one possible option. Had it been implemented in the lost decades, however, all too often Japanese managers simply would have selected close acquaintances for such positions. The regular appointment by Japanese managers of "friendly faces" engendered tacit gentlemen's agreements, which only contributed to the code of silence about problems among firms. Appointing directors from the outside did not actually discipline companies and Japanese firms' low MPK did not change.

The global financial crisis and government intervention

Following the 2008 Lehman Shock, conditions surrounding Japanese firms of course changed. As Toyama Kazuhiko explains in Chapter 4, the financial situation of the electronic sector took a definite turn for the worse. It was unable to properly respond to the twin challenges of globalization and digitalization, and momentum rose in favor of taxpayer-funded bailouts. For this, policymakers envisioned a scheme that resembled the Troubled Asset Relief Program (TARP) in the United States, which bailed out, for instance, General Motors. To finance troubled firms, the government set up government-supported companies such as the Innovation Network Corporation of Japan (INCJ) and the Enterprise Turnaround Initiative Corporation of Japan (ETIC), the latter reorganized in March 2013 into the Regional Economy Vitalization Corporation of Japan (REVIC). The proliferation of such government-supported corporations raised concerns over Japanese private firms' dependency on such companies, as well as the fear that reliance on such measures would become the normal state of affairs.

The aim behind such attempts to restructure and revive firms through government-supported corporations is to tackle problems in the economy left in the aftermath of the NPL disposal. Taken together, these problems formed a vicious circle. The combination of an industrial structure that was unable to respond to the challenges posed by a declining, and ageing, population and public uncertainty regarding increased public debt and the fate of social security dampened the possibilities of economic growth. The rigidity of Japanese society as a whole was reflected by the excess risk aversion and indecisiveness of Japanese corporate managers. As a result, Japanese enterprises showed a lack of initiative in opening new business fields, which led to further sluggish growth. The torpid economy put pressure on government finances, increased future uncertainty, and made society ever more rigid.

It seems to me that the solution to these problems entails a two-step approach. First, policymakers need to take measures to increase the nation's fertility rate, in order to revive the demographic balance in society. Second, in recognition of the demographic changes that have taken place, leaders need to implement reforms necessary for the sustainability of Japan's public finances and social security. This entails structural reforms accompanied by significant tax increases and cuts in social security spending. In short, if some sort of revival or restitution can be brought to public finances, social security sustainability, and the demographic makeup of society, Japan's future, at present so uncertain, may get brighter. If these things can be brought about, they will encourage companies to take the risk of active business ventures.

Nevertheless, such policies require an extremely long time to produce results. At present, Japan continues to flounder, with little visible progress. In the mid-2000s, policymakers at METI and similar bodies considered that the removal of the heavy NPL burden would stimulate lively economic activity based on free competition. Unfortunately, such hopes notwithstanding, the rigidity, or lack of decisive dynamics, shown by Japanese companies in their business activities only worsened, and few attempts were taken to open up new industrial fields. This is because, even after the disposal of NPLs due to Japan's demographic shifts and the accelerated accumulation of government debt, uncertainty significantly increased and thus depressed economic activities.

In order to properly understand the aim of the government-supported corporations such as INCJ and REVIC, it is necessary to understand how METI grasped the inner workings of the Japanese economic system. Their view differs considerably from the standard market-centered view of economics. According to orthodox economic thinking, the remedy for a rigid economy requires the establishment of a highly competitive market environment through deregulatory policies. Because of the uncertainty in the Japanese corporate world regarding demographic, fiscal, and social security issues, however, Japanese companies became averse to risk-taking activities. Deregulation alone was not enough to produce the will for competition and the resulting reallocation of resources. In actuality, interfirm business and trust networks play a major role in the real economy, even though they are usually discounted as a factor by orthodox economic theory. The characteristics of these "complex networks" are gradually elucidated by the theory of complex networks based on network science, which has made remarkable progress in the last decade. In an interview with a senior METI official who was also very close to INCJ, I was told the following:

> Interfirm networks create a distinctive "small worldness," where a limited amount of players function like hubs and have a major impact over the industry as a whole. Therefore, the revitalization and reorganization of firms that were key hubs through public institutional investors would propagate policy-led growth incentives through interfirm networks. And this would lead to the eventual revitalization of competition within the sector as a whole.[14]

This peculiar type of state capitalism is based on the assumption of market intervention by government-engineered institutional investors. The aim, however, was not to eradicate economic competition in the manner, say, of socialist intervention. Rather, the aim was to revitalize economic competition, as pointed out in the above comment by a senior METI official, who continued:

> As society grows immobile, if stimuli from the public sector is absent, firms also remain rigid, visionary businessmen are kept down, and the economy flounders. The INCJ's role is to provide such unorthodox yet visionary businessmen with resources and positions of management, in order to facilitate their corporate activities at the hubs of the market networks. In other words, the INCJ is responsible for regularizing newcomers' challenges to the traditional economy.[15]

Japan's demographic, fiscal, and social security problems, especially prominent in the later 2000s, prove that market competition does not always work along standard economic assumptions. These problems were also hard to get rid of, so policymakers made even more frequent use of public investment-led stimuli, intervention, to galvanize market competition.

The structure of the two lost decades

It is possible to argue that the fundamental problem in Japan over the past two decades has been a pervasive rigidity in public and private organizations, where decisions to revive economic activity came too late, and when the actions came they were insufficient. Organizational problems inhibiting flexibility common to many administrative organizations, banks, and private firms also played a part. This problem can be described as negative externalities (i.e., damage/costs caused by an organization for which it does not have to pay) stemming from "insider decision making." This section will explain the structure of negative externality by insiders.

Japanese organizations are peculiar for being relatively insulated from external discipline; and with the passing of time in the two lost decades, outside actors have become even less capable of exerting pressure. Discretion pursued by insiders is often neither interrupted by outsiders nor institutionally prevented. In the case of Japanese firms and banks, for example, the institutional environment of capital market actually constitutes the problem; in the case of administrative organizations, the institutional settings of government employees, which give them perverse motivations in relations with politics and the private sector alike, are the core of the problem.

Due to a growing insularity from discipline imposed by external actors, Japanese banks, private corporations, and public organizations developed into a sort of closed community. Insiders avoided situations that might damage their community, and they do not take into sufficient account the costs actually inflicted on outsiders. For example, Olympus, an optics and medical device company, developed a huge financial scandal on the loss-hiding of its mistaken investments made in the asset bubble era. The loss-hiding scheme was discovered by a newly appointed CEO, Michael C. Woodford, whereas other Japanese directors kept silent or did not have the capability to look into the situation.[16] As a consequence, insider decisions were made that were perfectly appropriate for their own interests but were apparently illegal and caused major deficiencies – or negative externalities – on outsiders (i.e., shareholders).

This problem has been key in policy domains affected by decision making in government departments. In fact, it explains why government deficits have been left unattended, leading to the rapid expansion of public debt. It was the same with the lack of willingness to take effective countermeasures to address the problem of an ageing society characterized by a low birth rate. What was happening was that do-nothing governments kept prioritizing minimizing the costs affecting their policy stakeholders over alleviating the burden on future generations. Such patterns of Japanese organizational avoidance during the two lost decades persist today.

Theoretical explanation and policy implications

Administrative organizations, banks, private firms, and the like developed into closed communities of this sort, composed of traditional managerial cadres, financial investors, and ministerial and agency heads, among others. This inward-looking environment allowed certain vested interests to impose substantial costs on outsiders, a negative situation that qualifies as a coordination failure within society as a whole. In this section, I will use game theory to analyze the nature of this coordination failure.

For simplicity's sake, I will take the government as a representative insider and citizens as their external counterpart, the outsider. Insider and outsider interact with one another through a particular strategic game. In this case, the government has the choice of two strategies: maximize the government's utility – that is to say, its own insider interests – to the people's detriment, or maximize citizens' utility through instituting stringent regulation. The downside of the former option, or the cost to society, is insufficient reallocation of resources and, in comparison with the latter, shrinking economic activity. On the opposite side, the citizens have a choice of opting for active political participation and stern monitoring of governmental activities, or an absence of political participation and no monitoring of government activities. The people's active political participation will incur costs for which citizens have to pay. The penalty for the government if it pursues policies to the people's detriment is the possibility of a regime change.

Of course, the desirable result is a "good equilibrium," meaning that the government maximizes citizen's utility and that citizens participate in and monitor the governmental activities. However, first of all, if the government's expectation of penalties that the citizens can impose on it are too small, and the costs for citizens' political participation are too high (too much time being spent, for example, due to insufficient reliable information), the government will be able to maximize its insider interests and thus impose costs on the nation as a whole. Furthermore, as far as the expected damage for a citizen due to her/his absent participation in politics is lower than the costs of her/his active participation, a rational citizen will keep not monitoring. Therefore, shrinking economic activity might not be prevented in such a "bad equilibrium." In short, in the case that the expected penalty for the government is too small (e.g., almost no chance of a regime change), or that the costs associated with citizens' active participation in politics are too high (e.g., insufficient disclosure of information about the government activities), the government tries to maximize its insider interests by imposing the costs on citizens. The coordination between the government and citizens is lost and the social welfare is significantly damaged.

Two reform options can solve this coordination failure: one is to increase the penalties that may be placed on the government through monitoring by citizens. The other is to decrease the costs on the people for their active political participation.

This structure and choice of reform options also applies to the interaction between the management in firms (insiders) and shareholders (outsiders), and bank managers (insiders) and depositors (outsiders). Arguably, empowering outsiders through easier monitoring mechanisms and enabling them to provide stronger penalties would be an important first step in increasing flexibility within Japanese society.

Conclusion

The two lost decades in Japan grew out of years of rigid decision-making processes and the avoidance of responsibility. To be sure, these problems originated from a sluggish economy; however, they also impeded economic growth on their own merits. Cause and effect work both ways, and Japan has been experiencing a bad equilibrium in which insiders (e.g., the government, corporate management, and bank management) maximize their own interests by deprioritizing interests of outsiders (e.g., citizens, shareholders, and deposit holders respectively) for quite a while.

Once the economy gets stuck in this bad equilibrium, it is insufficient to rely on market competition to bring about any reversal or comeback. Strong political initiatives or policy-driven big pushes are essential. A massive external shock, sufficient to smash the rigid social structures, is probably necessary to stop the inertia behind Japan's lost decades. A Japanese government bond (JGB) crash, for example, would be one such shock.

As of 2013, Japan's current account balance maintains a surplus. The trade balance has fallen into the red, however, so a sudden JGB crash would not seem out of the realm of possibility. The social costs of such an eventuality would of course be immeasurable, and every step must be taken to avoid it. It is imperative that the Japanese people push their government to carry out reforms, avoid economic turmoil induced by a crisis, and once and for all shed dependence on a system that has characterized the country's economy throughout the lost decades and continues to do so to this day.

Notes

1 Shigeru Matsushima and Harukata Takenaka, eds., *The Japanese Economy and Macroeconomic Policies from the Beginnings of the Bubble to the Overcoming of Deflation (History, Volume 3): Record of the Japanese Economy – An Oral History* (Tokyo: Saiki Insatsu, 2011), pp. 261, 302.
2 Ibid.
3 Ibid., p. 222.
4 Official statistics of industrial production, shipments, and inventory, monthly reported by the Ministry of Economy, Trade, and Industry.
5 A large body of research on balance-sheet variables were pioneered by Nobuhiro Kiyotaki and John Moore in "Credit Cycles," *Journal of Political Economy*, 105, no. 2 (1997), pp. 211–48; and Ben S. Bernanke, Mark Gertler, and Simon Gilchrist, "The Financial Accelerator in a Quantitative Business Cycle Framework," in John B. Taylor and Michael Woodford, eds., *Handbook of Macroeconomics* (New York: Elsevier, 1999), vol. 1C, chap. 21.

6 Shigeru Matsushima and Harukata Takenaka, eds., *The Japanese Economy and Macroeconomic Policies from the Beginnings of the Bubble to the Overcoming of Deflation (History, Volume 3): Record of the Japanese Economy – An Oral History* (Tokyo: Saiki Insatsu, 2011), p. 321.

7 Ibid., p. 221.

8 Economic Reform Study Group, "On Economic Reforms," http://www.esri.go.jp/jp/prj/sbubble/data_history/5/makuro_kei12_1.pdf.

9 Economic Planning Agency, "Annual Report on Japan's Economy and Public Finance 1999–2000," 1999.

10 Japanese Cabinet Office, "SNA (National Accounts of Japan)," http://www.esri.cao.go.jp/en/sna/menu.html; U.S. Bureau of Economic Analysis, "National Economic Accounts, http://www.bea.gov/national/Index.htm.

11 Japanese Cabinet Office. "SNA (National Accounts of Japan)," http://www.esri.cao.go.jp/en/sna/menu.html; U.S. Bureau of Economic Analysis, "National Economic Accounts," http://www.bea.gov/national/Index.htm.

12 In February 2014, the Financial Services Agency published the Stewardship Code "to promote sustainable growth of companies through investment and dialogue," a small step for the reforms of institutional investors.

13 Statement by an ex-METI official in interview with the author, July 30, 2013.

14 Statement by METI official in interview with the author, July 29, 2013.

15 Ibid.

16 Olympus Corporation, "Investigation Report by Third Party Committee," http://www.olympus-global.com/en/common/pdf/if111206corpe_2.pdf.

4 The curse of "Japan, Inc." and Japan's microeconomic competitiveness

Toyama Kazuhiko

Corporate Japan during the lost decades

Many Japanese companies that had once dominated world markets suffered from a declining market share and sluggish profitability during the lost decades (1990–2010). The fundamental problems arose due to the matured state of Japan's economy and also from external influences that were triggered by new trends – globalization and the digital revolution, which transformed the world of international business. The inability of Japanese companies to come to grips with these trends and to adopt corporate governance models to comply with the new world economic order led them to lose ground quickly in the global economy. Their demise is easily discernible from a glance at *Fortune*'s Global 500 List: in 1995, readers found 141 Japanese companies, but astonishingly only 71 in 2010.

Japan's single most abundant resource after World War II was its population, which meant the availability of a cheap yet educated workforce. In the 1950s labor costs rose, but the nation underwent a major structural shift from labor-intensive to capital-intensive industries through government-led policies, and this improved industrial productivity sufficiently to justify the higher labor costs. Once Japan had established a big enough domestic industrial base to support high economic growth in the 1960s through export-oriented production and external trade, domestic demand, sustained by an increasing population with a growing dispensable income, enabled in the 1990s the final transformation of the nation into a knowledge-intensive economy. This economy emphasized services and businesses reflective of twenty-first century needs. However, in the final stages, many major Japanese companies stumbled.

During the first half of the lost decades era, Japanese corporations suffered a setback when Japan's asset bubble collapsed in 1990. Management practices founded on lifetime employment and an outdated socioeconomic system (based on the "main banking system" and weak safety measures for responses to bankruptcy and merger and acquisition situations) impeded speedy economic recovery in the private sector. Problems surfaced related to excessive corporate debt, superfluous numbers of employees, and production overcapacity.

The stagnation that Japan underwent after the burst of its economic bubble was a complete first-time experience. Nothing like this had happened before in Japan or indeed any other country in the world. Japan's political classes were initially slow to identify and come to grips with the problem. Financial institutions dealt with accumulated nonperforming loans in an inefficient manner and market failure prevailed. The situation continued until Prime Minister Koizumi's administration (2001–2006), which swiftly launched initiatives to deal with the problem. The delay that resulted from the tardy response, however, contributed to the lack of any significant turnaround in the Japanese economy. (The EU is facing a similar situation now with the postponement of post-recession measures).

The resulting economic slowdown was so consuming in terms of time and energy for many Japanese companies that they could not direct their attention to the reforms that were necessary to stay competitive in a new environment that had been utterly transformed. There was also a strong home market bias that sidetracked product development and diverted corporate resources to domestic market needs, with little consideration given to product competitiveness from the perspective of a global customer base.

In this chapter, I will try to explain the drop in overall competitiveness during the lost decades with a look at the less-than-suitable management models that were applied by Japanese companies and that led to their failure to utilize the competitive advantages they had gained. The term Japan, Inc. has been used widely in media to illustrate mutual collaboration between governmental and corporate interests in Japan. In this chapter, we use this term to label the established domestic corporate system which was developed in the period of high economic growth and was sustained by three fundamental practices founded on lifetime employment, a system of seniority, and a harmonious relationship between management and labor unions. I will look at the example of the well-known electronics manufacturing company Sony, which even now is struggling in the face of stiff global competition. My view is that even putting aside internal factors, the responsibility for the drop in competitiveness lies mainly with the use of traditional approaches to corporate management and business models. These approaches had contributed greatly to Japan's previous success, but are now outdated: they could no longer handle changes to the new international business environment, which was fundamentally altered by globalization and the digital revolution. I will use Sony to highlight the strategic and structural failures and the causes that have affected the entire Japanese corporate sector.

Globalization in the 1990s and the decline of competitive advantage

Globalization, a profoundly overused term, tends to have various meanings depending on one's perspective and intended audience. In this chapter, I employ the term to describe a state in which the traditional definitions and categories of markets were fundamentally changed. Up until the 1990s, the world was divided into advanced and developing economies, and geopolitically separated – separated into blocs – by the Iron Curtain. When the Berlin Wall came down in 1989, borders opened, the Cold War system crumbled, and the economies of East and West united and transformed into something new. Many nations opened their markets and took a proactive role in new trading activities, which could now take place on a global scale. Globalization is founded on cross-border integration and the mutual exchange of people, products, services, capital, and ideas. Historical borders grew much less important than they had been before, and traditional strategies of manufacture and export were seen to have reached their limits.

The markets that emerged were ones that expanded rapidly and offered new opportunities for everyone involved in this new era of competition. Japanese companies were keen to exploit these opportunities. They faced several problems, however, in accessing the markets. For one thing, they were too focused on the traditional large markets in North America, Western Europe, and Japan, which in the 1990s still represented the largest portions of the world economy – this was a further reason why during this period the Japanese companies' home share shrank significantly. Data from the International Monetary Fund (IMF) for GDP shows that Japan's economy represented about 15 percent of the world economy in 1990, but shrank over time to 8 percent by 2012. In the 1990s, Japanese companies were consequently less proactive than their Western competitors in relocating their strategic capabilities overseas, especially to emerging economies such as Brazil, Russia, India, and China (the so-called BRIC countries). Most Japanese companies abroad typically had only a minor footprint, with only local sales and a small marketing presence or production site.

To some extent, already during the 1970s and 1980s, a new movement for cross-border integration aimed at seizing market openness and mutual exchanges began to modify the traditional strategy of manufacturing goods and providing services to customers. It became important to provide products at highly competitive prices by utilizing production localization, off-shoring, outsourcing, and other strategies used by all the corporations that were able to achieve their own cost leadership and maintain their competitive advantage in developed countries. Japanese companies were keen to locate new business opportunities and to find cost-competitive production sites overseas. They were less proactive, however, about bringing a long-term vision to their strategically integrated capabilities and shaping the markets in emerging countries so that they could be equivalent to their already established main overseas markets in North America and Europe.

Japanese corporations invested during the early 1990s in Southeast Asia (Shiraishi Takashi discusses the politics behind such decisions in Chapter 11). However, as the currency crisis hit the "Asian Tiger" nations, many enterprises had to downsize local operations or withdraw completely, retracting their operations, and return home. This suggests that these local operations were nothing more than low-manufacturing-cost centers. Simply put, the "new" strategy Japanese companies were employing at this time was just an extension of Japan's classic trade policy as a "processing" nation (employing cheaper labor at a local site and exporting goods to the rich consumer markets of developed countries), which had given Japanese companies their comparative advantage over American and European ones.

In the meantime, foreign direct investment had brought about a transformation in the industrial capabilities of these emerging nations. Further, as local industries became increasingly stronger, it became much easier for these nations to gain access to capital markets – and this accelerated local industrialization. Vigorous competition within these emerging economies started to erode the conventional advantage that had once been enjoyed by the major Japanese companies, in the electronics industry for example, that at one time had been able to dominate tradable goods markets.

There were two reasons why the traditional economic model that had been based on simple processing and external trade (the model that lay behind the Japanese economic miracle during the era of high economic growth) was no longer valid. First, the strength of the Japanese yen together with high labor costs undermined the ability of Japan to compete directly with companies from emerging economies in terms of manufacturing costs if they wished to preserve Japanese domestic assembly operations. Second, globalization led to a larger-than-expected market diversification, and Japan's focus on mainly North America and Western Europe became less ideal as emerging economies positioned themselves to become larger contributors to global growth.

Adaptation to globalization

As globalization proceeded, European and U.S. companies with overseas operations began to hire more local business talent with the requisite local market insight, with a view to increasing operations in regional markets. Clearly, it was essential to have a range of key decision makers for success. Japanese companies hired local staff but continued to entrust control at top levels within the organizations only to Japanese managers. Needless to say, globalization impacted the world of business both domestically and abroad. Their tardiness in diversifying their markets and involving local human capital meant that Japanese corporations were slow off the mark in identifying market potential in comparison with their Western counterparts. Even today there is a marked lack of diversity in their executive boards and management circles, not only in terms of nationality but also of gender – women are still significantly underrepresented in the Japanese workforce. (Andrew Gordon explores these issues more fully in Chapter 5.)

Japanese companies were on the whole unsuccessful in dealing with globalization. European and U.S. companies, which had languished in the shadow of Japan's success in the 1970s, generally handled the need to adapt much more skillfully and produced significant results. During the years during which Japan had reigned supreme, some European and U.S. companies had been forced to exit the market. But others took the opportunity to reform their management models and strengthen their operational capabilities. In some cases they adopted an action-oriented decision-making process (sometimes by studying Japanese management practices such as total quality management and reconfiguring their corporate businesses portfolios accordingly) that eventually led them to outpace the Japanese management systems. The results of these strategic reforms are clear to see in a famous study by the MIT Commission on Industrial Productivity, "Made in America." Neither European nor U.S. companies did at all well in the Japanese domestic market at this time. The trade friction caused by structural impediments eventually developed into a political issue, but the truth was that Western corporations simply looked down on the Japanese market and failed to fully grasp the increasingly refined needs of domestic consumers. Notwithstanding their perception of Japan as a small and distant island in the Far East, strong Japanese competitors had already emerged.

Japanese corporations were on the whole enjoying great success abroad, and most business leaders still believed in the worth of their traditional corporate model. A similar trend can be seen today in the Chinese automotive industry where U.S. and European manufacturers dominate the market, despite their geographical distance from China.

The latest studies show that innovation practices created in emerging markets nowadays, such as those of India, are being transferred back to developed nations through a similar process of reverse innovation, with excellent results. This is in sharp contrast to most Japanese companies, which for the most part remain locked in their own practices and continue to underestimate the need for low-cost products in emerging markets.

New competitors and repetitive history

The era of the lost decades was the first time that Japanese firms had to face new Asian competitors: companies from Korea, Taiwan, and China. Somehow Japan, or Japan, Inc., had completely shut its eyes to these emerging market champions and ignored them as worthy competitors, only to discover that this was a grave mistake. Such behavior resembled the actions of European and American major companies toward Japanese companies in the 1970s and 1980s.

In contrast to Japan, Inc., European companies had come to grips with their own geographic constraints and the lack of scalability in their domestic markets, so they lost no time in establishing well-globalized operations. Japanese corporations clearly played a much safer game and relied extensively on their own domestic market. Japan had after all been the second largest economy in terms of GDP until 2010, before being overtaken by China. The traditional export-oriented trade business model was based on decisions being made at Japanese headquarters, and there was consequently never the need to evolve into a fully globalized corporate structure. The business model was extremely simple: raw materials were imported to natural-resources-lacking Japan, processed into finished goods, and then sold in the Japanese domestic market or exported mostly to Organisation for Economic Co-operation and Development (OECD) destinations. This model made overseas operations quite manageable, with sales and marketing offices in OECD countries and production sites in emerging countries. The only exception was a number of OECD countries where a manufacturing presence was maintained for political reasons, such as to prevent trade-related friction and secure local political support.

Given this structure, it comes as no surprise that all core managers in these operations were Japanese and the most important actions and decisions were carried out in Japan. Most Japanese managers did not catch on to the fact that globalization had brought a completely new environment, in which products and services were developed, produced, marketed, and managed in a much more delegated way, with much less centralized control. Even today, despite the shrinking and ageing population that Seike Atsushi describes in Chapter 1, the fiscal deficit as explained by Kuttner, Iwaisako, and Posen in Chapter 2, and the related macroeconomic issues summarized by Kobayashi Keiichiro in Chapter 3, Japanese corporate structures remain firmly attached to traditional principles – trapped by their glory days.

The digital revolution and changes in the game

The rise of digital technology in the early 1990s fundamentally changed the way products and services were designed, produced, and delivered, as well as how people communicate and interact every day. For a variety of reasons, however, the digital revolution did not suit Japanese companies and their management models.

The first reason was that modular designed technology eroded the value of the assembly process, which was where Japanese companies had always displayed a strong competitive advantage. The shift to this modular architecture was problematic for Japanese companies in that they relied on concurrent engineering and interdivisional coordination – the underlying keystones of integrally designed technology. This contrasting approach and capability was based on the long-term accumulation of technological and business expertise, enabled by the stable employment system provided by Japanese corporations.

Various strategic approaches were adopted by companies to deal with the changes brought by the arrival of the digital revolution, especially in regards to the value chain. Some Western companies focused solely on a specific layer in the value creation chain and became known as horizontal ("layer") champions. Microsoft, with its operating systems and office productivity products, was one such example. Others outsourced the less value-added manufacturing or the fabrication process. This became a popular move in the semiconductor industry, with Texas Instruments and Freescale establishing themselves as "fabless" players. This strategy allows for focusing and dedicating internal resources to technology development, product design, and marketing, while using external manufacturers for the actual fabrication.

To respond to manufacturing outsourcing needs, a new type of company with a pure focus on the assembly process also emerged. This business model, exemplified by Foxconn, relies on concentrating production to regions with a low labor cost. As manufacturing technology became widely accessible and commoditized and was pursued on an intensive global scale, the company became large enough to secure global orders from final assembly manufacturers that were shifting to a horizontal specialization model. The emergence of these competitors complicated the situation for the Japanese electronics industry, which was trying to preserve its traditional structural competencies based on vertical integration business models and a focus on high-quality products with high labor costs. Total solutions providers, such as GE, IBM, or Siemens, represented another approach. Japanese manufacturers cannot pride themselves on having adapted this model, as they have traditionally depended on the added value of their products as the main contributor to their value proposition instead of focusing on comprehensive turnkey solutions.

The digital revolution increased horizontal specialization efforts, which allowed for the breakdown of value chains in the industrial structure. The information and communications technology (ICT) sector particularly followed this trend. Strategic decision making was required to reassess each company's business strengths, during which their true competencies in specific layers of the value chain were apparent. Customers were willing to pay the most for delivered high-added value. In addition to traditional corporate portfolio management theory, competition called for an ongoing "choose and focus" strategy, which concentrated on a given company's value chain. This strategy required flexibility, speediness, and extremely dynamic strategic behavior for the execution of large-scale transformation or disposal of business units and functions, as was seen in the case of IBM selling its personal computer business to Lenovo in 2005 or Apple's "fabless" strategy with a focus only on design, marketing, and user interface.

Semiconductor memory chips, large-size LCD displays, and other similar devices once relied on complicated production technology and the need for highly skilled workers. Japanese electronics manufacturers had previously dominated their markets. With the digital revolution, however, this changed significantly when these device products became scalable. At the same time, core production technology was shifting to manufacturing equipment producers: if sufficient capital funding could be obtained, technology-related competitive obstacles vanished, which lowered the barriers to the market. In this business domain, financial muscle combined with an ability to make speedy and bold investment decisions to overpower technological capabilities and competition became a power game in which Japanese companies slowly lost their competitive edge. The initial successes of Elpida in DRAM chip manufacturing and Sharp's concentrated effort in LCD displays were made possible by this "choose and focus" strategy. However, this technological predominance as a competitive advantage was not sustainable.

Machinery and automotive manufacturing also felt the influence of the digital revolution, but because their business models centered on concurrent engineering and vertical integration they continued to function well and suffered less significantly than players in the Japanese electronics industry.

The second reason that Japanese companies did not fit well in the digital age was that the so-called productivity enhancement that IT systems brought into the corporate environment did not in fact bring about the desired effect.

Unlike their Western competitors, the Japanese proved unable to gain the full benefit from the cost savings that were supposed to accompany productivity enhancement, since the established system of lifetime employment did not allow for replacing labor in a comparably radical way, due to productivity increases gained through enhanced IT technology scaling. Despite the common notion that Japanese companies did not invest in IT technology as much as their Western competitors, this is not quite true – a 2008 Yano Research Institute survey concluded that Japanese corporations on average spent more than twenty-one months customizing enterprise resource planning (ERP) solutions (business management software) to their specific needs, whereas American firms spent only eighteen months. The overall process of externalizing and outsourcing routine work functions in Japan was much slower and structural reorganization was often blocked due to employment laws and protective labor practices. Such problems abounded across all industrial sectors, and from the 1990s into the 2000s overall productivity in Japan was improving at a much slower rate than in the United States.

With increased attention to IT stemming from the so-called Y2K problem, many large enterprises in Japan began introducing and adopting ERP (Enterprise Resource Planning) systems. Nevertheless, the lifetime employment system still prevented corporations from making any significant staff reductions that might have led to streamlining and operational optimization. The internal decision-making process, characterized by an institutionalized requirement of consensus, combined with an aversion to general process standardization throughout the corporation's global operations, prevented the implementation of large-scale corporate reorganization measures. Most surprisingly perhaps, ERP solutions tended to be customized to fit in with established organizational practices – not the other way around. As a result, system-related cost reductions were never met and standardization of indirect operations, such as accounting, never made. This morass led to the loss of the opportunity to improve overall corporate productivity by slashing heavy and fixed costs.

The third reason why increased digitization did not suit Japanese corporations was that the fast-growing industries established by the new wave of internet technology generally supported younger and much more agile corporations. These venture players in this new and fast-growing area were less vertical and more horizontally integrated in terms of hierarchy and they had a direct, streamlined decision-making process. The companies in "Japan, Inc." were by their very nature much more conservative and slow moving, and they found it difficult to adapt. Even in the United States, with the introduction of personal computers into the workplace and downsizing, horizontal integration with its focus on the same level of the value chain led to an emerging class of new technology companies – Microsoft and Intel, for example, as competitors to large, well-established, and technologically strong enterprises such as IBM. Google and Facebook later eroded Microsoft's dominant position with the emergence of social media, and Intel Company had to defend its leading position from Qualcomm, a microchip manufacturer that had been aggressively expanding due to the explosion of mobile devices. Apple, which had at one time been on the verge of bankruptcy due to the Wintel alliance (the combination of Windows and Intel processor-power computers), managed to completely resurrect itself by attracting customers back during the internet and mobile device revolution.

Moreover, the new approach of what is called "open innovation" proved to be much more efficient than the traditional closed model. By foregoing complete control and inviting external solution developers to resolve issues, open innovation has proven to be the principal driver of growth in the ICT industry, and it continues to be so even now. As a result, in the business-to-customer (B2C) domain, young entrepreneurs thrive with the use of their particular brand of executive leadership skills, but the large and well-established electronics companies of Japan were handicapped. Even the once globally dominant Sony was not spared difficulty, as we shall see later.

In short, Japan, Inc. was not able to come up with adequate responses to establish a new "industrial ecosystem" in the new digitized environment that would nurture risk taking. This was absolutely key in the creation of new ventures that thrived in new competitive regions such as Silicon Valley. As a result, companies in this high-tech space had to face fierce new realities. In fact, in the 1980s the Japanese government had already identified shortcomings and had made attempts at countermeasures. Financial institutions, at the center of this effort, made efforts to shape the conditions necessary for nurturing new business and attracting venture capital. Nevertheless, no significant results were achieved. In Silicon Valley, we find fundamental differences in the ways in which industry and educational institutions collaborate and in the nature of the culture of the industrial community. It is only very recently that we have seen some progress with the start of comparable ventures in Japan that attempt to target global markets from their very inception, in companies such as LINE, a Japanese messaging application provider that was launched in 2011.

The Galapagos syndrome/one-village mentality/home-market bias

Another trait that is identified with the lost decades was the emergence of what is now popularly referred to as the "Galapagos syndrome." This term was originally coined to refer to Japanese 3G mobile phones that dominated Japanese markets and that had developed a great number of specialized features using the miniaturization so favored by Japanese electronics manufacturers, but that were totally different from any comparable device offered by global competitors – and thus unable to be used outside Japan. The name Galapagos refers of course to the highly evolved but thoroughly singular flora and fauna that Charles Darwin encountered on the Galapagos Islands that led him to make key connections in the development of evolutionary theory, and draws a parallel with the highly evolved nature of these phones and their complete divergence from anything outside of the islands of Japan.

Japanese cellular phone companies designed products solely for the Japanese domestic market, targeted for usage in Japan only. The highly complex functions of the phones relied heavily on the high-spec hardware components inside them, and the industry ignored the potential sales of such equipment overseas. This way of thinking eventually determined the fate of the phones, as the advances of smart phones and mobile applications, which made further customer adaptation and customization easier, overtook them. In essence, there was a neglect of any strategic aims to further develop the software capabilities of Japanese phones and the manufacturers failed to foresee how the digital revolution would fundamentally change the competitive landscape of the global consumer electronics market.

Not all Japanese management groups failed to understand the need to evolve and adapt to business in the outside world – Sony and other companies did attempt various reforms. But, as I explain later, the very success that Japan had experienced with its long-term communitarian *"kaisha* model" (*kaisha* means "company" in Japanese, with connotations of an essentially inward-looking operation – a "firm" that is set in its established ways) characterized by lifetime employment, a seniority system, and internal labor unions, made it difficult to effect a shift in the corporate mindset.

The most defining characteristic of the communitarian *kaisha* model was the decision-making system, which itself was strongly based on the "one-village" mentality, in which all action and decisions take place within a tightly controlled and confined arena, mostly limited to one company, or one company and its close partners. The single most important aim of this decision-making process is the preservation of internal harmony. The opinion in each division is coordinated through consultation, which is extremely time consuming: all related parties meet face-to-face and a consensus is formed through a bottom-up decision process. After decisions are made, progress to the execution stage is usually smooth, which makes the process highly suitable for integral (nonmodular) manufacturing and business operations.

As long as business conditions change at a slow, continuous pace, the coordination that this process enables, within a set of careful and yet precise moves, works. However, the new era of globalization and the digital revolution brought choppy, discontinuous change, requiring speedy decisions in which people had to "choose and focus." Dynamic shifts in strategy were the order of the day. In many cases, with the necessity to make decisions that were radical and sweeping, this brought huge distortions in previously harmonious internal arrangements. Moreover, often seen even though top management became aware of the need for speedy decisions, all measures continued to be decided within the scope and timeframe of the one-village consensus framework. Such constraint inevitably resulted in only small-scale changes. Ultimately, the Galapagos syndrome was a byproduct of the one-village decision-making system.

The results of Booz & Company's thirteenth annual examination of CEO succession trends, which was released on January 17, 2013, and covered the largest 2,500 public companies according to market capitalization, perfectly illustrates the characteristics of this one-village mentality. These statistics show that 97 percent of Japanese corporate CEOs are internally promoted, a much higher percentage than in North America and Western Europe, as well as in the BRIC and other emerging countries. Additionally, 75 percent of Japanese CEOs have worked at only one organization, as compared with other countries where the figure lies between 7 and 20 percent. This study also suggests that whereas the global average age for a CEO is fifty-three years of age when they take up the position, the figure for Japan is six years older, at fifty-nine years. Furthermore, only 1 percent of CEOs in Japanese corporations are non-Japanese. In short, Japanese top management is selected from a rather small cohort of people. Such people can be expected to read any given situation from a position that is at once narrow and very much on the inside, which is to say that they will probably lack a global perspective.

Escaping from the *kaisha* model

As previously explained, many Japanese corporations faced difficult times in the 1990s. It is worth noting that in many cases the systemic problems were acknowledged and discussed. Japanese companies were still sending many employees abroad to the United States to study at top universities. These people gained exposure to, for example, the internet-related innovations that were starting to happen in Silicon Valley. Japanese companies were among the first to expand overseas operations into China. The issue of accelerating consolidation, for example in memory chips (DRAM) or in LCD devices, was raised at an early stage. Questions regarding the nature of these industries, how to leverage economies of scale, and how to take product design modularity on to commoditization were the frequent subject of debate.

Nevertheless, despite having a sufficient knowledge of the latest trends, corporate leaders were unable to propose any effective solutions that would define the necessary course to be taken for their organizations in the future. The causes behind this powerlessness were deeply rooted.

Many of the largest Japanese companies had become highly successful in the business environment that had prevailed from the 1960s to the 1980s. They had utilized their competitive advantages under the Japanese management system, or the *kaisha* model. Their business practices, systems, and regulations all arose out of this management model. Lifetime employment, for example, was originally nothing more than a voluntary labor arrangement between employers and employees practiced mainly at large companies, and had been designed to overcome a labor shortage during the 1960s. Later, court decisions made this practice the norm for most regular workers in any kind of company and instituted a form of employment for life. The dual-tier industrial organization comprised large corporations and small- to medium-sized enterprises. At the same time, a vertically collaborative system known as *keiretsu* (informal groupings of enterprises) grew, and worked effectively to produce top-notch quality products with cost flexibility in the manufacturing sector based on vertical integration strategy model. The "main bank" system, which involved close long-term ties between corporations and single large financial institutions, worked for the financing of corporate activities and in providing oversight in cases of sudden underperformance. The government's rigid regulation policy served to further banking stability by promoting this main bank system.

For thirty years, this arrangement had functioned well: the key socioeconomic structures like managerial and labor practices, the industrial structure, and the financial system all worked together, reinforcing one another. In the 1990s, this system was already entrenched both at the macroeconomic and the microeconomic levels.

In short, the very success of Japanese business practice and culture up until this time served to place business leaders under a kind of curse – a psychological trap that became all the more difficult to escape in the face of a business environment that in the 1990s suddenly started to undergo rapid change. In addition, in most cases even if CEOs had summoned up sufficient determination to try to transform their companies, few leaders of conventional large Japanese enterprises would be able to implement drastic reforms – they would instead be likely to encounter great internal resistance. And even had they convinced their own organizations to change, they would still have had to face steep hurdles originating in the rigid social establishment. The Japanese industrial community became immobilized, completely trapped by the narrow confines of its own one-village mentality, which ironically had slowly enveloped it during the years of high achievement. And the first companies to suffer from the dilemmas arising out of changing business conditions were the major electronics companies – their business models and organizational nature made them extremely vulnerable in the new environment.

The Japanese companies that did not deal well with the new business environment usually either missed the chance to invest in growth opportunities because they were unable to abandon underperforming business units (such companies tended to be manufacturers of general electric devices); or because they pursued a power game, driven by frequent zero-based redesign of new products, which did not match their core competencies (semiconductor and large-size LCD TV manufacturers); or because they became overly fixated on the growth potential of B2C information technology devices, which were outside their core capabilities.

In contrast, the companies that came out in a better position in the lost decades consistently adopted a "choose and focus" approach in their strategy and instituted a strong CEO-based model in corporate governance, one that had been adapted specifically to Japanese corporate situations, synchronizing organization and corporate architecture with an internal workforce comprising regular, skilled employees who had been trained up within the company.

In the end, the most effective key to global competitiveness lay in adopting an appropriate corporate architecture, one that would suit the Japanese socioeconomic environment, and at the same time enabling swift internal strategic decision making.

Overcoming the curse

The Japanese companies that successfully dealt with globalization and the digital revolution fall into three groups. The first group comprised newly established companies led by their owner/founders – they include Softbank, Rakuten, and First Retailing. These entrepreneurial companies were (and are) comprised mostly of younger people, extremely flexible, and relatively free from the conventional practices of the old Japanese management system. Power is kept to a few, strong figures at the top, enabling swift strategic decisions to be taken, something that is essential in the digital revolution age.

The second group comprises small but globally excellent companies and niche top companies in manufacturing. These companies focus on their core competence and establish unique and strong strategic positions (typically taking more than a 50 percent market share) in the small- to medium-size market segment. Most of these companies are the business-to-business (B2B) players in mechatronics (a fusion of mechanics and electronics), or in the manufacture of component or specialty materials, where their core competence allows for technology accumulation based on long-term business experience. They usually have a close relationship with their customers. Their products are not so significant in the cost volume arena, but represent extremely critical components for their customers – and so suppliers rarely switch. Despite their relatively small size, they are not subcontractor companies who stick to supplying large domestic manufacturing companies, but remain independent, selling products to a customer base all over the world. Such companies include Hirose Electric Co. Ltd., a manufacturer of specialized connectors for mobile phones, and Mani, Inc., a manufacturer of medical and dental instruments. These companies sell their products on a worldwide basis and have attained a dominant position in their respective global markets.

The third group comprises large manufacturing companies like Komatsu, Daikin, and Bridgestone. These companies conducted reforms successfully – under strong leadership they overcame structural problems and implemented long-term managerial changes. They have evolved significantly, retaining their edge as Japan-based manufacturing companies and building strong positions in the global market – continually reshuffling their product lines and functional units in order to keep these positions in competitive markets. Their corporate governance is a hybrid of Japanese and American styles, and they are very internationally minded.

Some companies even in the problematic electronics industry, which is perhaps the most affected by globalization and digitalization, have demonstrated positive results. Hitachi, Mitsubishi Electric, and Panasonic all successfully adopted the "choose and focus" managerial approach and pursued reforms in their corporate governance systems. Importantly, they were strongly aware of their core competencies and organizational capabilities as old, large, and well-established Japanese corporations. Despite substantial economic losses suffered in their organizational struggles during the lost decades, they appear now to be applying and profiting from the lessons learned. The on-site/first-line capabilities of many Japanese manufacturing companies are still intact and remain at world-class levels. With the correct reforms in their decision-making processes, these companies should be able to reap tremendous benefits in the coming decades.

A case study: The struggles of Sony

The consumer electronics company Sony played a major role in the development of Japan's economy as a major exporter during the 1960s, 1970s, and even the 1980s. In the 1990s, however, its power seemed to dwindle, and it became known for its fading brand name. Its fall from dominance as a once-renowned electronics giant derives from a series of inappropriate decisions that relate to the company's business portfolio strategy and tardy adoption of digitalization solutions, despite ongoing efforts in corporate governance reform. Sony was still making financial losses in the late 2000s, and has yet to make a full recovery. Here I will concentrate on the problems directly linked to managerial issues and on the one-village mentality that contributed to its problems.

From its very beginnings, Sony was an atypical Japanese company. Originally founded by Ibuka Masaru, it made a name for itself by creating markets for new technological devices and "cool" products, which were sought after for their quality, functionality, and portability. When cofounder Morita Akio became president in 1971, the company was highly entrepreneurial and capable of making fast and calculated decisions – quite different from other Japanese companies at the time. However, in the 1990s, when the founding generation of executives retired, the company made some questionable decisions, aggressively expanding into new businesses – the entertainment media, financial services, electronic components (semiconductors), and chemical materials – and it became too diversified. The company lost the ability to define its own strategic focus.

Despite such mistakes, Sony remained a player during the early stages of the digital revolution in the 1990s. It introduced the PlayStation into the video game market and the VAIO brand in the PC arena. In 1995, Idei Nobuyuki, a Sony lifer since graduation from university, was appointed president, initiating a period of "salaried" top management. This was a typical Japanese management practice in which employees advance from their initial employment after university graduation and, in line with the internal seniority policies, potentially progress to a CEO position (usually in four- to five-year rotation periods) at about sixty years of age. Idei appears to have grasped the challenges facing Sony in an increasingly globalized world and the changes required by digitization, and identified three main issues that the company had to address. The first was to create and nurture strong leadership in the organization in the post-owner/post-founder generation. The second was to enable management agility and control – the company employed over 200,000 people and was a highly diversified, autonomous business with a global reach. The third was the problem of ossification that had clearly beset the company and the one-village mentality characterizing its internal relations – a problem that beset all old and well-established Japanese companies (and Sony was now one of these).

Simply put, Sony's management needed reform. It was quite clear that no company could survive in the digital age by keeping basically to the *kaisha* model with a few piecemeal adaptations and continuing to only depend on nonconfrontational and harmonizing planning among business unit heads for setting the corporate direction. Sony accordingly initiated a series of corporate governance reforms. The position of CEO was introduced into the corporate architecture. The company also decided to adopt American-style management practices – with power exercised through a top-down decision-making structure, with stronger executive power. The rationale for this was that the company now needed strong leaders to enable fast and decisive steering at the corporate helm.

When Sony initiated its corporate governance reforms in 1997, it was one of the first companies in Japan to introduce a mostly independent board and a system of corporate executive officers dividing the supervision and execution of tasks. In addition, a focus on value creation was introduced by implementing economic value added (EVA) models for measuring performance. Several of its publicly traded subsidiary companies were delisted. These dramatic changes frequently brought Sony into business media headlines as the pioneer in modernizing corporate governance in Japan. CEO Idei proposed a new vision for the company based on the key term of "regeneration" (rejuvenating Sony), making every effort to stimulate innovation and attract new customers, because young and old alike were now fascinated by digital technology.

Sony also adopted an American style of management and a new corporate vision, in the hope that – even though many on the corporate board were now external directors – it could resuscitate its fortunes and remain a player in the new digital age. Other corporations also thought that this was a progressive way to deal with the changing business environment and emulated Sony. In Sony's case, however, these reforms did not work well.

Sony's difficulties

The challenges Sony faced involved the very core of its organization. The new wave of innovation related to the digital revolution impacted most of its central businesses. The new Internet business wave favored much younger entrepreneurial companies led by charismatic founders. The company's last resort was to truly shake up things internally, and these changes demanded a shift in the strategic, top-down decision-making process, which had already been made by Sony's American competitors. However, Sony's CEO did not have the same role and powers as his Western counterparts or the influence that Morita once held. The nature of Sony's organization, which began to resemble other Japanese competitors, did not allow this sort of adaptation.

Sony had fallen into the same trap as many other large and well-established enterprises. It was unable to keep pace with the internet age that thrived on the discontinuous and radical, spontaneous innovation of the B2C information technology sector.

Due to duplicate products and services, Sony's brand had become diluted and the company lost time in dealing within the internal chains of command. Yet, past successes led to the self-perception of superiority in terms of technology and products. Sony had become convinced of its principles of self-sufficiency and the corporate mentality was weighed down by its own bureaucracy.

Although Sony was looking for opportunities to utilize its technological prowess (even now Sony is acknowledged as an excellent innovation leader) in elemental technology as its competitive advantage in the digital B2C sector, it is not clear that any decisive actions were taken concerning how to deal with non-core and loss-bearing businesses in terms of reconfiguring the corporate portfolio. In the end, the company lost the opportunity to invest in growing businesses due to its inability to divest itself of its firmly entrenched, pathological Japanese-style decision-making behavior. Sony continued to keep its particular internal assembly process (equipment and workforce), despite seeing Western competitors flexibly adapt to changing trends in the assembly process. It was not long before the "Sony shock" occurred.

The "Sony shock"

Latent problems in Sony started to surface around 2002 when profit margins began to shrink, producing what was later labeled the Sony shock. In the light of the losses, Idei Nobuyuki, then CEO and chairman of Sony, turned the company's focus to restructuring and reducing redundancy. The biggest problem was not his initiatives, but the internal resistance that he encountered. He eventually resigned. In 2005, the company took a further measure to deal with the poor internal state of governance and appointed Sir Howard Stringer as CEO in an attempt to escape the trap of the one-village mentality.

This move improved the company's fortunes somewhat during the high consumption period prior to the world economic recession. Sony began shedding production facilities and other fixed assets, while laying off employees at various stages. Unfortunately, fundamentally nothing changed. The problem was that no one wanted to make unpopular and drastic decisions such as divesting the company of the loss-bearing TV and game businesses, or making the radical shift to the fabless business model. It seems that not even a non-Japanese CEO could overrule the divisions that arose from the bottom-up decision process. As a consequence, Sony tried various options to adapt to the digital revolution, but these did not always deliver the desired gains. Before long, the company had merely become another old and large corporation in which the decision-making process had been altered superficially but at heart remained what it had always been and driven by the same operating principles as any other ordinary Japanese company.

Another factor behind the organizational inertia was the system of hiring of employees. In its owner/founder management days, Sony had the same human capital acquisition practice as most American venture companies and acquired many of its key leaders from outside and from untraditional career tracks. In fact, Sony had a considerably diversity within its management layers in the 1970s and 1980s because, unlike its competitors, it was still an entrepreneurial company and strove to attract the best talent from the outside. Ohga Norio, Sony's CEO prior to Idei, had been an aspiring opera singer before joining the company. Unfortunately, this practice of acquiring leaders from untraditional career tracks lapsed over time and the company began systematically hiring university graduates and offering lifetime employment. The results were typical of most of Japan, Inc. Despite having a foreign CEO, the majority of its outside directors were corporate officers who had been lifelong Sony employees since graduation from university. This naturally increased the inertia of the *kaisha* model.

Sony's problems and struggles

Despite the transformation initiatives since the mid-1990s, many superficial discussions took place in which top managers were held responsible for the failure to innovate because they did not have engineering backgrounds. They were blamed for the fact that management provided only a conceptual vision, which was far removed from the everyday operations of the company. However, I believe that such discussions did not get to grips with the real problem. The key issue was the nature of people in the organization of the old and large Sony. The late founder of Apple, Steve Jobs, did not offer specialized engineering expertise to his company. When, after leaving Apple once, he returned to the company, his grand vision and his charismatic (some might say dictatorial) leadership were enough to take Apple on to eventually dominate the field with portable audio devices and the smartphone business.

Would it have been possible for Sony to come up with an effective strategy in response to the iPod and the iTunes ecosystem created by Apple? Sony had the technical capability; the main issue was how to establish similar integrated internet-based services. Organizationally, however, it was an entirely different story. Apple was a small, flat, and simple organization with a young and charismatic leader. Sony was a huge, hierarchical, and complicated group of business units with a "salaried" CEO at its helm. The key problem was how to bring the various parts of each business together to achieve the best fusion of capabilities in hardware, software, content, internet access services, and payment processing. Such a conglomeration also required an extremely fast response time, as the new digital age demanded agility. Overcoming organizational torpidity was the greatest hurdle to successfully countering Apple products and services. And the main problem was that the new game was not designed for large, diversified, decentralized, and old organizations. Apple, Google, and Facebook were all young and small, a model that will always win in a game in which radical and fast-moving innovation is required.

Core issues and challenges ahead

Sony's issues were not just related to management and corporate governance. Transforming Sony involved addressing its corporate culture, organizational habits, and the behavior of its managers and employees. In many ways this poses an even greater challenge than strategic change, as it takes time to catch up in order to coordinate the synchronization of new systems and people. Sony's management should have tried to stay more aware of what was happening in the organization. It should have spent more time and energy in encouraging not just strategic change but also cultural and behavioral transformation at the lower and middle layers of its companies. One might argue that Sony's main business domain did not allow for such a time-consuming approach, but this was the reality of Sony in the early twenty-first century. Haste does indeed make waste.

Should Sony have attempted to redefine its business portfolio based on its core competence and adopted the "choose and focus" strategy, despite its lumbering and massive organizational structure? Should it have brought in young and charismatic talent to resuscitate itself? This is what many middle-aged Japanese were wistfully wondering, as they recalled the original founders of Sony, who were so innovative. Opinions on the subject remain divided.

One U.S. company whose foundational story is similar to that of Sony and that faced a similar dilemma in the 1980s was General Electric (GE), a company founded by the king of inventors, Thomas Edison. Under Chairman and CEO Jack Welch, GE chose not to pursue the romantic path of innovation. Instead, "Neutron Jack" made GE focus on segments – jet engines, power generators, medical devices – the technological competitive edge in these segments was "integral" rather than "modular," "cumulative," or "zero-based." But GE was not the only company to transform itself. Similar transformations happened at other technology giants such as IBM, Intel, and Microsoft. In Japan, Komatsu, Bridgestone, and Hitachi also overhauled themselves. The success of these companies demonstrates that first identifying organizational capabilities and then linking them to specific business strategies can offer large and well-established corporations an effective method for change.

If Sony had done this, it would have had a huge effect on the rather romantic image of the company in the imagination of the public. In addition, the question remains as to what extent it could effectively leverage its nature as an established and large organization and coordinate it with a focus on strategic domains, where its core competence could be more effectively utilized. Such a move requires a drastic change of corporate architecture and requires time.

Sony still has the option to bring in younger leaders and to pursue innovation, in keeping with what it did in the days of Ibuka and Morita. Such an achievement would provide a brilliant success story in management history if Sony were able to combine a reliance on technology accumulation and B2B focus, in addition to the option of challenging discontinuous innovation serving the B2C segment, as no other company managed to pull this off before. As such, Sony is at a crossroads and whatever option it chooses to follow, it will not be easy. If Sony manages to utilize the experience it has gained over the past twenty years and fundamentally reshape its own organization in its corporate values, behavior, habits, and decision-making process, then the young Hirai Kazuo, newly inaugurated as CEO in 2012, and his team may have a better chance to put the company back on the right course.

Conclusion: The end of the curse of Japan, Inc.?

In this chapter, I have examined trends in the lost decades that showed how the traditional corporate model in Japan was unsuited to the new world of globalization and digitization. Globalization joined up markets all around the world, making the traditional view of individual, separated markets completely outdated. The digital revolution created a new era in which radical and disruptive innovation flourished. Its ever-changing nature forced companies to move away from core capabilities that had been shaped through technological expertise and the accumulation of know-how, typical for corporations established on linear and continuous innovation. The Galapagos syndrome had driven Japanese product development to extremes, so that many Japanese companies were making highly complex products that could only suit narrow markets; it had also narrowed the country's ability to see what was happening in the wider, newly expanding global market. A strong bias toward the domestic market had sidetracked the corporate strategic mindset, which remained too focused on high-price/high-quality solutions and products without trying to challenge and proactively penetrate emerging markets.

The inability of Japanese companies to cope with globalization and digitization was deeply rooted in the organizational fabric of Japanese corporate management. At one time, the codes of practice in Japanese companies were supremely efficient – but they were now long past their expiry date. Unfortunately, most of the Japanese business community remained unaware of its lack of capacity. Those companies that did manage to initiate transformational changes fall into two categories: ones that recognized their outdated nature and successfully transformed themselves by utilizing organization-specific capabilities, and ones that grew new businesses to a sustainable scale under the direction of their founders.

While Sony was relatively young, it was able to pit itself against older, more established Japanese electronics giants and win. During the years of the lost decades, however, when the company had gained an established position and was run by "salaried," lifer executives, it had to compete with new, global technology champions such as Apple and Google. These competitors attracted a much younger generation of engineers and product developers, and they also had strong visionary leaders who could execute more agile and dynamic strategic decisions through a top-down approach.

Managers at Sony and other Japanese companies did become conscious of the mismatch between their corporate strategy and management styles and the new environment. They tried various measures – introducing a system of independent directors, for example, and instituting company and performance-based evaluations. However, these attempts failed to address the problems deeply enough, resulting in patchwork corrections that never took systematic or consistent root, and the gap between organizational behavior and capabilities grew. The failure can be compared to computer users who do not wish to change their old operating systems but still try to upgrade their computers and use the latest applications by buying new hardware components. Piecemeal improvements mean the computer will not run well and there is actually even a greater likelihood of errors or failures. Changing the operating system in an organizational management structure is not easy. Integrity and consistency also have to be installed into the system: all informal relationships have to be thrown out, power relations that have grown up over the years, with accompanying assumptions, have to be dismantled, and attitudes of employees and stakeholders reset. The enormous and yet delicate managerial effort necessary to accomplish all this requires considerable time. The longer the old operating system has been in place, the harder it is to overcome old and entrenched behavior. This is possibly why such transformations that did occur over the long lost decades were so slow in coming.

The lessons of the lost decades and the struggles that many Japanese companies went through have universal relevance. Many companies in China and other Asian countries will soon face comparable issues, once their founders retire and new management comes on the scene. Continued success inevitably brings the risk of inertia taking hold. In any successful organization, internal and external stakeholders will have vested interests and will want to prioritize harmony and the status quo at the expense of rational, clear-headed adjustment to external change.

I will end this chapter on a positive note. I firmly believe that Japanese corporations still possess the capacity to acquire technical expertise and business know-how, as it is one of their greatest strengths to focus on the long-term horizon and continuity in product development. Japan's current problems, which include an ageing population as Seike Atsushi describes in Chapter 1, and a looming energy crisis resulting from the Fukushima accident as outlined by Kitazawa Koichi in Chapter 7, will not be easily solved. But these challenges in fact have the potential to offer fantastic opportunities for the private sector and could lead to an expansion of technologies and business models in, for example, energy management, medical devices, and services for an ageing society – fields in which all the developed economies, including those of China, India, and Russia, will need products. Japanese corporations have been given a precious opportunity to make an early start in securing a potentially highly advantageous market position.

To move back to the central theme of this book, I support the argument that demographics will play a decisive role in the direction that Japan chooses for itself in the future. In Japan, the first baby-boomers were born in the period from 1947 to 1949. This first post-war generation was nurtured in an environment based on traditional Japanese management practices and a decision-making process that reflected a one-village mentality. All this needs to change. The key to improving Japanese corporate governance and resolution processes lies in overcoming the inertia and apathy regarding alteration of the status quo. Japanese companies now need to start executing a top-down approach and to stop relying on middle management in making their strategic decisions.

The baby boomers in Japan are now reaching retirement age. The departure of such a large number of people will open up spaces in the corporate ranks. These leadership positions will more than likely be taken up by younger people who have a more individualistic set of values and a more results-oriented approach. The change of guard has the potential to lead to a break from the traditional one-village mentality that has characterized Japanese corporate decision making. I hope that the present upside-down pyramid composition of companies, with serried ranks of older people occupying the top positions, will be corrected, and excessive labor-related fixed costs will be reduced, and that it will become easier to escape from the old *kaisha* mindset.

For those old and well-established enterprises that have passed into the post-disruptive/nondiscontinuous innovation phase, it is essential to realize how important it is to bounce ideas off multiple corporate functions to obtain fine-tuned integrated outcomes. This part of the integral or hybrid (integral and modular combined) business approach needs to be emphasized as a key organizational core capability. With an adequate corporate architecture in place to encourage strategic decision making, this focus on continuous innovation could be leveraged as an advantage and utilized as a company's own core competence.

Looking at Japanese companies who have succeeded and those who have failed, we can extract some important clues for success in finding sustainable business approaches. There are key elements in enhancing strategic decision making and execution capability, driven by rationality and speed: the importance of keeping a strategic focus on core competence in the new and global competitive environment, and disregarding ungrounded or superficially competitive advantages or market fads; the importance of creating the right conditions for and nurturing strong leadership (this last includes instituting new systems to improve human capital development, CEO selection and empowerment, and the governance structure); and the importance of creating a globally diverse organization in terms of personnel and management style.

The good news is that the keys or clues all entail changes in attitude or focus toward strategy to be made by the upper echelons of the Japanese corporate community, that is to say the people at the very top. This means that most Japanese companies can duplicate this success. It also means that the fundamentals of the Japanese industrial community in terms of the basic caliber of the employees and their morale remain solid and competitive. All that is needed is for management to adopt the correct strategy and correct focus.

The years after the 1990s have seen many changes take place in Japanese business with significant revisions in corporate law, the bankruptcy code, and labor laws. Subinstitutional systems like the main bank system have less hold, and financial regulation policy has also been completely overhauled. Japanese banks are now much more focused on their own survival. The control exerted by the traditional main bank system is now limited by a new regulatory environment and the current health of cash positions on corporate balance sheets. The employment of external directors is also becoming a more common practice and is having an effect on corporate governance in Japan.

Obviously, obstacles and challenges remain, but they are steadily being dealt with. Even among the major electronics manufacturers, traditional and large companies are adapting management systems and strategies under the direction of visionary leaders. New ventures are appearing, based on disruptive and nonlinear innovation, and there are clear signs of a new potential for much more global players. All is not necessarily lost in Japan. The two lost decades, twenty years of struggle, may, in the end, bear fruit.

5 Making sense of the lost decades

Workplaces and schools, men and women, young and old, rich and poor

Andrew Gordon

Prologue: Talking about lost decades

Since the 1990s, an extraordinary change has taken place in the way Japan is understood and discussed both domestically and around the world. A country spoken of in the 1980s with awe or with fear, as model or as menace, came to be described as having a "soured" system, beset by profound problems in society, economy, and politics. These were said to affect the young and old, both men and women, in families, schools, and workplaces. Toward the end of the 1990s, the appellation that won the day (and still prevails) is that of the "lost decade(s)."[1] The term replaced an earlier discourse of "Japan as Number One," which had its heyday for a bit more than a decade, from the late 1970s through the start of the 1990s. This positive earlier take was never unanimous or unchallenged.[2] But the discourse of decline has been both more enduring and more confused – pregnant with contradictory assessments of what has been lost and where the problems lie. Any appraisal of Japan's experience of the past twenty years must begin by sorting through these diverse and divergent perspectives.

One of the most prominent views of Japan in this era is that the nation failed to change in ways that our globalized times demand. I argue in this chapter to the contrary: tremendous change has occurred over the lost decades, in public mood, socioeconomic practice, and state policy. In part, these changes reflect some of the issues that Machidori Satoshi analyzes in Chapter 8 on Japanese domestic politics and that Peter Drysdale and Shiro Armstrong point to in their discussion of Japan's foreign trade and investment in Chapter 10. But however profound they have been, the changes have not been unidirectional: for some they are negative and need to be reversed, for others they are positive but insufficient. The combination of opposing directions and opposing assessments produces an overall impression of stasis or insufficiency. Nevertheless, the changes have been substantial.

A second argument of this chapter is that change – even as it has been extensive – has unfolded in the context of existing and relatively enduring norms and structures. This truism was most memorably described by Marx as people making their history in a context where "the tradition of all the dead generations weighs like a nightmare on the brains of the living."[3] It bears repeating as a reminder that tossing long-established norms and systems overboard is never simple and not always wise (even if Marx certainly hoped that his readers would repudiate their inherited past). Toward the end of this chapter, I will develop the concept of a multidimensional "moral economy" as one way to characterize these enduring structures of the past.

A third argument is that any account of the lost decades and any prescriptions for the future must keep politics in focus. The views and actions not only of those at the center and top of society, but also of those in civil society standing in places "outside" or "below" or on the margins, are important. And the discourse of stagnation is always a value-laden claim with political valence. To put forward a view of Japan as lost is inevitably to call for some sort of action, whether for reform, moral regeneration, or a return to a better past.[4] Escape from the condition of "lostness" is not a technocratic matter of discovering the current global best practice and following it: it is a profoundly political challenge.

The discourse of "decline"

The discourse of socioeconomic deadlock and decline ranges across several related topics: employment systems and corporate management; the situation of youth in education and the transition to their working lives; the situation of women in the labor force and in families; the decline in birth rates, the ageing of society, and the plight of the elderly; and a rise in economic or social inequality. Policymakers, business and labor leaders, and scholars have long understood that issues of employment are intimately linked to questions of education, gender and social equality, and well-being.

Given their interconnected nature, one might start with any one of these topics. In this chapter, we begin with the workplace and move on to address matters of gender and social equality, with only brief mention of education and demography, topics addressed more fully by Seike Atsushi in Chapter 1 on demography and Kariya Takehiko in Chapter 6 on the Japanese education system. Toward the end of the era of "Japan as Number One," truly grand claims were being made about the brilliance of Japanese-style management. Itami Hiroyuki, a well-known professor of management at Hitotsubashi University, proclaimed in the mid-1980s his belief in the superiority of Japan's "human-centered corporate system." He argued that, "when we think of Japan's long prosperity, at risk of exaggeration perhaps, can we not say that we have arrived at a time to consider the self-conscious export of our civilization?"[5] In more muted tones, in 1991 Koike Kazuo proclaimed Japan's "skill formation and industrial relations" to be "a step ahead of world trends."[6]

The bursting of the 1980s financial bubble and the onset of the lost decades dramatically changed the context and generated a new flow of views on the defects of the Japanese workplace. Most prominent has been the neoliberal critique. As early as 1993, flagship carriers of this view such as the *Economist* were deploring the rigidity of long-term job security or seniority-based wages.[7] In contrast to Anglo-American-style "shareholder-first" capitalism, Japanese firms were criticized for adherence to a "stakeholder" capitalism that considered the interests of employees and managers to be as important as those of investors. At home, also from the mid-1990s, the business federation focused on employment issues, Nikkeiren, began to call for more flexible deployment of labor. A leading domestic supporter of this position, the *Nihon Keizai Shimbun* (Nikkei), ran a series in January 2003 on what it called the "Japanese disease" (a play on criticisms from the 1960s of a "British disease" of economic stagnation and entrenched labor power). The newspaper condemned Japanese business leaders for failing to implement much needed reforms in managing their companies.[8] Similar views had been put forth during the 1970s' recession and oil crises. But the recent round of criticism of Japanese workplace practice has been far more enduring and has focused not just on what employers should do differently, but on reforms that the government needs to initiate. Reformers have called for deregulation of labor markets to allow companies more freedom to dismiss workers and close unproductive facilities, greater reliance on outsourcing both to save on costs and to allow easier future adjustments, and increased use of "nonregular" workers on fixed-term contracts, for similar reasons.

The distinction here between "regular" and nonregular" labor has a particular legal and social meaning in Japan. A "regular" employee is someone hired with an indefinite time commitment rather than a time-defined contract. Decades of legal precedents, as well as agreements between unions and companies, established fairly strong protections for these workers, who were most often men. In legal battles over dismissals, courts ruled that before shedding regular workers, employers had to meet four standards of "reasonableness": business conditions had to necessitate retrenchment; the need for cutting back via outright dismissal as opposed to transfers or furloughs had to be clear; the selection of those persons marked for dismissal had to be fair and rational; and the procedure, including discussion with the union if present, had to be reasonable. In contrast, "nonregular" employees, typically hired on a fixed contract and often in part-time status, were only protected from dismissal during the contract period. They had no protection when it ended. At the same time, labor laws from the 1950s placed some significant restrictions on the industries and contexts in which workers could be hired on time-limited contract, in particular when hired through third-party labor brokers.

Regular status has in fact never been as protected in practice as it appeared to be through legal decisions. Beginning in the 1960s, companies devised an array of methods to cut back employment and ease out regular workers, and smaller companies in particular have been able to cut back with little fear that employees would go to court to protest. Nonetheless, the neoliberal critique from the 1990s took aim at the purported rigidity of Japanese employment law and practice.

But even as significant changes in employment did indeed take place (discussed in greater detail later), other voices emerged to lament the new situation equally as one of discouragement and decline. Reflecting the enduring force of the male breadwinner model as a dominant gender ideology in Japan, concern focused in particular on the ripple effect of the increase in nonregular employment for young men. Deregulated labor markets were said to have increased the numbers of poorly paid young men with insecure jobs and weak prospects for advancement.

These youths were seen to lack the means or the confidence to spend money and generate domestic demand, reinforcing an enduring negative cycle of deflation and economic stagnation. Their growing need for unemployment insurance, as well as corporate claims to state subsidies to sustain employment, put pressure on the national budget. Their situation was prominently connected in the public and bureaucratic mind to declining marriage and birth rates. Nonregular workers were understood to lack the confidence not only to buy things, but also to marry and have children. And a smaller working population would experience increased trouble supporting an ageing society.

The discourse of decline included a more generalized concern with youth and education beyond the confines of the workplace, although it was often related to employment and economic issues. The sense of crisis in education ran from elementary through advanced levels, and it is discussed in depth in Kariya's chapter. Of most relevant to this chapter is Kariya's depiction of a sense of crisis in secondary education, focused mostly on nonelite students. This must be set against a backdrop where, through the 1980s, the efficient placement of young male high school graduates into secure jobs with long-term prospect for advance in pay and skills had been a point of pride in Japan and among outside observers.[9] By the late 1990s and into the 2000s, school guidance counselors were uniformly lamenting the unraveling of this system due mainly to a sharp decrease in desirable job placements in manufacturing. Available opportunities for those without university degrees seemed increasingly limited to poorly paid and insecure service sector jobs.[10]

In higher education, the pessimistic trend discussed most widely not only in Japan but in universities elsewhere was the dramatic drop-off in the number of Japanese youths who studied abroad. It is important to set this decline in context; it followed a dramatic increase in overall study abroad from the mid-1980s through the early 2000s, and numbers going abroad in 2012 were still significantly higher than the numbers in the 1970s and 1980s. Fueling anxiety behind this decline was the pronounced decrease in Japanese students going to the United States in particular, especially when compared to the sharply increased numbers going to America from China or India.[11] As the Kariya chapter argues, this new comparative context is the critical element in producing a sense of crisis in the production of global talent in Japan. Explanations for the decline have abounded, ranging from the unwillingness of companies or government offices to sponsor young employees for study abroad, to the allegedly inward-looking mindset of risk-averse youths, to the (perceived) need of college students to stay in Japan to begin job-hunting even in their sophomore or junior year.[12] For government officials and some business leaders, the lack of global experience and ambition was part of the explanation for the failure of Japanese companies. Their reports and statements, which proliferated from about 2009 onward, lamented that younger workers did not seek a global stage for their careers, and that Japan trailed much of the world in English proficiency. They also said that the problem ran two ways: Japanese students and workers were failing to look to the world, while Japan was failing to attract students and workers from the world.[13] In this sense, such reports echo some of the Drysdale/Armstrong criticism in Chapter 10 concerning Japan's lack of ability to allow in foreign investment and to import global talent.

The gloomy discourse on youth was a gendered one, with roughly equal-opportunity lamentation about both women and men. Beginning in the late 1990s, observers in Japan began to write critically about "parasite singles," defined as young people who lived rent-free at home, with little ambition beyond shopping and enjoyment of leisure. The term first gained prominence with the 1999 book by the sociologist Yamada Masahiro, *The Age of Parasite Singles*.[14] Yamada argued for a rough equivalence in the numbers of male and female young parasites, but the mass media tended to see this as a female phenomenon, with the additional criticism of these women as "selfish" for neither forming families nor seeking serious careers. These labels gained currency around the world, helped by a feature article in the *New York Times Sunday Magazine* in July 2001.[15] Several years later, a male-centered term for failed youth came to prominence: the "herbivore." Coined in 2006, this label spread so widely that by 2010 government surveys were asking young men if they self-identified as "herbivores" (in one survey, 36 percent of teenage boys did so). The term typically conjured images of feminized young men interested above all in personal grooming and lacking both sexual drive and the career ambition of earlier generations.

While such pejorative buzzwords tended to lay the blame on young people themselves, other commentators found fault with the socioeconomic or political systems for failing to provide opportunity or empowerment to youths. The economist Genda Yuji argued with harsh passion in the early 2000s that "contrary to the belief that parasite singles enjoy the vested right to live at their parents' expense, the real parasites are the parents, the generation of middle-aged and older workers on whom society has conferred vested rights and who make their livelihood at the expense of young people."[16] An important related argument was made in some quarters to the effect that Japanese employers, mainly men, were failing to offer sufficient opportunities to young women and indeed to all women to use their talent and energy in productive ways. Many people saw this not just as a matter of justice or equity, but as one of national economic interest. A 2010 report by the Tokyo office of Goldman Sachs on what it called "Womenomics," argued that "if Japan could close its gender employment gap, we estimate that Japan's workforce could expand by 8.2 million and the level of Japan's GDP [gross domestic product] could increase by as much as fifteen percent." In addition, it noted, "against a backdrop of anemic consumption, female spending trends have been relatively resilient."[17]

Genda's claim that middle-aged and older employees, mainly men, were protecting their privilege at the expense of the young in some measure echoed the spirit of the neoliberal prescription for a corporate free hand in cutting back on expensive long-term commitments to employees. But his opinions sat uneasily with equally downbeat arguments, also made frequently and with passion, to the effect that the older generation (especially men) was being squeezed and cast aside in violation of the implicit understanding that long and dedicated service would be rewarded.

The *Asahi Newspaper* from November 8, 1997, began with a provocative headline: "Sayonara, Mainstream Consciousness!" The reporter argued that the prolonged recession and corporate restructuring had made once-secure jobs unreliable, while crashing land and stock prices and microscopic interest rates had eroded the assets of the middle-class population. The article related the nightmare of the forty-nine-year-old Mr. A, employed at a company that sold electronic equipment. He had been transferred to the "market development section," a posting widely understood by coworkers to be a dead-end dumping ground for those targeted by the company for "voluntary retirement." Explicitly told by his boss that he should volunteer for early retirement, Mr. A was discouraged, angry, and humiliated. He had worked for this company for thirteen years and had just taken out a loan to pay for a new four-bedroom home that he would be paying off until age seventy. He and his wife, who worked part time in a real estate office, were saddled with college preparation and tuition costs for three teenage children. Mr. A had not yet had the courage to tell his wife honestly of the extent to which he was under pressure to resign. The article quoted him as asking "Can my ever-so-average lifestyle be so easily snatched away from me?" Angry at the company's "insincerity" and determined to fight to keep his job, he had recently joined the Tokyo Manager's Union but his future on his job was uncertain.[18]

More dramatically, there were increasingly depressing reports of high numbers of suicides among middle-aged Japanese, men in particular. Typically attributing these acts to despair at personal economic and employment circumstances, government and media attention focused with keen intensity on a spike in suicides among men from precisely the moment when the story of Mr. A was published in 1997. Suicides by men in Japan jumped from 16,416 in that year, a level typical of the previous two decades, to 23,013 in 1998, an extraordinary increase of nearly 50 percent. Suicides have remained at this level ever since.[19]

The discourse of decline as it intensified over the course of the lost decades focused on one further important loss. A high degree of social and economic equality had been widely trumpeted as a key strength of Japanese society across the decades of rising postwar affluence. In the late 1990s, as the economy floundered, authors of best-selling books started to argue that equality was vanishing. Japan's middle class was fast dissolving into groups of winners and losers in the competition for income and wealth. The winners were epitomized by a handful of self-made billionaire entrepreneurs who were seen as heralds of a new free-wheeling economic order. The losers ranged from younger adults, men in the typical retelling, unable to gain a post-graduate foothold of stable employment, to more senior employees, such as Mr. A, eased out of their mainstream positions by corporate downsizing. In the mid-2000s, the dominant buzzword in discussions about this rising inequality was "stratified society." Then, sparked by a powerful two-hour NHK television documentary on the topic, broadcast in December 2007 *before* the global financial crisis (known in Japan as the "Lehman shock"), the appellation "working poor" came to public attention. The program focused on the growing numbers of conscientious, hard-working, well-intentioned men and women employed in low-wage, insecure jobs, unable to earn enough to meet their most basic needs for shelter, food, clothing, or even health care.

On the one hand, this downbeat catalog of decline is obviously full of apparently connected and reinforcing trends. A rigid employment system that protects jobs of veteran workers can be blamed not only for inhibiting nimble corporate strategy, but also for clogging or breaking down the school-to-work pipeline for youths when companies are not growing. And lack of job opportunities can discourage young men, perhaps indeed making them "herbivores." It can also discourage young women, leading them to become stay-at-home parasite singles. And these trends can discourage both young men and women from marriage and parenthood. The logic behind such connections is clear, but we should not assume there is always a strong causal relationship: in particular, Japan's demographic shift to a rapidly ageing society with a declining birth rate long predates the 1990s and the emergence of the key attributes ascribed to the lost decades.

On the other hand, the discourse of "lost Japan" is equally filled with contradictory and mutually exclusive perspectives. One observer's solution is another's problem. For some, the demographic shift is a crisis because there are *not enough* young people available to work and to generate the revenues to support their elders. For others, there are *too many* young people, unable to get their careers and their lives on track. For some, greater corporate flexibility in hiring and dismissing employees is crucial to allow businesses to compete in the global economy. For others, the resulting increase in nonregular labor inhibits domestic demand and drags down the economy. In the eyes of some, women are selfish parasites who need to get serious. To others, women are a valuable resource who are poorly treated and not given opportunities to enrich their own lives and that of the nation. Some condemn parasite singles, whether women or men, for spending irresponsibly. But others complain that nonregular workers – and by definition the great majority of parasite singles falls into this group – are underconsuming because of their low pay and uncertain future prospects.

Finally, although the specific configuration of these problems varies from place to place, at a general but by no means an empty level of abstraction, these ills are globally shared. Significant and rising inequality, a crisis in education in which youth are not taught the skills and knowledge that would put them on a path toward productive futures, a declining birth rate and worry about supporting an ageing society financially and socially, anemic job growth and job creation centered on part-time and insecure positions – this catalog certainly applies to many places in the advanced capitalist world.

The following section analyzes in more detail the social or economic trends that underlay these diverse negative perspectives. This presentation of the "facts" will, however, neither resolve dubious causal connections nor clarify which of the contradictory perspectives are true. I rather turn to look at the evidence that buttresses these perspectives to gain a better understanding of the three points made at the start: The lost decades have seen significant change. These changes, and the processes by which they have unfolded, have been embedded in longer historical contexts. And the ways in which the facts and the changes are construed are inevitably political.

Japan's "social-industrial complex" of problems

The Japanese employment system changed greatly in the 1990s and 2000s with new configurations of regular and nonregular employees, both men and women. Most significantly, across the entire society the rise in both numbers and proportion of nonregular workers was quite dramatic. But change in the treatment of regular workers has been far-reaching as well, in some ways leading to a convergence in the two types of employment.

Job security in major firms became notably weaker over the 1990s and 2000s. The practice of soliciting "voluntary retirements," already part of the tool box of corporate Japan since the era of the recession and oil crisis of the 1970s, became ever more common and occurred at earlier ages in a typical career. Likewise, interviews with personnel managers at major firms in 2010 suggest that employees were more likely than in the past to find their division in a large enterprise spun off as an independent company.[20] Such moves would likely narrow their later options. Those who remained faced increased workloads, especially as a company's fortunes improved and new hiring was pursued cautiously. In recent years, one extreme manifestation of this change in employees' status has been the emergence of so-called "black enterprises." There are at present no government surveys or official definition of such firms, but discussion in the media tends to focus on two sorts of brutally harsh corporate behavior: Such corporations seek to rid themselves of senior employees with a variety of tactics to bully them into leaving "voluntarily." And they exploit young workers by hiring them in regular status while treating them as disposable resources. Enterprises hire far more new employees than they plan to keep, impose impossible work norms, demand long hours of unpaid overtime, and squeeze out their labor until they quit, often in exhaustion or with damaged health. Young people sign on for such jobs drawn by promises of regular employment status in a difficult job market.[21]

In matters of compensation, the idea of "seniority-based pay," even for regular employees in large firms, has been transformed through a series of incremental changes that over time have produced a qualitatively different system. Building on policies since the 1960s, which introduced merit assessment into annual raises, many companies in the early 2000s introduced or expanded a "result-based" element in wage setting. This component was usually tied to an assessment of an individual's achievements; in this regard it did extend the long-established calculation of wages to reflect traits of the person more than traits of the job. But the spread among individual incomes at a given age or seniority nonetheless increased. This was all the more pronounced when bonuses were taken into account. Companies brought much greater managerial discretion into aggregate calculation of bonuses to reflect corporate revenue and profit, and they greatly increased managerial authority to allocate bonuses to individuals to reflect their performance. In aggregate terms, bonuses at one leading steelmaker in recent years (and steelmakers are often presented as among the more traditionally minded employers) have varied by nearly 100 percent from year to year (average bonuses in 2009 were 2.2 million yen; in 2010 they averaged 1.2 million yen). And at one of the major electronic firms, the bonus payment given to a strong performer over the course of a given year by 2010 stood at ten months' additional pay compared to four months' pay for a poorly rated person. Since the base monthly income itself was sure to be higher for the more highly rated worker due to better merit increases over time, the spread in bonuses between such individuals would be considerably greater than a 10-to-4 ratio.

Thus, even in the purportedly rigid world of regular workers in major firms, employees can no longer assume either that their jobs are secure over the long term or that their pay will reliably and steadily increase. Managers have a wide range of tools at hand with which to allocate labor and control personnel costs. More than ever, employees have come to face greater variability in earning power and a greater likelihood of reassignment to a subsidiary or a call to retire voluntarily. As described above, the particular mechanisms by which companies have come more strictly to control wage costs, adjust workplace numbers, and allocate human resources have developed within a framework of long-established practices that are in some measure distinctive to Japan. But the changes in these practices are nonetheless profound.

Equally profound has been the shift in the proportion of employees in the category of regular and nonregular workers. The latter include part-time and full-time employees on fixed-term, renewable (and easily nonrenewable) contracts made directly with an employer, as well as workers dispatched to a job from a third-party employment agency. Defining and measuring such nonregular employment is not a straightforward project, but the direction and scope of change is clear. Counting dispatch workers is difficult because the same person can be dispatched more than once in a given year, and government statistics count each dispatch as an additional worker. When the entire workforce is included, the proportion and numbers of self-employed and family labor declined sharply, the proportion defined as "regular employee" declined modestly from 58 percent (38 million) in 1992 to 52 percent (34 million) in 2007, and, most notably, the proportion and absolute number in the various nonregular categories nearly doubled, from 14.4 percent (9.5 million) in 1992 to 27 percent (18 million) in 2007.[22] These numbers and proportions have been relatively unchanged since 2007. In the "Labor Force Survey" of the Ministry of Internal Affairs and Communications, which excludes the self-employed and family labor from the denominator, the proportion of nonregular workers in relation to all employees is even higher – it reached 33.7 percent by 2009 and 35.2 percent in 2012 (see Figure 5.1).[23]

This expansion of contingent employment was accelerated by legal changes in the labor field, promoted and implemented from the late 1990s into the early 2000s, most aggressively under the Koizumi administration. A 2003 revision of the Labor Standards Law, while it ironically reaffirmed the four "reasonable" standards that had to be met to dismiss a regular worker, made it easier to hire workers on fixed-term contracts. A Dispatch Worker Law of the same year made it

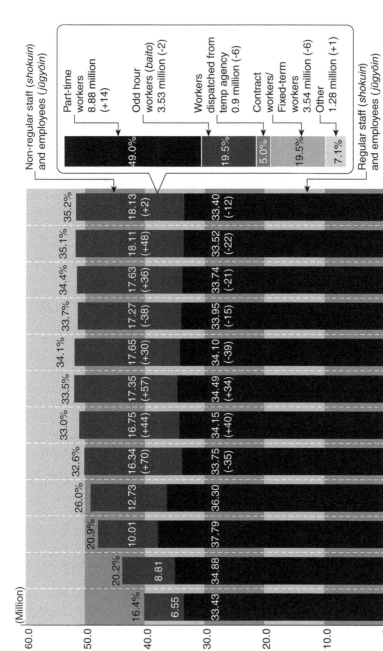

Figure 5.1 Shifts in regular and nonregular employees

Source: 1985–2000: Ministry of Internal Affairs and Communications "Labor Force Survey (Special Survey in February)" and 2005–2012: Ministry of Internal Affairs and Communications "Labor Force Survey (Detailed Tabulation) (annual average)."

possible for labor brokers to enlist and dispatch workers in virtually any industry (until then this sort of employment had been limited to a handful of industries). These reforms were certainly of some consequence, but it is important to note that even in the 1970s and 1980s, large manufacturing firms outsourced significant elements in their operations to subcontractors, and those employees had weaker protections. The expansion of nonregular employment gained headway from the late 1980s, well before these legal reforms.

One important indication that employment in Japan has become more flexible (or insecure, depending on one's perspective) for both regular and nonregular employment is found in evidence that losses and gains in employment have become significantly more responsive to the performance of the overall economy. The economist Arthur Alexander found some years ago that from the 1950s through the 1970s, for a given change in GDP, employment in Japan fell or rose only one-fifth as much as in the United States. That is, Japan's elasticity of employment with respect to GDP was only 0.2 (or 20 percent), whereas the elasticity in the United States (in both cases measured over a two-year period following a given shift in GDP) was 1 (or 100 percent). This was a striking difference, a clear macroeconomic statistical indication that jobs in Japan during the high growth era were significantly more secure when compared to the United States. But beginning in the 1980s, and especially in the past two decades, the gap has closed significantly. By 2009, employment elasticity in Japan as measured by Alexander had reached the realm of 0.7 to 0.85, still lower than in the United States by 15 to 30 percent, but much narrower than in the past.[24] It is hard to doubt that the combination of greater flexibility (or insecurity) in the jobs of regular workers, combined with increased hiring of workers in nonregular, contingent jobs, were the factors producing this tighter link between employment and economic performance. This is an important change. It makes the Japanese scene much more like that of the United States (and less like Europe). It casts doubt on oft-repeated claims that a rigid employment system is the root cause of lagging corporate performance.

A key critique of changing employment patterns is that increased flexibility to hire contingent labor has various negative effects, most notably weaker consumer demand and declining rates of marriage and reproduction. Commonly cited is a sharp rise in nonregular employment among men, and in particular among young adult men. The number of male nonregular employees nearly tripled from 1995 to 2013 (from 1.9 million to 5.4 million), and the number of nonregular male employees aged twenty-five to forty-four rose nearly fivefold (from 360,000 to 1.69 million) (see Figure 5.2).

As a proportion of all male workers, nonregular employment rose from 7.4 percent in 1985 to 19.7 percent by 2012.[25] The younger men in this status are the very people who in the past would have been starting and building careers as regular employees in medium- to large-scale corporations, with some realistic hope of building a long-term career in their organization. For commentators in the mass media and for the general public, educators, and labor bureaucrats, the fact that so many young men, the expected breadwinners and household heads of the nation,

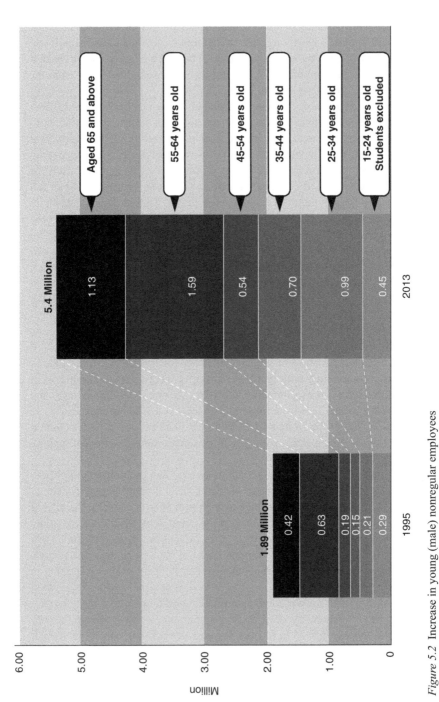

Aged 65 and above

55-64 years old

45-54 years old

35-44 years old

25-34 years old

15-24 years old
Students excluded

5.4 Million

1.13

1.59

0.54

0.70

0.99

0.45

2013

1.89 Million

0.42

0.63

0.19

0.15

0.21

0.29

1995

Million

6.00

5.00

4.00

3.00

2.00

1.00

0

Figure 5.2 Increase in young (male) nonregular employees

Source: Ministry of Internal Affairs and Communications "Labor Force Survey (Special Survey)" and "Labor Force Survey (Detailed Tabulation)."

have been unable to enter the mainstream of regular employment constitutes a change with far-reaching social and economic consequences. Their concern is bolstered by good evidence that nonregular male workers in their twenties and thirties were only half as likely to be married as regular male employees of the same age (see Figure 5.3).

These changes have been considerable and are important. But they are neither the only nor necessarily the most important element in the story of rising numbers of nonregular workers. Over these same years, from 1985 through 2012, the proportion of women in contingent employment, mainly in the category of part-time workers, rose even more dramatically; it almost doubled, from 32 to 54.5 percent of all women workers. And the absolute number of part-time women workers far more than doubled, from 4.9 million nonregular women workers in 1985 to 12.8 million in 2012.[26]

The long-accepted understanding and justification for this preponderance of women in the part-time labor force was that the great majority of them were married and raising children. They were seen to take up part-time work voluntarily to supplement a family income earned mainly by their husbands. But with an increase in single-mother families as a result of a rising divorce rate, the growing numbers of working women in various types of nonregular employment no longer fit the model of the supplementary wage–earning wife and mother, even as the growing numbers of men also did not fit the model of primary wage earner. By

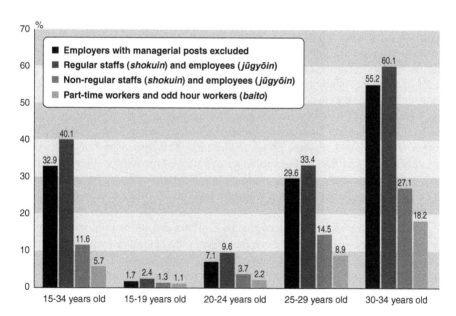

Figure 5.3 Comparison of the percentage of married young males based on employment status

Source: Ministry of Internal Affairs and Communications "Employment Status Survey" (2012).

2012, among the 7.8 million women engaged in part-time work, nearly 1.2 million (15 percent) were either the head of the household or were supporting themselves on their own. And one-fifth (20 percent) of the 2.75 million women in the categories of dispatch labor or contract employee were household heads or self-supporting. Taking a slightly different perspective, data provided by the Ministry of Health, Labor and Welfare also shows that in 2010 only four million (about one-third) of all nonregular women workers fit what we might call the "pure" case of a part-time female employee of prime working age (fifteen to fifty-five) married to a full-time working husband.[27]

In sum, the twin trends of rising nonregular employment for men and women, coupled with changes in the social and economic responsibilities of working women, have rendered the male breadwinner model significantly out of alignment with the life situation of people in Japan. Increasing numbers of nonregular male and female workers are employed in this category because regular work is not available, although many would prefer full-time "regular" jobs. A government survey in early 2013 found that as many as one in three nonregular male employees and one in six nonregular female employees were working in this status against their wishes.[28] This proportion among women nicely matches the percentage of women in part-time work who are either household heads or self-supporting.

In addition, an important government survey of 130 companies across all industries and of all sizes, covering over 42,000 applicants for regular employment in the "comprehensive" career track in 2010–11, implies that there is in Japan not only a glass ceiling to promotion, but also a closed glass doorway for women even entering such jobs. Looking at the entire applicant pool and all applications to these companies, whereas 5.8 percent of men who applied for these positions were hired, only 1.6 percent of women applicants were. Looking at the breakdown by gender once companies had filled these posts, women accounted for only 11.6 percent of all new hires. If female applicants had been hired at the same ratio as the men, they would have constituted nearly one-third (32 percent) of all new employees.[29] It is hard to imagine that the merits of the female applicants were so much weaker as to justify these results. One cannot help suspecting that employers, for other reasons, prefer to hire men. The consensus among government officials, and the staff of employer and union organizations queried about this in 2013, was that a key factor leading to lower rates of hiring for women was a concern among employers that women would be unwilling to accept transfers to distant offices.

Changes in the security offered regular workers and in the numbers and proportion of nonregular workers have thus been quite extensive over the past two decades or more. These changes have been framed by modifications, though not abrupt ruptures, in law. They have been accompanied by important shifts in customary treatment of regular employees. The ongoing historical context for these changes includes persisting norms of a gendered division of labor, with women continuing to dominate the ranks of contingent labor. At the same time, changing social patterns have made this division particularly out of sync with the life situation of women and young men. This story of change embedded in shifting structures and norms of the past brings us to our third theme – politics. How have contending parties sought to use a discourse of the lost decades to push for a particular sort of change or defended elements of the status quo within a changing world?

For men, the key political divide has centered on what can be called Japan's "moral economy" of employment.[30] By moral economy, I refer to a set of ideas that define a concept of a just or moral regulation of economic life, in this case the regulation of employment. I juxtapose such a concept to a neoliberal belief that unfettered markets – in this case job markets – produce the best and indeed the fairest or most just outcomes for all concerned. The moral economy of labor in Japan is a cultural configuration. It is not "cultural" in the simplistic and static sense of a centuries-long inheritance carried forward from some imagined "traditional Japan." It is a dynamic cultural configuration produced in the modernizing course of the twentieth century and always subject to change. Concern with status and respect was expressed in disputes of railway engineers in the 1890s; in the insistence that bosses respect the "character" of workers as humans in the 1910s; in the calls for improved treatment such as regular pay raises, bonuses, or secure jobs in the 1920s; and again in early postwar demands for the elimination of status discrimination between blue collar and white collar staff, or disputes of the high growth era both between unions and companies over decisions to eliminate jobs and dismiss workers.

Over time, the outcome of such struggles, reinforced by legal decisions in lawsuits brought by individual workers in defense of their jobs, was to define a moral economy as one in which male workers had a right to keep their jobs and employers were obligated even in the face of hostile market conditions to make all possible efforts to preserve these jobs. This value remains alive, if under greater pressure and more qualifications than in the past, not only among many working people but also among employers, politicians, and state bureaucrats. It is only against this background that we can understand the powerful impact of the setting up of a Dispatch Workers' Village over the New Year's holiday of 2008–09, when the Lehman shock led hundreds of Japanese companies to lay off thousands of their nonregular dispatch workers. An effective coalition of nonprofit organisations (NPOs), lawyers, community unions, and media on very short notice set up a tent village in Hibiya Park for 500 of the laid-off workers. The village gained extraordinary attention, with much sympathy for the workers and strong criticism of the companies and the government policies that made these workers so vulnerable.

In some cases the contract workers had been ousted from company housing in violation of the law or work rules, and in some cases contracts had been abrogated illegally. However, it seems fair to say – and to me, this is the key point – that even if all these layoffs had been implemented in accord with the letter of the law, the very fact of these mass dismissals would have gathered huge attention and been seen as a violation of Japan's moral economy of labor. One pithy example of this sense of violation came in a letter to the *Asahi Newspaper* from a junior high school student from Kyushu: "I am upset at the recent news that dispatch

workers are being fired by companies. Until now, they had worked hard to support the company, yet they are so easily fired. . . . Don't the companies have some
responsibility?"[31]

This episode led some major companies to reduce their reliance on dispatch
workers and resulted in a modest shift toward greater legal regulation in a revised
Dispatch Workers Law in March 2012, passed with bipartisan support. Although
a retreat from early drafts under the Democratic Party of Japan (DPJ) administration, the law prohibited short-term dispatches, required the dispatch agencies
to make public their revenue margin above the amount paid to the workers they
supplied, and included provisions that would encourage firms to convert dispatch
employees to regular workers.[32] The question of how far to go, and in what ways,
toward systems of more flexible deployment of labor remains deeply contested
within an enduring framework of social values.

For women, the employment issue in its wider context plays out on a different sort of moral landscape, because – with some notable dissent from feminist
scholars and activists – the moral economy of labor in Japan as it evolved in the
twentieth century accepted a secondary role for women as not just legitimate but
desirable. The widely accepted view of the best way to balance women's commitments in the spheres of reproductive and productive labor had historical roots in
the cultural configuration of the idea of the "good wife and wise mother." To be
sure, from as early as the 1890s, when a widespread consensus emerged (mainly
among men) that women must give priority to these twin roles, productive labor
for wages was not necessarily seen as a violation of these commitments.[33] But to
the extent that work was validated, it was for the sake of the family and the nation
or for women's ability to support themselves just in case they had the misfortune
(from war or disease or a dissolute mate) to find themselves without a breadwinner husband.

As with the issue of a moral economy of regular employment, one finds no consensus on the issue of women's proper or desirable role in economy and society.
In recent years, the balance of opinion (if not necessarily of behavior) appears
to have shifted considerably in favor of encouraging women to work outside
the home. This is not unambiguously a new formulation of the moral economy
of labor. Those who take this position make claims not only or even mainly on
grounds of justice or equity (the moral side), although such values do seem to sit
just beneath the surface and motivate the argument. They also advocate increased
participation for women as a plus for economic productivity and growth (the
economy side).

The 2010 Goldman Sachs analysis of Womenomics mentioned earlier argued
that increased employment opportunities for women would boost Japan's GDP
and consumption in general. It further introduced strong evidence that around
the world increased labor force participation for women correlates to increased
rates of childbirth. The report specifically identified forty-four companies whose
stock prices were likely to rise as women played stronger economic roles, and
it claimed that a similar list compiled in 2005 had indeed outperformed other
investments.[34] This sort of Japan-focused analysis is reinforced more generally

by recent macroeconomic research focused on the American economy. Work by Peter Klenow and colleagues argues that the opening of career opportunities to women and to African Americans in the United States over the half-century since 1960, in essence a more efficient allocation of talent in the economy, may explain 15 to 20 percent of growth in aggregate output per worker. And Klenow's work concludes that further removing what the paper calls "frictions" in job allocation offers potential for additional "substantial gains" in productivity.[35]

The policy and political case for gender equality in the workforce also posits such an outcome as a solution to the nation's demographic dilemma. It is well known in Japanese policy circles and in public debate that across the advanced capitalist world, high rates of employment for women correlate strongly with high birth rates (mainly in nations of northern Europe plus Australia and North America). Conversely, countries with the lowest rates of female labor force participation (Korea, Italy, Spain, and Japan) are also the places with by far the lowest birth rates.[36] An intriguing eight-year longitudinal survey of 2009, carried out by the Ministry of Health, Labor and Welfare, offered suggestive evidence that if Japan's employment practices moved in a "northern European" direction, so might its demography. The study found that compared to what we might call a traditional "modern" couple where the husband held a regular post and the wife worked part-time (or in otherwise nonregular employment), married couples where both partners held regular positions not only desired slightly larger families but did in fact have more children.[37]

But despite such evidence and supportive rhetoric from those in authority, including the Abe administration in 2013, which is in favor of bringing women more fully into economic life outside the home, the mainstream of corporate, political, and bureaucratic elites seems ambivalent about pushing vigorously in this direction. Calls for women to act as "good wives" by earning money or contributing to the economy are frequently met by admonitions for them to be responsible and dutiful by staying home and having children. Although its wording was vague enough to be understood as gender blind if one were so inclined, the Liberal Democratic Party's 2012 draft of a revised constitution included an article (24) on the family which, in its statement that the "members of a family are obligated to help each other," could be read as an implicit moralistic call by the state for women to bear the primary burden at home at the expense of their wider social participation. More specific tension over such a view of women's roles emerged in sharp relief in the spring of 2013 when the Abe administration proposed circulating a "Handbook on Life and Women" to teenage schoolgirls nationwide. The handbook would have contained information about pregnancy and childbirth with the aim of encouraging women to bear children sooner rather than later, arguing against the tendency of women to delay marriage and childbirth. The proposal was to distribute the handbook only to schoolgirls, not boys, a clear reflection of a view that men were exempt from reproductive responsibilities. This plan was roundly criticized by a wide range of women's and labor organizations, who called instead for economic and social policies to make it easier for families to afford to raise children and find childcare, and in short order the proposal was abandoned.[38]

Inequality

A purported rise in economic and social inequality is another aspect of the social-industrial complex of lost-decade problems that merits consideration. Like insecurity of employment, socioeconomic inequality cannot be measured easily. On the one hand, according to data collected and analyzed by the International Monetary Fund (IMF) in 2004 and at several earlier points in time, the income of Japan's wealthiest 20 percent was only 2.3 times that of the poorest 20 percent, and the ratio was little changed over the previous decade. This compared to an eight- to tenfold multiple for the United States and a twelvefold multiple for China, and in these societies inequality had increased sharply in the previous decade.[39] By this measure, Japan's inequality was not increasing, and it boasted the smallest income differential in the world.

On the other hand, according to the Organization for Economic Cooperation and Development (OECD)'s calculation of this ratio, which compared disposable (after-tax) income in 2003, 2006, and 2009 – essentially contemporaneous with the IMF data of 2004 – the United States only beat Japan by a moderate amount in the inequality Olympics. The OECD reported that Japan's top quintile earned about six times more than the bottom fifth, while the American top fifth earned about 7.8 times the bottom. And inequality was similarly rising in both societies. The Japanese top/bottom ratio was fivefold in 1985; in 1984 the U.S. ratio had been a multiple of 6.4 times.[40] In addition, recent OECD statistics for another measure of inequality, the so-called poverty index – which measures the proportion of people whose income is less than half the national average – found that in the year 2006 Japan's poverty index stood at 15.7 percent, a fairly significant increase from a 12 percent rate in 1995. In this inglorious race to the bottom, the United States and Japan are similarly unequal; Japan's poverty index ranked second worst among the advanced economies, beaten only by the United States where 16.8 percent of the population had incomes far below the average in 2006.

These divergent results are based on different data.[41] If one gives credence to the IMF data, one can reconcile the discrepancy between its top/bottom ratio and the OECD poverty index as follows: indeed more people than before are on the bottom rungs of Japan's economic ladder, and this is a change one must take seriously; but the ladder from rich to poor itself is shorter than in the United States or elsewhere. But a second and perhaps safer conclusion is that cross-national comparisons of inequality are unreliable. Some scholars in Japan believe that the Japanese data used by OECD, while accurate for Japan, exaggerates inequality compared to elsewhere because the Japanese data collection does a better job than other nations in tracking income among the poor.[42]

In this murky statistical situation, we might best focus our attention on changes over time in Japan rather than on comparative inquiry. After all, unlike comparatively inclined social scientists, most people in any society compare their situation not to other societies or nations but to their own society's past and their own personal past. And while comparative data is problematic due to different methods of data collection and different efficiencies in the process from place to place, we can be fairly confident that temporal data within Japan over this span was calculated consistently.

It seems safe to conclude that postwar Japan circa the 1960s through 1990s was far more egalitarian than it is today – even if, of course, never completely equal and certainly not inclusive or equal across gender lines. The inclination to view the complex data on inequality in this pessimistic way seems both empirically justified and culturally rooted in a roughly fifty-year history of pride concerning equality of both opportunity and to some measure of result. Against this background, recent changes have produced a profound sense of loss.

If the lost decades have been a time of significant change in the level of equality, the politics of the pursuit of equality are no less challenging or complex than the politics of employment or gender roles. Japanese society today, like many societies elsewhere, faces a perplexing dilemma in continuing to value equality of both opportunity and of result, when people inhabit a world of increased and increasingly unequal competition. Given that the higher proportion of nonregular jobs raises the proportion of low-wage earners, neoliberal prescriptions to unleash the market with further deregulation of employment markets would seem likely to generate more inequality, at least in the near-term. Is that a pill that people – whether among policymakers or the general public – are willing to swallow?

The answer is uncertain, but it is notable and not well recognized that Japanese income policies across the lost decades have in fact ameliorated what would have been a far more dramatic rise in economic inequality.[43] In 1985, the Japanese poverty rate as calculated by the OECD was essentially the same for pretax and after-tax income (12.5 and 12 percent). By 1995, a notable gap had opened (19 percent versus 13.7 percent). And by 2009, the pretax poverty rate stood at an astounding 32 percent. That is, one third of the population had pretax incomes that stood 50 percent below the median. The after-tax, disposable income poverty rate was "only" 16 percent. The quintile comparisons were no less stark. In 2006, pretax income earned by the top fifth stood at about ten times that of the bottom fifth; the after-tax multiple was "only" sixfold.[44]

The intuitive explanation for this shift in pretax to after-tax income would of course be income taxes themselves, which are assessed in progressive fashion in Japan as elsewhere. A second explanation might be the payment of direct welfare benefits to the poor. But economist Oshio Takashi reveals that neither taxes nor welfare benefits are a significant factor. The heart of the matter is an intergenerational transfer of income through the national social security system. It is well known that over the past several decades the elderly have increased substantially as a proportion of Japan's population. Those who are retired have virtually no pretax income, so pretax data places many of the increased numbers of the elderly into the poverty zone. Social security payments, which are calculated as after-tax income, then lift many of these elders above the poverty line and thus substantially reduce, both in appearance and in fact, the nation's poverty rate.[45]

It is important to note that the social security system that has buffered rising inequality both predates and has persisted across the lost decades. It is not a direct policy response to rising inequality. This is an incomes policy in result more than intent.[46] It is an open question as to whether the current Japanese government will take additional proactive steps to address rising inequality. The push underway in 2013 to revise the Livelihood Protection Law would be a step backward from an active incomes policy.

Future possibilities

Japan's state policies and corporate programs to address the web of social and economic problems surveyed in this chapter remain ambivalent. The center of gravity in the Liberal Democratic Party (LDP), the corporate world, and the bureaucracy appears to be a view that unleashing markets offers the best way forward. But over the course of the lost decades, a considerable body of opinion has also persisted that values community and solidarity and fears the decline of those things if markets are allowed to function without significant constraints. As one example, the leader of one of the nation's major business federations in the early 2000s spoke of the "moral hazard" of deregulation in discussions of revisions to labor law. In the end, these revisions affirmed some degree of protection for regular workers as a trade-off for allowing wider use of nonregular employees.[47]

Voices from civil society outside the political, bureaucratic, or business elites are similarly ambivalent, and muted. Japan's mainstream labor unions affiliated with the Rengo federation have been losing members and especially under the new LDP administration are on the defensive. Rengo unions in the best of circumstances face a dilemma in pursuing both protections for regular workers, who constitute the majority of their members, and at the same time reaching out to nonregular workers for new members. It is logical to pursue the latter, whose numbers in the workforce are growing and who need protection. Indeed, the only area of membership growth in both Rengo-affiliated and nonaffiliated unions is among nonregular employees, mainly in the service sector. But squaring the circle of protecting the former without imposing some costs on the latter is difficult, when corporate managers argue with apparent success to leading unions that without the flexibility afforded by a significant (and growing) buffer of contingent employees, the fortunate regular workers in these unions cannot be protected.

This fundamental and long-standing dilemma is not simply an ideological clash between supporters of a Japanese version of a regulated market economy undergirded by a moral economy of employment and a neoliberal vision of political economy where regulation is in principle counterproductive to the greater good. That friction is part of the story, but a second clash of views is also in play. The moral economy of employment as it took root in postwar Japan (and before) always accepted the exclusion of some – mainly but not only women – as fair. Confronting this view are calls for a society and economy grounded in what some call Womenomics, a society that gives to all its members the opportunity for secure and productive career paths on both economic and moral grounds. Reinforcing such calls is the fact that the acceptance of a subordinate role for women has lost much (but not all) of its legitimacy as a social norm in Japan today, making it all the more necessary in both moral and economic terms to find a way to a future where the old exclusions are broken down.

But those who pursue this new sort of equality continue to face the question of whether the goal should simply be the opportunity or the right of women to "lean in" and to work as long and as hard as men.[48] Perhaps such a goal is both socially and economically desirable. The survey data showing that married couples with two regular jobs have more children than "traditional" modern couples where the wife works part-time might support such a view. But can – and should – this trend be expanded and sustained when regular jobs so often demand long hours of overtime and acceptance of transfers? Is there any alternative?

In recent years, the opening up of a third way between insecure nonregular employment and the unlimited demands of "regular" careers has been much discussed as a possible solution. This category of employment is sometimes called "regularized nonregular" or "limited regular" employment.[49] Supporters characterize this as a form of employment that would offer possibilities for career development and increased responsibility and pay, with the understanding that the employee would not be asked to accept distant transfers but would also not have the job security that access to wide-ranging assignments might offer. Critics fear that rather than raise the prospects for formerly nonregular employees (mostly women) to be upgraded to such posts, this middle way might weaken the prospects for regular employees, men and women, whose posts would be downgraded and less secure. It is too soon to offer a confident judgment as to which outcome is more likely, although without strong advocacy by, or on behalf of, those moving into such posts, it is hard to be optimistic. But at a time when a return to a "golden era" of middle-class equality and stable long-term jobs for men – buttressed by limiting the opportunities outside the home for women – is neither economically practical nor politically or culturally attractive, efforts in this direction seem worth pursuing.

Notes

1 The first published use of this term in English appears to have been a *Newsweek* story in 1998; in Japanese, it was probably the same week, in a newspaper column that attributed the expression to foreign investors. Bill Powell, "The Lost Decade," *Newsweek* (July 27, 1998), p. 28. Takita Yōichi, "*Kokufu: Ushinawareta 10-nen no kyōkun*," *Nihon keizai shimbun* (July 21, 1998, evening edition), p. 3. Since magazines date their issues to the week after actual publication, the *Newsweek* story would have appeared one day before the Japanese newspaper article.
2 In English, the most famous challenge was probably that of Karel van Wolferen, in his *The Enigma of Japanese Power* (New York: A.A. Knopf, 1989).
3 Karl Marx, *The Eighteenth Brumaire of Louis Bonaparte*, 1852, https://www.marxists. org/archive/marx/works/1852/18th-brumaire/ch01.htm.
4 Richard Samuels, *3.11: Disaster and Change in Japan* (Ithaca: Cornell University Press, 2013) and J. Charles Schencking, *The Great Kanto Earthquake and the Chimera of National Reconstruction in Japan* (New York: Columbia University Press, 2013) frame the response to these two disasters in similar ways.
5 Itami Hiroyuki, "*Bunmei o yushutsu suru toki*," *Astaeon* (Autumn 1986), pp. 41–42.
6 Koike Kazuo, *The Economics of Work in Japan* (Tokyo: Long Term Credit Bank International Library Foundation, 1995), pp. 257–58. Original in Koike Kazuo, *Shokuba no*

rōdō kumiai to sanka: rōshi kankei no Nichibei hikaku (Tokyo: Tōyō Keizai Shinpō, 1977), pp. 313–15.

7 *Economist*, January 16, 1993, p. 66.

8 Ross Mouer and Hirosuke Kawanishi, *The Future of Work in Japan* (New York: Cambridge University Press, 2005), p. 254.

9 For example, Ezra Vogel, *Japan as Number One* (Cambridge, MA: Harvard University Press, 1979), pp. 177–78.

10 Mary Brinton, *Lost in Transition: Youth, Work and Instability in Post-industrial Japan* (New York: Cambridge University Press, 2011), pp. 98–104.

11 For students going to the United States, see Japan-U.S. Education Commission, "*Amerika ryūgaku no kiso chishiki*" (2011), http://www.fulbright.jp/study/res/t1-college03.html. For students going to other countries, see the Ministry of Education, Culture, Sports, Science and Technology, Japan, *Nihonjin no kaigai ryūgaku jōkyō*, http://www.mext. go.jp/b_menu/houdou/24/01/icsFiles/afieldfile/2012/02/02/1315686_01.pdf.

12 For one interesting perspective linking the decline in study abroad to the phenomenon of stay-at-home youths in the literal sense of those who never leave their house or apartment (*hikikomori*), see Genda Yūji, "No Place to Belong," in McKinsey & Company, ed., *Reimaging Japan* (San Francisco: VIZ Media, 2011), pp. 171–75.

13 Nihon Nōritsu Kyōkai, "*Gurōbaru jinji no jūten kadai to sono kaiketsu ni mukete*," February 2012; Nihon Keizai Dantai Rengōkai, "*Gurōbaru jinzai no ikusei ni muketa teigen*," June 14, 2011; Keizai Sangyōshō, "*Gurōbaru jinzai no ikusei, katsuyō ni yoru Nihon keizai no kasseika ni tsuite*," May 7, 2012.

14 Fukazawa Maki, "*U35 Danshi ma-ketingu zukan*," Vol. 5, Nikkei Business Online, October 13, 2006, http://business.nikkeibp.co.jp/article/skillup/20061005/111136/.

15 Peggy Orenstein, "Parasites in Prêt-à-Porter," *New York Times Sunday Magazine*, July 1, 2001.

16 Genda Yūji, *A Nagging Sense of Job Insecurity* (Tokyo: LTCB International Library Trust, translated by Jean Connell Hoff, 2005), p. 43.

17 Kathy Matsui, et al., "Womenomics 3.0: The Time Is Now," *Goldman Sachs, Japan Portfolio Strategy*, October 1, 2010.

18 *Asahi Newspaper*, November 8, 1997, Sunday "Weekend Economy" page.

19 For this data, see "*Keisatsuchō seikatsu anzen kyoku seikatsu anzen kikaku ka*," *Heisei 21 nen chū ni okeru jisatsu no gaiyō shiryō* (May, 2010), p. 4.

20 Author interviews with managers at Toshiba, IHI International, and JFE Steel, December 2009 and January 2010.

21 For one definition, see "'*Burakku kigyō*' *tte donna kaisha?*" *Asahi Shimbun* (May 23, 2013), p. 2.

22 Nitta Michio, "*Koyō portfolio system kaikaku no shiten*," *Gendai no riron* (Summer 2009), p. 3. See also Nitta Yoshio, "*Koyō no ryōteki kanri*," in Nitta Yoshio and Hisamoto Norio, eds., *Nihonteki koyō shisutemu* (Kyoto: Nakanishiya Shuppan, 2008).

23 Ministry of Internal Affairs and Communications, Japan Annual Labor Surveys ("*Rōdōryoku chōsa*").

24 Arthur J. Alexander, "Adaptation in the Japanese Economy," *Oxford Analytica* (July 20, 2010). Arthur J. Alexander, *In the Shadow of the Miracle: The Japanese Economy since the End of High-Speed Growth* (Lanham, MD: Lexington Books, 2002), pp. 223–26, makes a similar argument with slightly different modes of calculating elasticity.

25 Osawa Mari, *Social Security in Contemporary Japan* (Routledge, 2011), p. 72.

26 Ministry of Internal Affairs and Communications, Japan Annual Labor Force Surveys ("*Rōdōryoku chōsa*").

27 MIC Annual Labor Survey of 2010.

28 MIC Annual Labor Survey of 2013, January to March.

29 Ministry of Health, Labor and Welfare, "*Kōsu-betsu koyō kanri seido no jisshi shidō jōkyo*," 2011.

30 E.P. Thompson, "The Moral Economy of the English Crowd in the Eighteenth Century," *Past and Present* 50, 1971, pp. 76–136.
31 *"Wakai sedai, kei'eisha-gawa ni wa tsumetasa kanjita,"* Asahi Shimbun (January 18, 2009), p. 6.
32 *"Haken rōdō, kaizen e no ippo: kaizei haken hō, kyō seiritsu,"* Asahi Shimbun (March 28, 2012), p. 3.
33 Sharon H. Nolte and Sally Ann Hastings, "The Meiji State's Policy toward Women, 1890–1910," in Gail Lee Bernstein, ed., *Recreating Japanese Women, 1600–1945* (Berkeley: University of California Press, 1991).
34 Kathy Matsui, et al., "Womenomics 3.0: The Time Is Now," *Goldman Sachs, Japan Portfolio Strategy*, October 1, 2010, p. 31.
35 Chang-Tai Hsieh, Erik Hurst, Charles I. Jones, and Peter J. Klenow, "The Allocation of Talent and U.S. Economic Growth," working paper, version 3.0, published February 22, 2013. Accessed at http://www.klenow.com.
36 Ministry of Health, Labor and Welfare, *"Kakkoku no gōkei tokushu shusseritsu to josei shugyōritsu."* From OECD Family Database, 2009.
37 Special calculation by the Ministry of Health, Labor and Welfare, Labor Policy Advisory Bureau based on the Ministry's "Longitudinal Survey of 21st Century Adults" (2010). The couples with two regular jobs had on average 1.9 children, compared to 1.79 where the husband had a regular post and the wife a nonregular job. The survey also found only 1.09 children born to couples with a husband holding a nonregular post and a regular-employee wife, and 1.36 children where both husband and wife held nonregular jobs. However, the sample sizes in these two cases were only eleven and twenty-eight respectively.
38 *"Josei techō, haifu miokuri,"* Asahi Shimbun (May 19, 2013), p. 1.
39 International Monetary Fund, *World Economic Outlook*, October 2007, fig. 4.6, http://www.imf.org/external/pubs/ft/weo/2007/02/.
40 OECD statistics are located at http://stats.oecd.org/. For poverty rates and quintile ratios, search under "social protection and well-being," sub-category "income distribution and poverty by country."
41 The IMF survey uses household consumption data from the Family Income and Expenditure Survey provided by the Japanese Statistics Bureau for its measure of disposable income; the OECD looks at pretax and after-tax income-based surveys carried out by the Ministry of Health, Labor and Welfare Comprehensive Survey of Living Conditions Office, Social Statistics Division, Statistics and Information Department, Minister's Secretariat, Ministry of Health, Labor and Welfare, available at http://www.mhlw.go.jp/english/database/db-hss/cslc.html.
42 Personal communication from Moriguchi Chiaki, economist at Hitotsubashi University, October 28, 2013. Moriguchi has done extensive research on economic inequality in Japan.
43 For an example of nonrecognition of this trend, see the otherwise interesting paper by Marco Mira d'Ercole, "Income Inequality and Poverty in OECD Countries: How Does Japan Compare?" in *Japanese Journal of Social Security Policy* 5, no. 1 (June 2006). The author makes a persuasive case that Japanese income transfers are low in comparison to European nations in particular. But the clear increase in the impact of those transfers over the lost decades remains significant and worthy of analysis.
44 After-tax data is from OECD statistics cited above. For the pretax multiples, see Hiroshi Kaneko, "The Japanese Income Tax System and the Disparity of Income and Wealth Among People in Japan," *Proceedings from the 2009 Sho Sato Conference on Tax Law, Social Policy and the Economy*, p. 17, http://www.law.berkeley.edu/files/sho_sato_tax_conf_web_paper—kaneko.pdf.
45 Oshio Takashi, *Kōritsu to kōhei o tou* (Tokyo: Nihon Hyōronsha, 2012), chap. 3, sec. 1.
46 Kaneko, "The Japanese Income Tax System," p. 23.

47 For details see Andrew Gordon, *Nihon no rōshi kankei shi* (Tokyo: Iwanami Shoten, 2012), p. 471.

48 For many years, Kumazawa Makoto, among others, has been exploring this issue. See, in English, his *Portraits of the Japanese Workplace* (Denver: Westview Press, 1996), chap. 7.

49 For extensive discussion of this issue, see the July 2013 special issue of *Nihon rōdō kenkyū zasshi, "Hiseiki rōdō to 'tayō na seishain.'"*

6 The two lost decades in education
The failure of reform

Kariya Takehiko

Japanese education: Best in class?

Until the early 1990s, the education system in Japan was the object of admiration in a great number of developed nations, and perhaps especially in the United States. To be sure, a number of shortcomings were pointed out, but during most of the 1980s, when the Japanese economy seemed to be flying high, the view that Japan's economic success somehow *was* its educational success, that the one meant the other, became a kind of fashion in much academic research and in the media. The relationship, or the link, between the education system in Japan and its economy, in particular, came in for praise. Japanese company management practices; the high caliber of human resources in Japanese companies; the highly qualified people in charge of business administration who came not from the elite, but from the middle stratum of society; and the high caliber of the workers on the production lines, who actually did the manufacturing, were identified as factors of Japan's success. Toyama Kazuhiko discusses some of these elements in more detail in Chapter 4. Much was made of Japan's top-level higher education institutions, but it was the high quality of compulsory as well as upper-secondary education, responsible for the education and the preparation of mid-level and manual workers, that garnered the most attention.

Ezra Vogel's 1979 bestseller *Japan as Number One* was one book that underscored this perception. Vogel pointed out certain weak areas in Japan's education, such as its overemphasis on university entrance examinations and the low quality of education at many universities, but he clearly saw the relationship between high-quality compulsory and upper-secondary education on the one side and Japan's high-quality economy and society on the other. Other books, such as William Cummings' *Education and Equality in Japan* (1980) and the U.S. Department of Education's *Japanese Education Today* (1987), analyzed Japan's education and revealed similar issues. As Cummings' title makes clear, his study paid keen attention to the contribution of Japan's educational system, particularly its compulsory elementary education, to creating equality within Japanese society. *Japanese Education Today* extensively scrutinized the realities of Japan's education system and searched for clues useful to assist U.S. education policy, as might be expected of a government-produced study. Foreign experts understand education as part of the secret to Japan's economic success, and they published findings that seemed to uphold this conclusion in journals, newspapers, and numerous academic reports.

However, this enthusiasm for Japan's education came to a sudden halt in the second half of the 1990s. Almost in parallel with Japan's economic downturn, journalistic and academic interest in Japan's education (with particular regard to its success) withered. Certainly, this was in no small part due to the sometimes facile findings that equated economic with educational success. On the other hand, something did seem to have occurred to the fabric of Japanese education. Why did it lose its attractiveness in the eyes of foreign observers? This chapter centers on two questions in particular within an analysis of the overall transformation: What change(s) did Japanese education and society experience during these decades? And what was "lost" due to that change?

As well as looking at the effective changes in education, the target of my analysis focuses on the discourse of education policy documents. Policy documents advocating educational reform at this time clearly show the cognizance of the kinds of problems Japan was facing in education. Preoccupation centered on the role of education in society and the kind of reforms, or policies, that were going to be necessary to deal with certain issues. My study analyzes the debates that emerged from these questions, unraveling the concerns behind education reform and where possible clarifying Japanese society's idiosyncrasies, as well as the zeitgeist of public opinion.

In this study, I focus mainly on the social consciousness of the narrative of "playing catch-up with the West," an overarching ideology that was widely espoused in Japanese society and public opinion at this time. The diffusion of this narrative from the end of the 1970s through the 1980s exerted a determining effect on policy-debate responses to the socioeconomic changes that ensued after the bubble economy. Undoubtedly, it was the collapse of the bubble economy that initiated the two lost decades, but these were also the two decades when various educational reforms were discussed and implemented. In the context of the post-bubble reforms, the Japanese-style education system that had led to the success of Japan was seen as a yoke and, in an era of increasing globalization, obsolete. Reform became synonymous with dismantling the traditional system as quickly as possible; this was held as the formula that would solve the numerous problems that had emerged with the bursting of the bubble. Initially devised to catch up with the West, the education system was now suddenly conceived of as an impediment. The perception applied, jointly, to several policy fields, for example, the Japanese employment system with its lifetime contracts and seniority-wage system, the inter-firm cross-share-holding *keiretsu* system, and the "convoy banking system."[1] There was a paradox in this perception: the Japanese system, which had led the country to its success, was unable to respond to globalization, and this was now leading the country down the path of failure. The idea of achieving a catch-up with the West turned into a prism through which the traditional Japanese-style system was seen as containing the cause of its own deconstruction. It is possible to make the argument that this configuration of the postwar Japanese education system purely and simply in terms of being something devised to catch up with the West was a very crude and inappropriate oversimplification.

Anticipating my conclusion, the outline of my argument is as follows: Japan's stagnation, following the collapse of the bubble economy, was understood as resulting from an insufficient and slow response to the new issue of globalization. This mindset permeated Japan during the 1980s – it was gradually agreed that the catch-up process was to end, and this led to a considerable bias in views when leaders were trying to generate new plans and policies. As a result, the need for the dismantling of the Japanese-style system, understood in terms of a catch-up style system, was widely accepted because everyone had agreed that this was the best way to solve the problem. Consequently, it was thought that responding to globalization meant the eradication of the Japanese-style system. Deconstruction of the Japanese-style system proceeded full speed ahead in the heat of the moment and with little or no cool-headed discussion.

If my line of questioning and interpretations are correct, the idea of the "end of catch-up" distorted the way in which the two lost decades problem was configured. Thus, we need to clarify the kind of characteristics that this way of thinking carried with it. In what follows, I ask what kinds of policies were undertaken in the name of this idea and explain what contributions they made to Japanese society and education during the two lost decades. Finally, I clarify the limits of such a configuration by shedding light on some persistent problems in Japan's response to globalization (with regard especially to the problems of "studying abroad" and educating and training "global human resources").

The "end of playing catch-up with the West"

Before any discourse analysis of education policies, I would like to briefly introduce how and along which axis the ideas surrounding the "end of playing catch-up with the West" narrative surfaced in Japanese policy documents.

The end of playing catch-up with the West was first officially referred to in reports from Prime Minister Ohira Masayoshi's Policy Study Groups. Among the members of these study groups were prominent conservative academics who participated in some nine subcommittees, each of which submitted a report on August 1980. Report No. 1 presented a section titled "The Age of Culture":

> In the past there have been periods that strongly demanded countries to westernize, modernize, industrialize, and pursue economic growth. Then, the content of the needs of the times were clear, and there existed models we needed to aim toward. Since the Meiji period, such needs have denied, or even ignored, our own traditions, placed our nation as backward and low-level, and constituted a way to pursue alien aims.[2]
>
> [. . .] In order to "catch up" as speedily as possible with the advanced nations of the West, Japan has proactively pushed forward with modernization, industrialization and westernization since the Meiji Restoration. As a result, Japan succeeded in reaching the stage of a mature highly industrial

society, and everyone has come to enjoy freedom and equality, progress and prosperity, economic wealth and the convenience of modern life, high education and high welfare standards, as well as advanced scientific technology. These are all qualities we can be proud of in the world. Moreover, with the backdrop of enormous structural socio-economic changes, which were induced by industrialization and modernization, the nation's consciousness and its behavior have been undergoing major changes.[3]

Report No. 7, titled *Economic Administration in an Age of Culture*, added these three points:

[First,] Japan's modernization (industrialization and westernization) and the maturation of it into a highly industrial society imply the end of any models involving the need to align to, or to "catch up with." From now on, we need to find our own path to follow.

[Second,] Japan's culture made possible a speedy modernization as well as the attainment of high economic growth. Upon studying it, we have rediscovered many of its superb qualities. Many of these parallel recent trends among Western societies.[4]

[Third,] even more than before World War II, Japanese society after the war became devoted to "catching up" with Western advanced economies. The Japanese people's aim in life too was oriented toward "production," derived from an attempt to build a comfortable and efficient life environment that depended on the acquisition of as many goods and services as possible. In this way, "work" became life's foremost value.[5]

As is evident from the above reports, it was accepted that Japanese society had completed its catch-up with the West at the beginning of the 1980s and, more importantly, that Japan now needed to find its own path. This psychological mindset was responsible for a growing preoccupation with rediscovering what was "good" in Japan, which gave rise to yet more theories of Japanese exceptionalism and attempts to emphasize the special character of Japan's unique culture and society (known as *Nihonjinron*). The end of catch-up statements contained in the Ohira Study Groups were subsequently adopted by the most influential policy-making establishment in education in the 1980s under the Nakasone Cabinet: the Ad Hoc Council on Administrative Reforms (AHCER).[6]

The logic behind education reforms since the 1990s

Education policy discourse adopted the official views of the end of catch-up, giving rise to clearly identifiable changes in education policy and ensuing education reforms. Discourse analysis of these education policy documents, therefore, will reveal the logic behind education reforms since the 1990s, which led the reforms to "fail" during the 1990s and the 2000s.

Researchers in education believe that the course of education reforms from the 1990s was determined by AHCER in the mid-1980s. AHCER's proposed education policy was labeled, by AHCER itself, the "Third Great Education Reform." This succeeded the "First Great Reform," which had produced a modern education system following the Meiji Restoration, and the "Second Great Reform," which had established democratic education in the postwar years. The Third Great Reform sought an overall design of education reform that took into consideration the challenges and opportunities that would be posed by the twenty-first century.

Looking at AHCER's documents, it is possible to sum up the basic outlook as a consensus that Japan had successfully achieved its catch-up with the West. According to AHCER's understanding, the First Great Education Reform, which had been after the Meiji Restoration, was based upon the importation and adoption of Western countries' modern education systems, with the expectation that it would educate and train human resources to become central to building a "rich nation, with a strong army." The Second Great Reform followed the end of the Second World War and took the American education system as a model, with the aim of educating Japanese people to become the building blocks for a democratic and peace-loving state. This move was aimed at catching up with Western values of democracy. But most importantly, AHCER understood the logical aim of Japan's education reform to be based on the political ideology of international cooperation, which was premised on the East-West Cold War structure. Japan would be a member of the "Western camp," where the market economy and democracy were consecrated. This reform therefore aimed at educating and training the bearers of Japan's economic growth (or "human capital") as well. While the initial aim of establishing a democratic, peace-loving state was configured as a way to catch up with Western Europe and the United States, the process centered on economic growth as a political ideology, rather than on a politics-centered catch-up aimed at democratization. On the precedence assigned to catching up in terms of economic recovery and development, a passage from the AHCER Report states:

> From a wider perspective, reforms such as the extension of the number of years of compulsory education, as well as the popularization of higher education, brought by this "Second Great Education Reform," followed the course set by the "catch-up model" of modernization originally inaugurated in Meiji Japan. In this sense, we can say that the "catch-up" type of education installed during the Meiji era [seeking to be a "rich nation"] was complemented by the "Second Great Education Reform" in the postwar period [seeking the same thing but precluding the "strong army" idea].[7]

Based on this historical experience and understanding, the Third Great Education Reform aimed at ending the phase of catch-up and overcoming the West. As Japanese society faced the twenty-first century, the argument ran, Japan had to become its own master and to educate and train "idiosyncratic" and "creative" individuals, who would find and solve their own problems. In this sense, the end of the catch-up zeitgeist was at the very core of the new education system's

design. If we were to single out AHCER's First Report's most emblematic proposals, the following would be key:

> Since the Meiji era, Japan had set up "catching up" with the Western advanced
> industrialized countries as a state goal. Education aligned itself with this goal
> by educating and training the workforce according to the needs of the times.
> To accomplish this, the government implemented policies to institutionalize
> a national school-education system that would provide a common foundation
> of basic academic ability for the people, enabling society to utilize human
> resources widely from society and therefore to strengthen itself. Such efforts
> provided the vitality for Japan to successfully develop its economy and soci-
> ety and are deserving of praise. On the other hand, during the prewar period
> authorities emphasized the importance of education so much that it created
> a so-called "qualification-based society," where the education credentials of
> employees differentiated their wages and other benefits accordingly.[8]
> [. . .] We need to recognize that the "negative side-effects" of Japan's
> modern-industrial-civilization, its "catch-up model" of modernization, and/
> or the rapid economic growth in the postwar period, led to the deterioration
> of children's spirit, built a society upon foundations that damaged the physi-
> cal and mental health conditions of human beings, tainted interactions among
> people, and had negative influences on culture and education.[9]
> [. . .] We imported and adopted from Western advanced industrial countries
> such things as their advanced technology and systems, and we emphasized
> efficiency in order to swiftly promote their dissemination. From a broader
> perspective, in terms of both content and method, the result of nothing less
> than a rigidly uniform education system was preordained.[10]

The catch-up model of education was seen as the reason behind the "qualification-
based society," as well as "the deterioration of children's spirit" and what was
described as "a rigidly uniform education system." Japan had effectively caught
up with the West, but at the same time this had produced problems. This was the
lens through which the educational system was placed under the microscope. To
reform Japanese education with an eye to the twenty-first century, catch-up style
education now needed to be discarded. The following passage typified the way
the discussion was framed:

> However, it is undeniable that Japan's traditional education has mostly rested
> upon the tendency of cramming knowledge by rote memorization. The soci-
> ety of the future will require us not merely to acquire knowledge and infor-
> mation, but to further develop the ability to express, create, think with our
> heads, and to make an appropriate use of that knowledge and information.
> Creativity is closely connected to individuality, and only when individuality
> is fostered can creativity be nourished.[11]

This quotation shows how goals were configured as an extension of the Ohira
Policy Study Group, which was the first to expressly place them in a context of

playing catch-up. As the report put it, "[Japan's modernization implies] the end of any models to follow, to align ourselves with and 'catch up' with. From now on, we need to find our own path." In short, at the very moment that AHCER declared that Japan had caught up with and even overcome Western advanced industrial countries, the obsoleteness of the education up to that point was identified, and specifically in its inability to respond to the "changed times and needs of society."[12] Japan's education system was at once the cause behind various education problems and the impediment to their resolution.

The specific features of postwar education that needed to be reformed, according to AHCER, were its "equality and rigid uniformity." AHCER understood Japan's education as knowledge reception based, which had been useful for catching up with advanced countries, but now constituted a problem: "Rote memorization is an obstacle to the capacity to think and judge independently, and to the development of creativity, hence over-producing the same people with no individuality."[13] Seeking to break away from this straightjacket was considered important for twenty-first century Japanese education. According to this cognitive filter, the efficient importation and absorption of knowledge, which had been aided by rote memorization-based education, had been a driving force behind the catch-up with the West. Such a view overlooked other, much more positive aspects of traditional education. AHCER viewed such rigidly uniform rote memorization-centered education as the cause behind the noxious "entrance exam–based education," which was exemplified by the Joint First-Stage Achievement Test for national universities. The "knowledge-cramming," "rigidly uniform," "entrance exam–based" education was simply criticized as old-fashioned. However, it should be noted that no classroom surveys on the actual effectiveness of school lessons were undertaken, even though these had been the subject of praise by certain U.S. researchers who appreciated the emphasis on student-teacher interaction in Japan and Japanese teachers' education practices.

At first, AHCER arguments advanced the aims of liberalizing educational institutions (according to which cram schools would also be recognized as schools) and abolishing school districts as the way to break away, because these things were intimately linked with the catch-up model. Such arguments were dominant during the first two years of the reform debates. Rather than emphasizing the service-supplier side, these ideals emphasized choices on the demand side, that is to say the consumers, or students. In other words, these were attempts to effect a thoroughgoing change to a centralized education system from a neoliberalist standpoint.

Calls for the liberalization of education triggered a heated discussion within AHCER, with arguments both for and against such measures. But no specific policies were clearly mentioned in the reports because a radical liberalization of education would have harmed the vested interests of both the Ministry of Education Science and Culture (MESC, renamed MEXT in 2001) and the teachers unions. The revival of established education quarters forced an about-face from pro-liberalization arguments to arguments in favor of "respect of individuality." Arguments in favor of individualism and the full development of education centered on individually focused education shared in the criticism against knowledge-cramming, rigidly uniform, admissions tests–based education. However, in lieu of a radical market-centric reform, the principle of individuality-respecting education resulted in reforms that aimed at child-centered education, which acknowledged students' individuality and fostered creativity and capabilities for independent thinking. This was all referred to as "relaxed education."

For instance, the 1989 revised version of the Japanese national curriculum (a course of studies that was decided by the Japanese government) adopted a "new concept of scholastic ability." According to this view, reforming the catch-up style education model that overemphasized knowledge accumulation required the creation of a system that "fosters a self-driven appetite for learning as well as the ability to independently respond to social change; it emphasizes the basic and foundational teaching content, and supports education that revives individuality."[14] Based on the idea of Japan finding its own path to follow in responding to the changing times, the country urgently needed to develop "a self-driven appetite for learning as well as the ability to independently respond to social change." (This was later summarized in the slogan of a "zest for living"). A relaxed education, in which a child's individuality would be respected, was seen as indispensable to the formation of each child's progress. For that purpose, learning had to be shouldered more autonomously by each student and the system geared to encourage such behavior (this was "child-centered" education).

Concomitantly, the role of teachers was similarly required to change: teachers were to go from "lead" to "support." To realize these new plans, policymakers decided to introduce the practice of an "Integrated Learning Class," which would require no textbooks or evaluations. This reform institutionalized time windows dedicated to the promotion of students' independent learning, free from standard subjects. It involved not only scholastic and pedagogical changes, but also considerably reduced textbook content. In addition, authorities decided to shut schools on Saturdays. Thus, time in school and number of subjects taught were reduced, and the assumption was made that children would carry out their own learning based on their own desires. It was, in short, the adoption – and I would say, the overidealization – of the "independently learning and thinking" child.

Further, concerning university admissions, in the mid-1990s the Central Council for Education (CCE) forcefully pushed for a reduction of entrance examination subjects and for the introduction of reference-based admissions. This was done to eliminate the deleterious effects of the entrance exam–centered education. The decrease of the number of eighteen-year-olds in the population, together with higher university admission quotas, would have resulted anyway in more relaxed competition at the entrance examination. Regardless, authorities decided to reduce the stringency of entrance exams owing to continued criticism, a fact that would later trigger further complaints about the low level of scholastic ability among university students.

In this way, each policy turn aimed at moving away from the catch-up style of education. This did not mean, however, that any clear and feasible alternatives were presented. For instance, while there was no doubt that entrance examinations raised the incentive for students to learn, it was not clear whether fostering an appetite for independent learning could take the place of strict entrance examinations. Neither was there was any serious discussion on the likelihood of increased education inequality in the aftermath of the hasty dismantlement of the so-called rigidly uniform education (for example, through the introduction of a system of school choice). The rejection of knowledge-cramming education was also problematic, and with insufficient empirical surveys on the real practice of classroom instruction, education suddenly shifted simply to a "new concept of scholastic ability." Japanese teachers' excellent knowledge diffusion practices met with criticism, and were dismissed as "leading," "directing," or "cramming" students with knowledge.

The shortcomings of "relaxed education"

Thus, an education based on the respect of individuality was inaugurated in the 1990s. However, this education, too, presented major shortcomings, and ironically the reason was something that had already been pointed out by AHCER itself – insufficient investment in education resources. AHCER made arguments pushing for a qualitatively higher education, without actually increasing such investment. For instance, the largest class size in elementary and middle schools at that time was forty students. To reduce class size the number of instructors needed to be increased, along with the budget for public education. The government aimed for an education that respected every single child's pursuit of learning, however, without touching the balance sheet. With so many students in class, what sort of personalized teaching could be expected of instructors?

Not only were financial investments in educational conditions insufficient, but also instructors were offered insufficient training opportunities to acquire the new skills necessary for the new education practices. It was all very well to have the objective of fostering independently learning and thinking children, but this did not mean that teachers had necessarily already mastered the pedagogy to support such change. The acquisition of new skills that would enable support-centered pedagogy required preparatory time, as well as training. Yet reforms in education started without sufficiently providing for them. In other words, an ideal education was crafted at the policy level with neither additional resources nor sufficient finances at the level of implementation.

Unfortunately, when people framed these policies, the real state of education at the time was poorly understood by most of them. For instance, in the mid-1990s the image of overworked children swamped with homework constituted the dominant understanding within MEXT's CCE. However, if we track down the results of surveys on the conditions of schoolchildren, the amount of time spent studying at home was already decreasing at this time. In addition, an insufficient grasp of the actual facts of teachers' duties, as well as their pedagogical capabilities, led to a misapprehension of the situation, and schools themselves were blamed for the lack of effectiveness of educational reform. What allowed such a state of affairs to emerge was, yet again, the all-too-easy and easily shared fixed idea that Japan maintained an obsolete catch-up model of education, and these old forms of education needed to be dumped to respond to the changing needs of society.[15]

In the early twenty-first century, the problems arising from the relaxed education reforms for the first time gained public attention in the debate on "the crisis in scholastic abilities." MEXT initially lacked any specific opinion and even failed to initiate surveys that captured these changes in scholastic ability. In such a context, along with other scholars, I conducted surveys targeting elementary and middle schools in the Kansai region, to study the degree of change in pupils' scholastic ability during the 1990s. My results showed that the scholastic ability of both elementary and middle school children had clearly decreased and the gap between pupils' capabilities had widened. We did not control for social class in our data, but our analyses made use of information that clearly demonstrated the increased influence of family background on scholastic ability. These findings have not been discussed in MEXT council deliberations. In particular, the problem of widening gaps in education is a phenomenon that has been entirely overlooked in the policy-making process. The progression of inequality, under the guise of education, was the direct result of hasty attempts to make a clean break from the "egalitarian and rigidly uniform" postwar education. Until very recently, when the problem of widening income gaps within society as a whole surfaced, the problem of widening gaps within education was not given attention in policy debates.

After mounting policy-related criticism, Prime Minister Abe Shinzo's first cabinet (2006–07) attempted a reverse in these reforms, and now aimed at "revitalizing education." His plans consisted of reforms whose linchpins were a new attitude that was critical of the excesses of education policies based on respect for individuality and charted a policy centered on increasing scholastic abilities through a revival of education content and education "face-time." To these we should add the nationalistic revision of the Fundamental Law of Education and a new educational and explicit preoccupation with responding to globalization. All of these were basic policies that aimed at reversing the education plans and reforms that had overemphasized the independence of children and schools.

What got lost?

To detail what Japan lost in terms of education, we need to ask two distinct but related questions: First, what got lost in the domain of education? Second, what did Japanese society lose because of its ruinous education policies?

On the first question, we may do well to remember the axiom that education reforms call for other reforms. Education reform that is not accompanied by increased investment tends to fail, all the more so when the intent is lofty but the goals are not delineated. When education reform goes wrong and the policy itself is not called into question, but rather the schools' pedagogical capability, then the failure to deal with this will necessitate reforms in other areas. One example of this, following the reforms to the "relaxed education system," concerns the preoccupation with the decline of scholastic ability, which placed the blame on teachers in charge of putting the system into practice, rather than on the system itself. As a result, more reforms were called for, involving more changes from teachers, the need to institutionalize license renewals and teacher evaluations, and so on. The resulting chain of cookie-cutter reforms caused serious damage to the self-confidence of people in the world of education, as well as its credibility in society. When serious bullying incidents occurred in schools, teachers and members of the local education boards were obliged to appear in front of TV cameras and make the requisite apology. Symptomatic of this situation, teacher bashing was seen in the eyes of the public as a legitimate way to call for revitalizing education, leading to a wave of severe and even insulting criticism being leveled against teachers and schools. Educational circles were seen as guilty, and they became themselves a target of reform, and so the cycle continued. Reform of the board of education system became a longstanding goal; changes to the education administration structure and of its inspection and administrative practices were seen as constituting attempts at revitalizing the dormant state of things. This change was tied to the belief that education could not be changed if it depended solely on independently minded instructors led by the new pedagogies of a "new rubric of scholastic ability" and "integrated learning classes."

To put it plainly, all these attempted changes in education added to the list of what was lost during the two lost decades. These items together led to a total loss of self-confidence and credibility amongst those involved in education. The failure is ironic, because the ideas behind the reforms were to provide more autonomy to schools and more independence to teachers.

Properly speaking, education reform should have enhanced the quality of education. Yet, it actually resulted in the opposite, widening performance gaps and diminishing quality. By analyzing the results of various surveys, it is possible to verify a deterioration of learning behavior, motivation for learning, and scholastic achievement both at the compulsory education and high school levels. It is highly ironic that an education reform that was supposed to aim for the education of a stronger and better-trained labor force ended up producing a contrary result. Beyond this, any notable change in education was bound to have major consequences in Japanese society, and in this case it did, specifically in the phenomenon of growing social inequality in education. In the first of the two lost decades, with regard to learning behavior, learning motivation, and scholastic achievement, yawning inequality was evidenced, which often depended on the children's social class.

One undeniable development in Japanese education over these twenty years has been an increase in university education opportunities. Indeed, the percentage of students enrolling in four-year university courses rose from about 40 percent to more than 50 percent. If we were to include junior colleges and vocational training schools, the percentage of high school graduates who go on to tertiary education has reached more than 75 percent. For this generation, it is safe to say that the number of years spent in education has substantially increased.

Thus, on the one hand, the quality of education up to the high school level has deteriorated, and the gap among students has widened. On the other, the proportion of students who continue their education after high school has increased. This increase in the years of education might have substantially enhanced the performance of Japanese education as a whole, had the quality of higher education been high. Unfortunately, the quality of higher education is definitely problematic, and in fact only represents an additional difficulty for Japanese education. This is particularly true of universities.

In the two lost decades, changes in the higher education world occurred in tandem with major changes in the labor world. Specifically, due to the rise of nonregular employment that Andrew Gordon illustrates in Chapter 5, university graduates are no longer as able as they once were to secure regular, permanent jobs, because such jobs are on the decrease. In the context of a dwindling job market, who does succeed in securing such posts? As always in the Japanese context, where education credentials have long been the decisive factor in the labor market, the name of a prospective job hunter's university matters much more than the amount he or she has actually studied and achieved. In such circumstances, it is only to be expected that the erosion of quality of education up to high school level has been accompanied by widening gaps in employment based on social class. Such gaps would derive from the exclusion from opportunities to secure a stable job and long-term on-the-job training to enhance professional skills in the workplace and would be exacerbated by the sudden destabilization of the labor market. In other words, a decrease in education standards is negatively interconnected with the whole of society's destabilization and widening overall inequality.

The end of catch-up and the response to globalization

One very interesting element of the end of catch-up narrative lies in the perception that Japan had somehow managed to create a system that differed from the West, with which it had to catch up, by virtue of hastening that catch-up process. According to the way in which discourse on Japan's education was presented, Japan's education was based, as we have seen, on a fixed array of knowledge-cramming, rigidly uniform, and entrance exams–based elements. According to this mindset, the system helped in the catch-up with the West, but did not necessarily mean that Japan built up an education system similar to that of Western advanced countries (even if the models coincided, that did not mean that Japan had correctly imitated the models). In particular, Japan's education had failed to encourage independent thinking and learning capabilities, as well as creativity, in contrast to Western advanced countries. The preoccupation with this psychological incapacity was the main driving force behind educational reform. To put it into stronger terms: the creation of a Japanese-style education system that was quite different from the Western models made catch-up possible; but, at the same time, the environment that this had created was the very structure that would later make it so difficult for Japan to meet the changed times and needs of society.

I would now like to analyze this paradox in light of another dominant preoccupation in the public mindset, that is, the response to globalization, or internationalization. As mentioned in my introduction, upon entering the 2000s the imperative of a response to the challenges and opportunities posed by globalization quickly penetrated the nation's psyche, becoming yet another major issue that

113

education had to confront. To put it the other way, globalization, and the need to respond to it, exacerbated the awareness that Japanese education lagged behind.

Certainly, the idea of catch-up with the West was undoubtedly one of the ways in which Japan had responded to an early form of globalization. However, ironically, it was now seen that Japan's very success had made it harder for Japan to respond to globalization. In other words, the idea that Japan had now completed its catch-up gave rise to the contrary idea that it now found it impossible to meet the "changed times and needs of society."

To answer this question of why such a paradox emerged we ought to remember that, along with the above-mentioned fostering of independent thinking capabilities, the basic response to globalization in Japanese education centered on the development of English-language skills. For instance, English activity classes in elementary school fifth and sixth grades were introduced full-scale, nationwide, in 2011. MEXT is currently considering the adoption of these classes as school subjects.[16] In addition, since 2012, MEXT has been pursuing a policy of teaching high school English classes solely in English. At the university level, too, MEXT has pushed for the active use of the Test of English as a Foreign Language (TOEFL) for university entrance examinations and for an increase of classes taught in English.[17] To train a global labor force, it is deemed that the development of English communication capabilities should be assigned the highest priority. More recently, MEXT is adopting a "super global high school" system, where MEXT selects and supports schools that grant an international baccalaureate. This recent policy aims specifically at increasing the number of Japanese studying abroad. These reforms all originate from the identification of poor English language skills as the major reason behind Japan's slow response to globalization.[18]

Playing catch-up with the West was one of Japan's responses to globalization. Nevertheless, Japan's education was able to successfully achieve its goals through a thorough localization of knowledge. In other words, Japan pushed for catch-up through the *Japanization* of foreign knowledge and education undertaken in the Japanese language. As a result, Japan built a system able to capture globalized knowledge through the use of the Japanese language from primary to tertiary education – surely something that has not often been seen among non-Western nations. In Japan, even cutting-edge knowledge is readily available through translations into the Japanese language. I am not able to present detailed statistics, but it is my understanding that no other country publishes as many translated foreign (especially Western) books as Japan does. Topical writings and textbooks assigned at university are read in Japanese. Even though English is dominant in the field of science and technology, Japanese language material is adopted for basic education at the undergraduate level. In comparison to university education in other non-Western latecomer nations that *had* to rely on Western books, one might qualify Japan's catch-up in education as a brilliant success in terms of the localization of knowledge. Japan did not share in the problems experienced by other, latecomer nation-states. These nations attempted to catch up with the West through education, especially higher education, which depended to a great extent on utilizing Western languages such as English. In other words, Japan was able to develop an original knowledge market – in education, publishing, and journalism – that was, in turn, sustained and in some sense protected by the Japanese language. Even if capability in English was insufficient, Japan devised a method that was able to capture high-quality knowledge and information in its own "local dialect." Quite apart from dissemination of knowledge and information, for those on the receiving end, it arguably built a remarkably successful system.

Protected by its own language, a labor market developed that was free from the imperative of the requirement of foreign language ability, and that actually worked for the education and training of human resources. A research group organized by the Ministry of International Trade and Industry (MITI) used statistics from the OECD to tabulate the mobility ratios in OECD countries of highly educated social strata of foreign-born immigrants (that is to say, the proportions of inbound foreign-born immigrants holding university or higher degrees out of the total number of natives who have a similar educational background). Among OECD countries, Japan scores the lowest in terms of the inbound (1.4 percent) mobility ratios.[19] This low showing is in fact the sole reason why highly skilled foreign workers are not stealing a share of the job market from their Japanese counterparts. To put it differently, Japan's labor market for highly qualified workers presents substantial entry barriers to non-Japanese job seekers. In such an environment, regardless of the insistence on the importance of English skills in the public debate, understandably only a few young Japanese will see the practical benefit of the need to gain English language ability.

On the one hand, there are those who lament the poor English of most Japanese as a sign of Japan's tardy response to globalization. On the other, Japan has a history in which the traditional catch-up style of education obviated the need for foreign language study. Squeezed into the narrow gap between these positions, a response to globalization is unlikely to advance, and the ensuing frustration may find its only recourse in even more attempts at demolishing what is left of the catch-up style of education.

In recent years, the decreasing number of Japanese students going abroad has also received attention as an example of the country's slow response to globalization. However, in this case too, the labor market practices and employment customs – both premised on the original Japanese-style education of human resources – play a role. This is because, even as policymakers and business leaders bemoan the lack of a global Japanese workforce, in reality Japan's workplaces cannot yet handle creative and independent workers who speak their minds freely. Toyama Kazuhiko digests some of these recent trends and issues concerning employment and business in Chapter 4. Even today, many Japanese companies target the labor market composed of recent university graduates, starting with students in their third, and semifinal, year, and the system shows no sign of weakening. Moreover, under such conditions the content of education and time spent studying are usually not regarded as important when applying for a job. In fact, university grades bear little or no influence on employers' decisions. Even now, the rank of one's *alma mater* is the most powerful factor behind employment (firms assign priority to the student's admission to the institution, and not to his or her studies). Under such a system, even if one were to study abroad and display one's individuality by being able to speak fluently, this guarantees nothing when looking for a job in Japan. The lag in Japanese companies actively using women in the workforce stands out particularly. Japan has one of the lowest ratios of women in managerial positions, with the highest income differential between men and women in all of the developed countries. For this reason, firms still do not make good use of extremely capable women who study abroad. So despite calls from policy quarters for a globalized workforce, in the actual workplace there is no acknowledgment of such a need. It is on the basis of these contradictions – a shared awareness, as well as the reality, of the actual circumstances of gaining employment – that Japanese youth prefer not to study abroad. It is for similar sorts of reasons that education in English will not go into full gear. These are, shall we say, the rather paradoxical results of the "great success" Japan has had during its catch-up period, in knowledge localization.

Nevertheless, the reasons behind the great sense of urgency to respond to globalization relate more to competition not from the West but rather increasingly from Japan's neighbors. In particular, the success of globalization in Chinese and Korean education continues to spur Japanese policymakers' anxiety.

Conclusion

In this chapter, I have analyzed the changes in social awareness that have underlain the changes in education, in particular the end of the catch-up zeitgeist during the two lost decades and the peculiarities of the interlinking social and education issues that were understood through the narrow window of this bias. The reforms to solve imbalances in Japanese education went into effect during the two lost decades. However, many of them failed to reach their original objectives and gave rise instead to further problems. One cannot help but conclude that the idea of the end of catch-up was an oversimplistic way of reading the situation, so simplistic indeed that it made level-headed arguments somewhat impossible to usher forth. As a result, the policies ended up producing a variety of paradoxical outcomes. The reform of Japan's previously egalitarian education actually created inequality in education, and this overlapped with a widening inequality in the society as a whole. The stress of university entrance exams–based education was ameliorated somewhat, but if anything this was due to a decrease in the number of applicants, which in turn was due to an overall declining youth population together with an increasing number of university slots, rather than to actual restructuring. In the end, this lowered the quality of a university education. In short, education reforms did not in fact contribute to an overall rise in education quality. Policymakers did not devise feasible policies and they also ignored the real state of affairs because their understanding oversimplified Japan's education problems. The end of catch-up mindset acted as a cognitive bias that simply fed its own foregone conclusions. Immediately before the two lost decades, Japan realized, or imagined, that it had caught up with the West, a goal to which the Japanese had pinned their national self-image. Ironically, this apprehension of the situation merely distorted how the Japanese should have truly grasped the problem.

During the two lost decades, a further problem came to occupy public attention, namely the imperative of responding to globalization. The catch-up model of education that Japan had pursued in the postwar period was seen as the reason why Japan's response to globalization had gone so badly wrong. Japan had succeeded in localizing knowledge to an extreme, but at the same time that very success had impeded its response to globalization. This dilemma only added to the mounting anxiety about Japan's slow response. Yet, even if a feeling of impatience intensified among a portion of Japanese leaders, recovering the lost ground proved very difficult precisely because the habit of translating knowledge of the world into the Japanese language had ended up taking deep root in Japan – with evident success. This is the reason why, in actuality, even now only a narrow portion of the population earnestly accepts globalization both in the workplace and in universities. In short, it seems that Japan has yet to free itself from this impasse, which means, at least in education, that the two lost decades have yet to end.

Notes

1   Under the "convoy banking system," government regulations stopped weak companies from collapsing and enabled strong companies to make exorbitant profits.
2   *Bunka no jidai kenkyū gurūpu* [The Age of Culture Study Group], *Ōhira sōri no seisaku kenkyūkai hōkokusho 1 – bunka no jidai* [PM Ōhira's Policy Study Groups Report No.1 – The Age of Culture], Cabinet Councilor's Office, ed. (Tokyo: Ministry of Finance Printing Bureau, 1980), p. 2.
3   Ibid., p. 2.
4   *Bunka no jidai no keizai keiei kenkyū gurūpu* [The Age of Culture – Economic Administration Study Group], *Ōhira sōri no seisaku kenkyūkai hōkokusho 7 – bunka no jidai no keizai keiei* [PM Ōhira's Policy Study Groups Report No. 7 – Economic Administration in an Age of Culture], Cabinet Councilor's Office, ed. (Tokyo: Ministry of Finance Printing Bureau, 1980), p. 31.
5   Ibid., p. 42.
6   The opening paragraph of the Third Report, submitted to Prime Minister Nakasone in 1982, states: "The efforts towards modernization undertook since the Meiji period have borne fruits, and our country today has become a prosperous society, among the first in the world. In addition the income disparity among the components of society is, by international standards, low. We have almost reached the point of reaching the "catch-up"-style modernization. Parallel to this, the Japanese nation's interest and behavior, life style has become varied and multidimensional, along with the improvement in knowledge, education, income, properties, and health conditions. Housewives and elders' desire to participate in social activities too is on the rise. In such context, we are also arranging the conditions necessary to build a new autonomous and self-reliant society." *Rinji gyōsei chōsa kai* [Ad Hoc Council on Administrative Reforms], *Gyōsei kaikaku ni kan suru dai sanji tōshin – kihon tōshin* [Third Report on Administrative Reforms] (Tokyo: 30–7–1982).
7   Ad Hoc Council on Education (AHCER), *First Report*, *Kyōiku kaikaku ni kansuru tōshin*, 10 (Tokyo: Ōkurashō, 1988).
8   AHCER, *First Report*, p. 25; see also Jeremy Rappleye and Takehiko Kariya, "Reimagining Self/Other: Catch-up across Japan's Three Great Education Reforms," in David Blake Willis and Jeremy Rappleye, eds., *Reimagining Japanese Education* (Oxford: Symposium Books, 2011), pp. 51–83.
9   AHCER, *First Report*, p. 50; see also Jeremy Rappleye and Takehiko Kariya, "Reimagining Self/Other," pp. 51–83.

10 AHCER, *First Report*, p. 9; see also Jeremy Rappleye and Takehiko Kariya, "Reimagining Self/Other," pp. 51–83.
11 AHCER, *First Report*, p. 14.
12 Ibid., p. 278.
13 Ibid., p. 278.
14 1991 National Curriculum Council Report.
15 At the time MESC's spokesperson in charge of education reform, Terawaki Ken, told me about a debate published in the magazine, *Ronza* (October 1999), that "to state MESC's case, to be sure there is no available data, but I think there is, more or less, an internal consensus that the 'traditional education system is plain bad'" (Kariya, 2002).
16 With regard to English as a school subject too, new issues would dominate the debates, as schools are left with the problems of training instructors' skills and developing new teaching material. An analysis of the real-world causes behind Japanese people's poor English skills has not even been undertaken. Under such conditions, the promotion of English to subject status is worse than a drop in the bucket, since it could lead to the inefficient use of resources for compulsory education.
17 The adoption of TOEFL for university entrance examinations is meaningless, as long as authorities do not take into consideration major university reforms that link English capabilities measured through TOEFL, with those effectively required at university. With regard to the practice of English-taught university courses too, we ought to ask ourselves why Japanese universities need to teach courses in English. In the absence of such awareness, the number of English-taught classes will rise without students learning the necessary communication skills to become truly global human resources. The same applies to English language skills necessary at work. Without a precise analysis of English and communication capabilities required of global human resources, simplistic expectations, along the lines of "fluency solves all problems," interfere with proper debate over English-language education.
18 An additional issue is the relation between the already widening education inequality and the fostering of global human resources. By building up a superior elite-class education, how will education at the tertiary level evolve, considering the already evident gap within mandatory and high-school-level education? This issue has not been sufficiently addressed in the debate over the fostering of a global workforce.
19 *Kokusaika Shihyō Kentō Iinkai* (2009). The original data is from OECD Factbook (2007).

7   The Fukushima nuclear accident

Lost opportunities and the "safety myth"

Kitazawa Koichi

On March 11, 2011, an enormous tsunami, caused by a massive 8.9-level earth-quake, swept through the coastal areas of northeastern Japan. It was a natural disaster of a magnitude that is seen perhaps once every thousand years. At the Fukushima Daiichi nuclear power station, four nuclear units suffered serious accidents. When the water from the tsunami inundated the units and disabled their cooling systems, the safety devices, previously believed to be 100 percent fail-safe, failed completely. Three of the units suffered explosions due to a buildup of hydrogen gas, and radioactive substances started flowing into the surrounding land and sea. For a while, there were fears of a nuclear meltdown with apocalyptic ramifications.[1]

Immediately after the disastrous failure of these apparently invincible safety devices, the Tokyo Electric Power Company (TEPCO), which owned the nuclear units, issued a statement that the tsunami was so unprecedented that it was "beyond anyone's imagination."[2] However, before long it became clear that the breakdown of the cooling systems was not, in fact, as unavoidable as had been claimed, and that the ensuing catastrophic damage to the environment and to the lives of the residents in the neighboring towns and villages, as well as to the nation's economy as a whole, could have been substantially lessened had the emergency safety devices operated properly.

In the aftermath of the nuclear disaster, three separate commissions were established to investigate the causes of the problems in the safety and disaster-preparedness of the nuclear plant operations. All three commissions reached essentially the same conclusion: the failures of the cooling systems were not inevitable as TEPCO claimed and human error (in regulatory policies, company policies, management, and oversight) played an important role in the unfolding disaster.

In this chapter, I examine the way in which the safety devices failed to work properly to cool the unit cores, as well as analyze the role of human error in the debacle. My purpose here is not simply to apportion blame, but to describe the dynamics of the failures and to draw out lessons learned. No regulations or rules are perfect. No safety measures are 100-percent fail-safe and human beings make mistakes. The Fukushima disaster can be seen in terms of an overall systems failure. It emerged as the result of lax regulatory rule making, a management culture that is prone to "groupthink," and a decision-making structure that was held captive by rules and regulations. To put it another way, the real culprit behind this disaster was the illusion of perfect safety, a myth enshrined by Japan's nuclear power regime. To learn the real lessons of the Fukushima nuclear disaster, it is important that we examine the errors of the collective systems from a larger perspective.

According to the three investigation commissions, Japan would have been able to avoid an accident of serious proportions if it had conformed to internationally accepted improvements in safety measurements. There had been international calls for increased safety measures following the two severe nuclear accidents of Three Mile Island (U.S.) in 1979 and Chernobyl (former Soviet Union) in 1986. Countermeasures had been taken at many nuclear plants elsewhere in the world, and the related information was shared among countries, including Japan. Following the September 11, 2001 terrorist attacks, the U.S. Nuclear Regulatory Commission (NRC) urged foreign nuclear regulatory organizations throughout the world to enhance the security levels of their nuclear facilities, as the United States had done with the so-called B.5.b measures. These measures appealed for thorough preparedness and backup systems against any failure in the cooling systems and total power failures, vital to prevent the unit cores from heating up to dangerous levels. The three investigation commissions stated in their respective reports that the Japanese nuclear power community had failed to take the necessary countermeasures on the basis of the American suggestions and to implement more stringent training for the actual evacuation of residents.

In other words, even though there had been many opportunities to shore up disaster preparedness at nuclear power plants in Japan and to improve regulations, for three decades, from 1979 to 2011, these issues were never fundamentally addressed. This chapter examines what was lost as a consequence and why the chances were ignored.

History of Japan's nuclear power program

Before 2011, Japan was the world's third largest nuclear energy producer, with fifty-four nuclear units in use for commercial energy production.[3] Given the intense integration of Japanese government and business, Japan's nuclear power development progressed steadily under a symbiotic "government-led private management" system, meaning that it was directed and regulated by the government but owned and operated by private sector companies. Even so, there were many twists and turns in that history.

In the aftermath of World War II, during which Japan had two atomic bombs dropped on it at Hiroshima and Nagasaki, the U.S. occupation headquarters prohibited all matters related to nuclear technology, even going so far as to order the destruction of cyclotrons at RIKEN, Japan's leading research institute. Shortly afterwards, however, following the announcement of the USSR's successful development of a nuclear program, the United States did an about-face and decided, as President Eisenhower announced in 1953 at the UN General Assembly, to promote nuclear energy under the slogan "Atoms for Peace." The

United States and its allies subsequently started a movement to share information on nuclear technology, opening the way for nuclear energy to be pursued in Japan. Immediately, a group coalesced to push the program forward, led by a few Diet members, such as Nakasone Yasuhiro (later to become prime minister), and leaders in the business community. A request was made in the Diet to start investigating and planning for a nuclear power program and it quickly gained approval. The government founded the Science and Technology Agency (STA) to promote nuclear research and to build test units, and nuclear engineering departments were opened in major universities. The Science Council of Japan (SCJ), however, was rather reluctant to move toward the commercialization of nuclear power production. It stipulated three guiding principles for the nuclear program – "independence, democracy, and transparency" – with the aim of avoiding too much state interference in nuclear research, and these principles were stipulated in the 1955 Basic Law for Atomic Energy.

Initially, the relationship between the government and the electric utilities industry was quite tense, and competition among electric utilities was also very fierce. However, following the 1973 oil crisis, the political will grew to offer a stable supply of energy by assigning a monopoly to an electric power company for each of Japan's nine national district power grids. This rendered interaction among business, the government, and companies more cooperative, certainly with regard to the location of power plants and the ability to increase power rates.[4] Within the government, competition between the Ministry of International Trade and Industry (now the Ministry of Economics Trade and Industry, or METI) and the Science and Technology Agency (STA) turned into a tug-of-war over leadership. The former advocated the indigenization of foreign technology, while the latter firmly wanted to encourage in-house development.[5]

In the early 1970s, certain issues with nuclear power, such as where to locate power plant facilities and general safety concerns, emerged and remained unresolved. Nevertheless, the industry registered steady progress following decisive government action in the aftermath of the second oil crisis in 1979. This crisis left the public with the impression that Japan needed nuclear power because it was a country without energy resources. Japan's nuclear power program was an important part of its energy policy aimed at maintaining a diversification of energy resources with a stable supply and economic efficiency in mind. The Three Mile Island and Chernobyl nuclear accidents froze the growth of nuclear power generation in many Western countries from 1990 onward – but not so in Japan, where new units kept being constructed. In fact, in 2011 nuclear power supplied as much as 30 percent of electricity (13 percent of all energy) in Japan. And Japanese nuclear unit manufacturers gradually became a major global force in the nuclear power industry.

Characteristics of the Japanese nuclear safety regulation system

It has been pointed out separately and independently by the three investigation teams examining the Fukushima nuclear accident that there was a gradual deterioration in the oversight of nuclear safety. During the last three decades the apparently successful development of Japan's nuclear power business under the "government-led private management" system was in declining health. Indeed, the safety precautions and countermeasures that should have been adopted by the nuclear industry turned out to be surprisingly insufficient in comparison to what was taking place elsewhere in the world. The investigation teams learned that outside Japan the nuclear community consistently strengthened its countermeasures and during the period made sure to offer regular training in operating emergency contingencies.

The Independent Investigation Commission on the Fukushima Nuclear Accident (IICFNA), which I chaired, defined Japan's nuclear safety regulations as a "paper tiger," offering merely the appearance of safety but nothing in terms of content.[6] It is precisely due to this setup that Japan's so called nuclear "safety myth" emerged. In other words, safety regulations were a mere formality and lacked real teeth. The IICFNA stressed that opinions offered by many individuals from different nuclear safety organizations were never allowed to rise to the surface for serious and open discussion. It was difficult to achieve any significant change in the face of this all-encompassing safety myth. Consequently, the necessary safety countermeasures on a par with international standards were not introduced over the last three decades in contrast to the gradually strengthened countermeasures in the United States and in Europe.[7]

The promoters of nuclear energy adopted the "100 percent safe" catchphrase to persuade the Japanese people, especially communities in areas that hosted the construction of nuclear power plants. Although one cannot guarantee "zero-risk" with nuclear energy, the real key is to manage the risks below a publicly acceptable level. Unfortunately, the "100 percent safe" slogan gradually trapped the nuclear community into a bind. Even when nuclear technology manufacturers called for improved safety in the informal prespecification stages of reformation, these calls fell on deaf ears at the electric power companies because they had convinced themselves that it was logically impossible to improve an already 100 percent safe system. If they had responded and taken the called-for measures, this would have been tantamount to admitting that the system was less than 100 percent safe. For this reason, they actually eliminated wording in favor of "safety improvements" in their reform proposals and only approved "cost amelioration" specifications.

Japan's Nuclear and Industrial Safety Agency (NISA) was also reluctant to issue written guidance for safety improvements, instead limiting itself to verbal guidance to not leave any evidence of "less than 100 percent safety." Moreover, the NISA did not require Japanese electric companies to reply to the guidance, but merely recommended improvements, with no need to provide the agency with any feedback documentation.

This does not mean that the people on the promotion side of nuclear power believed in the safety myth, but merely that they fell into their own trap over the course of the lost decades. In other words, the nuclear power safety myth gradually gained its own inert power as interested parties preferred to stay with the status quo. The result of this was complacency at all levels of regulation, with policies that were never actually tested or that reflected a conscious sense of the actual potential for a disaster. Sadly, at the same time, while many knew the system was never as safe as it was touted to be, they were literally at a loss because no one within the nuclear community would speak out for change. What was lost was therefore a moment when a change in the regulatory structure could have imposed a system of oversight that did not crumble so easily in the face of a disaster.[8]

The Fukushima nuclear accident and regulatory safety

Fukushima was the first case of a long blackout of a nuclear power station. If the station had been ready for such an eventuality, it is possible that the severe accident could have been avoided altogether.

The nuclear units in the Fukushima Daiichi station lost both AC and DC electricity for several days due to the earthquake and tsunami on the afternoon of March 11, 2011. Units 1 to 3 suffered a series of grave problems, namely the meltdown of the fuel rods in their unit cores. The destruction of nuclear fuel rods then led to a release of radioactive material. As the accident grew in severity, the pressure and temperature in the pressure vessel rose (which is inside the containment vessel), releasing water vapor, hydrogen, and radioactive substances into the containment vessel, probably due to deteriorated seals. The pressure continued to rise in the containment vessel, leaking gases into the unit building. The released hydrogen reacted with oxygen in the atmosphere inside of the building, which created hydrogen explosions in Units 1, 3, and 4. Unit 4 was not in operation and the reactor core was empty of fuel on the day of the earthquake. But hydrogen seems to have leaked from neighboring Unit 3 into the Unit 4 building, and a blast occurred in the Unit 4 building as well. Although a hydrogen explosion did not occur in the Unit 2 building, the pressure and temperature in its containment vessel rose the most, and a break occurred somewhere at the bottom of the containment vessel, releasing a huge amount of radioactive material.

The release of total radioactive material amounted to about one-tenth of the amount released in the Chernobyl accident, the second highest in world history; as an event it was ranked at level 7 in terms of intensity – the highest – in the International Nuclear Event Scale (INES). The Fukushima accident shocked the people in charge of nuclear energy all over the world because once the loss of electricity threw the station into chaos, accidents occurred not at one particular single unit but rather at all four units at the site in succession. The tsunami affected most seriously the four units close to each other on the site. The hydrogen explosions occurred at three of them, causing the roofs of the unit buildings to blow off. One of the units, number 2, seemed to have escaped the hydrogen explosion but the inner pressure of the unit containment rose, causing great worry about the possible explosion of the unit itself. It was impossible to open the valve to release pressure due to the total power outage of the power station, and finally a part of the bottom of the unit containment was broken to release the steam. In the end, even the number 2 containment vessel or suppression chambers exploded, and the

March 15 leakage of radioactive material associated with the blast of the number 2 unit at the bottom of the containment vessel is believed to have been the largest. As a consequence of this nuclear disaster, as of January 2014, roughly 138,000 residents of the area remain evacuated from their homes.[9]

In addition to the release of radioactive materials in the atmosphere, underground water penetrating into the damaged units seems to be coming into contact with the damaged and radioactive fuel. This produces several hundred tons of contaminated water every day. At present, this contaminated water is being pumped up and stored in hundreds of tanks, and plans are in place for the removal of radioactive components such as cesium and strontium through a cleaning system called the Advanced Liquid Processing System (ALPS). Nevertheless, there are still problems in the decontamination process – the tritium, for example, cannot be removed chemically and has to be released into the sea. The situation feeds further public distrust of TEPCO and even now, years after the accident, keeps the process of decommissioning the units from being brought to a conclusion. It is imperative that the flow of underground water into the units is stopped. Efforts should be made to calculate how much radioactive substance has leaked from the unit cores into the natural underground water and how much there will be in the future.

The social impact of the accident

The economic damage caused by the Fukushima nuclear accident includes elements such as disruption to local agriculture, fisheries, and tourism; the cost of removing the traces of radiation in local schools and residential districts; and compensation to former residents of the area who can no longer live in their homes. The most liberal estimates for the total costs amount to between US $100 and 200 billion. Fukushima Prefecture makes up 4 percent of Japan's total area and 2 percent of its population, but roughly 10 percent of this land has been contaminated. Approximately 10 percent of the people in the prefecture have lost their homes. The prefectural economy revolves around agriculture, but sales of Fukushima-produced rice, vegetables, and fish have decreased, along with the number of tourists. For this reason, the regional economy has become impoverished and there is no sign of a return to equilibrium with full employment. The problem is partly real and partly psychological. But because it is difficult for consumers to clearly distinguish between what is safe to eat and what is not, they tend to avoid purchasing food from the Fukushima area. The local and central governments have instituted a system whereby all the agricultural and fishery products in the affected areas get measured for radioactivity, which has addressed people's concerns to some extent.

The greatest anxiety of the residents has been the question of whether they should return home or move somewhere else to start afresh. Their villages and towns are to a certain extent all contaminated with radioactive materials; where the safety lines should be drawn remains a controversial question. People's attitudes on this point vary depending on their age, profession, and personal circumstances.

Many elderly residents prefer to remain, notwithstanding higher radioactivity levels, while many younger people, especially if they wish to have families, choose to move away. Everyone is anxious over the potential effects of radiation exposure and the possibility of its effect on the incidence of child cancer.

Lost opportunities for nuclear reactor safety

The light water nuclear units that make up the majority of nuclear units for civilian use today are not designed as "fail-safe." To make nuclear power generation as cost-effective as coal-burning electric power plants, the heat generation density in the nuclear unit core is maximized by packing the nuclear fuel rods together as densely as possible. This, in turn, has an effect on the speed at which the water heats up and shortens the time before a potential meltdown occurs. When an emergency occurs, the unit shuts off by terminating the chain reaction that usually runs with the proper insertion of control rods. However, even if the unit successfully shuts off, the fuel rods continue to give off heat – about one-tenth of that given off when the unit is in operation. The heat comes from the radioactive decay of the accumulated nuclides in the fuel rods. The amount of heat is so large that several tons of water per hour are needed to prevent a meltdown. Once a meltdown occurs, radioactive material leaks out from the unit, resulting in a severe accident.

Various multistep braking systems are in place for such emergencies. Following the International Atomic Energy Agency's (IAEA) definition of "defense in depth," there are five different stages to consider when braking controls can be used.[10] The Fukushima nuclear accident exposed the relative defenselessness of Japanese units at the fourth and fifth stages. From the vantage point of preventing an escalation into a more serious accident and protecting public safety, countermeasures in Japan were weak compared to those implemented in other countries.

Why was the accident not contained?

The reason why the Fukushima accident escalated so quickly was, in a word, due to "unpreparedness." The investigation reports listed numerous examples, but below are the issues that I think are key.

First, even though the units were equipped with battery systems for use in emergencies, they ended up submerged in water. Why were reserves not placed somewhere nearby? Plenty of batteries were urgently procured but they were not helpful because of a mismatch in voltage. Second, there were emergency diesel electric power generators, but these were also flooded by the tsunami. Fundamentally, the two alternative sources of electricity for an emergency were useless. Why was none of this considered before? More than thirty electric power supply cars arrived at the station to assist, but none could be connected because the attachment plugs did not match. Any prior training would have revealed this discrepancy.

Unit 1 had an emergency cooler equipped to circulate water without the need for electric power to keep the fuel rods cool in the unit core for a while. However, the operators switched off the cooler but mistakenly thought that it was in operation because they saw steam coming out from the unit building. If the operators had more training on the emergency cooler system, they would have known that the cooler made a surprisingly high noise if it was operating. In a unit of the same type in the United States, the cooler is tested every four years and therefore operators know how noisy the equipment is. At the Fukushima Daiichi station, there had not been any exercise of this kind for more than thirty years! It was therefore not possible for an operator to judge whether the emergency cooler was functioning or not, which created a situation that left some room for false hope until it was too late.

The water level sensor is important to gauge whether enough water covers the heating fuel rods. After the Three Mile Island accident, it was learned that the water level sensor had not functioned properly inside the unit, and some European nuclear plants subsequently exchanged their sensors after learning this news. But at Fukushima they had continued to use the same kind of sensor, and there were questions as to whether it was malfunctioning at the time of the accident. The exact whereabouts of the water level is crucially important for operators to figure out when and how to execute the next emergency procedure. The strategy to reign in an accident is to try to maintain the circulation of water inside the unit by utilizing an emergency circulation pump that does not require electricity. In this case, because the amount of water is limited, the temperature and also the pressure can rise too high within just a few hours. If it is impossible to restore the electric power, external fresh water must be introduced to cool the unit. But the amount of fresh water that is available may be limited. If every step fails, the final solution is to bring in seawater, of which there is an endless supply, by routing seawater through fire engines and funneling it into the unit. This has two disadvantages. Pouring seawater into a nuclear unit is corrosive, and makes it impossible to use one ever again. And it requires a decision at the executive level – as it did in the Fukushima case. At Fukushima, it later became clear that there were no clear rules in place regarding swiftly taking such a decision. It was too late anyway; the accident had already escalated.

In addition to getting water into the unit core, another major task is to release the pressure inside the unit vessel and the containment vessel so that the water can be pumped in from fire trucks operating at a lower pressure. In association with this "venting" process, some radioactive materials leak out together with steam because the casing of the fuel rods is likely by then to be damaged. After the Fukushima accident, it was learned that the unit was not designed to vent easily in case of a station power outage – and it took an unexpectedly long time to do so after the decision had finally been made. Moreover, in the case of Unit 1, when the venting process was at last prepared, operators learned that some residents were still in their homes so they had to wait for another hour so those people could be evacuated. Once operators completed the venting, seawater could be poured into the unit. Even with these measures, it was not long after this that the hydrogen explosion occurred. The explosion seems to have been caused by the venting, which had taken place too late, and hydrogen that had leaked out from the containment vessel into the unit building.

The worst-case scenario

The IICFNA team uncovered in December 2011 the presence of a report prepared by the then chairperson of the Japan Atomic Energy Commission, Dr. Kondo Shunsuke, for Prime Minister Kan Naoto and titled *Worst Case Scenarios*. Authorities had fears, as voiced in the report, and held simulations for two possible scenarios in the case of further possible escalation of the Fukushima accident. The report estimated that in the worst case approximately thirty million residents would have to evacuate, and they would include people in the Tokyo metropolitan area. One of the worst-case scenarios included a possible explosion of the containment vessel itself. A few days after the earthquake, a problem occurred with Unit 2. First, the venting of Unit 2 did not go as planned, so the pressure and temperature were both increasing within the containment vessel. In the previous hydrogen explosions, the roofs of the unit buildings had essentially been blown off but the containment vessels remained mostly undamaged. If the containment vessel itself had exploded, however, the unit core would then have been scattered together with the fuel rods, as happened in the Chernobyl accident. Fortunately, the containment vessel as a whole did not explode and instead a part of the vessel had broken, allowing the release of pressure. It should be noted that the fate of the country ironically depended on this fortunate error.

Second, spent fuel rods had been stored inside the Unit 4 building. Spent fuel rods are highly radioactive and consequently no one wants to house them. In Japan, the spent fuel rods were supposed to be treated in the reprocessing factory in Aomori Prefecture, but the factory had not been functioning properly and was in fact stacked full of such rods. There were difficulties in both the temporary storage and the processing of spent fuel rods in each of the Japanese unit buildings. The fuel rods of Unit 4 that had been taken out of the unit core for repair had had to be stored in the fuel pool. The spent fuel pool is located near the top of the containment vessel as a temporary storage pool for the purpose of periodically exchanging spent fuel rods. At the time of the accident, spent fuel rods, which had been accumulating for more than several years, were being housed in the temporary spent fuel pool.

After the hydrogen explosion in Unit 3, a similar hydrogen explosion struck Unit 4, which was not in operation on the particular day of the accident and whose core was empty. It is thought that this explosion probably occurred because some hydrogen had leaked over from Unit 3 into Unit 4 through pipes that they shared in common. The roof of the building that covered Unit 4 was blown off and the spent fuel pool at the top was directly exposed to the atmosphere. Spent fuel rods are highly radioactive and generate much heat along with their radioactive decay. A few days after the earthquake, many people worried that if the water level of the pool diminished due to the failure to get more water circulating through it, then a meltdown of the spent fuel rods could also occur. The total amount of radioactive material in the spent fuel pool is in fact greater than in the unit itself. All of these potential disasters were unfolding right when the aftershocks of the earthquake were feared.

It was at this time that several nations issued advice to their citizens living in Japan to leave the country. A request from the Cabinet Office had the self-defense forces fly helicopters over Units 3 and 4 in an attempt to douse the spent fuel pool with water from above. Tragically, getting water into the fuel pool proved to be very difficult. Images captured from the helicopter flying over Unit 4 seemed to suggest light being reflected from the surface of the spent fuel pool. Luckily, this meant that the water had not yet dried up and was potentially still covering the spent fuel rods. The Cabinet Office then requested the fire department bring fire trucks equipped with long hoses to pour more water into the spent fuel pool from a portion of the building where the roof had been destroyed and thus offered access. The firefighters succeeded in locating the kind of equipment that could do the job and did indeed save the spent fuel pool. This unexpected piece of good fortune is thought to have been possible due to the accidental leakage of water brought about by the earthquake through a gap in the top of the pressure vessel where normally water would not be stored. The spent fuel rods had just been transferred from the unit core to the pool, which required the top of the containment vessel to be filled with water. This spent fuel rod pool is now regarded as the most dangerous spot that requires serious postaccident countermeasures. It is obvious that radioactive spent fuel rods should not be allowed to accumulate in places like a spent fuel pool, an unsafe place that can suffer damage during earthquakes and also easily become the target of terrorist activity.

It is worth noting that at every moment in this series of accidents, the fate of millions rested merely on serendipity and happenstance. It is extraordinary that the fate and functionality of a nation was wholly dependent on these twists of fate, and that a disaster of truly unprecedented scale was only narrowly avoided due to providence. The Cabinet Office limited disclosure of the *Worst Case Scenario* report to a select few and did not disclose the contents to the public.

The "hollowing out" of Japan's regulatory system

TEPCO's initial investigation pointed to the height of the tsunami as something "beyond imagination." However, after the three investigation commissions had expressed their opinions, the second investigation commission set up by TEPCO, headed by Anegawa Takefumi, acknowledged the main conclusions of these three commissions. In short, the reasons behind the lag in Japan's nuclear energy industry taking necessary countermeasures for serious accidents relative to elsewhere in the world were rooted in Japan's limiting administrative structure and differences in rules of command and control within nuclear management. In Japan, nuclear regulation moved according to its own internal inertia, so little change was implemented once rules were made. Moreover, even when individual leaders in various sectors hit upon the idea that some new safety countermeasures should be adopted, nobody was able to speak up to push such initiatives forward because it was believed to be impossible to improve an already 100 percent safe system. Last, the regulatory office was housed under the same administrative umbrella, in METI or the STA, which also served as a promotion agency for nuclear energy.

The Diet investigation team defined this tendency as "regulatory capture," where those in charge become too close to the group they are supposedly supervising. In other words, the regulators were weaker than their nuclear power–promoting partners. Regulation also ended up being trapped within a byzantine managerial framework.

The advisory council

I question whether it is possible to administer nuclear regulatory issues properly through Japan's advisory council system, which has been adopted by both the central and local governments. According to the Japanese administration system, important decisions can be taken through the authorization of bureaucrat-drafted regulations by a committee called the "advisory council." Advisory councils are staffed with "expert" members invited from outside the government administration offices. In the context of nuclear energy administration, both nuclear supporters and regulators adopted the advisory council system as the decision-making body because it fitted with the "government-led" philosophy of management. It was postulated that when the conventional way of doing things needed change, the advisory council would ponder and provide proper decisions because the members were knowledgeable individuals with neutral backgrounds who were externally appointed. To make the advisory council function smoothly there is also a "secretariat" – one for each council in the administrative organization in charge. This secretariat is a point of contention.

The advisory council may be composed of several subcommittees that are referred to as committees of experts because they are supposed to check administrative regulation and represent the people's interest. For this reason, each committee member is selected from among prominent intellectuals, including specialists from related particular fields, to represent "the citizens." The former Japanese Nuclear Safety Commission (NSC), a type of advisory council, provides the most important example that has led the country onto a path of real danger. The NSC was the top decision-making body responsible for nuclear safety guidelines. The Fukushima accident started with the power outage at the station. But it was the NSC that had stated in its guidelines: "The eventuality of a prolonged blackout of a nuclear power station need not be considered."[11] If we take the statement literally, then TEPCO cannot be held responsible for the accident because the accident was indeed triggered by the prolonged station blackout.

Missed opportunities to revise regulatory guidelines

The August 30, 1990 Japanese NSC decision entitled, "Regulatory Guide: Reviewing Safety Design of Light Water Nuclear Power Reactor Facilities," adhered to earlier safety guidelines prepared in the early days of nuclear energy in Japan by the Atomic Energy Commission (AEC). However, a research working group put together to analyze what needed to be done in the event of a station blackout, and labeled as a subcommittee in the NSC, was called in 1991 to discuss whether it was necessary to revise the basic guidelines for the safe regulation of nuclear power. At the time, various countries had already started changing their nuclear safety regulations, triggered by news of station blackouts reported in Taiwan and the United States. As a result, the subcommittee came to the following conclusion: "With regard to an enduring station blackout, it is expected that transmission lines and emergency power sources would be restored to normal so there is no need to deliberate on the matter."[12] The subcommittee decided to approve the existing guidelines. That meant they decided to do the exact opposite of what other countries were doing – which was taking a potential station blackout seriously and drawing up strategies to deal with a several-hour-long loss of electric power.

As investigations of the Fukushima accident progressed, a voluntary investigation team set up by Omae Kenichi, whose members mostly comprised engineers from nuclear power manufacturers, pointed out this massive gap in the NSC's safety plans inspection guidelines. The Diet investigation team then asked for documentation from the "secretariat" of the NSC and the procedures of this particular advisory board were made public. The secretariat was a part of the old STA agency that was responsible for the research working group in the event of a station blackout. The STA was an agency established in 1956 with the aim of promoting nuclear power development in the early days of postwar atomic energy. The STA's secretariat responsible for the examinations appointed a Tokyo University professor as head of the committee, and formed the subcommittee mainly from academics and executive engineers from private companies. According to memoranda of those meetings from this subcommittee, the deliberations are detailed below:

Following explanations from the secretariat, the committee head conferred with committee members on the necessary safety guidelines in the event of a station blackout. The secretariat claimed that, "provisions aimed at tackling a station blackout are expensive. Since power cuts in Japan are usually short, countermeasures are probably unnecessary." The committee members did not voice any objections. The committee head then asked members: "How shall we argue that countermeasures are unnecessary?" However, the committee did not come up with any proposals. Instead the secretariat's suggestions were as follows: "We will ask the loaned transferees from TEPCO and the Kansai Electric Power Company (KEPCO) in the secretariat to come up with reasons before the next scheduled subcommittee meeting." The subsequent subcommittee meeting then accepted the explanation provided by the secretariat, which stated: "First of all, power supply cuts in Japan are never longer than thirty minutes so there is no need to devise safety countermeasures following a blackout."[13]

Why the advisory council could not speak up

By the time of the Fukushima accident, the two major Japanese administrative offices for safety regulation were the Nuclear Safety Commission (NSC) and the Nuclear and Industry Safety Agency (NISA), belonging to METI and STA respectively, both of which fully supported the nuclear power industry. The advisory councils for safety regulations were both managed under the auspices of secretariats in METI or the STA. Because the secretariats needed members who had good knowledge of nuclear technology, they invited people as temporary staff from the electric power companies. Members of the advisory council were thus basically appointed by the secretariats. Each of the council members believed that all the other members would agree to the plan proposed by the secretariat and consequently it would be useless for one person alone to raise objections. There was also a fear that raising questions about secretariat decisions would risk one's membership in the advisory council.

In sum, three main reasons why the Japanese advisory council systems did not function properly in the case of nuclear regulation were: (1) the secretariat included members on temporary transfer from electric companies, and their voices dominated the discussions, (2) the secretariat for safety regulation belonged to the same administrative agencies responsible for the promotion of nuclear power, and (3) the secretariat had the power to select members of the advisory council.

Additional lost opportunities for improved safety countermeasures

Other important factors were crucial in these lost opportunities. Those who had been appointed to the head or important positions in NISA were high-ranking METI officers who remained in power for an average of two years. Otherwise they had little or no background in the nuclear energy industry. None of the prominent members of NISA raised any issues for serious discussion because they were not specialists in any related field and, in any case, after two years they would be transferred elsewhere – so there was no incentive to closely scrutinize problems. All that was needed was for them to just quietly wait until the end of their short tenure and avoid creating trouble. This complacency allowed the system to advance on the precedent established during the previous decades.

A typical example of NISA negligence occurred when it received a warning from the U.S. Nuclear Regulatory Commission concerning the B.5.b measures, which recommended preparations against terrorist attacks at many of the world's nuclear units after September 11, 2001. NISA officials considered the advice but ultimately ignored the suggestions, confining the information to a small number of people in the office without distributing it more widely to the electric power industry. This sort of negligence to protect people from possible danger in the event of a nuclear accident was typical of Japanese regulatory agencies until the Fukushima accident. The mismatch between the regulatory organizations and supervising ministries meant that NISA was essentially an offshoot organization of METI. Post-accident investigations noted that many high-ranking officials in NISA later found positions at TEPCO or related foundations after retirement. This enmeshing of regulation and promotion made it difficult for NISA to be independent of TEPCO or METI.

The birth of the nuclear village

After the Fukushima accident in 2011, the IICFNA investigation team interviewed more than a dozen former high-ranking officers of METI and of the former STA, who reflected on how they had administered the government's nuclear policy.[14] Surprisingly, many of them confessed to having felt rather helpless in their various positions. They all had an inkling that things were not quite right, but also that there was probably no other way to do things. Consequently, decisions were simply rubber stamped as a consequence of bureaucratic inertia. For the most part these officials felt as though they had been kept under the thumb of the electric power companies. However, when it came to the advisory council, the secretariat was responsible for determining the direction and tone of the discourse. Advisory committee members also joined pushing the programs forward. The IICFNA team's final report claimed that the formation of a "nuclear village," a sort of inward looking and closed system that was virtually solely controlled from within, greatly impacted implementation of Japan's nuclear safety regulations.

According to the report, this nuclear village was composed of politicians, both local and central, nine electric power regional monopolies, nuclear manufacturers, electric power company labor unions, academics, various foundations, and non-profit organisations (NPOs) involved in the promotion of nuclear power. Being a member of the nuclear village entitled the village members to a constant flow of various merits. For example, local governments and residents received their annual budget subsidies from the central government. They also received generous donations from electric power companies to establish cultural centers, music halls, libraries, elderly care centers, children's pools, sports centers, etc.[15] Politicians could count on votes under initiatives taken by the electric companies and the labor unions. University professors could expect extra research funds from electric power companies. There were other advisory council committees set up in the various fields of nuclear power by the central and local governments in which each committee member received generous rewards. Foundations sponsored by the electric power companies provided voluntary groups and NPOs with generous funding for their activities. Many education programs aimed at children to learn about radioactivity were provided in this manner through volunteer groups funded by the foundations.

The "government-led private management" system adopted by Japan just after World War II turned out to be a powerful promotion scheme for nuclear power. But it also created the safety myth within the culture of these nuclear villages.

The foundation of a new "Nuclear Regulation Authority"

A year and a half after the Fukushima accident, in September 2012, Japanese policymakers reflected on the problems raised in the three investigation team reports and abolished both the METI-dependent NISA and the STA-dependent NSC (at the time of the accident it was under the Cabinet Office's jurisdiction). The abolition of the preexisting regulatory organizations was accompanied by legislation establishing a new Nuclear Regulation Authority (NRA), independent of any government agency and ministry that might have a motive to promote nuclear power. This step was taken partially due to the final conclusions of the three investigation teams, which basically corroborated one another's findings and advocated the need to establish an organization whose activities are independent of the nuclear village. As if acknowledging the validity of this announcement, a new law was enacted taking into account the views of the government and of a supra-partisan group of Diet members. As such, the NRA was inaugurated in September 2012 and the prime minister appointed five starting committee members. The new NRA's task is limited to "the protection of people's lives, health and properties, the preservation of the environment and, along with that, the guarantee of the peaceful use of nuclear power." In other words, its task consists exclusively of assessing safety on the basis of the committee members' good conscience and from a purely technological standpoint. Importantly, considerations of energy security are not part of its mission.[16]

The new law also assures the independence of NRA members from pronuclear ministries and agencies. Their appointment and dismissal are recommended by the Prime Minister and approval is required by the Diet. Moreover, the secretariat of the NRA was removed from the previous jurisdiction under METI and MEXT, and now sits as an external organ to the Ministry of the Environment.[17] Moreover, according to the new law, those public officials who are assigned to managerial positions at NRA are not allowed to return to working in pronuclear positions in ministries, agencies, or companies. This so-called no-return rule is designed to avoid the influence of nuclear promoters on the nuclear regulatory decision-making process. In addition, the NRA is obliged to comply with strict transparency rules. The NRA's deliberations are made public and detailed minutes will be compiled. Decisions must also be recorded in detail.

Moreover, the so-called back-fit rule was introduced in the same year through another legislative amendment, and even preexisting nuclear units have to conform to these newly drafted nuclear regulatory standards to receive permission to operate.[18] According to this new regulation, preexisting nuclear units that are now suspected of having lied about active earthquake fault lines cannot operate unless the actual situation is studied and made clear. Due to the application of this new rule, investigations over the presence of active fault lines under a number of nuclear power plants is ongoing.

The Nuclear Regulation Authority was launched with a staff of 480 people. In addition, the independent administrative body that deals with safety inspections of nuclear units – the Japan Nuclear Energy Safety Organization (JNES) – acts together with the NRA by providing technical support, expanding the total number of personnel to 1,000. By contrast, America's NRC commands as many as 4,200 employees. As such, the lack of adequate staff in Japan has become a hot topic of debate. The effective functioning of the newly established NRA has already become a touchstone to test lessons learned over the course of the lost decades.

Conclusion

Sins of omission have characterized nuclear regulation in Japan for the last three decades. This negligence has been especially true with regard to countermeasures for the kind of nuclear power plants that were at the center of the severe

Fukushima accident. Countermeasures were taken abroad but never implemented in Japan. The direct reasons for this were simple: such measures were expensive, and people were complacent – until the Fukushima accident, no major nuclear accident had ever occurred in Japan.

The most important reason has also been, as discussed here, the unique administrative structure characterized by "government-led private management," and the "secretariat-led advisory council" system that maneuvered decisions for nuclear regulation in Japan. The decision-making process for nuclear regulation was constructed under the umbrella of ministries for nuclear promotion. This too cozy and ultimately harmful relationship also stimulated the growth of the so-called nuclear village. This loose conglomeration of entities has proved quite hardy; it runs according to its own logic and no individuals have been able to control it. The nuclear village mentality imbued itself with a "safety myth" that prevented efforts toward better safety standards due to the fallacy that no improvement was necessary if the system were already "100 percent safe."

This challenging and error-ridden decision-making system in Japan was dismantled in 2012 to establish a new independent organization, the NRA, to cope with this array of problems. The attitude of nuclear energy researchers in academia will be particularly key for future developments concerning whether the new NRA can properly maintain safety standards – observers who can be both neutral and critical are necessary for regulation to become healthy and effective. Considering the high frequency of earthquakes and other natural disasters, the management of nuclear power in Japan must of course aim at the very highest levels of safety.

Notes

1 For a full treatment of what happened at the Fukushima nuclear power plant, see the RJIF book, The Independent Investigation on the Fukushima Nuclear Accident (Mindy Kay Bricker, ed.), *The Fukushima Daiichi Nuclear Power Station Disaster: Investigating the Myth and Reality* (London: Routledge, 2014).
2 Okuyama Toshihiro, *Rupo tokyo denryoku genpatsu kiki ikkagetsu* (Asahi Shinsho, 2011).
3 Following the 2011 Fukushima Daiichi accident, none of these units is operational (as of February 2014).
4 Takeo Kikkawa, *Nihon denryokugyō hatten no dainamizumu* [Dynamism of Development in the Japanese Electric Power Industry] (Nagoya: Nagoya Daigaku Shuppankai, 2004).
5 Hitoshi Yoshioka, *Genshiryoku no shakaishi* [Social History of Nuclear Energy] (Tokyo: Asahi Shimbun Shuppan, 2011).
6 The Independent Investigation Commission on the Fukushima Nuclear Accident, *The Fukushima Daiichi Nuclear Power Station Disaster: Investigating the Myth and Reality*, (London: Routledge, 2014), pp. 50–62.
7 Ibid.
8 Ibid., pp. ix–x.
9 http://www.minpo.jp/pub/topics/jishin2011/2014/02/post_9275.html.
10 The Independent Investigation Commission on the Fukushima Nuclear Accident, *The Fukushima Daiichi Nuclear Power Station Disaster: Investigating the Myth and Reality*, (London: Routledge, 2014).

11 National Diet of Japan Fukushima Nuclear Accident Independent Investigation Commission, *Kokkaijikocho Houkokusho* (Tokuma Shoten, 2012), http://naiic.tempdo mainname.com/pdf/naiic_honpen.pdf.
12 http://sankei.jp.msn.com/affairs/news/120604/dst12060411340002-n1.htm. The original "Collection of guidelines for safety inspections of Nuclear Safety Commissions" is published by Taisei Pub. Co. in 1978, rev. ed. 1988.
13 http://sankei.jp.msn.com/affairs/news/120604/dst12060411340002-n1.htm
14 NHK Special "Safety Myth," "Road to the Nuclear Accidents: Neglected Cautious Views" (22:00–23:00, Sept. 18, 2011, Koichi Kitazawa, *J. Nuclear Soc. Japan*, March, 2014).
15 For a historical look at these issues, see Martin Dusinberre, *Hard Times in the Hometown: A History of Community Survival in Modern Japan* (Honolulu: University of Hawaii Press, 2012), especially chapters 10 and 11.
16 http://www.nsr.go.jp/english/e_nra/idea.html
17 The Ministry of Education, Culture, Sports, Science & Technology in Japan.
18 Backfit is defined as "the retroactive modification of or addition to systems, structures, components, or design of a plant or a facility to comply with the new manufacturing license requirements, under updated guidelines." The National Diet of Japan Fukushima Nuclear Accident Independent Investigation Commission, http://warp.ndl.go.jp/info:ndljp/pid/3856371/naiic.go.jp/wp-content/uploads/2012/08/NAIIC_Eng_Appx1_web.pdf.

8 The last two decades in Japanese politics

Lost opportunities and undesirable outcomes

Machidori Satoshi

Introduction

Japan's social and economic stagnation during the past twenty years is frequently blamed on problems in its political system, which has also been heavily criticized for its inadequacy in the face of the 2008 Lehman shock and the subsequent international economic crisis. During this period, decision making was severely delayed by gridlock in a divided Diet and the upheavals created by a succession of short-lived governments. Seen from the longer perspective, Japanese politics has often been viewed as failing to respond to broader changes both in the global political economy and Japan's domestic developments, in particular demographic changes such as declining birthrates and an ageing population. Each successive government championed policies, but these frequently lacked consistency and produced poor results.

Nevertheless, this does not mean that Japanese politics remained static during these two decades. From the first half of the 1990s through the early 2000s, reforms in the political system took place on a scale comparable to those of the Meiji era of modern state building and the period of postwar reconstruction. These late-twentieth-century reforms covered the Lower House electoral system, the cabinet and administrative bureaucratic systems, the relationship between central and local governments, and interlocal government relations. If we include the changes to the judicial system and special public-sector corporations, it would appear that almost all of Japan's public sector came in for reform. Furthermore, relationships between "decision-making domains" – for instance, between central and local governments, and the public and private sectors – also shifted considerably.[1] These widespread reforms reflected a recognition that politics had to adapt to the drastic changes taking place in the international environment and indeed in the domestic socioeconomic context that had supported Japan during its high-growth to stable-growth period. Politics changed. However, the changes did not produce the desired results.

The question to ask of Japanese politics in the lost decades, therefore, should not be why reforms were not implemented, but rather why the reforms were not properly achieved and what sort of mistakes or deficiencies these unsuccessful reforms reveal. The essential feature of Japanese politics during the lost decades was an energetic engagement with various challenges, but a broader failure to achieve adequate results. Those people who pressed for reform and implemented the changes arguably possessed an accurate understanding of the problems at the time. The measures they pursued were rational and appropriate to the perceived problems. Yet these reforms effectively failed. Why? What were the critical moments, the junctures, that determined the progress of the reforms? This chapter seeks to explore these questions.

The argument for reform

Two lines of thought fed the momentum for political reforms seen in the first half of the 1990s.[2] The first was a growing critical awareness of political corruption, as well as the pressures on politicians to seek large amounts of political funds generating such corruption. The combination of the 1988 Recruit scandal and the concomitant introduction of the consumption tax exposed the ruling Liberal Democratic Party (LDP) to severe criticism. The public perceived the Recruit incident as just the tip of the iceberg of political corruption. At the same time, the negative effects of the bubble economy, such as skyrocketing land prices, were also causing increasing economic hardship. The mounting dissatisfaction brought about the LDP's crushing defeat in the July 1989 Upper House elections and the loss of its majority, which led to the resignation of both Prime Ministers Takeshita Noboru and Uno Sosuke. The LDP attempted to respond with a set of ideas for "political reforms," starting with the *Political Reform Guidelines*, published in May 1989 by the newly established Commission for Political Reform, which was headed by Gotoda Masaharu and other young LDP Diet members such as Takemura Masayoshi. The *Political Reform Guidelines* focused on anticorruption measures and blamed many of the LDP-related problems – such as excessive political campaign financing and factionalism – on the multimember district (MMD) electoral system used to elect members of the Lower House. These reformers therefore advocated a radical shift to an electoral system based on a single-member district (SMD) system.

The second line of thought was a growing recognition that Japanese politics as it stood was incapable of responding to changes in the foreign and domestic environments. The prospectus of the Forum on Political Reform – established in October 1989 by the Social and Economic Congress of Japan – indicated that

> the diffusion of advanced information technologies (IT) and revived international friction demand an overhaul of Japan's traditional political, economic and social structures, as demonstrated by administrative, fiscal, and other reforms. [. . .] Since Japan's parliamentary system inadequately meets citizens' needs, the entire postwar political structure, which includes the parliament, the political parties, the electoral system, the issue of political financing, and central-local relations [also needs to be renovated]. Radical reforms to meet the challenges of the twenty-first century are a national priority.

The Forum on Political Reform was an organization that later led to the establishment of the Ad Hoc Committee on Administrative Reform and also the Congressional Forum for a New Japan. The core members of such organizations formed in the first half of the 1990s consisted of businessmen such as Inaba Hidezo (former head of the *Sankei Newspaper*) and Kamei Masao (former head of Sumitomo Electric), as well as journalists and academics such as Uchida Kenzo (professor at Hosei University and former editor-in-chief of *Kyodo News*) and Sasaki Takeshi (professor at Tokyo University).

The single most important issue that forged the reformers' perception of the need for political reform was Japan-U.S. economic friction during the 1980s. In this friction, the Japanese side, comprised of LDP members and bureaucrats from ministries and agencies, had proved itself utterly incapable of dealing with single-issue trade disputes, including car exports and orange and beef imports. Due to this inability, Japan depended heavily on U.S. pressure to advance various Japanese domestic issues – these included coordination of domestic interests for internal reform. To the reformers, such dependence on foreign pressure to catalyze internal change demonstrated the limits of postwar Japanese politics even more than political corruption.[3]

Behind these frustrations also lay a sense of despair with the Japanese Socialist Party (JSP), which had entrenched itself as the perennial party in opposition and grown complacent. The JSP usually secured about 20 percent of the Diet seats due to guaranteed support from labor unions and other groups, while offering an ideological and unrealistic foreign and security policy based on arguments against the constitutionality of the Self-Defense Forces and against the Japan-U.S. Security Treaty. The reformers believed that Japanese politics should generate interparty competition over specific policy issues; this would lead to greater adaptability in policy according to changes in the global and domestic environment. Such adaptation was made impossible by the prescribed dynamics between ruling and opposition parties, which were also related to the formation of collusive relationships among key political actors. As noted by Michael Green and Igata Akira in Chapter 9, following the 1991 Gulf War these views about the need for reform were shared by leading LDP politicians and key persons such as Ozawa Ichiro.

Joining these reformers was Hosokawa Morihiro who, as head of a subcommittee for the Council for Administrative Reform and governor of Kumamoto Prefecture, viewed the state of Japanese politics critically from the vantage point of central-local government relations. In 1992, on establishing a new party named Japan New Party (JNP), Hosokawa published an essay entitled *Declaration of Forming an Alliance for a Liberal Society*.[4] Diet member Takemura Masayoshi, another leading proponent in the debate on anticorruption measures, was also a former local politician; he had been governor of Shiga Prefecture. Due to these voices from local politics, decentralization reforms – which sought to reduce the excessive interference of central government bureaucrats in local governments – came to be seen as a critical factor in altering the status quo. As a result, reforms of national-level party politics, reforms of the bureaucratic administrative structure, and decentralization reforms came to be advocated as a single package during the early 1990s.

Overlooked issues

With the benefit of hindsight, it is clear that two issues were overlooked during the early period of reform.

The first concerned Japan's foreign policy strategy. As Akiyama Nobu-masa makes clear in Chapter 14, Japanese diplomacy rested on three pillars: cooperation with the United States, so-called UN-centrism (keeping to a UN-centered diplomacy), and an emphasis on Asia. The start of the twenty-first century saw a number of converging trends: dysfunction within the UN Security Council due to a strengthened U.S. unilateralism; the revival of Russia and the rise of China; and, as detailed by Togo Kazuhiko in Chapter 13, growing anti-Japanese nationalism in China and South Korea, which in turn spurred Japanese nationalism. The question of how to link the three strategic pillars of Japan's diplomacy – in other words, how to maintain a balance between cooperation with the United States, UN-centrism, and an emphasis on Asia – posed a fundamental point of contention for Japan's foreign and security policy strategy, as it does to this day.

At the beginning of the 1990s, Japanese policymakers and intellectuals assumed that Japan's goals of cooperating with the United States and keeping to a UN-centered diplomacy would get gradually easier due to the end of the Cold War. The Gulf War bolstered this perception. South Korea's democratization and the progress of China's reform were seen as a chance for Japan to gain further potential partner states in East Asia. Few predicted increased antago-nism arising in these states toward Japan. Due to the prolonged and sterile LDP-JSP confrontation over foreign and security policy in the postwar period, there was a strong preference that Japanese foreign policy should be based on a supra-party consensus. This meant that the question of how to connect the three strategic diplomatic pillars, or goals, to promote national interests remained above party competition and undifferentiated ideologically. In short, competing and differentiated foreign policy options ultimately did not emerge during this period.

The second political issue that was overlooked during the early reform period concerns demographics: the problem of declining birth rates and an ageing population. As explained by Seike Atsushi in Chapter 1, predictions of Japan's dramatic demographic decline and growing numbers of elderly people were already evident in the 1970s and incontestable in the 1980s. However, post-1945 Japanese governments have long viewed direct involvement in pro-natalist policies as taboo, and images of overcrowded cities and classrooms during the rapid economic growth period diluted any sense of urgency. The ageing population problem was conceived of at the political level as a com-paratively narrow policy issue, mostly concerning matters such as health care expenses for the elderly. Apart from demographic specialists and a small num-ber Ministry of Health, Labor and Welfare bureaucrats, very few people held the view that both the low birthrate and ageing society issues represented a national problem.

Majoritarianism as a key idea: Opting for the single-member district system

Many of those advocating political reform criticized the multimember district (MMD) electoral system and sought to introduce single-member districts (SMDs), which they believed were conducive to creating a competitive two-party system and fairly regular alternations of parties in power.

The lack of alternating parties in power has often been blamed for the stagnation and corruption of Japanese politics during the postwar period. Under the MMD system, between two to six representatives are elected from one electoral district. A candidate generally needs only between 15 to 20 percent of the total votes to get elected, thereby allowing socioeconomic minorities to be more easily represented. At the same time, the MMD system resembles a proportional representation (PR) system since shifts in the electoral strengths of parties are relatively small over elections. Generally speaking, proportional electoral systems generate coalition parties. Japan's system after the war, however, took the shape of a permanent two-party coalition government in 1955 when two major parties – the Liberal Party and the Democratic Party – established a unified party, the LDP, out of a conservative merger. This allowed the LDP to continue its one-party government rule, while the other remaining major party, the JSP, was permanently excluded from power.

This political stability generated by the LDP's predominance provided a firm bedrock for rapid economic growth, but it also produced a number of downsides. These include the entrenchment of relations between the ruling and opposition parties, the formation of factions within the LDP, a clientelistic and particularistic allocation of benefits, and the diminishing of the opposition party's ambitions to come to power and in particular to hone its policymaking capabilities. The particular allocation of benefits based on clientelism resulted in the formation of relationships that exchanged political support for political redistribution of goods between the LDP and its member politicians with various industries and interest groups. The transaction channels between patron and client stabilized due to frequent bureaucratic regulatory involvement. Over time, however, these exchanges led to excessively intimate and collusive relationships among politicians, bureaucrats, and interest groups. The agricultural, construction, and retail and transport sectors were particularly prone to this behavior, resulting in heavy regulations and high costs relative to productivity. Rather than foster government-led economic growth, the essence of Japan's "government-private sector cooperation," or "Japan, Inc." – widely used labels in the 1970s and 1980s – was the protection of inefficient sectors and industries left behind by economic growth. This protectionism in turn made reform of such industries and sectors difficult.

As a prescription for such inefficiencies, reformers argued for a party system that would allow for alternations in power. They believed parties should compete, not internally through factional infighting, but against each other through differentiated policy programs. From the electorate's viewpoint, votes could then be cast for parties based on national policy programs, rather than for the qualities of a particular candidate or the kind of services the candidate had provided to individual districts or specific industries. Britain's two-party system was considered a model. As a response to the problems of Japanese politics in the postwar period, the proposal to introduce SMDs appeared as a rational choice that went beyond a simple utopian view of British politics or two-party systems.

The shift toward majoritarian democracy

The decision to reform the Lower House's electoral system to one centered on SMDs was not only to determine whether Japan would have a two-party or multiparty system, interparty competition or intraparty competition, and votes cast based on candidate quality or party programs. In fact, as comparative political scientist Arend Lijphart notes, the shift to SMDs was of crucial significance since this particular electoral system plays a central role in "majoritarian democracies."[5]

Majoritarian democracies are characterized by the concentration of power in a single party, which has been given a mandate from the majority of voters and implements policy regardless of minority opposition. Japanese politics, in contrast to these majoritarian polities, had always emphasized consensus building and a mutually conciliatory attitude among multiple actors engaged in public policy making. The significance of choosing a majoritarian system was that it would weaken this type of policy making.

For instance, it was considered standard procedure to consult the opinions of interested parties – such as those in the economic and labor circles, relevant business sectors, and local governments – when drafting and deciding macroeconomic and microindustrial policies in Japan. The intimate cooperation between the government and industrial circles through the Ministry of International Trade and Industry (MITI) is a classic example, as we see in Kobayashi Keiichiro's Chapter 3 and research from Daniel Okimoto and Richard Samuels.[6] Similar consensus-based policy formation was achieved through personnel exchanges and other measures between central and local governments. Although this has been criticized as excessive centralization and oversight of local governments, it also encouraged local governments' active participation in policy formation through subsidies and local grants.[7] Administrative guidance by the central government over local authorities and the industrial sector rested upon an ambiguous legal mandate and often came under criticism. However, there were many instances in which local governments were granted a de facto veto without any formal legislative basis, such as in cases when local approval was informally required for the construction and operation of nuclear reactors.

This system thus carried with it both positive and negative effects. On the one hand, the decision-making process from drafting to implementation tended to proceed smoothly. On the other hand, political actors able to participate in this system of consensus building and mutual conciliation often formed collusive relations, excluding others.[8] From the vantage point of society as a whole, each business and local authority qualified as a minority group. For this reason it was no surprise that as Japanese politics leaned more toward majoritarian attitudes, the typical decision-making process involving intimate collaboration among business, central, and local governments came under attack.

Majoritarian democracies in Lijphart's model, characterized by the concentration of power in the central government, tend to weaken the independence of institutions such as the central bank, the judiciary, and local governments. Over the course of Japan's post-1990s political reforms, however, reformers believed that the independence of these external institutions had to be strengthened precisely because of a shift to majoritarianism.[9] For that reason, decentralization reforms, judiciary reforms, and revision of the Bank of Japan Law reinforced the autonomy of these institutions in tandem with a shift to majoritarianism. The reduction of government interference in society was also pursued through measures such as private sector deregulation and regulatory relaxation. Freedom of choice in education was expanded through the abolition of educational districts and the introduction of a public school choice system, for instance.

As evident from the analyses presented in several of this book's chapters, a major feature of the years after the 1990s has seen in Japan the parallel development of concentrating power within the central government while reducing government intervention into other decision-making domains (the separation of the domains of public and private life, government and business sectors, central and local governments, etc.). These reforms were based on the perception and experiences of the immediate challenges that Japan faced in the latter half of the 1980s, rather than on any firm theoretical foundation about their appropriateness. This particular package of reforms, which combine majoritarian reforms within the central government and the granting of greater autonomy to other domains beyond the central government, will be referred to as "Japanese-style majoritarianism" in the rest of this chapter.[10]

Specific reforms

The various reforms enacted in the context of Japanese-style majoritarianism have been analyzed in depth in other individual chapters in this book, as well as in a large body of existing literature. I will provide a brief sketch of three major reforms highly significant for the evolution of Japanese politics.

The first set of reforms involved the Lower House's electoral system. After the 1993 LDP split and subsequent change in administration in 1994, a mixed electoral system combining single-member districts and proportional representation blocs was adopted under the Hosokawa administration. Since the ratio of Diet seats assigned through single-member districts was high, these electoral rules were believed to bring about the effect of something closer to a purely SMD system. Yet these electoral rules did not mean that the smaller parties disappeared since it was still possible to secure Diet seats in the PR tier.

The second set of reforms involved administrative reforms centering on strengthening the functions of the cabinet (and Prime Minister's office). The Hashimoto Ryutaro administration began in 1996 and implemented administrative reforms in 1998, such as the Basic Law of the Administrative Reform of the

Central Government. Among these so-called Hashimoto Reforms, the strengthening of cabinet functions was a central element. The Council on Administrative Reforms's final report called for the formation of "a twenty-first century administrative system suitable for the formation of an equal and free society." Concrete measures to achieve this goal consisted of "securing strategic and integrated policy formation," "emphasis on agility," "securing transparency," and "the pursuit of efficiency and simplicity." To secure strategic and integrated policy planning and drafting, "a radical overhaul of the prime minister's office and cabinet" was deemed necessary. The goal of these measures to strengthen cabinet functions was to create "a cabinet-driven, especially prime minister–driven, management of national affairs." To this end, the new law established a Minister of State for Special Missions, expanded the Cabinet Secretariat and Cabinet Office's functions, and set up advisory bodies involved in macrolevel policy planning such as the Council on Economic and Fiscal Policy and the Council for Science and Technology Policy. Finally, a new and physically enlarged prime minister official residence and building was constructed to back up these strengthened cabinet functions.[11]

The third set of reforms involved decentralization.[12] In 1993 the Diet passed a Resolution on Decentralization Promotion, and in 1995 it passed the Decentralization Promotion Law. Various conflicts emerged over how to implement reforms, but the decentralization law passed in 1999, largely reflecting recommendations of a committee on decentralization that had been established in accordance with the law to promote decentralization. These reforms weakened the central government's control and intervention over local authorities, through measures such as the abolition of a system of agency-delegated functions and the transfer of administrative powers to local governments. Moreover, in 2005 the Koizumi administration enacted fiscal decentralization, which included the transfer of tax revenue sources to local governments. During this period a substantial number of municipalities merged, reflecting the pressures to reorganize small- and medium-sized municipalities that were seen as fiscally and administratively insufficient in capacity. In total, the number of municipalities in Japan decreased from 3,234 in April 1995 to 1,719 by January 2013.

Changes that resulted from the reforms: the apex

The impact of these reforms – particularly the centralization of powers within the central government through administrative and electoral reforms – became apparent during the Koizumi administration.[13] Koizumi Junichiro ran for the LDP leadership elections campaigning on the slogan of "Destroy the LDP" and won by securing the overwhelming support of local LDP party branches in 2001. Having become the LDP president and prime minister without relying on the support of intraparty factions and powerful LDP Diet members, Koizumi overturned the LDP's traditional bottom-up policy-making process originating in the Policy Affairs Research Councils (PARC) and predicated on interfactional cooperation. Koizumi pushed for top-down decision making coming out of the prime minister's office. Given authority over personnel decisions, Koizumi dismissed bureaucrats opposing his policy goals and actively exercised his prerogatives over LDP candidate nominations to punish Diet members who failed to toe the party line. The struggle over the passage of the postal privatization bill and consequent dissolution of the Lower House, called by Koizumi in 2005, was an illustration of the centralization of powers in the prime minister.

In terms of policy, two distinctive features emerged under Koizumi. The first was an emphasis on economic structural reforms. Such emphasis reflected a shift from a traditional particularism, which was focused on micropolicy, to a universalism, which was focused on macropolicy. "Particularism" in this context refers to policy making as a quid pro quo exchange based on the level of electoral support and mobilization for the LDP. Particularist policy making, whether pro-business or pro-labor/pro-minority, was determined by the nature of partisan support from, and particular conditions of, specific industries and interest groups. In contrast, universalism refers to the formulation of policies that target a wider range of individuals and groups and that tend to emphasize broader long-term policy goals for Japan, usually those concerning macroeconomic and fiscal conditions. Such universalist policy making, as the word implies, does not differentiate between the circumstances or partisan attitudes of specific industries or interest groups.

The Council on Economic and Fiscal Policy, established in 2000 under Minister Takenaka Heizo, played an especially large role in this shift in policy focus. Takenaka's post as the Minister for State and Fiscal Policy, one of the Ministers of State for Special Missions, was established as part of the Hashimoto Reforms measures to strengthen cabinet functions. While managing the policy council, Takenaka also appointed economists sympathetic to his ideas, such as Ota Hiroko, and reform-minded bureaucrats, such as Kishi Hiroyuki, to the cabinet and assigned them fiscal and financial policy responsibilities. These steps reflected the decline in influence of so-called policy tribe LDP Diet members who emphasized benefit-allocation policies and the preservation of the business status quo through close coordination between interest groups and the central ministries. As Japan's fiscal deficit worsened, public works spending – the glue, along with regulatory policy, that had melded together the LDP, the bureaucracy, and the business world – was cut drastically.

The second distinctive policy trait under the Koizumi administration was an unmistakable commitment to the U.S. alliance in foreign policy. Following the September 11, 2001, terrorist attacks and the War on Terror that followed, Koizumi consistently supported the George W. Bush administration's stance on the Iraq War. It seems that Koizumi's aim was to minimize the energy that needed to be invested in diplomacy by relying on the alliance with the United States so that he could concentrate on internal reforms focused on macroeconomic management. At the same time, Koizumi paid visits to the Yasukuni Shrine, presumably to demonstrate decisive leadership and also out of consideration to a certain portion of his domestic support base. His visits, as Togo Kazuhiko makes clear in Chapter 13, had a harmful effect on relations with China and South Korea.

A two-party system, but only partially emerged

Electoral system reforms also strongly reshaped Japan's party system.

Most prominent among the changes was the emergence of a two-party system resulting from the amalgamation of non-LDP opposition parties. In 1994, the New Frontier Party (NFP) was established through the merger of parties that had formed the core of the Hosokawa administration's coalition government. Following the dissolution of the NFP, the Democratic Party of Japan (DPJ) emerged as the second largest party. By the general election of 2000, there was two-party competition between the DPJ and the LDP. Both the NFP and the DPJ, especially in their early stages, sought to differentiate their economic policies from those of the LDP. In the meantime, the Japanese Communist Party (JCP) and Social Democratic Party (SDP; a successor to the JSP) continued to stress ideological differences vis-à-vis the LDP on foreign and security policy and saw their Diet seats dwindle. The Komeito party, too, only managed to maintain its seats through electoral cooperation and coalition with the LDP. The eventual alternation in power between the LDP and DPJ in 2009 and 2012 was a consequence of this shift toward a two-party system.

The electoral reforms, however, continued to permit not only the survival of smaller parties but also the formation of "microparties" (usually a handful of Diet members left after the breakup of larger opposition parties). The existence of these smaller parties stemmed from several features of the new electoral system: more than one-third of the Diet members are elected through PR, many of the Upper House seats are allocated through MMD and PR tiers, and no electoral threshold exists. As demonstrated by the performance of the Japan Restoration Party during the 2012 general elections, the PR system enables the emergence of additional, "third parties." The plethora of smaller parties also affected – amplified – the swing between the two major parties in elections. In addition, as the electoral system for local assemblies remained untouched, local party politics transformed into a two-party system only loosely.[14]

Although inclining toward a majoritarian system, Japan adopted a mixed electoral system for the Lower House to soften the impact of the electoral reforms and did not make changes to the electoral systems of the Upper House and local assemblies. This meant that Japan's shift toward a two-party system was incomplete. The DPJ's performance in the 2009 elections was indicative of this problem: the DPJ occupied more than 60 percent of the Lower House seats but did not have a majority of the Upper House and held less than 20 percent of seats in local assemblies, thus providing a weak foundation for the ruling party.

An incomplete transformation of the internal party organization

The ability of the LDP to avoid splintering over the long term under the old electoral system, despite the base that this system supposedly provided for multiparty dynamics, allowed the LDP to stay in power for many decades as a single-party government. This also came with the price, however, of weak leadership – a leader who was dependent on the support of other leaders of rank-and-file LDP Diet members. The leader was both president of the LDP and prime minister of the government.

Until the 1980s, the internal management of the LDP was based on the principle of bottom-up decision making, emphasizing the particularistic interests of rank-and-file Diet members' local constituencies and support groups. From the high-growth to stable-growth period, tax revenues steadily increased, public finances were relatively in order, and the demographic portion of young people was still large. For these reasons, much of the government's financial resources were spent on policy programs directly linked to the vote-gathering activity of LDP Diet members, including policies for regional development and the protection of weak industries. The compatibility of these spending programs with nationwide equity or macroeconomic fiscal policy was seemingly of secondary importance. These microeconomic and clientelistic policies based on the allocation of benefits were justified as a kind of redistribution policy since they ameliorated the drastic changes brought by economic growth, such as rural depopulation or the rapid decline of some sectors like the coal and textile industries.[15]

The reform of the Lower House electoral system, together with an awareness that the international environment and domestic context had changed, was expected to greatly alter the internal organization of the main parties, starting with the LDP. Indeed, as demonstrated by Koizumi's refusal to accept recommendations from internal factions when forming his cabinet, the influence of intra-LDP factions manifestly diminished after the reforms. On the policy side, too, Koizumi pushed for regulatory reform and cuts in public spending works that weakened the tendency toward clientelistic spending that had generated collusion and redistribution of benefits to favored industries.[16] These policy shifts, such as the privatization of the Japan Postal System and Highway Public Corporation, were undertaken by the prime minister's office and reflected the views of Koizumi and LDP executives instead of the interests of rank-and-file LDP Diet members.

However, changes in the parties' internal organization remain incomplete. While the party executive has secured predominance over rank-and-file members, there is no clear structure in which the party leader can secure support from others within the party executive. Members of the party executive – such as the party president, secretary general, and the deputy president – are roughly at the same career stage. This has meant that party leaders have not always commanded the full support of other executives, which in turn has meant weakness. This struggle for power has been seen in the DPJ, which has been divided by never-ending quarrels, and in the LDP, with the exception of when it was under Koizumi. The cabinet of the first Abe administration, which was filled with Abe's close personal friends who were seen as lacking the qualifications for their positions (and was mockingly referred to in the media as the "cabinet of Abe's friends") and which frequently resisted Abe, was an example of this kind of weakness.

Whenever differences have emerged within the party executive, it has been difficult to make sure that universalistic policies are chosen over particularistic ones. The reason for this is that when powerful ruling party members seek to challenge the party leader, they do so by increasing rank-and-file members loyal to themselves through the redistribution of clientelistic benefits. Such rebellious behavior is encouraged by the fact that the party leadership is often held responsible not only when the party suffers electoral losses in Lower House elections, but also for losses in Upper House and local elections. In other words, unless the party executive continues to win successive elections (of differing electoral rules and institutional purposes), it has trouble preventing the rise of antiexecutive factions or the particularistic politics of redistribution. The recurring outcome of this dynamic is short-lived governments and deteriorating public finances.[17]

An upper house still in need of reform

The stability of the long-lived Koizumi administration rested upon an unexpected piece of good fortune, little appreciated at the time: a continuous majority formed by the ruling parties (LDP and Komeito) in the Upper House.

Japan's Upper House cannot be dissolved. Half of its seats are up for election every three years and the ratio of Upper House representatives elected from MMDs (two or more representatives elected per electoral district) and PR districts is high. This results in a distribution of seats that is relatively stable across parties over elections. Moreover, due to severe malapportionment, rural districts are overrepresented. These features mean there is no guarantee whatsoever that the composition of the Upper House will be consistent (congruent) with that of the Lower House. The LDP lost its majority in the Upper House in 1989 and has since formed coalitions with other parties to keep a majority in both chambers. From 2000 onward, the Komeito was the LDP's coalition partner. Because the two parties controlled a majority in the Upper House, no decisive constraint on the government was offered by the second chamber.

If the goal of the reformers was the amalgamation of central government power based on majoritarianism, this bicameral system that provided excessive veto power to the Upper House should also have come in for reform. At the time, however, reformers – even experts on the outside – did not believe that the Upper House would generate a decisively negative influence on Japanese politics. It is also possible that those involved had run out of steam, having expended efforts in reforming the Lower House electoral system. Despite Japan being a parliamentary system (combining executive and legislative powers), there was also a deeply rooted normative predilection toward the separation of powers and a belief that the cabinet should not engage in reforming the Diet. The 1990s had in fact offered the perfect opportunity for comprehensive Diet reform including that of the Upper House, but the issue was left unconsidered and untouched.

Ironically, the Koizumi administration's very success led to the loss of opportunity for Diet reform. In 2005 the Postal Privatization Bill was rejected by part of the ruling party in the Upper House. Koizumi responded by dissolving the Lower House and calling for general elections. On that occasion it might have been possible for Koizumi to dissolve the Lower House while calling attention to the problems of the bicameral system and the Upper House. The prime minister, as to be expected, used his powers to implement his policy program. It would have been irrational for Koizumi to advocate Diet reforms during an election campaign that was called in direct response to the rejection of a specific law on postal privatization. Moreover, there was a broad consensus that central government reforms had basically been completed following electoral, administrative, and judiciary reforms (starting in 2004). What Koizumi needed to do was to reflect these institutional changes in actual policy making. The normative view of checks and balances, which meant that Diet reforms should be undertaken by the Diet itself, remained in place. Although Diet reform may have theoretically been possible under the Koizumi administration, it was very unlikely.

That two crucial opportunities to reform the Diet that were missed – in the first half of the 1990s and first half of the 2000s – proved decisively damaging for Japanese politics thereafter. In the 2007 Upper House elections, the LDP was unable to secure a majority of seats, even in coalition with the Komeito, leading to a gridlocked Diet. As two-party competition had been established in the Lower House, there were hardly any opposition parties willing to cooperate with the ruling party in the Upper House. The result was a government that kept stumbling into a deadlock on trivial matters. The change in government in 2009 to the DPJ hardly improved this condition, which became the major cause of a succession of subsequent short-lived governments, each with a lifespan of roughly one year. With the exception of Aso Taro and Noda Yoshihiko, all prime ministers between 2006 and 2012 (six in total) resigned for reasons other than defeat in general elections. In fact, these resignations stemmed largely from their inability to secure a majority in the Upper House. In a system where power is centralized in the national-level government, it is normal for the prime minister to take responsibility for political stagnation. In Japan, however, the Upper House maintains the ability to constrain the concentrated powers of the government as a whole. This issue remains one of the largest impediments in Japanese politics.[18]

Increased veto power of local governments

The single most distinctive feature of Japanese-style majoritarianism is the attempt to centralize power within the central government, combined with attempts to separate the relationships between the central government and other key decision-making domains. Central-local government relations in particular underwent active decentralization in Japan's shift to majoritarianism, unlike in the orthodox model of majoritarianism in which power is taken away from local governments and shifted to the center. Despite the decentralization in Japan, many areas of local-central government relations were left untouched, including the local allocation tax grants system. Local government bonds also continue to face only minimum levels of market pressures.[19] As a result, the fiscal decentralization of local government remains incomplete.

This has resulted in two larger problems for Japanese politics. First, this incompleteness has put in place a serious moral hazard involving local governments. Decentralization reforms increased the administrative autonomy of local governments vis-à-vis the central government. And as a two-party system emerged at the national level of politics, decentralization reforms made it easier for different partisan forces to govern at the local and central levels. At the same time, since central-local fiscal relations were left untouched, the risks increased of politically autonomous local governments carrying out programs while depending on the central government's financial guarantees. Calls by the mayor of Nagoya to cut taxes exemplified the increased risks of such behavior. Policies to reduce this moral hazard were gradually undertaken, such as the enforcement in 2007 of the Assurance of Sound Financial Status of Local Governments Law. However, reform of the local debt system and local allocation of tax grants – at the heart of the fiscal integration of central and local governments – have not progressed.

Second, despite decentralization, the problem of the inadequate governance capacity of local governments remains. Local governments in Japan adopt a "dual representation system" (a type of presidential system) in which the local chief executive is elected separately from the legislature. For this reason, the local assembly's policy-planning and administrative oversight capacities are on the whole weak, and assembly members focus on the goal of securing a portion of the budget for their own electoral base. Consequently, local assemblies either tend to rubber-stamp budgets based on the political preferences of the governor (or mayor) or criticize the executive without providing any constructive alternatives. Local policy areas where voter interests are high and the chief executive is actively engaged, such as education, end up being used as a means to secure short-term political support. These methods threaten chances for the kind of long-term policy development and specific planning that local governance requires. When local government expenditures comprise 60 percent of total government expenditures, it is highly likely that these sorts of local governance problems will cause severe headaches in the future.

Undesired yet explainable outcomes

Basic features of the past two decades

When looking back over the past twenty years of Japanese politics, two major features stand out. First, the reforms spanned an extremely broad range of areas. It is no exaggeration to say that Japanese politics pushed forward on a remarkable number of reforms including, among other things, the administrative system, the Lower House electoral rules, and political/administrative decentralization. However, some areas were left completely untouched, such as Diet reform. If one was going to concentrate power in the ruling party and prime minister's hands, it was also necessary either to dilute the Upper House's power or to develop conditions to ensure the same majorities in the two chambers. Similarly, the local fiscal and tax system was left intact. Since the central government is unable to control local government activity in detail, the financial guarantee given to local governments – whose autonomy had increased through a system of local grants and local bonds facing weak market pressures – constituted a source of moral hazard.

Second, the reforms throughout this period were undergirded by an idea. This idea involved combining the centralization of power while also separating ties between the central government and external domains (economic, social, or local institutions). I have labeled this package of reforms as Japanese-style majoritarianism. Although Japanese-style majoritarianism is similar to the orthodox model of majoritarianism in terms of concentrating power in the central government's hands, Japanese-style majoritarianism is different in that it reduces the links between the central government and external institutions. Leaving aside the validity of Japanese-style majoritarianism, the reforms were based on this manifest political and social vision, what could be called a clear "grand design" for Japan. Moreover, certain individuals continued to promote and make an effort to implement this grand design. In this sense, the view that Japanese politics did not have the ability within itself to reform is both inappropriate and superficial.

Desired changes

What changes, both in terms of the political process and policy outputs, were hoped for from the series of political reforms that had begun with the reform of the Lower House electoral system? Let me draw together the arguments that I have made so far.

First, the streamlining of decision making was advocated in terms of political processes. During the latter half of the 1980s a number of LDP politicians, bureaucrats, and business managers experienced first-hand Japan's dependence on foreign pressure to tackle domestic socioeconomic structural reforms. They also experienced Japan's unsatisfactory response – deemed "too little, too late" – to the First Gulf War in the early 1990s (as Michael Green and Igata Akira explain in Chapter 9). There also existed, at least in some parts of the mass media and academia, a kind of modernist perception that these problems stemmed from insufficiently independent individuals.[20]

In Chapter 6, Kariya Takehiko discusses the foundational vision for education reform as an attempt to foster children's "individuality" and "zest for life," ideas which exemplify this modernist worldview. Similar attitudes are also traceable behind political, economic, and social reforms. In other words, the reformers believed that more autonomous individuals or institutions would be able to undertake, collectively, a more rapid decision-making process. This in turn would enable Japan to avoid the kind of paralysis it suffered during Japan-U.S. economic disputes and during the Gulf War. As a result, reformers sought to separate the various domains of decision making while simultaneously seeking to centralize power within each area. Until the 1980s, the basic feature of Japanese politics was the maintenance of a harmonious decision-making process from policy drafting to decision, premised on a view that most issues were relatively clear and had precedents. The "harmony" that was achieved came about because of the creation of tacit cooperative relations among numerous policy actors who became policy insiders, while the separation of various domains (politics and bureaucracy, government and private sector, local and central governments) remained ambiguous.

By breaking this harmonious decision-making process, there were hopes that Japan would be able to better deal with unknown or unprecedented challenges, even those in foreign countries. There was also the hope that Japan would be able to engage in socioeconomic reforms that combated vested interests.

Specifically, this meant a shift from a particularistic allocation of benefits based on a microfocus, to the equalization of universalistic benefits and responsibilities based on a macrofocus. In terms of foreign policy, this implied a shift from dependency on U.S. protection based on Japan's unconditional support of the United States, to Japan becoming an autonomous and responsible player in the international world order. In this context, the reformers hoped that political groups would emerge which would be in favor of macrofocused economic policies domestically and be able to combine a more autonomous foreign policy in coordination with the United States. The reformers also particularly hoped for the establishment of clear-cut policy competition between two major parties.

At the same time, these changes would mean the increased likelihood of conflict and friction among the various decision-making domains, which were now acting more independently of central government intervention. To confront this problem, policymakers adopted countermeasures, such as reform in the judicial system and an increase in the number of lawyers, the establishment of a Committee for Settling National-Local Disputes to assist in decentralization reforms, and measures for increased government transparency through, for instance, the Administrative Procedures Law and the Freedom of Information Law. However, the reformers basically saw the increased autonomy of these external institutions as a general panacea, without paying too much attention to the potential for conflict and friction. In practice, this meant, for instance, that the private sector parties such as shareholders were deemed basically responsible for dealing with problems that arose, although the central government sought to tighten regulations of basic market competition rules through the strengthening of the Anti-Monopoly Law. The argument could be made that the Japanese government's role had changed; it was no longer responsible for achieving national goals such as economic growth and had become nothing more than a referee for various external domains such as the market. Following Chalmers Johnson's classic categorization, Japan had transformed from a "developmental state" to a "regulatory state."[21]

Reasons for the failure in outcomes

As we have seen, Japanese politics earned rather less than "full marks" for its attempts at reform during the 1990s and early 2000s. There are at least three reasons that explain the failure to achieve the full extent of reform as was initially hoped.

First, as has been argued already, certain areas were left untouched. As a result, the effect of implemented reforms – despite the enormous amounts of time and energy expended on them – was severely curtailed. With regard to Diet reforms, it may have been possible to push for reforms to weaken the influence of the Upper House or minimize the gap between the electoral results of the two chambers.

Such reforms could have been promoted at several moments: in the first half of the 1990s, when the reform of the Lower House electoral system was undertaken; in 2005, when Koizumi dissolved the Diet and called for snap elections over postal privatization; or even immediately after the 2009 "regime change," when the DPJ held an overwhelming mandate. One could also argue that it should have been possible to further separate local and central government domains in the local fiscal and tax systems during the first half of the 2000s. Despite the existence of a grand design of Japanese-style majoritarianism, the entirety of the Japanese political system – including politicians, bureaucrats, and public intellectuals – clearly lacked the strength to translate and implement this vision into a concrete plan for reform.

Second, the soundness of the basic idea of Japanese-style majoritarianism needs to be questioned. In particular, it is open to dispute whether it was appropriate to seek to minimize central government intervention in various other external domains. Certainly, the distinctive trait of Japanese politics, economics, and society until the 1980s had been the almost inseparable coordination between these different domains (such as those between politics and bureaucracy, the public and private sector, and the central and the local governments). This feature made policy decisions inward looking, increased the time necessary for policy adjustments, and also led to the exclusion of various groups and individuals from participating in the decision-making process. The deeply felt urge to cut through these collusive relationships is understandable. However, insufficient intellectual consideration was given to the consequences of reducing central government intervention in institutions such as local governments and the central bank. The reformers also were not fully aware that they were including elements that differed from standard majoritarianism.

These two problems, layered upon each other, have resulted in Japan suffering from what can be called "plural immobility." Plural immobility refers to a situation in which multiple actors with decision-making powers undertake diverging policy decisions independently, resulting in a loss of policy direction as a whole. The source of this immobility stems from the fact that the links between the central government and external institutions and groups have been reduced, permitting each of these groups to pursue autonomous actions. In conjunction with certain areas that were left untouched by reform, a deepening pluralization within the political system rendered decision making difficult. This outcome was not desired but it was, arguably, predictable. The Koizumi administration appeared to be able to act successfully within this structure, but the policy immobility of subsequent administrations caused by the separation of the central government and other institutions triggered intense popular frustration.

The effects of such plural immobility can be observed in the Futenma military base relocation issue that Sheila Smith examines in Chapter 12, as well as the restarting of nuclear power plants after the Fukushima accident in 2011 that is partially dealt with in Kitazawa Koichi's work in Chapter 7. Here I will present a brief case study showing the relationship between the government and the Bank of Japan (BoJ) over antideflationary policies. Kuttner, Iwaisako, and Posen in

Chapter 2, and others in this book, have noted that overcoming deflation has been Japan's biggest policy issue over the past twenty years. Such a perception became particularly strong after 2000.

Internationally, monetary policy replaced fiscal policy as the central pillar of economic policy in many advanced countries, including the U.S. and the UK. Japan's case differed, however. Prompted by scandals in the Ministry of Finance (MoF), reforms in the latter half of the 1990s sought to increase the independence of the BoJ. These reforms were an important part of Japanese-style majoritarianism, which sought to reduce central government intervention in external institutions. Prior to the revision of the Bank of Japan Law, which brought greater autonomy to the BoJ, the MoF wielded great clout over the central bank. For instance, the Ministry fully coordinated with the bank over bond issuance in the financial markets, and many bank governors originally hailed from the Ministry.[22] The BoJ did not differ from other central banks, such as the German Federal Bank, in terms of being strongly concerned about the damage caused by inflation to the value of money. But once given greater autonomy, the BoJ increased the money supply and brought interest rates to near-zero or zero levels in the short term, while itching to revert to its traditional anti-inflation measures. The appointment of MoF bureaucrats to the post of chairman of the BoJ became taboo and the government could do little more than check the bank through public statements, failing ultimately to control its behavior.

As a result, the BoJ did not coordinate its measures with the government, fostering the perception that it was not as active as the government in pursuing anti-deflationary measures. This in turn fostered expectations that there would be no inflation in the near future. Such a trend increased after the DPJ came to power, since the party had looked critically on coordination between the MoF and BoJ and saw it as "MoF dominance," calling instead for the increased independence of the central bank.[23] From the bank's point of view, it was not ignoring deflation and had carried out adequate countermeasures against it, some of them showing positive results. However, the impression of poor communication between the government and the BoJ hurt expectations and reduced the effects of Japan's monetary policy. Moreover, it undoubtedly contributed to a broader negative evaluation of both the DPJ government and the BoJ.

The third reason that the reforms failed to meet expectations was the absence of clearly defined and competing policy programs among the parties, the existence of which would have made the effect of majoritarian reforms more tangible to voters.

As mentioned previously, Japanese politics had long been defined by an emphasis on particularistic and clientelistic distribution of benefits in the domestic realm and Japan's role as America's junior partner in the diplomatic realm.

A possible alternative platform to the old LDP would have combined a macro-focused domestic universalism with an autonomous diplomatic stance toward the United States. Since, as in many other advanced countries, Japanese voters tend to place the most importance on economic policies, it is unlikely that the main policy differentiation could form only around foreign and security policy. One of the reasons why the JSP was never able to threaten the LDP lies precisely in the fact that it sought to differentiate itself from the ruling party mainly on diplomatic and security affairs. In a shift to two-party competition under majoritarianism, it is obvious that competing platforms of microfocus versus macrofocus policies (particularistic versus universalist policies) would be increasingly important. Indeed, in the early years of party formation, both the New Frontier Party and the DPJ sought differentiation along these policy divides.

But the DPJ strayed from this course during the Koizumi administration. Koizumi treated those in the LDP who focused on microeconomic policies as "reactionary forces" and carried out a sharp turnaround in economic policies at the domestic level. At the same time, he made the choice to emphasize even more strongly Japan's alliance with the United States in foreign policy. The DPJ thus faced a thorny challenge when Koizumi co-opted the very universalistic policies that the DPJ had been earlier advocating. If the DPJ had stuck to a more universalistic stance, when the LDP revived particularistic policies in the first Abe administration of 2006, DPJ politicians could have chosen to praise the importance of Koizumi's domestic policies, and advocate, once again, universalistic policy alternatives. Within the same universalistic framework, the DPJ could have also criticized the Koizumi administration's economic policies for leaning excessively toward business interests. There was the option of advocating the preservation or even expansion of social security programs. In this context, the DPJ's criticism of widening "socioeconomic disparity" and the LDP's abandonment of socially disadvantaged groups might also have led to the establishment of more clearly defined policy differences.

However, under the leadership of Hatoyama Yukio and Ozawa Ichiro, the DPJ chose to campaign on the ambiguous slogan of "People's Life First," blending universalism and particularism with bureaucrat bashing. The DPJ also opted to differentiate itself from the LDP on diplomatic policy by promoting autonomy from the United States, such as in the Futenma military base relocation issue, as discussed by Sheila Smith in Chapter 12. Such a strategy – which lumped the former ruling party, bureaucrats, and the United States as responsible for Japan's failures – was nothing more than an expedient to gain short-term political support. The strategy certainly helped bring about the DPJ's 2009 electoral landslide. But there is no denying that once they held the reins of government, this attitude harmed the DPJ administration, which was unable to achieve most of its policy promises, triggering further voter disillusion.

Nevertheless, it is unfair to put the blame solely on the DPJ for the arrested development of policy in Japan. After all, there were many issues that were not sufficiently recognized during the reform process. As argued earlier, the impetus behind political reforms of the 1990s can be traced back to a perception that the Japanese political system had been inadequate in getting to grips with Japan-U.S. economic friction in the late 1980s and with the Gulf War.

Clearly insufficient attention had been paid to the predictions that Japan's society and economy would undergo drastic and rapid changes from the so-called golden age of the 1980s. Planning for future scenarios was limited: What would the consequences be of a full-scale entry of women into the labor market? How would the combination of an ageing society and a low-birth rate affect Japanese society and the economy? What sort of policy and decision-making mechanisms would suit these changing demographic conditions? Several agencies and ministries had valuable information and estimates pertaining to these individual domains, but the political system failed to link them together to create comprehensive policy drafts and reform proposals.[24]

In terms of foreign policy, those who advocated reform emphasized Japan's pursuit of an enlightened national interest under the "international liberal order." Japan could have pursued this challenging yet feasible foreign-policy option of maintaining an intimate relationship with its traditional ally, while not falling into a simple follow-the-U.S. policy. The 1970s German Social Democratic Party's "Ostpolitik" was an example of such a strategy. As both G. John Ikenberry in Chapter 15 and Akiyama Nobumasa in Chapter 14 suggest, there was room to combine cooperation with the United States, UN-centrism, and an emphasis on Asia. But the experiential stance of the political parties, and the assumption that the three pillars of Japanese diplomacy were basically immutable from the way they had been seen in the early 1990s, meant that the opportunity to rebalance those three pillars under the rapidly changing international politico-economic order was lost. The LDP's inclination toward cooperation with the United States tended to underplay relations with the UN and Asia. The DPJ's arguments for greater autonomy vis-à-vis Washington were based on a fundamental error of judgment concerning how to pursue Japan's own national interest. In the end, what ultimately emerged was a breeding ground for the growth of a myopic nationalism that made futile attacks on various forces that were seen as "constraining" Japan at specific points in time.

Conclusion

There are at least three key turning points in Japanese politics since the 1990s. The first turning point occurred in the first half of the 1990s when reforms were initiated and when Japanese-style majoritarianism was selected as an underlying idea of these reforms. The context of this choice was a perception that the old way of Japanese politics – a decision-making process led by the national government and its bureaucrats that had built up long-term and integrated relations with local governments and the private sector – could not adequately deal with international and domestic changes. With this in mind, the reformers pursued the concentration of power in the central government, which included strengthening the role of the prime minister, while at the same time reducing central government intervention in other external domains (local governments, the private sector, the central bank, the judiciary, etc.). The decision is understandable in view of the evident decline of the Japanese system in the 1980s. As concentration of power in the central government proceeded hand-in-hand with reduced intervention in external domains, actors in these external domains came to reject decisions taken by the center. Responsibility for the resulting stasis was then seen to lie with the prime minister and ruling party executives who were the decision makers in the central government.

The Koizumi administration, inaugurated in 2001, constituted the second turning point. This period saw the concentration of powers in the central government, stemming from the 1990s reform, being used effectively. Since the ruling parties controlled a majority in both chambers, they remained largely indifferent to the need for Diet reform. Through a decision-making process that was led by the prime minister's office, the Koizumi administration turned around economic policy and strengthened ties with the United States. The shift in economic policy was particularly significant as LDP governments up to that point had simply pursued clientelistic policies favoring individual support groups and industries – the accumulation of microfocused and particularistic decisions constituted the entirety of Japan's economic policy. In contrast, the Koizumi administration pursued economic policies that emphasized macrolevel economic and fiscal indicators, reducing the emphasis on particularistic benefits and burdens. Koizumi's slogan to "destroy the LDP" signified a substantial break with the party's emphasis on local and industry interests.

This shift from particularism to universalism was not surprising considering the incentive structures that single-member districts place on ruling parties. But it probably mostly affected the DPJ, which, as the second-largest party, sought early on to create a policy cleavage to differentiate itself from the LDP. This is the third turning point. The DPJ did not want to follow the footsteps of the JSP which had sought to differentiate itself from the LDP mainly in foreign and security policy matters, a wholly sterile ideological confrontation; the DJP aimed instead to differentiate itself by providing counterproposals in domestic policy. Some of these were similar to the universalistic social security policies emphasized by European social democratic parties. When under Koizumi the LDP took up universalistic economic policies, the DPJ responded by criticizing the problems generated by these policies, such as the widening socioeconomic gap, and by proposing particularistic responses to these challenges, all the while bashing bureaucrats. It also advocated a shift in foreign and security policy. Waging an offensive on the Koizumi administration ought not to have excluded the possibility of a pursuit of alternative universalistic policies, and some of the universalistic social security policies instituted at this time have persisted, in fact, including countermeasures to Japan's low birthrate problem. However, in the post-Koizumi years, the overall difference between the LDP and DPJ became very hard to discern, and this lack of clarity did not disappear even after the DPJ's acquisition of power in 2009. Thus it was that the development of programmatic policy competition predicated on universalism and a basic consensus on foreign and security policy in Japanese politics never really got off the ground.

Notes

1 In this chapter I use the term "decision-making domains" to refer to areas of social and economic activity (government, the private sector, etc.). The relationships between

these domains include those between central and local government, the public and private sector, and politicians and the bureaucracy.

2 Taniguchi Masaki, *"Seido kaikaku"* ["Institutional reform"], in Sasaki Takeshi and Shimizu Masato, eds., *Zemināru gendai nihon seiji* [Seminars: Contemporary Japanese Politics] (Tokyo: Nihon Keizai Shinbun Shuppansha, 2011), pp. 225–61. Nakakita Kōji, *Gendai Nihon no seitō demokurashī* [Contemporary Japan's Parliamentary Democracy] (Tokyo: Iwanami Shinsho, 2012).

3 Sasaki Takeshi, *Ima seiji ni nani ga kanō ka* [What Can Politics Do Now?] (Tokyo: Chūkō Shinsho, 1988).

4 Hosokawa, *"'Jiyū shakai rengo' Ketto sengen," Bungei Shunju* (June 1992).

5 Arend Lijphart, *Patterns of Democracy* (New Haven: Yale University Press, 1999).

6 Daniel Okimoto, *Between MITI and the Market* (Stanford: Stanford University Press, 1984); Richard J. Samuels, *The Business of the Japanese State* (Ithaca: Cornell University Press, 1987).

7 Michio Muramatsu *Local Power in the Japanese State* (Berkeley: University of California Press, 1997).

8 Such collusion characterized the relations between members of the bureaucracy, the Diet, the financial sector, media and academia, as well as the vendors, who promoted nuclear energy in Japan – collectively referred to as Japan's "nuclear village" – who were harshly criticized following the nuclear accidents of 2011.

9 I received useful hints on this point from a conversation with Sunahara Yōsuke.

10 With regard to the contradiction between concentration of power in the central government and its separation from other decision-making domains in Japanese-style majoritarianism, the decentralization reforms offer a very interesting case. The leading proponent, Nishio Masaru, suggests that the reforms were originally driven by slightly different goals: "Decentralization reforms originated from the conflation of two trends: administrative reform from the 1980s, and political reform initiated by the Recruit Scandal of the late 1980s." See Nishio Masaru, *"Chihō bunken kaikaku"* ["Decentralization Reform"], in Sasaki Takeshi and 21 Seiki Rinchō, eds., *Heisei demokurashī* [Heisei Democracy] (Tokyo: Kōdansha, 2013), p. 78. However, it is also true that most reform proposals from public groups included decentralization. From interviews, it appears that to many the relationship between decentralization and majoritarian rule was not necessarily clear. The perceived compatibility between the two processes appears to have derived from intuitive logic, rather than from any theoretical basis.

11 As pointed out by Murai Tetsuya, a prime minister–centered policy-making process that made good use of human networks was also feasible in the past, when capable and idiosyncratic prime ministers such as Yoshida Shigeru were at the helm. Nevertheless, no legal structures for a prime minister office–led policy-making process had been put in place. One might say that the Hashimoto Reforms sought to ensure that the prime minister would have a central role in the policy process even when the person in question was not exceptionally skilled or idiosyncratic. Murai Tetsuya, *Sengo seiji taisei no kigen* [The Origins of the Post-war Political Regime] (Tokyo: Fujiwara Shoten, 2008).

12 For a brief history of these reforms, see for instance: Ikawa Hiroshi, "15 Years of Decentralization Reform in Japan," *Up-to-date Documents on Local Autonomy in Japan n. 4*, Council of Local Authorities for International Relations (CLAIR) and the Institute for Comparative Studies in Local Governance (COSLOG, GRIPS) (March 2008). Available at: http://www.clair.or.jp/j/forum/honyaku/hikaku/pdf/up-to-date_en4.pdf. For an excellent process analysis refer to: Kidera Hajime, *Chihō bunken kaikaku no seijigaku* [The Politics of Decentralization reform] (Tokyo: Yūhikaku, 2012).

13 There are many analyses of the Koizumi administration, but the following is of particular value: Takenaka Harukata, *Shushō shihai – nihon seiji no henbō* [Prime Minister's Rule: The Changing Face of Japanese Politics] (Tokyo: Chūō Kōron shinsha, 2006).

14 On the asymmetry of the party system and party organizations between the local and national level, please refer to the following articles: Soga Kengo and Machidori

Satoshi, "*Seitō saihen-ki igo ni okeru chihō seiji no hendō*" ["Transformations in Local Politics after the Period of Party Reorganization"], *Senkyo kenkyū*, 24, no. 1 (2008), pp. 5–15. Ken Victor Leonard Hijino, 2012. "Intra-party Conflicts over Gubernatorial Campaigns in Japan." *Party Politics*, 20, no. 1 (2014), pp. 78–88.

15 The investment of public resources in depopulating regions and decaying industries was not perceived as leading to waste and inefficiency, but rather its direct opposite: a view that these regions and industries needed political protection precisely because of their weaknesses. Kitayama Toshiya, "*Doken kokka nihon to shihonshugi no shoruikei*" ["The 'Construction State' of Japan and Typologies of Capitalism"], *Lebiasan*, 32 (2003), pp. 123–46.

16 Margarita Estevez-Abe, *Welfare and Capitalism in Postwar Japan* (New York: Cambridge University Press, 2008).

17 Benjamin Nyblade focuses on this issue, arguing that Japan suffers from a problem of "hyper accountability." See Benjamin Nyblade, "*Shushō no kenryoku kyōka to tanmei seiken*" ["The Strengthening of Prime-Ministerial Power and Short-Lived Governments"], translated into Japanese by Matsuda Natsu, in Hiwatari Nobuhiro and Saitō Jun, eds., *Seitō seiji no konmei to seiken kōtai* (Tokyo: Tōkyō Daigaku Shuppankai, 2011), pp. 245–61.

18 On the power of veto held by the Upper House, and on its consequences, please refer to Machidori Satoshi, *Shushō seiji no seido bunseki* [The Japanese Premiership: An Analysis of Institutional Power Relations] (Tokyo: Chikura Shobō, 2012). See also Ōyama Reiko, *Nihon no kokkai* [Japan's Diet] (Tokyo: Iwanami Shinsho, 2011).

19 Doi Takerō, ed., *Chihō bunken kaikaku no keizai gaku* [The Economics of Power Decentralization Reform] (Tokyo: Nihon Hyōron-sha, 2004).

20 "Modernism" here refers to a view of Japan as highly defective in comparison to modern Western society, seen to be rooted in Christianity and civic revolutions, and thereby advocating both spiritual and institutional change for Japan. Early postwar intellectuals Maruyama Masao and Ōtsuka Hisao are representative of this view. The 1980s was a period in which international praise for the Japanese-style management and economic success coexisted with domestic criticism of excessive collectivism in areas such as education. Modernism shares an emphasis on the autonomy of individuals with neoliberalism, an ideology which gained traction following the Nakasone administration.

21 Chalmers Johnson, "*Atarashii shihon-shugi no hakken*" ["The Discovery of a New Capitalism"], translated by Kengo Akitsugi, in *Lebiasan*, no. 1 (Tokyo: 1987).

22 Mabuchi Masaru, *Ōkurashō tōsei no seiji keizaigaku* [The Political Economy of MOF Control] (Tokyo: Chūō Kōronsha, 1994).

23 Rebuild Japan Initiative Foundation, *Minshutō seiken – shippai no kenshō* [The DPJ Government – A Study of Failure] (Tokyo: Chūō Shinsho, 2013), p. 117.

24 These shortcomings were particularly evident in the accidents at the Tokyo Electric Fukushima nuclear power plant following the 2011 Tōhoku earthquake and tsunami. For details, please refer to Chapter 7 in this volume by Kitazawa Koichi.

9 The Gulf War and Japan's national security identity

Michael J. Green and Igata Akira[1]

Introduction

On August 2, 1990, Iraqi Republican Guard units invaded Kuwait from the north and northwest as Iraqi aircraft bombed downtown Kuwait City. Within twelve hours, most Kuwaiti resistance had collapsed and the royal family had fled, leaving Saddam Hussein in control of the country. The invasion was met with immediate international condemnation and economic sanctions, followed by a war led by the United States to expel the Iraqis. In the first few days, political leaders and officials in Tokyo did not appreciate how fundamentally the conflict in the Gulf would challenge their assumptions about Japanese influence in the emerging international order. In subsequent days and months, however, the Japanese government realized what was at stake in the Gulf and watched in frustration as the clumsy response of Prime Minister Kaifu Toshiki was dismissed in Washington and the international community as "checkbook diplomacy" and "too little, too late." Together with the collapse of the economic bubble that same year, the Gulf War helped to destroy the so-called 1955 system, the party system that had remained in place in Japan since 1955, and ushered in a new era of diminished power and confidence in Japan.[2]

Nevertheless, the impact of Japan's experience in the Gulf War was different from the aftermath of the collapse of the economic bubble in important respects. The economic crisis was followed by a decade of ineffective stimulus packages, mounting national debt, and a dangerous deflationary spiral. In contrast, the decade that followed the Gulf War crisis saw successive Japanese governments implement important structural changes in national security policies and institutions. (In this respect, the findings of this chapter resonate with the conclusions reached by Toyama Kazuhiko in Chapter 4 concerning microeconomic policy and business.) As a result, when the United States was attacked on September 11, 2001, the response by the government of Prime Minister Koizumi Junichiro was far more effective than the Kaifu government's response to the Gulf War, a decade earlier.

Three factors account for this divergence in the impact of the security and economic shocks of 1990–91. First, the Gulf War illuminated underutilized areas of Japanese national power, whereas the economic crisis required comprehensive and painful restructuring of the entirety of Japanese politics, business, and society. Second, the humiliation of the Gulf War was followed by the tragedy of the Kobe earthquake, the Aum Shinrikyo subway terrorist attacks, and the Taiwan Straits crisis in 1995 (and in 1998 the North Korean *Taepodong* missile launch). This staccato drumbeat of crises eroded aspects of Japan's postwar pacifism that had underlain the poor response shown in 1990. The Gulf War thus immediately demonstrated what was missing in Japanese security policy. The debate was much slower to evolve on the economic side, where Japan was anesthetized by massive stimulus spending throughout much of the 1990s. Third, the management of security issues involved a much smaller universe of officials, politicians, and intellectuals than did the management of the economy; the experience of the Gulf War could thus be translated into concrete changes in policies more easily. Indeed, the lead architects of Koizumi's response to 9/11 were scarred veterans of the Gulf War debacle who were determined not to relive that earlier humiliation. Despite some shortcomings, they largely succeeded.

As we will see in this chapter, Japan's experience in the Gulf War ushered in the lost decades, but also witnessed the evolution of a new national security identity. Whether termed "reluctant realism" or "security normalization," that identity has become a defining element in Japan's world role today.[3]

The Japanese worldview before August 1990

In the years before Iraq's attack on Kuwait, Japanese politicians and intellectual leaders debated their nation's future world role, but did so with the sense that international trends were on their side. Throughout the postwar period, Japanese foreign policy followed the trajectory set early on by Prime Minister Yoshida Shigeru and followed by the ruling Liberal Democratic Party (LDP). Japan hewed closely to the United States in the Cold War and focused on economic revitalization and the steady restoration of Japan's reputation and influence in Asia and, more broadly, in international society. There were crises with the so-called Yoshida Doctrine as China reemerged in international society and Japan's own economic recovery led to calls from the United States for greater burden sharing, but these were met with adjustments in Japanese outreach to Asia or increases in Japanese host-nation support for the U.S. forces in Japan. These issues are dealt with more specifically by Shiraishi Takashi in Chapter 11 on the rise of China and by Sheila Smith in Chapter 12 on the Okinawa and Futenma issues. Overall, the bargain set by Yoshida with the conservatives at home and with the Americans in the 1951 Security Treaty generally held. The Japanese people were not entirely comfortable with their heavy dependence on the United States for security, but they generally assumed that dependence would wane as Japanese economic and therefore international political power accrued.

In the 1980s, Japan's growing economic clout seemed to align with the emerging importance of economic factors in international affairs. Prime Minister Ohira Masayoshi began the decade by releasing a report on Japan's potential for "Comprehensive Security" – a concept that enveloped energy, aid, and diplomacy as instruments of national power to offset Japan's self-restraint on the hard power side. After the rapid appreciation of the yen following the 1985 Plaza Accord, Japan came under pressure to recirculate its massive current account surpluses, providing seemingly bottomless resources to pursue a nonmilitary approach to leadership in international affairs and reduced dependence on the United States. The Japanese *keiretsu* (enterprise groupings) moved offshore to Southeast Asia and North America, Japanese Official Development Assistance (ODA) rocketed to the top rank among official donors, and Japan played a leading role in responding to the 1988 Latin American debt crisis. There was certainly friction with the United States. For example, in 1988 U.S. presidential candidate Richard Gephardt famously quipped that "the United States and the Soviet Union have fought the Cold War – and Japan has won!" – an attitude that Americans seemed to share in polling taken at the time.[4] However, economic resources were shaping new international accords and Japan was well-positioned to lead in the new era of economics over security that seemed at hand. Indeed, Japanese officials and scholars were not afraid to challenge the very underpinnings of Anglo-American economic ideology in the so-called Washington consensus – and to predict that Japan's influence would not be ignored. Characteristic of the pre-1990 confidence was Sakakibara Eisuke's famous book, *Japan That Surpassed Capitalism*, and comparable volumes in the United States predicting that Japan's new form of economic power would define the emerging international order.[5]

For those in the Foreign Ministry and the LDP who remained concerned about the credibility of the U.S.-Japan alliance, there were also reassuring precedents in the Far East. In the early 1980s, the government of Prime Minister Nakasone Yasuhiro had expanded Japan's ability to defend its own archipelago based on the existing interpretation that the nation could engage in "exclusively defensive defense." Nakasone promised to make Japan an "unsinkable aircraft carrier," and that was exactly what the Reagan administration had wanted.[6] With the Soviet military expansion in the Far East and the deployment of nuclear weapons ballistic missile submarines (SSBNs) in the Sea of Okhotsk, the Reagan administration initiated a new "Maritime Strategy" that aimed to bottle up and destroy Soviet submarines before they could escape into the Pacific Ocean. Indeed, the plan was for the Seventh Fleet to horizontally escalate against the Soviets in the Far East as a deterrent against attacks in Western Europe (so-called horizontal escalation). Under a division of roles and missions agreed upon in the Reagan years, Japan would serve as the "shield" to keep the Soviets back, and U.S. forces would be the "spear" that would go to strike enemy forces in the Sea of Okhotsk and the Soviet Far East. By dint of Japan's geographical position on the offshore island chain, Nakasone was able to contribute directly to containment and to the end of the Cold War from home without sending a single soldier abroad. Japan was providing real burden sharing and taking real risk, without appearing to do so, in a way that threatened the underlying pacifism of the Japanese people and the essence of the Yoshida Doctrine.

Before August 1990, Japan debated a future role confident that economic instruments would define international influence and that geography had rendered

Japan an indispensable security partner for the United States. Saddam Hussein's attack on Kuwait shattered both of those shibboleths.

Japan's response to the Gulf War crisis

In the immediate aftermath of the Iraqi attack, the Kaifu government considered itself swift and decisive. On August 3, only a day after Saddam Hussein launched his attacks on Kuwait City, the Finance Ministry rendered an administrative guidance to all Japanese banks to safeguard Kuwaiti assets in Japan. On August 5, the government announced its own economic sanctions against Iraq and Kuwait, consisting of an oil import ban, an export ban, discontinuation of capital and loan investments, and freezing economic cooperation with Iraq. Then, on August 10, the Finance Ministry revised the August 3 guidance to freeze all assets of Iraq and Kuwait and to stop all new loans and direct investments.[7] These measures – closely coordinated with Washington at a working level – were considered to be among the fastest of the major U.S. allies. Requiring first and foremost administrative guidance from the Finance Ministry and authorized by UN Security Council Resolution 661, the measures were well within the capabilities of Tokyo's elite bureaucrats and the framework of Japan's Constitution. The Japanese government was confident that it had "hit an out-of-the-park homerun" in its response to the developing Gulf War crisis.[8]

However, this turned out to be the high-water mark of Japanese effectiveness in the crisis as it unfolded. Japanese officials soon recognized that the punishment that the United States intended for Iraq was far more than just a slap on the wrist. On August 8, President George H.W. Bush announced that the United States was demanding the immediate and unconditional withdrawal of Iraq from Kuwait, and that he was deploying the 82nd Airborne Division and Air Force fighter squadrons to Saudi Arabia. He then spoke with Prime Minister Kaifu by phone on August 13. In response to Kaifu's plea that it would be "unthinkable for Japan to participate directly in the military sphere," Bush responded: "My bottom line is that when this chapter of history is written, Japan and the U.S. and a handful of other countries will have stood side-by-side."[9] In that instant, recalls then North American Affairs Bureau Treaty Division Director Okamoto Yukio, the Japanese government realized that this was not just another war between two Middle East states. The crisis was now being framed in Washington as a defining moment for American global leadership and the stability of oil supplies in the Middle East. On both points, Japan had to stand up and be counted.

On August 29, Prime Minister Kaifu announced what his cabinet thought would be a dramatic assistance plan to assist help U.S. and coalition efforts in preventing further Iraqi aggression and restoring the *status quo ante* in Kuwait. Through the plan Japan would provide contributions in four areas: transportation, equipment and materiel, medical assistance, and financial support. Aside from $10 million earmarked for refugee aid in Jordan, however, there were no specifics.[10] Criticism of this proposal was quick and harsh. One senior American official complained to the media that in the midst of an acute military crisis in the Middle East, "there's a limited number of Girl Scout cookies that can be used."[11] Stung by such criticism and urged in a phone call from President Bush to do more, Kaifu had his government spokesman announce that Japan would contribute an additional $1 billion package the day after the initial announcement was made. The Foreign Ministry's spokesman declared that Japan would pay $1 billion "and not a penny more," leaving the impression that his government was resentful and acting under pressure from the United States.[12] This was entirely counterproductive, particularly since Japan's $1 billion contribution was by far the largest from any U.S. ally up to that point.[13] But the attitude in Tokyo only invited the worst possible combination of resentment and further pressure from the international community.

The Kaifu government had actually listed financial contributions last in its August 29 four-point plan, but it was the money that Washington needed most. Knowing this, and obstructed by opposition control of the Upper House of the Diet, Kaifu eventually retreated from all the points in the plan but the fourth. The demise of each point deserves brief mention, but the scene was set by the fight over funds, and the narrative should begin with that. As the crisis became more acute and the United States and the coalition forces moved toward war, the pressure on Japan to provide funds mounted. On September 7, Secretary of the Treasury Nicholas Brady visited Tokyo to pressure the Kaifu cabinet for further financial contributions totaling $3 billion. On September 14, the Kaifu government announced its second batch of financial contributions, $1 billion for the coalition and $2 billion for the regional countries (Egypt, Turkey, and Jordan).[14]

On November 29, the Security Council passed Resolution 678, which gave Iraq until January 15 to withdraw from Kuwait and empowered states to use "all necessary means" to force Iraq out of Kuwait after the deadline. Foreign Minister Nakayama Taro traveled to Washington to meet with Secretary of State James Baker just before the deadline and agreed to pay for all yen-based costs for U.S. forces beyond the $2 billion already committed up to that point. It was a step that eased the burden on Washington without directly implicating Japanese funds or personnel in the coming war itself. But it was clearly not enough. Nakayama returned to Tokyo and joined Kaifu for an emergency session of the Security Council of the Japanese cabinet, where it was agreed to set up a crisis response headquarters in the Prime Minister's office and to consider other forms of support.

On January 21, Finance Minister Hashimoto Ryutaro met Treasury Secretary Nicholas Brady at the Stanhope Hotel in New York to discuss the issue of further financial contribution. This meeting was unusual, since Brady had asked in advance to meet with Hashimoto in private for the beginning of the meeting. Hashimoto sensed that Brady would ask for a vast amount. However, he also felt that taking a hardline approach in negotiating the amount would be inappropriate, given that the American soldiers were now on the ground and fighting. Hashimoto was "prepared to accept the amount proposed by Brady, no matter how high the price tag may be." At the meeting, Brady asked for $9 billion, and Hashimoto accepted this amount without asking how the amount "$9 billion" would be calculated.[15] Following this meeting, Kaifu officially offered a ¥1.8 trillion ($9 billion) contribution on January 24, which had brought Japan's total contribution close to $13 billion – the first batch of contribution was $1B on August 30, the second tranche was $3B on September 14, and the third was $9B on January 21. This brought the total to $13B, making Japan the largest funder after Saudi Arabia.

At ¥10,000 per Japanese citizen ($75), this was a substantial contribution, and the Finance Ministry Budget Bureau and Diet balked. Initially, the cabinet envisioned a tobacco tax to cover the costs, but then shifted to a combination of corporate tax increases, gasoline taxes, and government budget cuts because of political pressure in the Diet. At each turn the Foreign Ministry collided with the Finance Ministry Budget Bureau, which had been flush with confidence over the economy, resented foreign pressure, and did not fear the Prime Minister enough to relieve the diplomats from their agonizing tap dance with the Americans.[16] The impression of Japanese recalcitrance was worsened by demands from the Komeito party that it would not help the government overcome opposition in the Upper House unless the money was used for purely nonmilitary purposes. With U.S. and coalition forces now in combat, it seemed a particularly petty point to the observing allies. Eventually, the U.S. Central Command (CENTCOM) was desperate enough for the funds that it agreed to use them only for nonlethal "logistical support." It still took the Japanese government until late March to pass the budget – weeks after the fighting had already stopped on the ground in Iraq and Kuwait. By then, the value of the yen in dollars had fallen almost US $0.5 billion (the dollar tends to rise in value in a crisis), and Tokyo and Washington had to haggle over whether the contribution was originally intended to be calculated in yen or dollars. Japan agreed to make up the difference as part of a supplemental and barely face-saving "postwar" reconstruction contribution. The public perception was of a frustrated American government shaking down a passive and unhelpful Japan for money.

The commander of the coalition forces, General Norman Schwarzkopf, later stated that "[h]ad it not been for the Japanese, Desert Shield would have gone broke in August. While Western newspapers were complaining about Tokyo's reluctance to increase its pledge of one billion dollars to safeguard Saudi Arabia, the Japanese embassy in Riyadh quietly transferred tens of millions of dollars into Central Command's accounts. We were able to cover our day-to-day operations before anybody in Washington could lay claim to the money."[17] Yet this fact did not matter in terms of Japanese prestige or influence. The key actors – Finance Minister Hashimoto and LDP Secretary General Ozawa Ichiro, in particular – worked long, intense hours with their colleagues in the Foreign Ministry to deliver an impressive demonstration of Japanese support, if not leadership. They did not want Japan's role to be defined purely in terms of money, let alone reluctant contributions, but that is exactly what happened. The greater irony was that the desperate political and bureaucratic work of delivering a financial contribution sucked all of the life out of the other three parts of the four-part plan.

As Japan's initial financial contributions were being rebuffed as insufficient in Washington, exasperated alliance managers in the National Security Council, the State Department, and the Department of Defense urged their Japanese counterparts to dispatch personnel to the region, whether in the form of minesweepers, logistical support, or humanitarian support for refugees from Kuwait.[18] The most visible part of the August 29 four-part plan was to have been transportation: Japanese planes and Japanese ships under the national Japanese flag, delivering support to the coalition on the ground, with full coverage from CNN and NHK. But it never happened.

Immediately after the August 29 plan was announced, objections to the transportation proposal were raised with respect to Article Nine of the Constitution, and so the government turned to the private sector. First, a request for air transportation to deliver supplies was initially refused by Japanese airline companies due to opposition from both the pilots union and the flight mechanics union.[19] Japan Airlines reluctantly agreed to provide aircraft but imposed such strict conditions that the government decided it could not use them.[20] Ozawa, scarred by the disastrous negotiations over monetary contributions, urged Kaifu to announce that Japan Self-Defense Forces (JSDF) personnel would be sent, and on January 18 the Japanese government revealed that the SDF was considering sending transport planes to the Gulf to assist the coalition in rear-area missions. The Cabinet Legal Bureau had determined the planes could be sent for "training" without challenging the Constitution or requiring an amendment to the SDF Law, but an *Asahi Newspaper* poll found that 78 percent of the respondents expressed opposition to sending any SDF personnel to the Middle East.[21] Operationally, the government was also hamstrung by the fact that its two recently ordered VIP 747s were not yet ready, leaving only shorter-distance C-130 Hercules aircraft from the Japan Air Self-Defense Force (JASDF). Kaifu was already nervous about the opinion polls as it was, and on February 6 he stated in the Diet that the JASDF planes would only be sent if there was a request from the International Organization for Migration, something that was not expected and therefore provided a convenient excuse to pull the plug. In the end, the Japanese government had to hire the private American company Evergreen International Airlines to conduct "Japan's air transportation assistance." As it turned out, there was no Japanese national flag flown and no CNN coverage.[22]

The Kaifu government had somewhat more success with sealift maneuvers. There was some trouble with the shipping companies, which were reluctant to send their ships to an area where the government was not willing to send military ships, particularly given the high insurance costs involved. In addition, the painful memory of the loss of Japan's commercial fleet during World War II still ran deep among the sailors, and the All Japan Seamen's Union was hesitant to go into harm's way for the first time in almost fifty years.[23] Nevertheless, the Ministry of Transport convinced the progovernment shippers and their union to send two ships for sealift operations. The problem was that the domestic political process of convincing the shipping companies and the Komeito party to cooperate consumed the Ministry of Foreign Affairs, and nobody seemed to notice the actual cable from Washington detailing what kind of ships the U.S.-led coalition needed. The Ministry of Transport chose to send "lift-on/lift-off" ships used in Japanese commercial ports, but CENTCOM actually required "roll-on/roll-off" ships that could be used in ports that lack special equipment for loading heavy cargo and equipment.[24] In addition, there were limitations to what these Japanese ships could carry since "weapons, ammunitions, and troops" were considered off-limits under Japan's Constitution.[25] The issue subsequently became one of face-saving and the Ministry of Foreign Affairs had to convince (the Japanese media wrote "beg") Washington to accept the entirely unsuitable ships.[26] Operationally and politically the sealift operations had little impact on coalition views of Japan's contribution, but they did allow the government to claim at home that it had "shown the flag."

The second element of the four-point plan, material assistance, faced similar difficulties. For instance, construction materials for building runways were deemed a violation of the Japanese cabinet's "Three Arms Export Principles" – an export ban in effect since the 1960s.[27] Trucks with reinforced hoods and tops were also banned because they could potentially mount heavy weapons.[28] At the end of the day, material assistance proved less controversial than transportation assistance, but involved similar inconvenience for coalition forces as Japanese bureaucrats navigated the political and regulatory constraints on Japanese security policy.[29] For nations with troops in the fight, the minutiae of Japanese postwar pacifist constraints on material contributions was somewhere between laughable and infuriating.

Medical assistance, the third element of the four-point plan, seemed as if it might be an area where even the most conscientious objector to war could play a useful role. And yet here again, the Japanese government was surprised by domestic political, ideological, and bureaucratic obstacles. The initial plan was to send up to 200 doctors from national hospitals, but Japan's Red Cross Society declared that it would not send any nurses for the operations due to fear for their safety and underlying pacifist sentiments.[30] In the end, a total of six doctors ended up volunteering for the job, but even they were unable to operate in field hospitals out of concern that this might violate Japan's self-imposed ban on exercising the right of collective self-defense through a rather convoluted logic: because the soldiers who were treated by these Japanese doctors could end up going back to the battlefield, it would be possible to interpret the treatment of wounded soldiers as part of exercising the right to collective self-defense.[31] The six passionate and highly skilled Japanese doctors then sought to volunteer at hospitals away from the front lines, but were told that they were superfluous by the Saudi government, eventually returning home exasperated.[32]

In sum, the only part of the Kaifu government's "bold" four-part plan to come to fruition was the financial contribution. The government's effort to have a comprehensive multifaceted role collapsed in the struggle to sustain the one element that the Americans and the coalition wanted most. Unable to send people, Japan's large financial contribution looked even more like the rich man's way to avoid risk – like wealthy Unionists who hired "substitutes" to take their place during the American civil war. Japan's action ultimately engendered as much resentment and ridicule as encouragement and appreciation.

The struggle to prepare a longer-term role in mid-crisis

In the midst of the collapsing four-part plan, the Kaifu government also introduced legislation that would help Japan to recover its international reputation and
prepare for future crises. This effort to put in place a longer-term framework to
permit Japan a role in international crises helps to explain why the disastrous
response to the Gulf War was followed over the next decade by substantial progress on reforming national security laws and policies. Of course, these longer-
term initiatives did little to assist the U.S.-led coalition in the immediate crisis in
the Gulf and initially faced obstacles as daunting as the four-part plan.

The major thrust in this regard was the Kaifu government's effort to pass legislation that would authorize the JSDF to participate in UN peacekeeping operations
(PKO). The Gulf War was a UN Chapter Seven mission and not actually PKO
related, but the point was to demonstrate that Japan was willing – eventually – to
show the flag and do work that is (as the papers liked to report at the time) "difficult, dangerous, and dirty." That said, the politics of the PKO law proved highly
contentious from the start, particularly with respect to the question of whether the
JSDF or civilians could be dispatched under the new law.

In favor of a civilian force was Prime Minister Kaifu, whose pacifist leanings
were revealed in his statement to Foreign Ministry officials that a dispatch of the
JSDF was "out of the question."[33] Kaifu went so far as to state that he "recalled
the Manchurian Incident" upon hearing the arguments of those who favored JSDF
dispatch.[34] (The 1931 Manchurian Incident saw elements of Japan's military in
China stage a bombing close to a railway as a pretext for an invasion of China by
Japan.) Minister of Foreign Affairs Nakayama was also against the dispatch of
the JSDF because of the Cabinet Legislation Bureau's interpretation that military
forces' participation in peacekeeping operations might cross the line of the ban
against collective self-defense.[35] Importantly, Vice Minister for Foreign Affairs
Kuriyama Takakazu was also against the dispatch of forces. In his memoir, he
recalls that he opposed a JSDF role for two reasons: first, the public would not
support it; and second, sending SDF abroad would trigger sharp criticism
from surrounding countries that were wary of Japan once again becoming a military superpower.[36] Kuriyama's own family was placed under house arrest during
the Second World War by the military, and he reportedly blurted out, "I regard the
Self Defense Force as a monster," in the midst of the policy debate over the PKO
Law.[37] Other alliance managers in the Foreign Ministry were appalled at their
Vice Minister's opposition and worked around him with supporters of the JSDF
in the LDP.

Among the strongest supporters of dispatching the JSDF were LDP Secretary
General Ozawa, LDP Chairman of the Policy Research Council Kato Mutsuki,
and Minister of Finance Hashimoto Ryutaro.[38] Denizens of the powerful Tanaka
faction that controlled the LDP and that once championed normalization with
China were also the leaders of a postwar generation of conservative politicians
who wanted a more "normal" Japanese national security policy. They acted not
out of passion for the U.S.-Japan alliance, though the credibility of the alliance

was one factor in their thinking, but also out of a determination to demonstrate Japan's leadership and ability to move beyond merely standing as an "ATM" for the United States.

However, these two opposing groups failed to develop any consensus. One official from the Ministry of Foreign Affairs sadly recalled endless meetings in the prime minister's office and the LDP headquarters where nothing was decided as the Gulf Crisis unfolded before their eyes.[39] As time passed and the LDP fault lines were laid bare, new public opinion polls showed growing opposition to dispatching the JSDF under the new PKO law. Without cover from the prime minister, politicians in the center began opposing a role for the JSDF.[40] Despite these divisions, the government tried to ram through the Diet legislation that revised the JSDF law in October 1991, before finally surrendering and pulling the bill on November 9. Designed as a symbolic demonstration that Japan could step up in a future crisis, the ill-fated PKO law instead reinforced the impression of Japanese dithering and passivity.

By then the Gulf War had been over for six months, but Ozawa and the other realists were determined not to surrender the field with respect to the UN PKO law. They eventually prevailed on the newly installed Prime Minister Miyazawa Kiichi to introduce a revised UN peacekeeping bill to the Diet in November 1991. The Komeito party now supported the bill with new conditions, including a ceiling of 2,000 JSDF personnel that could be deployed abroad; requirements for UN neutrality, a ceasefire, and concurrence by all relevant parties that Japanese forces would be welcome; the use of side arms only for self-defense; and the right to unilaterally withdraw Japan's PKO contingent if any of the aforementioned conditions collapsed. Even that modified bill came under incessant criticism from the *Asahi Newspaper* and other media. It took Miyazawa until the summer of 1992 to pass the bill, after agreeing to additional conditions such as mandatory Diet approval for each JSDF PKO mission. Defense experts warned that the bill was so riddled with conditions and exceptions that Japanese forces would end up being a liability to their UN partners, but the new bill at least demonstrated the Japanese government was prepared in principle to put boots on the ground in future crises . . . as long as it was safe.

The Japanese government also did eventually show the flag at sea, albeit after the fighting had stopped. Based on prior planning completed by the Nakasone government during the Iran-Iraq War, Tokyo announced on April 24 that it would dispatch a Japan Maritime Self-Defense Force (JMSDF) flotilla of minesweepers and support ships at the request of Saudi Arabia. The minesweepers engaged in "clean-up" (as opposed to military) operations – after most mines had already been cleared by the U.S. Navy. Because the ships appeared to be removed from ground combat and because the public now recognized the international criticism of Japan's role up to that point, the JMSDF minesweeping operations received sufficient political and public support to proceed. There was also greater internal support for the mission in the JMSDF, which has always been more international and more sensitive to U.S.-Japan alliance issues than there had been for the PKO law within the leadership of the Ground Self Defense Forces, whose recruits had joined not expecting to ever go abroad. Operationally, the minesweeping mission did not make a significant difference, but it did set a precedent for JMSDF refueling operations a decade later and demonstrated the importance of planning.

These were investments – and limited investments at that – for the future. In terms of the Gulf War itself, Japan's failure to send personnel and the obvious internal divisions and weak leadership in Tokyo did enormous damage to Japan's international reputation. Japan was not included in a significant way in the diplomacy surrounding the Gulf War or the postwar planning (unlike Germany, which had a seat at the table thanks to its membership in NATO). Publicly, Japan's contribution garnered little appreciation. When the government of Kuwait took out full-page advertisements in major newspapers around the world to thank the members of the U.S.-led coalition, Japan was not mentioned (even though countries like Botswana, which had made very small symbolic troop deployments, were mentioned).[41] It was only after a strong protest from the Japanese government that the Japanese ambassador secured a seat at the allied forces victory parade that took place in Washington, DC.[42] Other examples abounded that showed how Japan's international reputation had suffered despite sizable monetary contributions. As former U.S. ambassador to Japan Michael Armacost lamented, "the Gulf crisis appeared ideally suited for close US-Japanese collaboration and a redefinition of Japan's international security role."[43] The result was an exaggerated but lasting image of impotence.

Why the failure?

The Japanese government's failure in the Gulf Crisis was not the result of diffidence or disinterest. Politicians and officials worked around the clock to put Japan on the map again after August 1990. Moreover, the roughly $13 billion Japan contributed was enormously important, as none other than General Schwarzkopf testified. If the Japanese goal was to support a successful U.S.-led coalition to compel Saddam Hussein to leave Kuwait and to assert the durability of the neo-liberal international system, then the policy was a success. In terms of Japan's most basic security interests, that should not be discounted. In broader context, however, Japanese failures were significant. From August 1990 to August 1991, the Japanese government projected indecisiveness and impotence. In terms of international influence and domestic confidence, Japan paid a major price. The U.S.-Japan alliance did not recover from the damage to Japanese credibility until the mid-1990s and the 1995 Nye Initiative, which stated that "[t]here is no more important bilateral relationship than the one we have with Japan," and that the "security alliance with Japan is the linchpin of United States security policy in Asia."[44] Discredited on the security side, Japan had few defenders in Washington as trade friction peaked in the late Bush and early Clinton years. Japan contributed in important ways to the maintenance of broader stability in the international system, but exposed major weaknesses in its own national security.

Four major factors explain what went wrong. First, Japan's strategic elites did a poor job of assessing the emerging international order on the eve of the war.

So much of the debate about Japan's role in the 1980s had focused on how Japan would use its massive economic power (measured primarily in current account surpluses) that little objective attention was paid to the nature of hard power in the international system. Even international security experts took too much comfort from the Reagan administration's Cold War strategy against the Soviets in the Pacific, which hinged on the geostrategic position of the Japanese archipelago – a nonfactor in the Gulf. The value and influence that Japan gained as a U.S. ally in the 1980s because of its frontline position against the Soviets was almost irrelevant as the United States formed an international coalition on the other side of the globe. The Gulf War was a stark reminder that hard power, geography, and decisiveness were still key ingredients in international security affairs.

Second, Japan suffered from weak leadership. Prime Minister Kaifu came to power with expertise on education and a generally positive outlook on the U.S.-Japan alliance, but he had no power base of his own and survived in office precisely because his political weakness served the interests of the powerful Tanaka faction, which still controlled the LDP. To be sure, Nakasone had also been kept in place in the 1980s by the Tanaka faction, but he managed to solidify the U.S.-Japan alliance by force of personality, generally high popularity ratings, and ideological conviction. Kaifu was not such a leader in any respect. It is probable that under the leadership of a Nakasone, Hashimoto, or Koizumi, the Japanese response to the Gulf crisis would have been more decisive. The roulette wheel of Japanese political leadership just happened to land on the wrong spot in 1990. Indeed, Kaifu was arguably a more typical Japanese politician of that era than Nakasone had been.

Third, Japanese crisis management was crippled by bureaucratic stovepiping. Institutional changes to strengthen the prime minister's office undertaken earlier by Nakasone were highly personality dependent. Under Kaifu, the small crisis management office was weak and the ability to coordinate policy across ministries was underdeveloped. Given Kaifu's own weak political base, cabinet ministers often had greater clout than the prime minister himself. Information sharing from the Foreign Ministry to other ministries such as Finance and Transport was done in a patchwork manner. The North American Affairs Bureau took the lead, but had to contend with antimilitary sentiments in the private sector, civil society, and other ministries that had never been brought in to support the alliance in the 1980s. In fact, Nakasone and Reagan had turned Japan into an "unsinkable aircraft carrier" to contain the Soviet Union with a relative limited number of supporters in the Foreign Ministry, Defense Agency, LDP, and industry. The Gulf War response required a buy-in from a much broader set of constituencies that were not yet empowered or animated by the U.S.-Japan security alliance.

Fourth, the U.S. side provided little help in crafting and branding Japan's response. While President Bush understood the importance of Japan, he set high expectations and left it to Secretary of State Jim Baker and Secretary of the Treasury Nicholas Brady to badger Tokyo to provide assistance. Neither secretary had ever demonstrated a deep commitment to working on the alliance (Baker ended up taking a total of only three trips to Japan as secretary, compared with two for

Mongolia and over a dozen to the Middle East). Moreover, the alliance managers who had helped Nakasone and Reagan build up a stronger relationship were now gone, including key architects like Secretary of Defense Casper Weinberger, Secretary of State George Schultz, former Deputy Assistant Secretary of Defense Richard Armitage, and National Security Council Senior Director for Asia Gaston Sigur. Ambassador Mike Armacost and officials like NSC Japan Director Torkel Patterson struggled mightily to ensure that the U.S.-Japan alliance came out of the Gulf War stronger and more credible. However, that was not a priority for the principals on the U.S. side.[45] It would not be so until a decade later.

The Gulf War shock and shifting Japanese views of security

The Gulf War punctuated the beginning of Japan's lost decades, but that was not the end of the story with respect to Japanese security policy and the U.S.-Japan alliance. While demographic problems, political fluidity, and economic stagnation continued or grew worse, the conservative realists in the Japanese government and the LDP used the Gulf War shock to institute important changes in security policy in the 1990s and 2000s. Some of these efforts ended in failure or frustration, but others led to an improved (if imperfect) performance by Japan's national security institutions and the U.S.-Japan alliance. Broadly speaking, the crisis in Japanese diplomatic performance in the Gulf War led to intense debate and action on two fronts: collective security and the U.S.-Japan alliance.

With regard to collective security, President Bush described the international response to the Gulf War as the first act in a "new world order" based on collective security, rather than the bipolar deterrence model of the Cold War. The UN Security Council had authorized the use of force for the first time since the Korean War. In an era where hard power now mattered again in unexpected ways, the UN route appeared to offer Japan influence over decisions to use force in international relations, as well as a legitimate framework for Japan to contribute its own forces consistent with Article Nine of its Constitution. Two important strategic documents produced in the wake of the Gulf War captured this logic. The first was an LDP Policy Research Council study group led by Ozawa Ichiro that focused on what security JSDF role Japan's Constitution would allow in the wake of the Gulf War experience. The LDP's expert panel held a series of meetings at LDP headquarters in 1992, focusing initially on whether Japan needed to revise the Constitution – a long-standing but controversial plank in the party's policy platform. In the end, the group concluded that the right path to expand the JSDF role in future international crises was through UN collective security actions, and specifically PKO, which the group argued would be consistent with the Constitution.[46] Ozawa continues to this day to hold the view that the JSDF can only be dispatched abroad with a UN mandate – a consistent position on his part but one that looks much less practical given the fracturing of the UN Security Council and the rise of threats within Asia since the Gulf War.

The second document reflecting the new collective security priorities of the Gulf War was the 1993 Higuchi Report – the findings of an expert group assembled to provide strategic guidance for Japan's first National Defense Program Outline (NDPO) after the war.[47] The Higuchi Commission emphasized "multilateral security" as one of three pillars for Japan's future security policy, symbolically listing it ahead of the U.S.-Japan alliance.[48] The report's emphasis on multilateralism reflected both the economic and diplomatic architecture that had begun to emerge in Asia after the Cold War and also the UN-centric lessons of the Gulf War. When the official NDPO came out in late 1995, the U.S.-Japan alliance was given greater weight than the important but secondary role of Japan in security multilateralism – in part because of intensive U.S. engagement with Japan after the release of the report, and in part reflecting a growing recognition that multilateralism would be insufficient in terms of deterring traditional security threats from North Korea and China.

The Gulf War collective security experience also led the Foreign Ministry and internationalists in the LDP to redouble their efforts to secure a permanent seat on the UN Security Council (UNSC). The PKO issue gained new importance in this context and Japanese peacekeeping missions in Cambodia and elsewhere have been an important tool for the government, though the original PKO law has been little changed and the JSDF are still capped at 2,000 personnel for external PKO missions. Japan's diplomatic bid for a permanent UN Security Council seat went into high gear after the Gulf War, as Akiyama Nobumasa explores in Chapter 14. The high-water mark for that effort probably came with the formation of a common effort with India, Germany, and Brazil under the G-4 to expand the size of the Security Council in 2004–05. However, the G-4 ultimately backfired as jealous neighboring countries (Pakistan, Korea, Argentina, etc.) unified in opposition to all four candidates and the United States was forced to withhold support because the G-4 proposal would have made the UNSC too big (U.S. support for Japan remained strong, but not for Japan's new friends in the G-4).

The second line of effort after the Gulf War came in the areas of strengthening crisis management and enhancing alliance capabilities. The Gulf War clearly demonstrated the weaknesses of the Japanese prime minister's office in terms of crisis management, in spite of Nakasone's introduction in 1986 of a Cabinet Councilor's Office on External Affairs, a Cabinet Security Affairs Office, and a Cabinet Information Office (none of which Kaifu utilized effectively). Hashimoto championed crisis management in the years after the Gulf War, particularly when he was secretary general of the LDP during the Murayama administration, during which time he quietly ran a series of crisis management studies within the party's Policy Research Council. The 1995 Kobe earthquake and the March 1995 Aum Shinrikyo attack on the Japanese subway system reinforced the political consensus that Japan needed stronger crisis management capabilities, and the subsequent 1995–96 Taiwan Straits crisis and 1998 launch by North Korea of a *Taepodong* missile added further impetus. Key changes included:

- The establishment of Cabinet Intelligence and Research Office/Cabinet Crisis Management Center in 1996.

- The establishment of a deputy chief cabinet secretary for crisis management in 1998 and later three assistant chief cabinet secretaries and one cabinet councilor for crisis management.
- The establishment of the Foreign Policy Bureau in the Foreign Ministry to handle long-term strategic planning and immediate crisis coordination.
- The passage of special contingency legislations in 2003 with 90 percent support in the Diet to enhance governmental authorities in a national security crisis, which allows the government to mobilize the SDF in a particularly urgent situation, such as an attack on Japan, before the plan of action is endorsed by the Diet.

The shortcomings of the alliance response to the Gulf War also spurred action on bilateral defense cooperation. After a period that Funabashi Yoichi has termed as an "alliance adrift" in the immediate aftermath of the Gulf War, Prime Minister Hashimoto Ryutaro and President Bill Clinton signed a bilateral security declaration in April 1996 that expanded the scope of the alliance cooperation in areas ranging from defense planning to missile defense and intelligence sharing. Then the 9/11 terrorist attacks of 2001 forced senior officials on both sides of the Pacific to brace for another test of the alliance. Deputy Secretary of State Rich Armitage, Assistant Secretary of State Jim Kelly, Senior NSC Director Torkel Patterson, and other senior officials who had served in the previous Bush administration still carried the bitter memories of what they had experienced in 1990–91. The same was true for senior Japanese officials, politicians, and advisors, like Okamoto Yukio, foreign policy advisor to Prime Minister Koizumi Junichiro and a veteran from the frontline diplomatic trenches of the first Gulf crisis. As director for Japan at the NSC, the author was repeatedly told stories of the 1990–91 Gulf Crisis and admonished not to allow a repeat of that debacle. In Tokyo, Okamoto began his first briefing to Chief Cabinet Secretary Fukuda Yasuo by stressing that Japan needed to be bold and decisive and never again repeat the mistakes of 1990–91. Prime Minister Koizumi was bold and decisive by temperament and popular with the Japanese people for just that reason.

Within days of 9/11, the U.S. media carried pictures of Japanese destroyers escorting a U.S. carrier out of Yokosuka. Koizumi announced a plan within weeks of the incident that included a role for the JSDF, acting on recommendations from Okamoto and the JMSDF that Japan refuel U.S. and coalition ships operating in support of Operation Enduring Freedom (OEF) against the Taliban.[49] When the United States and allies launched Operation Iraqi Freedom (OIF) two years later, Koizumi pledged $5 billion and offered to President Bush to lobby European and Gulf States to follow Japan's lead – a reversal of roles from 1990–91 that was not lost on the president or his staff. Koizumi then authorized the dispatch of Japanese forces to Samawah in southern Iraq for humanitarian relief operations.

Okamoto and some on the U.S. side had hoped that Japan would do much more to have a real operational impact in both OIF and OEF, but the political, symbolic, and ultimately geopolitical impact was significant.[50] Though Koizumi's support for OIF was controversial in Japan, overall support for the U.S.-Japan alliance reached record highs in both countries, and the alliance projected a more resolute stance within East Asia at a time of North Korean provocations and pronounced Chinese military modernization. The unfinished work of the alliance is daunting, including the problem of American bases on Okinawa that Sheila Smith describes in Chapter 12, but there is no doubt that the lost decades that followed the Gulf War and the collapse of the economic bubble were not entirely "lost" in terms of upgrading the U.S.-Japan alliance.

Conclusions and observations on the way forward

The Gulf War experience demonstrates that for Japan not all was lost – not even during the lost decades. This also explains why Japan has become more pragmatic on security issues overall in the past two decades. As a long-term strategy paper prepared by the Foreign Ministry several years after the Gulf War stressed: "If our foreign policy dependence on economic strength remains unchanged, we must reconsider where we should find the sources of our national power that would support diplomacy."[51] Although it would be difficult to assess Japan's response toward the Gulf War as a success, the experience served as a wake-up call for Japanese political leaders and alliance managers. It became obvious that the assumptions of the 1955 system about the sources of Japanese influence and prestige in the international system were flawed. New thinking was necessary with respect to security policy, crisis management, and alliance management with the United States. In that sense, the Gulf War was an important "teachable moment."

Notes

1 The authors would like to thank Teraoka Ayumi of RJIF and CSIS who gave helpful research support.
2 See Machidori Satoshi's discussion in Chapter 8 on the collapse of Japanese political equilibrium.
3 For the term "reluctant realism," see Michael J. Green, *Japan's Reluctant Realism: Foreign Policy Challenges in an Era of Uncertain Power* (New York: Palgrave Macmillan, 2000). For an argument that Japan's security policy is "normalizing," see Christopher Hughes, *Japan's Re-Emergence as a 'Normal' Military Power* (New York: Oxford University Press, 2004). For an argument that such fears are misplaced, see Andrew Oros, *Normalizing Japan: Politics, Identity and the Evolution of Security Practice* (Stanford: Stanford University Press, 2008).
4 For instance, the percentage of Americans that regarded Japan as a "dependable" ally or friend was only 44 percent in 1990. This number has steadily increased in the later years, with 60 percent in 2000 and 79 percent in 2010. Ministry of Foreign Affairs of Japan. *Beikoku ni okeru tainichi yoron chōsa (Heisei 22 nen)* [Opinion Poll on Japan Taken in the U.S. (2010)], http://www.mofa.go.jp/mofaj/press/release/22/6/PDF/060102.pdf.
5 Eisuke Sakakibara, *Shihonshugi o koeta nihon: Nihongata shijō keizai taisei no seiritsu to tenkai* [Japan That Surpassed Capitalism: The Establishment and Evolution of a Japanese Style Market Economy Structure] (Tokyo: Tōyō Keizai Shinpōsha, 1990). For the comparable English volume, see Eisuke Sakakibara, *Beyond Capitalism: The Japanese Model of Market Economics* (Lanham, MD: University Press of America, 1993).

6   Urban C. Lehner, "Nakasone Plan to Boost Japan's Defenses Irks Opposition Parties and Soviet Union," *Wall Street Journal*, January 25, 1983.

7   Teshima Ryuichi, *Gaikō haisen: 130 oku doru wa suna ni kieta* [Diplomatic Defeat: 13 Billion Dollars Have Perished in the Sand] (Tokyo: Shinchō Bunko, 2006), pp. 136–38.

8   Iokibe Makoto and Miyagi Taizō, eds., *Hashimoto Ryūtarō gaikō kaikoroku* [Memoir of Hashimoto Ryūtarō on Foreign Policy] (Tokyo: Iwanami, 2013), p. 25.

9   Cited from memorandum of telephone conversation between President George H.W. Bush and Japanese Prime Minister Toshiki Kaifu, August 13, 1990 (declassified through a Freedom of Information Act request by the National Security Archive and posted June 20, 2012, http://www2.gwu.edu/~nsarchiv/NSAEBB/NSAEBB382/.

10 Gaimushō, *Chūtō ni okeru heiwa kaifuku katsudō ni kakawaru wagakuni no kōkensaku* [The Contribution Plans of our Country Regarding Activities for Restoring Peace in the Middle East], August 29, 1990.

11 Steven R. Weisman. "Confrontation in the Gulf: Japan Promises Grants and Food, But Lack of Arms Aid Nettles U.S." *New York Times*, August 30, 1990.

12 Gaimushō, *Kishakiken ni okeru naikaku kanbō chōkan hatsugen yōshi* [Summary of the Statements Made by the Chief Cabinet Secretary in the Press Conference], August 30, 1990.

13 Teshima, *Gaikō haisen*, pp. 284–85.

14 Ibid., pp. 286–90.

15 Ibid., pp. 314–21. Iokibe and Miyagi, *Hashimoto Ryūtarō*, pp. 37–43.

16 For details on how Japan's diplomacy was divided into two between the Ministry of Foreign Affairs and the Finance Ministry, see Teshima, *Gaikō haisen*, pp. 328–403. Interview with Utsumi Makoto, August 13, 2013.

17 General H. Norman Schwarzkopf with Peter Petre, *It Doesn't Take a Hero: The Autobiography* (New York: Bantam Books, 1992), p. 424.

18 Michael H. Armacost, *Friends or Rivals? The Insider's Account of U.S.-Japan Relations* (New York: Columbia University Press, 1996), p. 102.

19 Nakayama Tarō, *Jinsei wa wakaranai kara omoshiroi* [Life Is Interesting because You Never Know What May Happen] (Tokyo: Chūō kōron shinsha, 2012), pp. 175–76.

20 Iokibe Makoto, Itō Motoshige, Yakushiji Katsuyuki eds., *Okamoto Yukio: Genbashugi o tsuranuita gaikōkan* [Okamoto Yukio: A Diplomat Who Stuck to His Principles] (Tokyo: Asahi Shimbun Publications, 2008), pp. 176–78.

21 "*Jieitai Haken ni 78% ga Hantai Houan Sansei wa 21%*" ["78% Opposes SDF Dispatch, 21% Supports UN Peace Cooperation Bill"], *Asahi Shimbun*, November 6, 1990.

22 Courtney Purrington, "Tokyo's Policy Responses to the Gulf War and the Impact of the Iraq Shock on Japan," *Pacific Affairs*, 65, no. 2 (Summer 1992), p. 166.

23 Interview with Terashima Kiyoshi, August 26, 2013.

24 Interview with Murakami Nobuo, August 15, 2013.

25 This has been confirmed in the response to questions in the 119th Diet, Special committee on United Nations Peace Cooperation, 8th Meeting.

26 Iokibe et al., *Okamoto Yukio*, p. 180.

27 Ibid., pp. 194–95.

28 Ibid., pp. 196–98.

29 Interview with Terashima Kiyoshi, August 26, 2013.

30 Interview with Nakayama Tarō, August 29, 2013; Mikuriya Takashi and Watanabe Akio, *Shushō kantei no ketsudan: Naikaku kanbō fukuchōkan Ishihara Nobuo no 2600 nichi* [Decision of the Office of Prime Minister: 2600 Days of Ishihara Nobuo as the Deputy Chief Cabinet Secretary] (Tokyo: Chūkō Bunko, 2002), pp. 81–82.

31 Former Foreign Minister Nakayama argues that the danger was the main reason for the doctors in declining to work at the field hospital, while the deputy chief cabinet secretary Ishihara argues that the concerns of violating the Constitution was also a factor.

Interview with Nakayama Tarō, August 29, 2013. Mikuriya et al., *Shushō kantei no ketsudan*, pp. 81–82.

32 Interview with Nakayama Tarō, August 29, 2013.
33 Iokibe et al., *Okamoto Yukio*, p. 168.
34 Kaifu Toshiki, *Seiji to kane: Kaifu Toshiki kaikoroku* [Politics and Money: A Memoir of Kaifu Toshiki] (Tokyo: Shinchōsha, 2010), p. 123.
35 Interview with Nakayama Tarō, August 29, 2013.
36 Kuriyama Takakazu, *Nichibei dōmei: Hyōryū kara no dakkyakku* [Japan-U.S. Alliance: Departing from Drift] (Tokyo: Nihon Keizai Shinbunsha, 1997), pp. 39–40.
37 Teshima, *Gaikō Haisen*, p. 185.
38 Kaifu Toshiki, *Seiji to kane*, pp. 122–23.
39 Iokibe Makoto, Itō Motoshige, Yakushiji Katsuyuki, eds. *Gaikō gekihen: Moto gaimushō jimujikan Yanai Shunji* [Revolution in Diplomacy: Former Vice-Minister of Foreign Affairs Yanai Shunji] (Tokyo: Asahi Shimbunsha, 2007), p. 54.
40 Paul Midford, *Rethinking Japanese Public Opinion and Security: From Pacifism to Realism?* (Stanford: Stanford University Press, 2011), pp. 69–75.
41 Murata Ryōhei, *Murata Ryōhei kaikoroku (ge)* [Memoir of Murata Ryōhei, Vol. 2]. (Tokyo: Minerva Shobō, 2008), p. 120.
42 Ibid., p. 121.
43 Armacost, *Friends or Rivals?* p. 99.
44 U.S. Department of Defense, *United States Security Strategy for the East Asia-Pacific Region* (Washington, DC: Department of Defense, Office of International Security Affairs, 1995), p. 10.
45 Okamoto Yukio reflects that this was a major factor in the Japanese side's own confusion about how best to respond to the crisis. Interview on July 31, 2013.
46 Green, *Japan's Reluctant Realism*, p. 19.
47 Bōei Mondai Kondankai, *Nihon no anzen hoshō to bōeiryoku no arikata: 21 seiki e mukete no tenbō* [The Modality of the Security and Defense Capability of Japan: Outlook for the 21st Century], http://www.ioc.u-tokyo.ac.jp/~worldjpn/documents/texts/JPSC/19940812.O1J.html.
48 The Japanese government dismissed the idea that the order mattered, but panelists on the commission at the time told the author that there was great debate and deliberateness about placing multilateralism ahead of the alliance.
49 Interview with Okamoto Yukio, July 31, 2013.
50 Okamoto and others in the JSDF and U.S. government were aiming for something more than the incubated humanitarian mission at Samawah – a relatively quiet sector in Iraq under British and Dutch protection. When a senior U.S. commander in Iraq met Okamoto and other Japanese officials, he praised their courage for taking such a critical mission – until his staff pointed out that the JSDF contingent was going to Samawah and not the hotbed of insurrection and heavy U.S. combat operations at *Samarra*.
51 Cited in Green, *Japan's Reluctant Realism*, p. 32. See also http://www.mofa.go.jp/policy/other/challenge21.html.

10 Foreign economic policy strategies and economic performance

Peter Drysdale and Shiro Armstrong[1]

Postwar trade and industrial transformation

The first four decades after the Second World War saw Japan effect a remarkable and successful trade and industrial transformation that allowed the economy not only to recover from the disastrous waste of war but also to catch up to the per capita income levels and living standards in the advanced industrial world. Postwar, the General Agreement on Tariffs and Trade (GATT) – later the World Trade Organization (WTO) – along with the global international institutions underpinning the Bretton Woods arrangements, put in place by the United States and its allies, were critical to renewing confidence in global economic engagement.

Japanese trade policy strategy over this forty-five-year postwar period was directed at establishing access to global markets. Market access was a prerequisite to acquiring the low-cost capital goods, technologies, industrial raw materials, and international food supplies that could bring industrial success and prosperity to a population-dense, resource-deficient economy such as that of Japan's. During the first twenty years, diplomatic energies were focused on extending the practice of the "most-favored-nation" (MFN) principle. This strategy offered Japan the promise of access to international markets and established Japan as a member of the Organisation for Economic Co-operation and Development (OECD) club and an Article IV member of the International Monetary Fund (IMF). While the lowering of barriers to imports came more slowly through successive rounds of GATT negotiations and through bilateral pressures from the United States (with significant and generally accepted exclusions like agriculture), this was still a period of substantial progress in the liberalization of Japanese markets for tradable goods.[2]

There was also pushback against the liberalization in the trade regime – in the form of restrictions on trade negotiated bilaterally outside the system – that controlled the growth of trade in textiles, for example. The precursor of more general restrictions that came to govern trade in textiles was the U.S.-Japan Cotton Textiles Agreement of 1962; these restrictions were not wound back until the Uruguay Round of trade negotiations in the 1980s.[3]

Yet, even at the height of Japan's participation in multilateral liberalization and despite formal adherence to the idea of all-round trade liberalization, strong currents of mercantilism remained in Japan's practice of trade policy.[4] The focus was on the promotion of exports and opening export markets more than on the liberalization of import markets in sectors in which Japan had a strong comparative disadvantage. A corollary of this current of mercantilism was an undervalued currency, faster growth of exports than of imports, and the steady accumulation of trade balances and current account surpluses, although these surpluses were mainly the result of other causes of the growth of Japanese net savings.[5]

Becoming a global player

While Japan remained a relatively small economy and held a relatively small share in international trade, it could get away with mercantilist, asymmetrical trade liberalization. However, as the economy grew and Japan became a large economy (and less of a "price taker" in international markets) whose trade policy behavior was of greater and greater importance to other major trading economies, the pressure mounted on Japan to undertake broader trade liberalization.[6] Reform of the international monetary system after 1971, growing flexibility in international exchange rates, and strong appreciation of the yen all put increasing pressure on the tradable goods sectors in the Japanese economy (excluding agriculture, which was insulated from international markets by quantitative barriers to trade) to maintain competitiveness through globalizing production. The 1980s saw a massive shift in Japanese production of labor-intensive activities offshore as the yen appreciated rapidly after the 1985 Plaza Accord, especially into Asia, driving a large growth of direct foreign investment and the expansion of international production networks.[7]

Argument in outline

The 1980s were the heyday of Japan's economic success. The catch-up with the advanced industrial economies was achieved. The currency was appreciating rapidly, foreign investment in Asia and around the world was expanding, and world economic leadership seemed within Japan's grasp. The country was assuming an important role in fashioning a new economic order in Asia and the Pacific. But the 1990s saw all this come tumbling down with the bursting of the asset bubble and the financial system in crisis.

This chapter explores the international economic policy dimensions of Japan's economic performance in the two decades that followed. We identify the three pillars of international policy strategy that underpinned Japan's success in the 1980s: it was a period of reform, trade liberalization, and large-scale investment by Japanese corporations abroad. It was also the era of the rise of the yen during a time of international monetary reform, when Japan was at the forefront of economic diplomacy, that provided new confidence in Asia Pacific economic cooperation. In the 1990s, but especially after the Asian financial crisis of 1997, Japan took a sharp turn away from commitment to the multilateral economic regime, of which it had been a significant beneficiary in the postwar period and an exemplar of its success, choosing a path of preferential bilateralism in trade policy to secure its regional trading interests. During the lost decades, Japan failed to develop a coherent strategy for playing a significant role in the international monetary system, and the limitations of foreign economic diplomacy over these years can be presumed to have affected economic performance more generally.

Grand Asian trade and economic reform strategy

Japan's trade growth and industrial development, which sustained higher-than-average growth in Japanese manufacturing productivity and put a safety net under Japanese economic performance even through the lost decades, was facilitated by three major initiatives in international economic policy in the 1980s. The first was commitment to liberalization of the international capital account and allowing the yen to appreciate strongly. The second was early commitment to the Uruguay Round of trade negotiations and becoming a collective player in broadening the GATT agenda to embrace dismantling the restrictions that had constrained exports of labor-intensive commodities (importantly textiles and clothing) from emerging economies, mainly Japan's neighbors in Asia. The third was a commitment to join with Australia in shaping the Asia Pacific Economic Cooperation (APEC) process that entrenched open trade and investment regimes across the region, including ultimately in China.[8] These commitments were the pillars of the foreign economic policy strategy that fostered remarkable Asian economic growth, collective commitment to economic reform and liberalization, and captured the gains from deeper integration in the East Asian and Pacific economies.

Steady appreciation of the yen from the late 1970s onward and the pressure of appreciation following the Plaza Accord in the 1980s forced Japanese manufacturing offshore to maintain industrial competitiveness. The share of Japanese manufacturing output produced offshore has accelerated sharply over the subsequent quarter century. Japanese corporations in the textiles and consumer electronics sector led the push into shifting the labor-intensive end of their activities abroad, first into Southeast Asia and later into China and elsewhere.[9] Japanese direct foreign investment into Asia surged and Japanese production networks, once characterized by their impenetrability by foreign suppliers,[10] led the way to the establishment of the complex, and open, supply-chain networks that typify the high degree of trade and investment integration in the East Asian economy today.[11]

Opening regional trade and investment

This development would not have been possible without a commitment in most economies across the region to open trade and investment regimes. An initiative important to entrenching East Asian economic openness was Japan's active role in helping to secure an emerging economy agenda in the Uruguay Round of GATT trade negotiations. Meanwhile, Malaysia and other Southeast Asian economies, as well as China, had established Special Economic Zones (SEZs), and they provided a platform for launching extensive offshore assembly production facilities, predominantly from Japan but also from other countries. The Uruguay Round saw the elaborate quantitative restrictions on the textiles and clothing trade gradually dismantled and agriculture brought into the negotiating agenda. Later, the Information Technology Agreement under the WTO reinforced the process of offshore manufacturing and assembly in electronics and electrical goods.[12]

A complementary strategy involved Japan's leadership with Australia in establishing the APEC forum as the primary framework for regional economic cooperation. The move to set up APEC signaled a newly emerging economic and political order in East Asia and the Pacific in the late 1980s, and Japan was a principal player.[13] The Asia Pacific region is characterized by massive economic and political transformations, whose scale and impact on the global economic system have centered dramatically on the growth of China in recent years. Japanese strategies toward regional cooperation needed to recognize that this process of transformation would continue, that it was positive, and that choking it off would damage prospects for regional prosperity and political and economic security. In Chapter 11, Shiraishi Takashi argues that these consequences were not anticipated, at least by Japanese leaders, who did not foresee that China's rise would eventually overshadow Japan's Asian leadership ambitions. Indeed, very few forecast accurately what these developments would set in train, even if their broad shape was not much in doubt.[14]

From the beginning, Asia's integration into the regional and global economy and its approach to regional cooperation was organized around a strategy of inclusiveness, born of the interest in continuing economic, political, and social change in East Asia. That interest is where the idea of open regionalism originated. It was important in this part of the world that regional cooperation be open in terms of the principles informing economic policy strategy, to realize the continuing inclusion of new players in the process and new opportunities for regional growth, trade, and development. Through the 1990s, China joined in this process and with successive unilateral trade liberalizations (especially those announced at the APEC Osaka Summit in 1995) as staging posts along the way eventually negotiated accession to the WTO in 2001.

These three pillars of Japanese international economy strategy, laid down in the 1980s, have sustained the competitiveness of Japan's core manufacturing sector over the past two to three decades. They are a significant factor behind Japanese manufacturing industry's superior productivity performance, and the baseline established to protect Japan against lower real income growth per head as the nonworking population grew with a rapidly ageing Japanese population, as detailed by Seike Atsushi in Chapter 1.[15] Since the East Asian financial crisis in 1997, Japan has not given significant priority to APEC, and it has launched a bilateral "free trade agreement" (FTA) strategy as the principal instrument of its foreign trade diplomacy. And yet, the three pillars remain in place and have had by far the most dominant impact on Japanese external commercial relations.

By the end of the 1980s, a model built on export-oriented growth was no longer sustainable. The combination of a strong yen after the Plaza Accord with an expansionary monetary policy fed a massive asset price bubble that eventually flattened in 1991.[16] Reliance on export-led recovery from the recession that followed was no longer a formula that worked. Japan's integration into the global economy was of course still critical to maintaining productivity (and income) growth, as explained above. But the country was not able to rely on export demand as a major driver of the economy's growth (although after China's 2001 accession to the WTO, the spurt of Chinese demand provided a new fillip to Japan's externally driven growth). Unwinding the mess in which Japan's leading financial institutions found themselves mired was a slow process.[17] The political will to deal with the structural problems that Japan faced in both the financial sector and in the vastly overinvested real economy was grossly absent.

Tactical retreat to bilateralism

The trade policy response to Japan's economic malaise of the 1990s, notably after the Asian financial crisis and failure to launch a new WTO round in 1997, was to retreat from the multilateral system and principles and ostensibly to seek revival of trade growth through embracing a strategy that put FTAs at the center. This aim was a significant shift in trade policy philosophy. Japan had stood out as a major trader that had eschewed discrimination in its approach to trade negotiations and clung resolutely to the MFN trading principle up until the 1990s.

Asian financial crisis and loss of faith in Washington

Regional institution building until the Asian financial crisis was limited to APEC and had required the involvement of the United States, as political estrangement between major East Asian countries made regional cooperation difficult. East Asian economic integration was market led, with APEC as the platform of cooperation and the concept of open regionalism allowing trade cooperation between East Asian neighbors without discriminating against those outside the region. This meant financial and monetary cooperation was at an embryonic stage when the Asian financial crisis hit and arguably allowed the crisis to emerge in the way it did.

The Asian financial crisis of 1997 and 1998 was an important turning point for East Asia. As growth in East Asia hit a wall in 1997, with Japan in the midst of its banking crisis and already facing half a decade of slow growth, the region looked to Washington for help – help that never came. Consequently, confidence in U.S. leadership and engagement in Asia was severely shaken.

As the then-second largest economy in the world, Japan played an important role in the process of putting together the rescue packages for the East Asian economies and was in fact their main donor under the 1999 aid initiative known as the Miyazawa Plan. But Japan was less successful in influencing the substance of the rescue packages or defining strategies – such as through the proposed creation of an Asian Monetary Fund – for dealing with future crises, due to a lack of capacity to provide overall leadership, which in turn was due to its own financial and economic problems.[18]

The Asian financial crisis was the proximate cause of the collapse of the status quo that triggered the emergence of the new regionalism in East Asia. A more exclusively East Asian regionalism and preferential trading initiatives gained sway: this was partly driven by the complex political response to Washington's weak role in dealing with the 1997 financial crisis, the inability of Japan to lead the region because of its own economic problems, and a loss of faith in APEC's ability to resolve contemporary financial problems. Those forces were both economic and political and they drove the marked shift in thinking about regional cooperation in East Asia and the Pacific.[19]

Ambitions for an East Asian community

Previously, former Prime Minister Mahathir of Malaysia had proposed but failed to form an East Asian Economic Caucus. However, the circumstances in the late 1990s were quite different. The mismanagement of the crisis coupled with the failure to launch a new WTO round of trade negotiations in Seattle, which had been so central to APEC's trade liberalization agenda,[20] came to justify heading in a new direction through the ASEAN+3[21] enterprise and the negotiation of bilateral preferential trade arrangements in East Asia.[22] ASEAN+3 is now at the core of East Asian arrangements, including the East Asian Summit. The East Asian financial crisis provided an imperative for deeper financial and trade cooperation within East Asia. However, Japan's own domestic financial market was hit hard by the crisis, and its call for an "Asian Monetary Fund" met with little support, even within the East Asian region. Japan had little willpower or capacity to avert the U.S. retreat from a new WTO round in Seattle in 1998, and impetus on the issue of trade liberalization within the APEC framework waned. It was against this backdrop that the emergence of ASEAN+3 reflected the regional interest in regrouping, constructing a framework for institutionalizing economic cooperation within the East Asian region.[23]

To the East Asian governments, ASEAN+3 was a convenient insurance policy for East Asian dealings with Washington and an expression of regional solidarity through socioeconomic cooperation and interdependence. This concept of an emerging East Asian community gathered momentum in the coming years, although the leadership contest between Japan and China gnawed at its core. Finally, by January 2002 in Singapore, Prime Minister Koizumi Junichiro proposed extending the East Asian community to include cooperation beyond trade and financial issues to promote regional integration, with Australia and New Zealand among its members. In 2005, when the first East Asian Summit was convened, Australia, New Zealand, and India were invited to participate in union with the ASEAN+3.

Neither the ASEAN+3 group nor the ASEAN+6 group was able to formalize into trade arrangements measures that were being advocated by some who wanted more binding cooperation. The real value gained from the East Asian arrangements was the institutionalized cooperation and resulting institution building done on East Asian terms. ASEAN+3 in particular provided a framework for demonstrating East Asian leadership and influence on regional and international affairs. The focus in ASEAN+3 was very much on financial cooperation. China came to this arrangement, embracing Japan, with unexpected enthusiasm. This was a deeply political decision, much more than an economic policy strategy. China's interest in ASEAN+3, encouraged by political events like the bombing of its embassy in Belgrade and the Cox Report in the United States, also acted as an insurance against continuing problems in the U.S.-China relationship.

Alongside the development of regionalism under the ASEAN+3 and ASEAN+6 framework, many countries in the region looked to strengthen ties, and bilateral deals offered a relatively easy way forward.

Bilateral preferentialism

Japan's advocacy of and the priority it attached to the multilateral trading system started its end in favor of preferential trade agreements in 1998.[24] This occurred not because of any purposeful decision that had been debated in Japanese policy-making circles or because of a strategic leadership decision, but in the lead-up to South Korean President Kim Dae Jung's visit to Japan. The context was the Asian financial crisis, Japan and East Asia's quest for stronger institutional ties, the desire for stronger political ties within Asia, and a search for Korea-Japan rapprochement.

The *White Paper on International Trade* that the Ministry of International Trade and Industry (MITI) issued in 1998 still espoused the supremacy of the multilateral system for Japanese trade, and the only mention that FTAs received in it was negative.[25] Yet, by late 1998 Japan and Korea were embarking on plans for an FTA, culminating in the launch of a joint study of a Japan-Korea Free Trade Agreement by December that year with ministerial support. That agreement has yet to be negotiated, as political differences among the parties and an inability to liberalize have stymied the process.

Japan's first foray into negotiating FTAs was with Singapore in 2002. A Japan-Singapore agreement was proposed in December 1999 and a joint study launched in 2000, halfway through the lost decades. This was not only Japan's first bilateral trade agreement but, significantly, the first bilateral FTA between two Asian countries. The agreement was termed an economic partnership agreement (EPA) and was relatively easy to promote, given that Singapore had virtually no tariffs and that agriculture could be excluded because Singapore did not have an agricultural sector.[26] The 1999 *White Paper on International Trade* from MITI revealed a shift in philosophy towards FTAs, while still noting their dangers for the multilateral system.[27] The argument in favor of FTAs was that they could "provide models of rule-making for multilateral fora including the WTO" and were "able to advance multilateral negotiations stuck in deadlock."[28] Unfortunately, subsequent white papers from METI (the Ministry of Economy, Trade and Industry, formerly MITI) have not explicitly nor actively directed FTAs towards strengthening the multilateral system.[29] Given the lack of liberalization that the Japan-Singapore EPA brought with it, its significance was mostly symbolic in the message it sent to the rest of the region. The Japan-Singapore Economic Agreement signaled a retreat from Japan's strong support for the multilateral system and the MFN principle. It also encouraged China to quickly negotiate an FTA with ASEAN, and FTAs have since proliferated among Japan's neighbors and trading partners.

Apart from Singapore (which, as stated above, has no agricultural sector) and Switzerland (not a major trading partner of Japan), Japan's FTAs to date have all been with developing countries. Japan took measures to offer investment and economic cooperation to these countries while keeping its own agricultural sector largely protected.[30] The same strategy allowed Japanese service industries to be excluded from its trade agreements. Japan's negotiations with developed countries that are also major agricultural exporters, such as Australia, stalled because of these tactics.

Yet, the trade and investment diverted away from non-FTA members have not been as damaging to economic relations, and therefore have not significantly undermined political relations in Asia as much as many studies had predicted.[31] The reason is not because FTAs took into account the interests of third parties and the multilateral system, but rather because they were not comprehensive enough and had no real economic bite.[32]

Divorce of trade policy from national reform objectives

Japan has EPAs under negotiation with South Korea, Australia, the Gulf Cooperation Council, Canada, Mongolia, Colombia, and the European Union. While the rhetoric might suggest otherwise, the impact of the agreements thus far has been limited and piecemeal – protecting against, rather than promoting, needed reforms in agriculture and services, advancing particular, limited interests in partner economies (such as investor protection and aid procurement) – and not directed toward any strategic national reform and growth goal. Japan's early FTAs were not entered into after careful deliberation of their economic costs and benefits but were politically, diplomatically, and strategically oriented.[33]

Major reforms of regulatory institutions and competition policies that would lift Japanese productivity in services (effectively the nontradable sector) cannot be delivered through negotiating trade agreements, even with advanced economies such as the United States.[34] These reforms have been entirely absent in the negotiating agendas of the Japanese bilateral FTAs put in place with a range of developing country partners. The pattern of Japanese international trade diplomacy over these years aimed to avoid negotiation of sensitive, reform-embracing issues with advanced country partners such as Australia or the United States. The FTAs that describe Japan's international trade and economic policy strategy over the past two decades have specifically avoided the difficult reforms. Indeed, avoiding the challenge of agricultural trade liberalization has been a critical factor in determining the priority in FTA negotiations. Extant agreements have been called EPA arrangements and aimed at securing treatment of Japanese investment abroad and access in partners who have little leverage in opening Japanese markets. There is hope among Japanese advocates for delivering a broad economic reform agenda

through the Japan-EU FTA and through the Trans-Pacific Partnership (TPP) negotiations. However, that may be misplaced, too, unless those negotiations are taken
as a symbol of commitment to much broader reform beyond what would actually
be included in the negotiations themselves.

Bilateral and preferential trade agreements could have been directed at making
progress on some priority areas of reform and liberalization in Japan. A heavily
protected and subsidized agricultural sector, although a relatively small part of the
economy and shrinking over these decades to only 1.5 percent of gross domestic product (GDP) in 2005, is a drag on Japanese government revenues and has
hamstrung Japanese economic diplomacy.[35] To put it succinctly, Japan chose to
negotiate only with partners with whom the agriculture issue could be avoided.
Liberalization of this sensitive sector was minimized because of the agricultural
lobby's stranglehold on Japanese lawmakers.[36] Trade agreements could have been
used to break the deadlock in some of Japan's most protected sectors before opening up to the rest of the world. This strategic intent was absent from Japanese
negotiating strategy; FTAs were acquired more as diplomatic trophies than pursued as elements in a serious economic reform strategy. The contrast between
Korea's and Japan's approaches to FTAs could not be more stark.

Contrasting Japanese and Korean strategies

Japan's trade policy strategy contrasts sharply with that of its neighbor South
Korea, which negotiated major bilateral agreements with the United States and
Europe and used them to effect significant domestic reforms in services and agriculture. Korea was strategic in its trade policy approach, using FTAs to open up a
wide range of industries – such as financial, insurance, and other service sectors
as well as agriculture, automobile, and other industries – to more international
competition. While liberalization through FTAs has its drawbacks, given the preferential and limited nature of liberalization (and Korean FTAs were no exception
in their discrimination against other partners such as Australia), Korea used this
policy tool for broad economic reform, not merely diplomatic purposes.

Korea's FTAs have been the most comprehensive in Asia. Nowhere else in Asia
has an FTA strategy been so successful in liberalizing protected sectors and so
closely connected to furthering domestic reforms. The challenge now for Korea
is to remove the distortions that FTAs have introduced into its trading structure
by opening up to the rest of the world, including Japan and China, so that it can
increase competition and contestability in its market through extending access to
lower cost and more efficient suppliers of goods and services.[37]

The most significant example in the region of how to connect domestic reform
priorities to external trade policy is that of China through its progress via accession to the WTO in 2001. China used the run-up to WTO accession to liberalize
and to open up unilaterally on an unprecedented scale, while also using platforms
like APEC to deliver on its reform agenda. Signing up to the WTO entrenched
and extended the domestic economic and institutional reforms that were required
across the country. While the circumstances of China's accession to the WTO

were completely different from the challenges that Japan faced over the past two decades, the lesson is one of how leadership in one case did, and in the other case did not, mobilize external arrangements to promote critical domestic reforms.

It is perhaps ironic that Japan's initial shift in policy toward FTAs came with the exploration of an FTA with Korea − only to be put on hold because it could not manage political cleavages or embrace the difficulty of negotiating a comprehensive trading agreement with its important neighbor, while Korea went on to sign meaningful agreements with its major advanced-economy trading partners.

Failure to internationalize the yen

The economic rise of Japan made it the second largest economy in the world − on a trajectory at one stage that seemed poised to overtake the United States as the largest. As Japan's weight in global transactions increased, the prospect that the yen might become a significant international reserve currency appeared real. The yen had the potential to be widely used for invoicing international trade and to be held in reserves for exchange management and as insurance against financial and economic shocks. The potential of the Japanese yen as an international currency gained attention in the mid-1980s and again after the Asian financial crisis at the end of the 1990s. In the earlier period this was encouraged by the rise of the Japanese economy and later an anxiety about overreliance of the East Asian region on the dollar. The yen satisfied some of the prerequisites for development as an international currency, with Japan's political stability and large economy; but what was absent were deep, broad, and efficient financial markets, and the liberalization of the capital account was incomplete.

In the 1980s, domestic political ambivalence over currency strategies prevented decisive steps necessary to internationalize the yen. In part this was due to the long dependence on the dollar.[38] The Bank of Japan was reluctant to lose its macroeconomic policy autonomy by relaxing capital controls, and there was a split within the Ministry of Finance over whether to proceed.[39] Domestic opposition to financial liberalization resulted in underdevelopment of short-term financial markets, making it less attractive for nonresidents to hold yen. The forces opposing the internationalization of the yen feared that less control over the yen, if it became a reserve currency, would mean Japan would likely have to run a current account deficit. Holdings of yen reserves by Asian countries grew from 15 percent of their total holdings in 1983 to 30 percent in 1987, mostly due to the appreciation of the yen after the Plaza Accord, but they fell to 17 percent by 1990.[40]

In the late 1990s, there was a second wave of interest in the internationalization of the yen with the prospect of the emergence of the Euro currency zone in the aftermath of the Asian financial crisis. The crisis provided strong incentive in Japan to promote the use of the yen in East Asia. Dependence on the dollar, including pegging regional exchange rates to it, was seen as one of the causes of the crisis. But by then Japan was in the middle of the first decade of economic stagnation, and promoting the international use of the yen was even less likely than it had been in the 1980s. The yen's role as a vehicle currency for trade between third countries had also been negligible. Much of Japan's large volume of trade with its East Asian neighbors was invoiced in dollars because many of these countries pegged their exchange rates to the dollar and the final destination for goods resulting from the Asian production networks was the United States. All of its resource trade was transacted in dollars. But it was the lack of financial market development that fundamentally hampered the use of yen-invoiced trade.

Japanese financial and capital markets were never fully deregulated in the 1980s – and in the late 1990s, when policymakers revisited the internationalization of the yen, this situation continued. Even as late as 1998, there were major constraints on yen transactions in domestic capital markets, especially in short-term capital markets, which stymied the use of the yen internationally.[41] There was a need for risk-free assets and highly liquid financial products, which are important as a benchmarking tool in developing financial products and also for deepening the financial and credit markets. The lack of liquidity and financial market development meant that the Japanese market did not establish a yield curve, and that restricted access to risk-hedging measures. Japanese yen balances and assets held by nonresidents was, and still is, low.

Some in Japan argue that language difference is a significant reason why the yen did not internationalize. But this barrier would seem to have been insignificant compared to the failure to commit to developing liberalized, deep, broad, and efficient financial markets. Rather, policy indecision and the failure to undertake the financial market reforms that are necessary for currency internationalization were the major reasons why Japan missed the opportunity to become a significant player in the international financial system. How did these weaknesses in foreign economic policy strategies affect Japan's economic performance? This is the core question in this chapter. In order to answer it, first we need to define the benchmarks whereby Japan's economic performance might be judged objectively. This can be done by measuring Japan's economic potential and assessing how fully it was realized.

Japan's economic potential

We can start by asking how Japan's economic performance compared with similar economies over the years of the lost decades. This question is critical to a careful assessment of whether Japan's economic performance was an inescapable consequence of its economic and demographic destiny, or whether the policy choices that were made over these years led to underachievement and a failure to realize the country's true potential. If the economic indicators for other economies – in similar circumstances, beset by similar problems – reveal a better performance than that of Japan, the sobriquet "lost decades" is apposite. These comparisons provide a metric by which Japan's performance can be judged objectively and some scientific precision brought to bear on the question.

At the core of Japan's economic bind is the management of the dramatic impact of its shrinking population. While this demographic transformation is of a kind that is now more common among mature industrial economies, nowhere else is it quite as intense, it seems, as in Japan. This is fully described by Seike Atsushi in

Chapter 1. With a shrinking workforce having a strongly negative effect on output per head of population, the only way to lift economic growth is to lift productivity substantially. Japan can only get more output from its shrinking population by encouraging or requiring that a larger proportion of the population actively engage in work or by lifting the average product of labor employed. There are also, of course, the options of lifting the population base over time through immigration or pro-natal policies.

Table 10.1 sets out data that shows how Japan's performance measures up objectively in comparison with other economies that have characteristics that, in one dimension or another, match those of Japan. As Column 1 in the table demonstrates, Japan's overall growth in real income per head of population has been below average OECD growth rates for most of the period after 1990, as well as all individual OECD economies selected here, except for France for the five years from 1990 to 1995 and Italy and the United Kingdom (which it matched) for the five years from 2005 to 2011. But, after adjusting for the shrinkage in the workforce and the ageing of the population, Japan's GDP growth rate per working-age population is highest among industrialized countries over the 2000 to 2010 period.[42] Japanese overall performance by this measure, it is argued, is not as bad as it looks from the measure of output per head; and there were periods, for example during the Koizumi years, when Japan actually did relatively well. Yet, as shown in Column 6, which sets out comparative labor productivity performance after 1990, only in the period 2000 to 2005 was Japan's annual rate of productivity growth unambiguously better than those of the OECD economies selected for comparison. For most of these years, productivity growth was not especially high. It certainly was not able to significantly overwhelm the effects of the shrinking workforce on overall growth, as reflected in Column 5.

An analysis of the contribution of labor, capital, and total factor productivity (a measure of the impact of increased efficiency and improved technology in lifting output per unit of factor input) to GDP growth in Japan and the selected OECD economies is more telling. Except for the years 2000 to 2005, total factor productivity growth in Japan was lower than that of major comparable OECD economies and, even in that period 2000 to 2005, the United Kingdom and the United States both had higher total factor productivity growth than that of Japan. In short, while Japan's total factor productivity has grown moderately well, it has not grown as rapidly as that of the best performing comparable economies.[43] It should be added that Japan's performance on all these measures over the entire period has fallen well short of that of Korea, although it might be argued that Korea, with a lower per capita income, still had some catch-up potential that it could take advantage of at that time. While productivity in Japanese firms remains higher than in Korean firms, there is much evidence that Korean firms caught up very rapidly over these years.[44]

Japan's international performance

How does Japan's mediocre, or at best average, economic performance relate to its external economic strategies? One way of assessing the efficiency and

Table 10.1 Comparative measures of Japan's potential and actual economic performance during the lost decades

Period	Country	GDP Growth	Factor Contribution to GDP growth		Employment growth	Total hours worked growth	Labor Productivity growth (per person)	FDI Performance (Inward Stock)	Trade Performance Export	Trade Performance Import
			Labor	TFP						
1985–1990	Canada	2.8	2	−0.6	2.6	2.6	0.3			
	France	3.2	0.8	1.6	1.0	1.0	2.2			
	Germany	NA	NA	NA	1.9	0.8	1.4			
	Italy	3.1	0.7	1.4	0.9	0.9	2.3			
	Japan	4.9	0.3	3.2	1.0	0.4	3.9			
	Korea	9.9	1.9	6	3.9	2.3	6.3			
	Netherlands	3.3	1.3	1.1	2.4	1.7	0.9			
	United Kingdom	3.3	1.5	0.4	1.8	1.8	1.5			
	United States	3.2	1.5	0.8	2.0	2.0	1.2			
1990–1995	Canada	1.7	0.1	0.7	0.1	−0.1	1.6			
	France	1.2	−0.6	1.1	−0.1	−0.7	1.3			
	Germany	NA	NA	NA	−0.1	−0.5	2.1			
	Italy	1.3	−0.6	1.2	−0.7	−0.8	2.0			
	Japan	1.4	−0.5	0.6	0.8	−0.7	0.6			
	Korea	7.6	1.8	3.8	2.4	2.2	5.3			
	Netherlands	2.3	1	0.5	1.3	1.4	0.9			
	United Kingdom	1.6	−0.9	1.3	−0.8	−1.2	2.8			
	United States	2.5	1	0.8	1.2	1.3	1.3			

1995–2000	Canada	4	1.6	1.2	2.1	2.1	2.0			
	France	2.7	0.5	1.3	1.6	0.7	1.1			
	Germany	1.8	0	1.1	0.8	0.0	1.0			
	Italy	1.9	0.7	0.4	1.0	1.0	0.9			
	Japan	0.8	−0.9	0.7	−0.5	−1.2	1.3			
	Korea	5.1	−0.3	3.6	0.7	−0.4	4.4			
	Netherlands	4	1.7	1.2	2.6	2.3	1.5			
	United Kingdom	3.4	0.7	1.3	1.3	0.9	2.3			
	United States	4.3	1.6	1.5	2.0	1.9	2.3			
2000–2005	Canada	2.5	1	0.5	2.0	1.7	0.5	0.31	0.39	0.37
	France	1.6	0.2	0.7	0.6	0.2	1.0	0.34	0.43	0.38
	Germany	0.6	−0.6	0.8	−0.2	−0.8	0.8	0.30	0.43	0.38
	Italy	1	0.6	−0.4	1.2	0.8	−0.3	0.22	0.40	0.36
	Japan	1.2	−0.5	1.1	−0.1	−0.6	1.3	0.18	0.36	0.33
	Korea	4.4	0.2	2.8	1.6	0.3	2.9	0.18	0.49	0.36
	Netherlands	1.3	−0.2	0.9	0.3	−0.3	1.0	0.29	0.48	0.38
	United Kingdom	2.9	0.5	1.3	0.9	0.6	2.0	0.37	0.41	0.37
	United States	2.4	−0.1	1.8	0.3	−0.1	2.1	0.35	0.38	0.43

(Continued)

Table 10.1 (Continued)

Period	Country	GDP Growth	Factor Contribution to GDP growth		Employment growth	Total hours worked growth	Labor Productivity growth (per person)	FDI Performance (Inward Stock)	Trade Performance Export	Trade Performance Import
			Labor	TFP						
2005–2011	Canada	1.4	0.7	−0.1	1.3	0.9	0.1	0.40	0.41	0.37
	France	0.8	0.1	0.1	0.4	0.2	0.5	0.43	0.42	0.38
	Germany	1.6	0.5	0.7	0.9	0.6	0.7	0.37	0.44	0.39
	Italy	−0.2	−0.2	−0.5	0.2	−0.2	−0.4	0.25	0.41	0.37
	Japan	0.3	−0.5	0.6	−0.3	−0.7	0.5	0.22	0.39	0.34
	Korea	3.7	−0.7	3.3	1.0	−1.0	2.8	0.21	0.52	0.40
	Netherlands	NA	NA	NA	0.9	0.7	0.4	0.38	0.50	0.42
	United Kingdom	0.3	−0.1	−0.5	0.2	−0.3	0.4	0.42	0.41	0.38
	United States	0.9	−0.4	0.8	−0.3	−0.4	1.2	0.38	0.41	0.42

Note: In Columns 1 to 6, annual growth rates here are calculated as annual compound growth rates. In Columns 7 to 9, the numbers are ratios or convert to percentages.

Source: OECD statistics and authors' calculations.

contestability of national markets is to compare how Japan's actual trade flows and investment flows compare with potential flows and how much of potential trade and investment was captured relative to comparable economies. The data in Columns 8 and 9 of Table 10.1 provide an idea of the extent to which these OECD economies have realized their trade potential on this measure. The ratios of actual trade flows (exports and imports) to potential trade flows (estimated from the frontier of best performance derived from the analysis of trade flows and economies' location, endowments, and size) provide an econometric measure of the openness and efficiency of each economy's integration into international trade. These ratios are reported in Columns 8 and 9 of the table for the last two periods in the sample. Similarly, the ratios of actual inward investment flows to potential inward investment flows (derived from a frontier of best investment performance in a way analogous to that for the trade frontier) are seen in Column 7.

Trade integration has become deeper and the realization of both export and import potential has risen somewhat for most countries over the two periods for which these data are available. But Japan's trade performance – the ratio of its actual trade flows to potential trade – was extremely low over both periods when compared with similar economies in Asia and in the industrial world. Japan realized only 36 percent of its export potential and 33 percent of its import potential in the period from 2000 to 2005, and 39 percent of its export potential and 34 percent of its import potential in the period from 2005 to 2011. In both periods for which these calculations are made, Japan achieved less of its export and import potential than any of these OECD economies. This gap implies that Japanese trade policies and institutions were significantly less open than those of comparable economies. The contrast with Korea's performance is marked. Korea had significantly higher and rising export and import performance over these years, with exports at 52 percent and imports at 40 percent of potential in the last period, significantly closer to its trade frontier than Japan.

Investment flows are another important channel allowing us to see the benefits of integration into the international economy. Foreign direct investment (FDI) outflows reflect the capacity of a country's businesses to reap the rewards of the capital, know-how, and technological and marketing assets it has accumulated through investment abroad. More importantly, inward investment flows reflect the contribution through investment that foreign firms bring to a country's economy through their capital, know-how, and technology. High levels of engagement in foreign investment are critical to the ability of mature economies to stay close to the global technology frontier and to maintain access to the latest management and technological capabilities.

Japan's inward investment performance, at 18 percent of potential in 2000–05 and 22 percent in 2005–11, is markedly worse than all these OECD economies, except for Korea. In respect of openness to foreign investment, Korea's performance was similar to that of Japan. Most other OECD countries were almost twice as open as Japan to foreign investors in both periods. The Japanese foreign investment policy regime and related institutions and policy settings limit flows of foreign investment into Japan and stymie productivity, innovation, and growth.

Although Japan's outward foreign investment is extensive, especially in production networks around Asia, similar analysis also reveals that Japan's performance on this front is also well below potential, at 30 percent in both periods compared with close to 50 percent for most other OECD economies except Korea.

The story of Japan's poor foreign investment performance is related to a number of institutional impediments beyond controls of investment at the border. For one thing, the difficulty for foreign investors to acquire established firms through mergers or acquisitions relates to still-entrenched Japanese capital market institutions that cosset local firms. Additionally, Japan's major cities fail to provide international business environments on a par with London, New York, and Shanghai. Regulations on floor-area ratios, for example, limit accessible high-rise residential buildings in metropolitan Japan. Obstacles to setting up international schools and to allowing foreign doctors to practice, which are important amenities for attracting foreign firms and personnel to Japan, discourage the sojourn of professional and management personnel in Japan.[45] Poor foreign investment performance is closely related to remarkably low rates of migration and movement of skilled and professional people into and out of the country, as also described in by Seike Atsushi in Chapter 1, on demography. Japan has the lowest net migration rate (0.2 per 1,000 people for 2005–10) among the G7 countries and is the only OECD country that does not have a policy for the integration of noncitizens. In a disturbing trend, the number of Japanese students enrolled at American universities has also dropped 38 percent over the past decade. All these factors suggest that Japan has failed to translate gains from trade, foreign investment, international know-how, and skills into economic growth.

Figure 10.1 compares the ratio of inward stock of investment to GDP in a number of countries in Asia and the Pacific, including Japan. The extremely low ratio for Japan confirms its impenetrability to foreign investment compared with countries as diverse as the United States, China, and India. Figure 10.2 provides an OECD index of foreign investment restrictiveness across another diverse range of economies that reveals Japan as the third most restrictive investment regime among the group, topped only by Indonesia and China. As Figure 10.3 shows, Japan also lagged behind the world in the dynamic area of services trade growth, with a growth rate around 62 percent that of the global average rate of growth and lower than all countries reported here.[46]

While average product growth per person in the workforce was respectable in the decade after the year 2000, there was great variation across sectors of the economy, with poor performance in services and in other sectors insulated from international competition. Studies of cross-sectoral productivity performance suggest that the best performers were manufacturing sectors that liberalized or service sectors that were subject to privatization or deregulation.[48] A number of features distinguish the poor performing sectors in the Japanese economy. The first and most important is that it remains relatively closed. A second and related feature is the extent to which these sectors are burdened by government regulations and restrictions. Last, the extent to which those sectors of the economy have been burdened by supporting failing firms has taken a toll.[49]

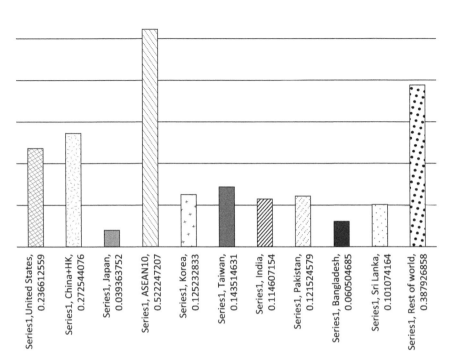

Figure 10.1 Inward FDI stocks relative to GDP, 2010 (ratio)

Source: United Nations Conference on Trade and Development (UNCTAD), UNCTADStat.

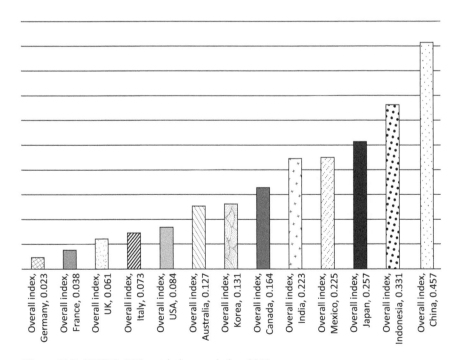

Figure 10.2 OECD's FDI restrictiveness index, 2010

Source: Kalinova, Palerm, and Thomsen (2010).[47]

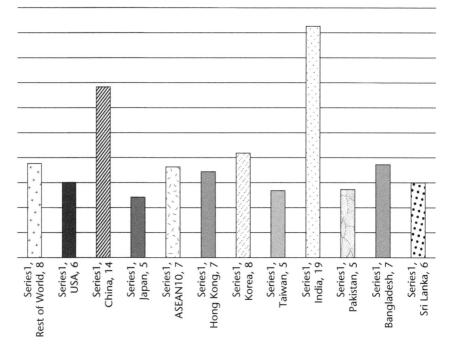

Figure 10.3 Growth rates of services exports 1995–2009 (percent)
Source: UNCTAD, UNCTADStat.

If productivity performance had been uniformly high across sectors, Japan's growth would have been considerably higher over these decades. It appears that the international contestability of markets (obviously in some commodities like agricultural goods but more importantly in services and capital markets) was an important factor that impeded Japanese growth over these years.

Governments, through the past two decades, have not articulated a comprehensive strategy for reform and have been more focused on particular symptoms of the problem than its fundamental causes. A failure to reform labor market institutions to allow more flexibility in the reallocation of labor and the increased participation of women when the supply is shrinking are both cases in point, as detailed by Andrew Gordon in Chapter 5 on labor and globalization and Seike Atsushi in Chapter 1 on demography.[50] An inability to break the deadlock on agricultural reform is another fundamental issue.[51] The Japanese government continues to work in silos when the interdependence of policy making is paramount to progress. This inability means that Japan does not articulate an international economic strategy that has comprehensive domestic structural reform as its centerpiece.

And yet, under the burdens that appear among other things to have condemned Japan to two decades of stagnant growth, the manufacturing sector (unlike services and agriculture), continually exposed to intense international competition, has achieved a strong turnaround.[52] While manufacturing firms cannot change the institutions that impede adjustment, for example in the labor market, they can maneuver around them. Such actions help explain why a third of the Japanese workforce is now employed as nonregular workers (non-lifetime employed).[53]

Manufacturing corporations have raised competiveness by taking production of low-valued activities offshore into Asia and China on a large scale. Japanese firms that compete internationally have, on average, higher labor productivity. Those firms that export or are engaged in FDI are more productive than purely domestic firms.[54] Over a third of the output of Japanese manufacturers is now produced abroad, significantly in Asia.[55] Globalization of production and off-shoring has not produced the same strains at home that are evident in North America, among other reasons because the labor force is shrinking. The drift in international economic policy strategy has produced an economy that has an incredibly efficient manufacturing sector but is burdened by inefficiencies and low productivity growth in services and agriculture. In manufacturing, decades of trade liberalization and a measure of capital penetration have delivered internationally contestable markets that have maintained the pressure for productivity improvement and change. There is a strong correlation between openness to international competition and contestability and cross-sectoral productivity performance in the Japanese economy.[56]

Foreign economic policy as an instrument of national reform

What is clear is that over the past two decades Japanese governments have not enunciated a comprehensive strategy for reform. Japan's economic performance has suffered. High impediments to achieving trade and investment potential, relative to comparable economies, are one important part of the problem. Many of the reforms that would deliver higher economic growth in Japan are largely domestic: they have to do with fixing the public and service sectors that relate to managing an ageing society through social benefits, the health sector, the pension system, taxation, and migration policy. But there is also an important international dimension to the structural reforms that Japan needs, related to how Japanese firms, especially those in the service sector, are to become more integrated into the global economy. Currently, the ratio of Japan's trade (exports plus imports) to GDP is only one-third of Germany's,[57] and services trade as a proportion of GDP is low, with slow growth (Figure 10.3). With very little proactive policy change from Japan toward China during the period 1990–2010, China went from accounting for 3.5 percent of Japan's total merchandise trade to being by far the largest trading partner at 20.7 percent (Table 10.2). That remarkable shift in Japan's trade relations occurred despite Japan's political tensions with China. The bilateral trading relationship is now the third largest in the world and is continuing to grow.

Japan's domestic circumstances also infect the psychology of economic diplomacy and foreign policy. The strategic inconsistencies in the politics and economics of relations with China are little remarked upon, if indeed they are understood and accepted (see Shiraishi Takashi in Chapter 11, on China; and Togo Kazuhiko in Chapter 13 for related points). There seems to be more and more acceptance

Table 10.2 Japan's top 10 trading partners (percent share and US $ mil)

	1990	1995	2000	2005	2010
China	3.5	7.4	10.0	17.0	20.7
United States	27.6	25.4	25.0	18.1	13.0
South Korea	5.6	6.2	6.0	6.4	6.2
EU	4.6	5.6	6.3	5.5	5.2
Australia	3.7	2.9	2.7	3.3	4.1
Thailand	2.5	3.8	2.8	3.4	3.8
Indonesia	3.4	3.1	2.8	2.7	3.0
Hong Kong	2.9	3.9	3.4	3.4	3.0
Saudi Arabia	2.6	1.6	2.0	3.0	2.9
Malaysia	2.1	3.5	3.3	2.4	2.8
Rest of world	41.5	36.5	35.8	34.7	35.4
Total	521,746	779,032	858,984	1,110,807	1,462,460

Source: UN Comtrade; authors' calculations.

of Japan's middle power and dependent status internationally. This change is not necessarily bad or unrealistic but it appears as a consequence of drift rather than the product of deliberate national strategic choice. Foreign and security policy have not adapted to these circumstances. Whether this will be sustainable in the long term given Japan's deeper and deeper economic interdependence with China's growth remains a critical question.

Regulatory barriers and protected markets

As shown in the above analysis, Japan has maintained low degrees of openness to foreign investment and talent and international linkages compared to other industrial economies. The share of foreign investor participation in the Japanese economy is very low compared with that in other industrial countries. Attracting FDI and foreign talent requires structural reform that makes doing business in Japan easier, and it also means addressing the immigration issue. Indicators from 2010 show just how badly Japan has performed relative to the rest of the world in its business environment for foreign firms and foreign workers. The World Economic Forum's Global Competitive Index (GCI) ranks Japan at eighth overall in 2010, up from 13th in 2008 for the competitiveness of its economy.[58]

But the rankings of Japan's external economic engagement in the GCI's Enabling Trade Index paint a different picture. Japan is ranked 25th overall internationally (of 125 countries) with the indicator for *market access* ranked 121 – close to worst in the world. When market access is divided into its domestic and foreign components, it shows not only how protected Japan is from foreign entrants in the market – ranked 124, or second to last globally – but also how poorly it is ranked with respect to market access for new domestic entrants – at 98th globally. There are also issues in Japan's regulatory environment according to the Enabling Trade

Index, with Japan ranked 77th in openness to foreign participation due to the dif-ficulties in hiring foreign labor (111th globally), prevalence of foreign ownership (89th), and the business impact of rules on FDI (92nd).[59]

The World Bank's Doing Business index ranks Japan 15th overall in ease of doing business, but looking at the components that comprise that overall score exposes similar problems to those identified in the GCI index. Japan ranks 90th in the ease in starting a business, 40th in employing workers, and 123rd in paying taxes.[60] The Fraser Institute's Economic Freedom of the World index for 2010 paints a similar story, with Japan ranked 60th globally in freedom to trade inter-nationally. Other aspects of Japan's economic environment rank relatively highly in the less aggregated categories of the GCI's Enabling Trade Index, with border administration ranked 16th, transport and communications infrastructure ranked 14th, and the business environment ranked 34th. Yet Japan, by these rankings, still does not score well for an advanced economy that is the world's third largest economy.

These rankings confirm what underlies the low performance as an FDI recipient (Table 10.1). For Japan to have open, efficient, and contestable domestic markets, it needs more open market access to both foreign and domestic firms. This cannot be done without significant regulatory reform, which is crucial to attracting more foreign investment and skilled foreign labor. The lack of deregulation of the non-manufacturing sector in the past two decades (and earlier) has led to productivity in those sectors (construction, retail and wholesale trade, real estate, agriculture, finance and insurance, and hotels and restaurants) to fall steadily behind the pro-ductivity of the manufacturing sector, which has been trade exposed.[61]

A paradigm shift in international economic policy thinking

Unless foreign economic policy strategy is conceived of as an instrument of struc-tural reform, there is little chance that it will contribute to the alleviation of Japan's economic malaise. There is scant evidence that the conception or the delivery of foreign economic policy was so directed over the past decades. This change will require a paradigm shift in trade and in the thinking about international economic policy. One problem may have been that the locus of trade policy development, in the Ministry of Foreign Affairs (MOFA) and, to a lesser extent, METI, was locked into a negotiating mentality not effectively informed by, or connected to, a well-outlined national reform agenda. Trade and economic diplomacy should be thought of as instruments for structural reform, not as the end goals in themselves with the objective of merely signing more international agreements.

The position of Japan in the geopolitical and economic world has changed sig-nificantly since the 1980s. It is not clear that either policy making or policy think-ing has come to terms with Japan's new circumstances. Japan already sees Korea as a major competitor and threat to many of its prized and symbolic brands glob-ally. Korea also challenges Japan's former position in Asia as a dynamic force in regional and global leadership. Korea has hosted a number of regional and global summits, such as the G20 Summit in 2010. The economic ascendancy of China and the emergence of India both mean that Japan's position in the region is very different from what it was at the end of the 1980s. Japan's new geopolitical and economic circumstances after the beginning of the 1990s required a fundamental reconception of how it might successfully manage its foreign economic and national policy agenda. Failure to accept and to integrate these circumstances into the framing of policy and to set national priorities accordingly was bound to leave the country on the back foot in realizing its economic and political potential in this new international environment. Though the shift to dealing with China in the framework of the new ASEAN-based East Asian arrangements is evidence of appreciation of the need to grapple with these changes and establish new modalities for doing so, as Shiraishi Takashi hints in Chapter 11 the mindset change necessary to capture Japan's new moment in history was largely absent. Many clung to atavistic thinking about Japan retaining a role in Asia as first among equals, and claimed the status of first among equals without doing much about the need to earn it. Nowhere else is this thinking more palpable than in Japan's reception of the elevation of the G20 meetings to global summit level after the global financial crisis. Japan's negative attitude was reflected in a deep reluctance to yield its status as Asia's special representative in the G7 group rather than enthusiasm about the new opportunity to elevate Asia's role in global governance. To revitalize its economy, Japan needs to play an active role in helping shape regional and global institutions and in engaging closely with China and India on the international dimensions of their ongoing reform.

The 2000s saw the Japanese economy buoyed by the external sector, mainly a byproduct of China's entry into the WTO. The Japanese economy enjoyed one of its longest economic expansions in the postwar period in the first half of that decade. Yet that was achieved because business had focused on the opportunities in Asia that were created largely by China's WTO accession. Japanese policy making not only lagged behind business but shut itself out of the main game decisively in the period from 2001 to 2006, which saw relations with China turn unnecessarily sour and a suspension of leadership visits. The management of the baggage of political history with China continued to threaten to throw the development of the Japan-China relationship off course, as Togo Kazuhiko discusses in Chapter 13 and Shiraishi Takashi explains in Chapter 11, although on the trade front there is little evidence that this has yet limited the expansion of trade and investment.[62]

Trade and investment between Japan and China grew rapidly despite Prime Minister Koizumi's repeated visits to the Yasukuni Shrine – where fourteen Class A war criminals are enshrined – to honor Japan's war dead. These visits caused diplomatic relations to fall to an all-time low since normalization in 1979. There is no clear explanation behind Koizumi's actions, apart from narrow party political imperatives, since his diplomatic starting point was the promotion of China's accommodation into the international system. Yet his action was symbolic of the inability of Japan's policy leaders to guide Japan's foreign economic policy toward a new strategy on China. At a time when China was changing the global economic and trading landscape and opportunities were opening up in China with its accession to the WTO, Japan instead sought only trade agreements with smaller countries and avoided significant trade-policy-driven economic reform.

The economic association with China is now a central element in Japan's external economic relationships. There is a great reform still underway in China, likely next to encompass a change of the financial markets, a liberalization of payments, and a new role for China in the international financial system. Given its proximity to development in China, Japanese business is an active beneficiary from China's economic transformation – and the benefits of its already large dealings with and experience in China will only grow. The costs of Japan's further distancing itself politically from China are immense.

Early on, Japan played a crucial role in the development of production networks in East Asia and also played an active part in East Asian economic integration. Its location and circumstance suggest a significant role in the next phase of Asian growth and integration if it can relate successfully to a grand new vision of Asian trade and financial integration. This new vision is likely to unfold around services, financial and capital account reform in China, the establishment of the ASEAN economic community, and the reinvigoration of reform in India. Japan has an integral role in this unfolding Asian drama.

Throughout the 1990s but more so in the 2000s, Japanese government investment in infrastructure and connectivity in Southeast Asia and later South Asia began to make a significant contribution to bringing new countries into supply chains and creating opportunities in the region's less-developed economies. While the primary motivation was to assist Japanese multinational enterprises (MNEs) in exporting equipment, machinery, and engineering services across the region, and this was business- not government-led, this does not change the reality that the positive externalities of these activities are large. Japan's policy leadership in precisely these connectivity-building dimensions of regional development is both an important public good and opportunity for national economic gain. What has been missing for Japan is the connection of those foreign economic policy strategies to domestic reforms. The Japanese economy needs deep structural reform; if this reform were done in tandem with an external economic strategy that brought South Asia into an integrated East Asia, the benefits would be compounded.

Regional and global economic diplomacy

What is obvious is that the global trade regime, rather than narrowly bilateral trade arrangements, has been crucial to the gains from growth through trade and investment between Japan and China.[63] Beyond trade, Japan's success in capturing the economic benefits from the relationship will also derive from an overarching strategy to manage and develop the increasingly important area of finance and investment relations within broader global and regional frameworks. Looking forward, on the trade and investment side, China is not a participant in the TPP and is unlikely to be one for the immediate future. This would suggest a rapid elevation of attention to the Regional Comprehensive Economic Partnership (RCEP), in which China is a participant, and the entrenchment of RCEP in a broader framework for reform of global trade and economic governance.

If Japan fails to reposition in its relations with China, it is likely to be overwhelmed by a "reverse Nixon shock" (the initiative that Nixon as U.S. president took to open relations with China that blindsided Japan in the early 1970s). Japan is now open to being caught off guard again in China's relations with the United States. China is already taking big initiatives in that relationship with its proposal for a bilateral investment treaty and, more recently, discussion of a comprehensive FTA with the United States.[64]

Even if Japan commits to significant liberalization through the TPP, it will only deliver on a small part of the reform that is necessary for lifting growth potential in the Japanese economy. The value of the TPP for Japan lies in the symbolism that it might bring in the triumph of good economic policy over status quo vested interests, and as a signal that policymakers are willing to challenge vested interests. Agricultural reform is especially important to this symbolism of commitment to reform, though the overall economic gains from it will not be large. Services reform is more significant to overall economic performance, but much of the action has to be beyond TPP, domestically and perhaps through RCEP. Avoiding commitments in TPP or RCEP and continuing the practice of traditional "trade-free agreements" will simply represent another major wasted opportunity.

Another problem, of course, is that the global institutions, such as the GATT/WTO, have weakened or become less relevant to the challenges that Japan now confronts. These institutions underpinned the heyday of Japan's international economic diplomacy by providing an appropriate framework and set of principles to ensure success.

The international structural reforms that Japan needs to undertake are germane to the emerging agenda in the G20. Japan's reluctance to embrace the G20 process fully, and especially to embrace the role of its Asian neighbors in the G20, means that it has not taken a forward position on reform of global governance in the areas of importance to Asia. G20 efforts to rehabilitate the WTO by resuscitating the MFN principle and nondiscriminatory liberalization and to refocus the WTO on issues related to structural reform could, if successful, help the Japanese economy in making this transition. Though there are few signs of it yet, it is to be hoped that the Japanese government will recognize its weakness and help push this agenda through the G20.

Nor has Japan grasped the significance of the infrastructure investment agenda to regional growth objectives. Rather, its role in the G20 has been narrowly diplomatic in nature. Although this might be construed as central to managing Japan's big economic and political partnerships in Asia, there appears little connection between the strategic coincidence of its interests in regional and global governance in the APEC, ASEAN-based, and G20 forums. The structural reform agenda has, over the past half-decade, become a focus of regional cooperation with APEC. But despite Japan's role in founding APEC, it has not played an active role in framing the structural reform agenda in a way that would support its own domestic reform. This may be partly because of the shift to FTA diplomacy and partly because Japan has not embraced the structural reform agenda in APEC as its own.

Conclusion

In this context, it is correct to observe, as Shiraishi Takashi does in Chapter 11, that Japan's decline was in some sense a byproduct of Asia's rise. Indeed, Asia's rise, including that of China, presented an array of opportunities for Japan to ameliorate and forestall the effects of the demographic crunch and transition to economic maturity that it was fated to confront over these years. That China and the rest of Asia were opening up and achieving such sustained and remarkable growth, despite the hiccup of the Asian financial crisis, was a blessing that expanded Japanese economic frontiers and opportunities. Many of these opportunities were clearly seized. This was a period in which China become Japan's largest trading partner, delivering both low-cost imports and export markets in China at scale. It was a period in which Japanese investment into China surged and output in Asia became a large share in the output of Japanese manufacturing corporations. These Japanese gains from Asia's rise buttressed Japanese corporate competitiveness and strength. The regret, as we have seen, is that Japan could have made more of these opportunities – other countries in the region did. This is reflected in their relative economic performance compared with that of Japan. And Japan's failure to do better was not the result of business capacities or a culture that was not alive to new openings. Rather it was the product of a failure of government to reinvent policy strategy as the new circumstances demanded – a failure to make the right policy choice. In Shiraishi's words, Japan's instinct in foreign diplomacy was to think about what was all around it through the prism of "Japan and Asia" and not "Japan in Asia." In the end, that was as damaging to national economic policy outcomes as it was diminishing to Japan's foreign diplomatic outcomes.

The loss of coherence in international economic policy – connected at the hip to the absence of a long-term strategic vision about how to respond to national economic challenges – distinguishes Japan's past two lost decades from what went before. Getting the choices right going forward will depend on reestablishing the link between an international economic diplomacy that is connected to an agenda for national economic reform. This change will also demand that Japan more actively engage with China in Asia's grand new set of reforms. This strategy is essential to the next phase of Asian economic transformation through the "middle income trap." Such moves demand new engagement at the global level, to strengthen and adapt the norms and rules for global economic governance that will be at the core of Japan's potential prosperity in Asia in the years ahead.

Notes

1 We are most grateful to Son Chu for research and statistical assistance, to Ryan Manual for comments on our draft, to Barak Kushner and Itō Kai for editorial input, and to Funabashi Yōichi and our colleagues on this project for sharpening our perspectives.
2 Peter Drysdale, *International Economic Pluralism: Economic Policy in East Asia and the Pacific* (Sydney: Allen & Unwin, 1988).
3 Warren S. Hunsberger, *Japan and the United States in World Trade* (New York: Council on Foreign Relations, 1964).

4 Robert Z. Lawrence and David E. Weinstein, "Trade and Growth: Import-Led or Export-Led? Evidence from Japan and Korea" (NBER Working Paper No. 7264, 1999).
5 Gary Saxonhouse, "Japan's Intractable Trade Surpluses in a New Era," *World Economy* 9, no. 3 (1986), pp. 239–58.
6 Funabashi Yōichi, "Japan and the New World Order," *Foreign Affairs* 70, no. 5 (1991), pp. 58–74.
7 Matsui Noriatsu, "Changing Manufactured Imports of Post-Plaza and Post-Bubble Japan," in Raj Aggarwal, ed., *Restructuring Japanese Business for Growth* (Boston: Springer, 1999), pp. 295–308.
8 Peter Drysdale and Terada Takashi, *Asia-Pacific Economic Cooperation: Critical Perspectives on the World Economy*, 5 vols. (London: Routledge, 2007), p. 1744.
9 Peter Drysdale, "Australia and Japan: A New Economic Partnership in Asia" (a report prepared for Austrade, 2009).
10 Dieter Ernst, "Searching for a New Role in East Asian Regionalization: Japanese Production Networks in the Electronics Industry" in Peter J. Katzenstein and Shiraishi Takashi, eds., *Beyond Japan: The Dynamics of East Asian Regionalism* (Ithaca: Cornell University Press, 2006), pp. 161–87.
11 Andō Mitsuyo and Kimura Fukunari, "The Formation of International Production and Distribution Networks in East Asia," in Itō Takatoshi and Andrew K. Rose, eds., *International Trade in East Asia* (NBER-East Asia Seminar on Economics, 2005), vol. 14, http://www.nber.org/chapters/c0194.
12 Michael Borrus and Stephen S. Cohen, "Building China's Information Technology Industry: Tariff Policy and China's Accession to the World Trade Organization," *Asian Survey* 38, no. 11 (1998), pp. 1005–17.
13 Peter Drysdale and Terada Takashi, *Asia-Pacific Economic Cooperation*, p. 1744.
14 Ross Garnaut, *Australia and the Northeast Asian Ascendancy* (Canberra: Australian Government Publishing Service, 1989).
15 Peter Drysdale, "Australia and Japan."
16 Okina Kunio, Shirakawa Masaaki, and Shiratsuka Shigenori, "The Asset Price Bubble and Monetary Policy: Japan's Experience in the Late 1980s and the Lessons," *Monetary and Economic Studies* (Special Edition) 19 (2001), pp. 395–450.
17 Hayashi Fumio and Edward C. Prescott, "The 1990s in Japan: A Lost Decade," *Review of Economic Dynamics* 5, no. 1 (2002), pp. 206–35; Hoshi Takeo and Anil Kashyap, "The Japanese Banking Crisis: Where Did It Come From and How Will It End?" *NBER Macroeconomics Annual 1999* 14 (2000), pp. 129–212.
18 Peter Drysdale, "Beyond East Asia's Economic Crisis: Development Paradise Lost?" in Inoguchi Takashi, ed., *Japan's Asian Policy: Revival and Response* (New York: Palgrave MacMillan, 2002), pp. 55–80.
19 C. F. Bergsten, "East Asian Regionalism: Towards a Tripartite World," *Economist* 356, no. 8179 (July 13, 2000), pp. 23–26.
20 V. K. Aggarwal "APEC and Trade Liberalisation after Seattle: Transregionalism without a Cause," in Maria Weber, ed., *Reforming Economic Systems in Asia: A Comparative Analysis of China, Japan, South Korea, Malaysia and Thailand* (Cheltenham: Edward Elgar, 2002), pp. 149–78.
21 ASEAN is the Association of Southeast Asian Nations.
22 Hadi Soesastro, "Towards an East Asia Regional Trading Arrangement," in Simon Tay, Hadi Soesastro and Jesus P. Estanislao, eds., *Reinventing ASEAN* (Singapore: Institute of Southeast Asian Studies, 2001), pp. 226–42.
23 Douglas Webber, "Two Funerals and a Wedding? The Ups and Downs of Regionalism in East Asia and Asia-Pacific after the Asian Crisis," *Pacific Review* 14, no. 3 (2001), pp. 339–72.
24 Ogita (2002) reviews the policy announcements and White Papers from METI and MOFA indicating the shift in policy position towards FTAs during 1998/1999.

25 Ogita Tatsushi, "An Approach towards Japan's FTA Policy" (IDE APEC Study Center Working Paper Series 01/02 – No. 4, 2002).
26 The trivial commitments to liberalize agriculture by Japan in the Singapore EPA had already been made in the context of the WTO (Terada, 2005).
27 Ogita Tatsushi, "An Approach towards Japan's FTA Policy."
28 MITI (Ministry of International Trade and Industry, Japan), *Tsūshō hakusho: Sōron* (White Paper on International Trade: General Remarks, 1999), pp. 293–94.
29 Ogita Tatsushi, "An Approach towards Japan's FTA Policy." Japan is not alone in its inconsistency on multilateral objectives being pursued through FTAs, which are usually WTO-consistent only in rhetoric while their preferential nature directly undermines the core principle of Article I of the GATT, namely MFN and nondiscriminatory trade: see Jagdish Bhagwati, *Termites in the Trading System: How Preferential Agreements Undermine Free Trade* (Oxford: Oxford University Press, 2008). Prior to the conclusion of the Japan-Singapore EPA, there were studies that showed there would be limited gains from pursuing narrowly bilateral deals relative to progress at multilateral talks. Lee estimated trivial benefits [Hiro Lee, "General Equilibrium Evolution of the Japan-Singapore Free Trade Agreement," in Peter Drysdale and Ishigaki Ken'ichi, eds., *East Asian Trade and Financial Integration: New Issues* (Canberra: Asia Pacific Press, 2002)], and even the most optimistic scenarios in Urata and Kiyota estimated that a comprehensive agreement for Japan with Korea, China, Taiwan, Hong Kong, and ASEAN would add only 0.5 percent to Japan's GDP: Urata Shujirō and Kiyota Kōzō, "The impacts of an East Asian FTA on Foreign Trade in East Asia" (NBER Working Paper 10173, 2003). Scollay and Gilbert also estimated small benefits and argued that an FTA strategy would damage trade relations with other non-FTA member countries: Robert Scollay and John Gilbert, *New Pathways for Regional Trade Arrangements in the Asia Pacific* (Washington, DC: Institute of International Economics, 2001).
30 Andō Mitsuyo and Kimura Fukunari, "Japanese FTA/EPA Strategies and Agricultural Protection," *Keiō Business Review* 44 (2008), pp. 1–25.
31 These studies include Scollay and Gilbert, *New Pathways, for Regional Trade Arrangements*, and Bhagwati, *Termites in the Trading System*.
32 The rates of utilization of preferences in FTAs (that is, the proportion of trade that is conducted under the preferential tariff rate rather than the MFN rate) in Asia have been low [see Richard Baldwin, "Multilateralising Regionalism: Spaghetti Bowls as Building Blocs on the Path to Global Free Trade" (mimeo) (Geneva: Graduate Institute for International Studies, 2006); and World Bank, "Trade Issues in East Asia: Preferential Rules of Origin," *Policy Research Report, East Asia and Pacific Region* (Washington, DC: World Bank, 2007).] A 2006 JETRO study found that only 5.1 percent of the 729 Japanese firms that were surveyed had used the preferential tariff rates when trading with firms in FTA partner countries (JETRO, *FY2006 Survey of Japanese Firms' International Operations*, JETRO, 2007). Some of the highest estimates of preference utilization rates are found in Kawai and Wignaraja who show, from firm surveys, that 22 percent of trade in Asia utilized FTA preferences in 2007, and up to 28 percent in 2010 [see Kawai Masahiro and Ganeshan Wignaraja, *Asia's Free Trade Agreements: How Is Business Responding?* (Cheltenham: Edward Elgar, 2011)]. According to that study Japanese firms are average in their utilization of FTAs – around 29 percent of Japanese firms who trade with an FTA partner opting to use preferential rates. With all of these studies, these shares represent not the value of trade that utilizes preferences but rather the proportion of respondent firms which utilizes preferences. Ex ante computable general equilibrium models usually overestimate benefits from FTAs as they assume full utilization of preferential tariff rates.
33 Ogita Tatsushi, "An Approach towards Japan's FTA Policy."
34 Such reforms are best done unilaterally and not through negotiation with a small number of external partners. Besides, there is little evidence that preferential services

commitments deliver much in terms of liberalization outside of Europe: Joseph Francois and Bernard Hoekman, "Services Trade and Policy," *Journal of Economic Literature* 48, no. 3 (2010), pp. 642–92.

35 See Andō Mitsuyo and Kimura Fukunari, "Japanese FTA/EPA Strategies and Agricultural Protection," pp. 1–25.

36 Aurelia George-Mulgan, *Japan's Agricultural Policy Regime* (London: Routledge Curzon, 2005).

37 Shiro Armstrong, "Korea: Beyond Preferential Trade Deals," *Korea's Economy 2012* (Washington, DC: Korea Economic Institute, 2012).

38. Saori N. Katada, "From a Supporter to a Challenger? Japan's Currency Leadership in Dollar-Dominated East Asia," *Review of International Political Economy* 15, no. 3 (2008), pp. 399–417.

39 Ibid.

40 George S. Tavlas and Ozeki Yuzuru, "The Internationalization of Currencies: An Appraisal of the Japanese Yen" (International Monetary Fund Occasional Paper 90, Washington, DC: International Monetary Fund, January 1992).

41 Satō Kiyotaka, "The International Use of the Japanese Yen: The Case of Japan's Trade with East Asia" (ICEAD Working Paper Series Vol. 98–16, 1998).

42 Fujiwara Ippei, "To Awaken its Dormant Economy, Japan Must Confront an Age-Old Problem," *Conversation*, September 19, 2012, http://theconversation.com/to-awaken-its-dormant-economy-japan-must-confront-an-age-old-problem-9401.

43 Fukao Kyōji and Hyeog Ug Kwon, "Why Did Japan's TFP Growth Slow Down in the Lost Decade? An Empirical Analysis Based on Firm-Level Data of Manufacturing Firms," *Japanese Economic Review*, 57, no. 2 (2006), pp. 195–228.

44 Fukao Kyōji, Inui Tomohiko, Kabe Shigesaburō, and Deqiang Liu, "An International Comparison of the TFP Levels of Japanese, South Korean, and Chinese Listed Firms" (CEI Working Paper Series 2007–13, Center for Economic Institutions, Institute of Economic Research, Hitotsubashi University, 2008).

45 Yashiro Naohiro, "Strategic Zones to Revitalise the Japanese Economy?" *East Asia Forum*, September 8, 2013, http://www.eastasiaforum.org/2013/09/08/strategic-zones-to-revitalise-the-japanese-economy/.

46 Fukao Kyōji, "Service Sector Productivity in Japan: The Key to Future Economic Growth," (Policy Discussion Papers 10001, Research Institute of Economy, Trade and Industry (RIETI), 2010).

47 Blanka Kalinova, Angel Palerm, and Stephen Thomsen, "OECD's FDI Restrictiveness Index: 2010 Update," *OECD Working Papers on International Investment*, 2010/03, OECD Publishing, http://dx.doi.org/10.1787/5km91p02zj7g-en.

48 Peter Drysdale, comment on Fukao Kyōji, Inui Tomohiko, Kawai Hiroki, and Miyagawa Tsutomu, in Itō Takatoshi and Andrew Rose, eds., *Growth and Productivity in East Asia* (NBER-EASE Volume 13, Chicago: University of Chicago Press, 2004), pp. 220–22.

49 Hoshi Takeo and Anil Kashyap, "Why Did Japan Stop Growing?" (Report Prepared for the National Institute for Research Advancement (NIRA), 21 January 2011), http://www.nira.or.jp/pdf/1002english_report.pdf.

50 See also Yashiro Naohiro, "Why Labour Market Flexibility in Japan is So Difficult," *East Asia Forum*, April 6, 2011, http://www.eastasiaforum.org/2011/04/06/why-labour-market-flexibility-in-japan-is-so-difficult/.

51 Honma Masayoshi, "WTO Negotiations and Other Agricultural Trade Issues in Japan," *World Economy* 29, no. 6 (2006), pp. 697–714.

52 Hoshi Takeo and Anil Kashyap, "Why Did Japan Stop Growing?"

53 An adverse side effect of this development, however, has been increased social vulnerability: Yashiro Naohiro, "Why Labour Market Flexibility in Japan Is So Difficult," *East Asia Forum*, April 6, 2011, http://www.eastasiaforum.org/2011/04/06/why-labour-market-flexibility-in-japan-is-so-difficult/.

54 Wakasugi Ryūhei, Todō Yasuyuki, Satō Hitoshi, Nishioka Shuichirō, Matsuura Toshi-yuki, Itō Banri, and Tanaka Ayumu, "The Internationalization of Japanese Firms: New Findings Based on Firm-Level Data" (RIETI Discussion Paper Series 08-E-036, The Research Institute of Economy, Trade and Industry, 2008).

55 Drysdale, "Australia and Japan: A New Economic Partnership in Asia."

56 Itō Takatoshi and Andrew Rose (ed.), *Growth and Productivity in East Asia* (NBER-EASE Volume 13, Chicago: University of Chicago Press, 2004); Hoshi Takeo and Anil Kashyap, "Why Did Japan Stop Growing?"

57 Itoh Motoshige, "The Japanese Economy: Tackling Structural Problems," *East Asia Forum*, June 9, 2010, http://www.eastasiaforum.org/2010/06/09/the-japanese-economy-tackling-structural-problems/.

58 The World Economic Forum's *Global Competitive Index* and *Enabling Trade Index* can be found at http://www.weforum.org/content/pages/competitiveness-library.

59 Many of these indices do not go back to, or do not have comparable time series data for, the 1990s. The indicators and ranks in 2010 show how poorly Japan fared at the end of the lost two decades, which helps explain Japan's underperformance as we demonstrate in our chapter.

60 Japan's rank has fallen to 114th in the 2012 rankings. Japan ranked first in ease of closing a business in 2010.

61 Hoshi Takeo and Anil Kashyap, "Why Did Japan Stop Growing?"

62 Shiro Armstrong, "The Politics of Japan-China Trade and the Role of the World Trade System," *World Economy* 35, no. 9 (2012), pp. 1102–20.

63 Ibid.

64 See, for example, Peter Coy, "The Powerful People Arguing for U.S.-China Free Trade," *Bloomberg Businessweek*, May 23, 2012, http://www.businessweek.com/articles/2013–05–23/the-powerful-people-arguing-for-u-dot-s-dot-china-free-trade.

11 Japan's Asia/Asia-Pacific policy in flux

Shiraishi Takashi[1]

If we look back at the past two decades of Japan's economic stagnation and ask what was lost politically, many will agree that it was the sense of a common vision about Japan's position in and toward Asia and the Asia-Pacific region in the immediate years of the post–Cold War era. This vision, held by the public and policymakers alike, was based on a shared consensus on region-wide economic dynamism, with frontiers stretching from the Asian newly industrialized economies (NIEs) of Taiwan, South Korea, Hong Kong, and Singapore to Thailand, Malaysia, and Indonesia and thence to the coastal regions of China, the Philippines, and Vietnam, and, in the imaginable future, Burma and beyond.[2] Such a vision took for granted the "flying geese pattern" of regional economic development, with Japan as the lead goose and the others following behind, with the promise of ever-expanding possibilities for Japanese business and freedom of action. What made this notion so appealing for the Japanese public was, as Okazaki Hisahiko puts it, the possibility that for the first time in its modern history Japan could be simultaneously Asianist and internationalist.[3] That is to say, Japan could play a role in the creation of an open regionalism in the Asia-Pacific region while harmonizing its own economic expansion in the region with the Japan-U.S. alliance.

This ideology had some basis in reality in the late 1980s and early 1990s. The countries of East Asia and Southeast Asia (Prime Minister Takeshita Noboru referred to these regions as "East Asia" for the first time in a prime minister's policy speech in 1989) had emerged as areas of growth. Japan had become a leading market for manufactured goods from the NIEs and the Association of Southeast Asian Nations (ASEAN) member countries. Japanese investment in East Asia was expanding and, along with the United States, it was a major investor and trade partner with NIEs and ASEAN countries. China, especially its coastal regions, had joined in the export-oriented regional economic development, and intraregional trade for the first time exceeded the region's trade with the United States.

This region-wide economic dynamism within the framework of the Japan-U.S. security alliance informed Japan's Asia policy in the post–Cold War years. Japan's economic cooperation no longer meant trade promotion and resources procurement, as it had in the 1970s, but the promotion of Asian economic dynamism with Japanese direct investment, Japanese aid for infrastructural and human resources development, and Japanese imports from the region. It meant encouraging market-driven and open regional economic dynamism without any political initiatives on the part of Japanese government for regional institution building, which might invite unnecessary suspicion on the part of the Americans that Japan was creating a "kinder, gentler 'Co-Prosperity Sphere'" in East Asia and awaken Asian misgivings about a resurgent Japan.[4] These goals also informed Japan's geopolitics. Democratization was on the move in the Philippines, Taiwan, and South Korea during the late 1980s. There was also the assumption that as China became increasingly integrated into the global economy, the living standard of mainland Chinese people would improve and Chinese nationalism would be moderated, whether the party state remained in power or not. Finding itself between America and China, Japan hoped that Southeast Asia would be an area open to the world and an arena for international cooperation. It was this vision that informed Japan's support for peace building in Cambodia, for Thai initiatives calling for the transformation of Indochina from a battleground to a marketplace, and for the expansion of ASEAN membership to include Vietnam, Laos, Cambodia, and Burma/Myanmar.

In retrospect, it is easy to say that Japan's goals were too optimistic, if not naïve. The first and most important false assumption that eroded the potential for this vision to come true was that Japan would remain a Gulliver in a region of Lilliputians, even though the pattern of regional economic development at the time pointed to a near future in which many of the countries in the region would grow faster than Japan. Even then, there were already indications that this pattern would translate into a radical redistribution of wealth, as well as power, in just a few decades. The Japanese economy constituted 14 percent and 14.6 percent of the global economy in 1990 and 2000 respectively, but its share declined to 8.7 percent in 2010 and is expected to fall further to 6.1 percent in 2018. This development, combined with the rise of other Asian economies, has changed the regional distribution of wealth radically. All the East Asian economies combined (China, Hong Kong, Taiwan, South Korea, ASEAN-5, Vietnam, and India) constituted 50 percent of Japan's GDP in 1990 and 70 percent in 2000. By 2010, however, China's GDP alone was already larger (108 percent) than that of Japan, and the combined East Asian economies were almost twice as large. Japan's relative decline is also evident in business. In 1991, forty-one out of the top fifty firms in Fortune's Global 500 Asia list were Japanese, while five were South Korean. No mainland Chinese firm was in the list. But by 2011, the number of Japanese firms in the list had fallen to twenty-two, while the number of Chinese firms in the list had shot up to eighteen. Five Korean firms made it to the list. Japanese electronics firms, such as Sony, Panasonic, Toshiba, Hitachi, and Sharp, which looked invincible in the early 1990s, were in tatters amidst the global financial crisis of 2008; the stock market value of Samsung alone was larger than the value of all the Japanese electronics firms combined.

Japanese policymakers have had to adapt to a changing environment defined by Japan's alliance with the United States, the rise of China and ASEAN, and the persistent question of Japan's wartime history in the context of Japan's own domestic politics and institutions. Not surprisingly, successive governments have tended to opt for the path of least resistance. And precisely because Japan had been so successful during the postwar era, neither its public nor its political leaders have seen any compelling reason to tinker drastically with the formula that had made Japan peaceful, stable, and prosperous.

How then has Japan engaged with regional developments in Asia, and what changes has Japan's position in and toward Asia undergone in the past two decades? This chapter identifies four major episodes, or moments, that mark the recalibration of Japan's post–Cold War East Asia/Asia-Pacific policy. The first is Japan's involvement in the Cambodian peace process and the end of the Cold War in Southeast Asia. The second is the landmark "Miyazawa Vision," which set the direction of Japan's engagement with East Asia/Asia-Pacific and spelled out the major directives – namely, a redefined Japan-U.S. alliance, the question of historical narratives of Japan's wartime past, and Japan's regional initiatives and greater involvement in regional security – that Japan would address in its region-building effort. The third is the Asian financial crisis of 1997–98 that called into question the assumptions on which the Miyazawa Vision was based, thereby spurring Japan's efforts to create an East Asia community. (It is worth noting that all these three episodes happened under the watch of Miyazawa Kiichi when he was finance minister from 1986 to 1988, prime minister from 1991 to 1993, and finance minister from 1998 to 2001. In this sense, Miyazawa is the key figure behind Japan's adjustment to the transition from the Cold War to post–Cold War eras.) The last episode involves the rise and increasing assertiveness of China, which has given rise to the "power politics" that has heightened the tension between the U.S.-led regional security system and the regional trade system in which China has become an indispensable central player, a tension that further undermines the Japanese foreign-policy assumptions that seek to link its "Japan in Asia" and "Japan and the U.S." policies.

The Cambodian peace process

The post–Cold War era began with a rude shock for Japan in the form of the Iraqi invasion of Kuwait. As Michael Green and Igata Akira point out in Chapter 9, the Gulf War in 1990–1991 shattered assumptions about Japan's future security requirements. U.S. military might still mattered, but Japanese economic power did not translate into global strategic influence and Japan's financial contribution of more than US $13 billion to the war coalition was derided as mere checkbook diplomacy. The day after Iraqi forces occupied Kuwait in August 1990 and the United Nations Security Council adopted the resolution to demand the unconditional withdrawal of Iraqi forces, the Japanese government immediately sent administrative guidelines to all Japanese banks to safeguard Kuwaiti assets and imposed trade sanctions on Iraq. Yet the Japanese public was deeply divided and no political consensus emerged on how to be part of the war coalition until after the war ended in January 1991.

The Gulf War episode was deeply traumatic for Japan's alliance managers. In its wake, Japan's participation in UN peacekeeping operations emerged as a major political issue. The LDP (Liberal Democratic Party) and other parties drafted a new bill for UN peace cooperation in September 1991. But there was a curious coincidence in timing: while the bill for international peace cooperation was being debated in the media and in the parliament, the Cambodian peace process was finally coming to a successful conclusion in Paris in July 1991. Since Japan had been actively engaged in the Cambodian peace process, Japanese foreign ministry officials such as Ikeda Tadashi believed that Japan's active participation in Cambodian peacekeeping operations would offer a good opportunity to restore Japan's international reputation and involve Japan in the process of shaping the post–Cold War regional order in Southeast Asia.[5]

The American war in Indochina came to an end in 1975 with the unification of Vietnam and the victory of the Khmer Rouge in Cambodia. By 1986, the Vietnam Communist Party elected the reformist Nguyen Van Linh as party secretary general and formally called for *doi moi* (renovation) as the guiding principle for economic reform. Vietnamese Foreign Minister Nguyen Co Thach expressed Vietnam's willingness to be part of ASEAN in 1988. Calling for the transformation of Indochina "from a battlefield to a marketplace," Thai Prime Minister Chatichai Choonhavan normalized Thai diplomatic relations with Laos and invited Cambodian Prime Minister Hun Sen to Bangkok. Prince Norodom Sihanouk proposed at the 1988 UN general assembly that the UN Security Council convene an international conference for the resolution of the Cambodian issue. In 1989, Vietnam and Cambodia under Heng Samrin agreed on the complete and unconditional withdrawal of Vietnamese troops from Cambodia.

Japan became active in the Cambodian peace process toward the end of the 1980s. It was the first time that Japan had become engaged in an international peace-building effort of this kind. As the second largest economy in the world, Japan was expected by the UN, the U.S., ASEAN, and other countries to make significant financial contributions to Cambodia's postwar reconstruction. The Japanese public had been unhappy with American criticism of Japan as a "free rider" intent on making money without any significant international contribution. Prime Minister Takeshita had presented his foreign policy doctrine in the name of "Japan contributing to the world," talked about his international cooperation initiatives, and committed himself to beefing up Japan's overseas development aid budget to US $50 billion for the fiscal years of 1988–1992, an amount twice as large as its budget for 1983–87.

Cambodia emerged in 1991 in Japan's foreign policy community as the perfect arena for a Japanese international peace initiative. Because neither the public nor parliamentary members were very interested in the Cambodian issue, MOFA (Ministry of Foreign Affairs) officials had more room to take the initiative without attracting negative media and domestic political attention. Japan was invited to the Paris International Conference on Cambodia in July 1989. Japanese officials wanted to engage the peace process proactively in part because they did not want another instance of checkbook diplomacy that would mean Japan having to pick up the bill after the Paris International Conference was over, and they contacted Hun Sen despite American opposition. The Japanese government coordinated with the Thai government to organize a meeting in 1990 in Tokyo, where Hun Sen and Prince Sihanouk agreed on a joint statement about the power-sharing formula in the Supreme National Council to be established in the wake of the peace agreement. Shortly after the Tokyo meeting, the United States decided to change its Indochina policy to engage Vietnam while preventing the Khmer Rouge from coming back to power in Cambodia. The Cambodian peace agreement was signed in Paris in October 1991.

Throughout these same months, the bill for international peace cooperation was being debated in the Japanese media and the parliament. In the meantime, UN Deputy Secretary General Akashi Yasushi was appointed as head of the United Nations Transitional Authority in Cambodia (UNTAC). Hun Sen asked Japan to provide military personnel for UNTAC. Prime Minister Miyazawa emphatically argued in April 1992 that since the Cambodian peace process was in its most important stage with the UNTAC peacekeeping operation and Cambodia had sent a request for Japan's cooperation, failure to pass the international peace cooperation bill would have a negative impact on Japan's international reputation. In September 1992, Japan sent an army engineering battalion and civilian police personnel for the UNTAC operation.[6]

Mapping Japan's Asia-Pacific policy: The Miyazawa vision

Prime Minister Miyazawa also took initiatives to map out Japan's Asia Pacific policy in the early 1990s. He organized an advisory committee on "21st Century Asia Pacific and Japan" in 1992. In the committee's first meeting, Miyazawa said that at a time when the world was embarking on building a new world order, it was important to ask what position Japan should occupy in the world, what path it should take, and what role it should play. "Japan has been in a position to enjoy the benefit of world peace," he explained; however, "Japan is no longer allowed to be in that position, now that Japan has become an economic power." "[A]s a country in the Asia Pacific, Japan should play a proactive role to maintain peace and prosperity in this region."[7] In its report, the committee made three points: that regional economic development was the main engine for building the Asia-Pacific region; that Japan would not, and should not, become a military power; and that Japan should proactively contribute to the making of a peaceful and prosperous world. With the American democracy project in mind, the committee stated that while there was no question that while "freedom and democracy are the objectives to be pursued in the Asia Pacific," they agreed that "there should be different paths to reach the destination." The Miyazawa Vision, as enunciated by the committee report, was without a doubt one of the most important attempts to spell out Japan's Asia-Pacific strategy in the early post–Cold War years. The committee understood the strategic importance of the Japan-U.S. alliance and free trade, but hinted at Japan's uneasiness over the American's "democracy project" and noted the need for Japan to engage in regional security dialogue for common defense. It was also aware of Asian misgivings about a resurgent Japan and the need to address Japan's wartime past nationally and internationally.

Japan had long treated ASEAN as one of its key partners (along with the United States), since the 1970s when Prime Minister Fukuda Takeo called for creating a "special," "heart-to-heart" relationship with the ASEAN countries. Japan suspended its assistance to Vietnam as a sanction against the Vietnamese invasion of Cambodia, in part at the request of ASEAN. Japan supported ASEAN initiatives on UN resolutions on Cambodia and worked closely with ASEAN in the Cambodian peace process. It was not surprising therefore that Japan started to promote regional security in the wake of the Gulf War. Foreign Minister Nakayama Taro proposed in 1991 that post-ministerial conference (PMC) dialogues on security be institutionalized. The ASEAN countries were lukewarm about the proposal, but the ASEAN summit in 1992 agreed to promote regional security with the PMC as a framework.[8] ASEAN invited all its members, observers, dialogue partners, and guests to establish the ASEAN Regional Forum (ARF). Its inaugural meeting was held in Bangkok in July 1994, and this was the first time in history that the foreign ministers of the United States, Russia, China, and Japan were seated together at the same table to discuss security issues in the Asia Pacific. The second ARF meeting held in Brunei in 1995 agreed on the ARF process of confidence building, preventive diplomacy, and approaches to conflict.

Japan's regional initiatives in Asia went hand-in-hand with its attempt to redefine its alliance with the United States. The new alliance was no longer limited to guaranteeing Japan's national security, but would become an instrument for maintaining an American presence in the region. This process started under the administration of Prime Minister Hosokawa Morihiro (1993–94), the first non-LDP prime minister since the 1950s, who appointed an advisory group on defense in 1994 and asked for a defense guideline for the post–Cold War Asia. By the time the group completed its assignment, Hosokawa as well as his successor Hata Tsutomu (1994) were gone and the report was submitted to Prime Minister Murayama Tomiichi (1994–95). The report called for a close alliance between Japan and the United States and urged the government to allow Japanese military forces to take part in peacekeeping operations. It also called for the integration of Japanese defense capabilities with the Japan-U.S. alliance and the UN collective security system. The Murayama cabinet decided on the new defense program outline in 1995 and reaffirmed the importance of a Japan-U.S. security treaty for regional peace and stability.[9]

In view of Asian neighbors' misgivings about Japan's wartime past and their latent fears of a resurgent militarism in Japan, Prime Minister Miyazawa also initiated the process to address its wartime history, which culminated in Prime Minister Murayama's statement in August 1995 (for a detailed discussion, see Chapter 13).

As Yamakage Susumu has noted, Japan's grand strategic debate in the those years was framed simultaneously in terms of a discourse of "Japan in Asia" and a discourse of "Japan with the U.S."[10] The point of contention was straightforward. Although the United States was an indispensable trade partner of Japan, trade conflicts between the two countries took place one after another. Economic relations with East Asia, on the other hand, were expanding and the region was becoming increasingly integrated. Those who called for "Japan in Asia" argued that embedding Japan in Asia would place the country in a better position to deal with the United States in matters of trade and security. This debate was linked with the debate about East Asian regionalism (such as the East Asia Economic Group/Caucus that Malaysian Prime Minister Mahathir Mohamad proposed) as opposed to Asia-Pacific regionalism. Japan opted for the Asia-Pacific Economic Cooperation (APEC) which started in 1989 as an Australian initiative with Japanese support. To encourage ASEAN member states' participation, the nature and style of APEC were patterned after those of ASEAN. APEC would be a consultative body of diversified economic entities. It was to work on a consensus basis with minimal organizational structure. Its membership was identical with ASEAN PMCs.

APEC underwent evolution in the 1990s, but not as an instrument of trade liberalization as the United States wanted. Japan was opposed to a regional free trade agreement like the North American Free Trade Agreement. Japan was not eager to liberalize its own trade because liberalizing trade in agricultural products was politically sensitive. Japanese officials were confident that Asia's network-style market integration made it possible for Japan – in the form of economic instrumentalities such as trade, investment, and official development aid – to promote de facto market integration "from behind." And Japanese policymakers understood that such a scheme might forestall U.S. protectionism. They did not want to choose between the United States and ASEAN. They saw economic cooperation as APEC's function and wanted to emphasize the facilitation of trade and investment liberalization rather than liberalization itself. Japan was interested in furthering de facto market integration in Asia, while maintaining its market access to the United States. Japan's relative economic position in Asia was best served by "shallow" rules with the World Trade Organization (WTO) as the anchor of the international trade system and not by intrusive regional arrangements.

The turning point: The Asian financial crisis

The debate in the early 1990s about "Japan in Asia" and "Japan with the United States" was more notional than real because the U.S.-ASEAN relationship was not in crisis. The U.S. presence in Asia was taken for granted and there was no need for Japan to choose one or the other side. It was the Asian financial crisis in 1997–98, during which the United States and the International Monetary Fund (IMF) made blatant interventions in crisis-hit countries to dismantle their developmental state regimes, that brought about a substantive recalibration of Japan's vision for Asia, one hitherto based on the Miyazawa vision of growth-driven regional peace, prosperity, and stability.

In retrospect it is clear that the crisis in 1997–1998 marked a major watershed in the history of East Asia region-making. The ASEAN + 3 (China, Japan and Korea) framework, inaugurated with the first summit meeting held in December 1997, has since become institutionalized, with summit and ministerial meetings held every year. The crisis also marked the beginning of Japan's new regional engagement, as evidenced by its call in 1997 for the establishment of an Asian Monetary Fund (AMF), the new Miyazawa initiative in 1998 to stimulate economies hit by the crisis, the Chiang Mai Initiative that Japan promoted in 2000 as a mechanism to create a zone of currency stability, the conclusion of the Japan-Singapore Economic Partnership Agreement in 2001, and the proposal that Prime Minister Koizumi Junichiro made in Singapore in 2001 for the Japan-ASEAN economic partnership as the first step to build an East Asian community.

The crisis first hit Thailand. The real estate bubble flattened in Thailand in 1995–1996. A state bank estimated that there were 275,000 housing units left unsold at the end of 1996 when Thai financial institutions experienced sudden deterioration in their balance sheets. In the meantime, the U.S. and Japan agreed in 1995 to let the dollar appreciate vis-à-vis the yen, leading to an export slowdown in Asian countries whose currencies were pegged to the dollar. In 1996 Thai exports declined by 0.8 percent and with the Mexican currency crisis still fresh in memory, the Thai baht came under attack. The IMF advised the Thai monetary authority to deal with the insolvent banks and to take a more flexible approach toward the de facto dollar peg system in June 1996.

When the crisis began in Thailand, the Japanese government's response was quick. The Japanese monetary authority had known it was coming – the Thai government had consulted with its Japanese counterpart in June 1995 – and had decided to work with the IMF. When the Thai government decided to float Thai baht and came to the IMF for assistance in July 1997, Japan hosted the meeting in Tokyo to conclude a rescue package for Thailand in cooperation with the IMF.

Japan and the IMF, however, disagreed on the causes of the crisis. Japanese policy-makers agreed with the IMF that there were problems with poor prudential supervision of banking systems in Thailand and other East Asian countries. But they saw these countries' economic growth as testimony to the underlying soundness of their policies and argued that the root cause of the crisis lay in the global finance system that escaped multilateral oversight. When one's house is on fire, they argued, one should first put out the fire rather than try to fix the structural deficiencies that might have caused it. Japan also had a big stake in the region. Since the mid-1980s, after the Plaza Accord, Japanese manufacturing industries, the mainstay of Japan's economy and hence national welfare, had moved their production facilities to East Asian countries, built transnational production chains, and became regionally embedded. This development had redefined Japan's economic cooperation: it no longer meant trade promotion and resource procurement as it did in the 1960s and 1970s, but the encouragement and promotion of regional economic development with Japanese FDIs, Japanese aid for industrial, infrastructural and human resources development, and Japanese imports from Asian NICs and ASEAN countries. Japan's economic cooperation sought to extend its productivity politics beyond Japanese borders and into the region.[11]

Japan's response to the crisis needs to be understood in this context. It was clear from the outset that the entire region, now increasingly integrated economically, was vulnerable to the crisis, and that a crisis would deal a big blow to Japanese firms and financial institutions which had regionalized their operations. The Japanese government thus reacted quickly when the crisis hit Thailand and came to Thailand's assistance through the IMF with a rescue package in which Japan and the IMF provided $4 billion each in support of Thailand. The Thai government initially wanted to deal with the crisis through foreign reserve borrowing and joint interventions in the foreign exchange market. But the IMF insisted on budget tightening and the floating of the Thai baht. Japan supported the IMF because it had to rely on the IMF to monitor Thai foreign reserves and macroeconomic conditions and because it was too risky to provide financial support to Thailand without a multilateral framework provided by the IMF. But Japan also wanted to create a mechanism to deal with the liquidity crisis regionally. It called for the creation of an Asian Monetary Fund to provide liquidity support to Thailand, as well as to other countries threatened by the outflows of short-term capital.

The IMF and the U.S. government, by contrast, insisted on structural reforms. Treasury Secretary Robert Rubin and Deputy Secretary Lawrence H. Summers with Federal Reserve Chairman Alan Greenspan were deeply involved in fashioning remedies for the Asian crisis. Their view was that the root cause of the crisis lay in misguided economic policies that East Asian governments had pursued for many years. In their discursive framing of the crisis, close government ties with business elites, which had been the hallmark of developmental states, nurtured "crony capitalism" and generated moral hazard when states gave de facto guarantees that encouraged businesses to take undue risks. The Korean economy was no longer a miracle but a nightmare. The Thai, Malaysian, and Indonesian economies were no longer tiger economies but crony capitalism purveyors. This ideological recasting of authoritarian developmentalism as a "problem" offered the United States and the IMF the opportunity to dismantle crony capitalism and create, as Greenspan put it, "the Western form of free market capitalism."[12]

The United States was opposed to the Japanese proposal because the AMF would undermine the authority of the IMF to impose structural reforms on the crisis-hit states.[13] U.S. Deputy Secretary of Treasury Summers even remonstrated with Japan's Vice Minister for International Finance Sakakibara Eisuke, saying: "I thought you were a friend."[14] Nor was Japan in a position to go ahead with establishment of an AMF without U.S. and IMF support, because its own banking system was in crisis and Japan had to rely on IMF support to monitor crisis-hit economies.

The disagreement between Japan and the United States also manifested itself in the making of an IMF-led rescue plan for Indonesia in the same month. At issue was whether or not to demand structural reforms as part of the IMF conditionality. The Indonesian economy did well in the late 1980s and early 1990s with a 6.7 percent average annual growth in the post-Plaza Accord boom years of 1987–96. When the crisis started in Bangkok, the Indonesian economy was still doing fine. Its economy was growing by 7.5 percent annually, its export was increasing by

10.4 percent, its budget deficit was below 2 percent of the GDP, it had US $21 billion in foreign reserves, its inflation was under control, and the rupiah looked stable. Confident of sound economic fundamentals, Indonesian technocrats seized the opportunity of the "mini-crisis" to persuade President Suharto to introduce the structural reforms that they deemed fit with the IMF assistance and to address structural problems, such as expanding bad loans in the banking sector and the dependence of business groups on short-term dollar-denominated funds from foreign sources. They persuaded Suharto to ask for IMF assistance to sustain the international confidence in Indonesia.

In support of its technocratic allies in the Indonesian government, the IMF came up with a rescue package that was larger than the one for Thailand but with a conditionality requiring, among other things, the restructuring of sixteen private banks (including the one owned by Suharto's son), the suspension of the national car project (which another son of Suharto controlled), and the curtailment of government subsidies. The Japanese government argued for a less ambitious package aimed at the stabilization of the Indonesian rupiah in the foreign exchange market, but went along with the IMF because this was what Indonesia's technocrats wanted. Japan pledged US $5 billion when the US $40 billion rescue package was agreed on for Indonesia.

But the IMF rescue package did not work as had been hoped. Upon signing the agreement, the Indonesian government immediately closed sixteen troubled banks as the IMF conditionality required. This, however, caused bank runs and led to a systemic crisis of the Indonesia's banking system. The Indonesian government also announced the suspension of government projects, but in a few days many of the projects, most of them controlled by Suharto's children and cronies, were revived.

The disagreement widened further between Japan and the United States in the following months as the crisis in Indonesia worsened. When it was announced that Suharto would not be attending the ASEAN summit in December 1997 because of his illness, the crisis was almost instantly transformed into a political and social crisis as well. The Indonesian rupiah plummeted by 70 percent in less than a month. Unable to repay their dollar-denominated loans, many business groups, including those owned by Suharto's relatives and cronies, went bankrupt. The informal funding mechanism of the state, a mainstay of Suharto's longlasting power, was also destroyed. Prices of goods, including rice and cooking oil, rose steeply. The social crisis manifested itself in increasing unemployment, widespread anti-Chinese riots, lootings, disturbances, and rising criminality. The United States continued to insist on structural reforms. By the time the second IMF package was agreed on in January 1998, however, it was clear that the United States wanted Suharto to go. Suharto understood the U.S. position very well and wanted to wage what he called "guerrilla warfare."[15] Shortly thereafter, Prime Minister Hashimoto Ryutaro visited Indonesia, met with Suharto, persuaded him not to introduce the currency board system, and opened the way for yet another IMF rescue package, which was to be agreed on in April 1998. But it was too late to bail out Suharto. In the wake of massive riots in Jakarta in mid-May 1998, Suharto stepped down.

The showdown between Japan and the United States came a few months after the fall of Suharto, when the Malaysian government under Prime Minister Mahathir introduced capital control and ousted Anwar Ibrahim as deputy prime minister and finance minister in September 1998. During the 1980s and 1990s, Prime Minister Mahathir had shifted his developmental emphasis from the public sector to the private and privatized public corporations to create a Malay business elite. But this transformation created its own problem and set the stage for the power struggle between Mahathir and his deputy Anwar Ibrahim, in the crisis years of 1997 and 1998. Working closely with the IMF, Anwar called for the fiscal tightening and criticized cronyism, while Mahathir opted for an economic stimulus package and wanted to bail out troubled Malay firms and banks. When the crisis spread to Malaysia, Anwar announced a strategic plan for the economic and fiscal stabilization in December 1997 with a high interest rate and tight fiscal policy package. This put a considerable number of firms and banks into trouble. Anwar also challenged Mahathir for the leadership of the United Malays National Organisation (UNMO), unsuccessfully, at its party congress in June 1998.

Mahathir fought back. The Malaysian government announced the introduction of capital control and the fixed foreign exchange rate system on September 1, 1998. The next day, Anwar Ibrahim was ousted as deputy prime minister and finance minister. On September 4, he and his allies were expelled from the UMNO. Young middle-class Malays were outraged at this development and at the way Anwar was subsequently treated (arrested, tried for sodomy, and sentenced to imprisonment). U.S. government officials were also outraged. The Japanese government supported Mahathir and defended his policy of capital control, because Mahathir's actions were in line with Japan's understanding that the crisis was one of liquidity and East Asia economies needed economic stimuli.

By then, however, the crisis was spreading beyond East Asia. The United States had argued until this point that the crisis was regional and had insisted on structural reforms wherever a country was hit by the crisis. The United States and Japan made a deal: the United States could go ahead with establishing a special account at the IMF to bail out Brazil, while Japan would start the new Miyazawa initiative in East Asia as an international Keynesian policy to revive East Asian economies and provide financial support to Malaysia, which had become the target of criticism in Washington and New York because of the imposition of capital control and the ousting of deputy prime minister Anwar Ibrahim. Mahathir survived the crisis.[16]

The new Miyazawa Initiative, announced in October 1998, marked a clear departure in Japan's engagement of East Asia. It made available US $15 billion short-term capital for financial and currency stabilization, and another US $15 billion long-term capital for economic recovery. East Asian economies were devastated by the crisis – the Thai economy contracted by 10.2 percent in 1998, the Malaysia economy by 7.5 percent, and the Indonesian economy by 13.2 percent. The aim of the new Miyazawa Initiative was to provide funds for stabilizing their currencies and finances and for economic stimulus measures to expand domestic demands, to create jobs, and to provide social safety networks for maintaining social stability. By February 2000, US $13.5 billion was provided to Thailand,

Malaysia, the Philippines, South Korea, and Indonesia within the framework of the new Miyazawa initiative and spent largely on public works and job creation. The initiative also made available up to US $5 billion and US $2.5 billion each to South Korea and Malaysia for short-term currency and financial stability. This paved the way for the Chiang Mai Initiative in the future.

With hindsight, it is clear that Japan became increasingly frustrated with the way in which the crisis was dealt with by the IMF and the United States, in part because of its different understanding of the nature of the crisis and in part because Japanese interests in the region were different from those of the Americans. Japan worked with the IMF when Thailand went into crisis in 1997, went along with the IMF to support Indonesia in 1997–98, but chose to support Mahathir in disagreement with the United States when Malaysia fell in crisis in 1998. The cooperation and rivalry between Japan and the United States affected the way in which the crisis ran its course in Thailand, Indonesia, and Malaysia (as well as South Korea, though that subject is beyond my discussion here), although of course the political economic structure in each country was also a large factor. The 1997–98 crisis, in which the crisis-hit countries experienced U.S. interventions, gave impetus to closer regional cooperation in the form of ASEAN+ processes with the regional framework of East Asia.

The rise of China

Whereas in the wake of the Asian financial crisis, it was intervention by the United States that was seen as a risk to be hedged; in the current conjuncture of circumstances, a rising and increasingly assertive China has become the main concern among the countries in the region. The global financial crisis which manifested itself dramatically with the collapse of Lehman Brothers in September 2008 marked the moment at which it can be assumed that China's party state leadership understood that the U.S. hegemony was in decline and made a strategic decision that China should depart from Deng Xiaoping's dictum of "hide and bide" and assert itself more forcefully.

In 1980 – a little over a year after the Chinese Communist Party under Deng Xiaoping decided on reform and opening up – China's economy was valued at just over 19 percent of the Japanese and 7.3 percent of the U.S. economy. Twenty years later, in 2000, China's GDP was 26 percent of that of Japan and 12 percent of that of the United States. By 2010 it had surpassed that of Japan. China's foreign reserve also expanded from US $166 billion in 2000 to US $1,809 billion in 2008, and China overtook Japan as the government with the largest foreign reserves in the world. In the years of its spectacular economic expansion, China's interdependence with the global economy deepened considerably. Its trade dependence increased from 12.5 percent in 1980 to 44.3 percent in 2009, peaking at 67 percent in 2006 before the global financial crisis hit. China's trade with the ASEAN countries expanded from US $35 billion in 2000 (which was 27 percent of Japanese and 26 percent of U.S. trade with ASEAN) to US $231 billion in 2008, surpassing Japan to become ASEAN's largest trading partner. China's defense budget has also expanded by more than 10 percent annually since 1991 (when it was US $6.2 billion) and reached US $70 billion in 2008 while the Japanese defense budget stood at US $44 billion in the same year.

There is no doubt that the weight of China has increased dramatically and significantly in regional affairs. The question is how the region is changing with the rise of China, and how Japan has responded to this rise and to its regional effects.

Fashioned under American hegemony in the early Cold War years in a way that was comparable to, but different from, the West European regional system, trade in East Asia was informed by two strategies. One was double containment: containing the Soviet Union and communist China on the one hand, while also containing Japan. This was achieved by integrating Japan's military power into the U.S.-led regional security system, and by U.S. control over Japan's energy supply. The U.S.-led regional hub-and-spokes security system was built on this strategic decision. The other was the fashioning of a triangular trade system of the United States, Japan, and Southeast Asia (and later Taiwan and South Korea). Japan's two most important prewar trading partners were the United States and China. Although Japanese businesses wanted to trade with China during the early years of the Cold War, the United States did not want the prospect of Japanese trade to undermine its containment of China. The United States encouraged Japan to go south, eventually leading to the creation of a system of triangular trade among the United States, Japan, and other countries in "Free Asia."

China was not originally part of this trade system, but embarked on modernization from 1978 onwards, initiating its own version of productivity politics, which meant reforming its socialist economy while opening and integrating China with the regional trade system.[17] Prime Minister Ohira Masayoshi stated that Japanese economic cooperation with China was part of U.S.-led global initiatives, cemented by China's decision to join the IMF and the World Bank in 1980.[18] Regional economic development from the mid-1980s to the late 1990s also worked for China's transformation and development and led to the integration of China, above all its coastal regions, into the regional economy.

These developments led to the evolution of an East Asian regional system that is structurally different from that of Europe. Toward the end of the 1980s, democratic revolutions took place in Eastern Europe, culminating in the collapse of the Berlin Wall, the unification of Germany, and the disintegration of the Soviet Union. These changes soon led to the North Atlantic Treaty Organization's (NATO) eastward expansion, as well as the deepening and expansion of European integration and the bloody civil wars in the former Yugoslavia in the 1990s. Nothing of this sort took place in East Asia. Democratic transformations did take place in the 1980s, not in socialist countries, but in America's client states of the Philippines, South Korea, and Taiwan. Although there were democracy movements in China and Burma, no socialist state in East Asia collapsed. China and Vietnam remain party states, while Myanmar has been undergoing significant economic and political changes since 2011.

China actively engaged its neighboring states in the 1990s. It normalized its diplomatic relations with its neighbors in two waves: with the United States,

Japan, Thailand, Malaysia, and the Philippines in the 1970s; and with Brunei, Indonesia, Singapore, South Korea, and Vietnam in the early 1990s. The end of the Cold War coincided with the U.S. and European imposition of economic sanctions on China in the wake of the Tiananmen incident. Its diplomatic normalization with East Asian states, as well as the visit of the Japanese emperor to China as its state guest, were in part efforts to break free from international isolation.

The 1990s, however, also saw the emergence of thorny security issues between China and its East Asian neighbors. In 1992, China enacted the Law on the Territorial Sea and the Contiguous Zone, in which its "territorial land" was defined as including "the mainland and its offshore islands, Taiwan and the various affiliated islands including Diaoyu Island, Penghu Islands, Dongsha Islands, Xisha Islands, Nansha (Spratly) Islands and other islands." China also embarked on military modernization and redefined the People's Liberation Army's mission as the maintenance of the maritime environment and defense of maritime interests. The enactment of the Law on the Territorial Sea and the Contiguous Zone instantly created territorial disputes in the South China Sea between China on the one hand and Vietnam, Brunei, Malaysia, and the Philippines on the other. Vietnam and China scrambled to occupy as many features in the South China Sea as they could in the same year. Tension mounted between China and Vietnam over oil exploration, prompting ASEAN to issue a declaration of concern urging the parties involved to exercise restraint and settle their disputes peacefully.[19] In 1995, however, while advocating a bilateral approach in settling the disputes, China occupied the Mischief Reef, which is claimed by the Philippines. This development again prompted ASEAN foreign ministers to issue a joint declaration urging all the parties involved to refrain from actions that may threaten peace and safety in the South China Sea.

The ASEAN Regional Forum was established in 1994, in part to engage China in a multilateral framework. Initially, China was not an active participant. It did not want the Taiwanese question to be raised there, it chose to deal with territorial disputes in the South China Sea bilaterally, and it did not want its freedom of action to be constrained multilaterally in a framework dominated by the United States and Japan. Toward the end of the 1990s, however, China adopted a new security concept that led to the establishment of the Shanghai Cooperation Organization (SCO) in 2001 and to its multilateral engagement of its neighbors in East Asia. China also became active in creating a regional framework for East Asian economic cooperation. In 1999, it proposed the institutionalization of financial cooperation with ASEAN+3 as a framework. China also agreed to hold a summit meeting between China, Japan, and South Korea in the same year and to institutionalize it the following year. In 2002, China and ASEAN concluded the Framework Agreement on Comprehensive Economic Cooperation and the Joint Declaration on Cooperation in the Field of Non-Traditional Security Issues. China and ASEAN also signed the Declaration on the Conduct of Parties in the South China Sea as a guideline for interstate behavior. The situation in the South China Sea stabilized. In 2005, the national oil companies of China, the Philippines, and Vietnam signed a three-year joint marine seismic project to explore waters off the

Philippines. In the meantime, China signed the Treaty of Amity and Cooperation in Southeast Asia – ASEAN's signature pact of association – in 2003. In 2004 China and ASEAN upgraded their relations to enhanced strategic relationship. This took the form of a five-year Plan of Action (2005–10), which included a joint commitment to increase regular high-level bilateral visits, cooperation in the field of nontraditional security, security dialogue, and military exchanges and cooperation. Put differently, China engaged ASEAN in the creation of a free trade area, promoted economic cooperation, and largely succeeded in calming fears of China as a threat.

Against this background, the mainland Chinese party and state leadership adopted the policy of building good relations with China's neighbors and making them its partners. This policy also informed the Chinese approach to Japan. In 1999, China agreed to a summit meeting of China, Japan, and South Korea when the ASEAN+3 summit was held. When President Jiang Zemin met with Prime Minister Mori Yoshiro (2000–01) in New York, he told Mori that Asia could not develop without Sino-Japanese friendship and cooperation. Premier Zhu Rongji stated in the same year that regional economic cooperation was an important area of collaboration, expressing his hope to promote China's cooperation with Japan in the region of East Asia. Prime Minister Koizumi (2001–06) welcomed his statement and called for the East Asia community building, appreciated the role that China was playing in regional cooperation, and underlined that the rising China offered opportunities – and not a threat – to Japan.

The strategic decision the Chinese party state leadership reached in the wake of the global financial crisis, however, changed the benign state of affairs in the region. The Chinese government became far more assertive on territorial and sovereignty issues, while it grew more confident of its management of the socialist market economy. It is against this backdrop that China's neighbors have come to be increasingly concerned about China's assertiveness. Carl Thayer documents this development in the South China Sea well.[20] It suffices to note that China's increasing advances in maritime territorial claims in the South China Sea have led to frictions with Vietnam and the Philippines. The Chinese government created a county-level town in Hainan Province with administrative responsibility over the Paracel and Spratly Islands. The Vietnamese government announced that, in 2009 alone, China had seized thirty-three Vietnamese fishing boats and 433 crews in the maritime area that both states claim. All of the claimant states except Brunei have built structures and garrisoned the features they occupy. Tension over territorial disputes has also mounted in recent years in the East China Sea between China and Japan, leading to the Japanese government's decision in 2010 to enhance its naval and surveillance capabilities in its southwest region and in 2012 to "nationalize" the Senkaku Islands.

The region of East Asia now finds itself caught between the United States and China geopolitically and geo-economically. The global financial crisis has accelerated China's rise, military modernization, and influence in regional affairs. The United States has responded by beefing up its military presence in and engaging with East Asia, both bilaterally and multilaterally. These forces have led to friction in the maritime domain and strategic competition for influence. In regional cooperation, ASEAN insists on its status as the hub in region making. Interestingly, however, ASEAN decided in 2010 to expand the East Asia Summit (EAS) to include the United States and Russia, in addition to the previous ASEAN+6. ASEAN has also sought to develop regional security architecture, such as the ARF and more recently the ADMM-Plus (ASEAN Defense Ministers' Meeting-Plus) process, which puts ASEAN in a position to set the agenda and to make decisions. Key Southeast Asian states have also reacted by adopting self-help measures to shore up their defense capabilities, while aligning themselves with the United States and its allies to pursue hedging strategies as a response to the geopolitical transformation now unfolding in the Asia Pacific.[21]

The change in Japan's East Asia/Asia Pacific policy needs to be understood in this context, as well as the change in government from the LDP-led coalition to the DPJ-led coalition in 2009 and back to the LDP-led coalition in 2012. Japan under the DPJ-led coalition reaffirmed its alliance with the United States, after Prime Minister Hatoyama Yukio (2009–10) briefly flirted with the idea of an East Asia community as a way to make the triangular relations among Japan, China, and the United States "equilateral." Prime Minister Abe Shinzo called for strengthening the Japan-U.S. alliance, embarked on security dialogues and cooperation with Japan's partner states, established the National Security Council (NSC), visited all the ASEAN member countries in a year, and decided to participate in the TPP negotiations in 2013. While Prime Minister Abe has made inroads in reinvigorating the economy, his decision to visit Yasukuni Shrine in December 2013 has undermined his initiatives on the diplomatic front and made Japan-China relations – and the as-yet-unresolved question of Japan's wartime past – the most crucial strategic issue for Japan in the years to come.

All of these developments have led to a shift in the framework for regional cooperation from East Asia back to the Asia-Pacific.

Conclusion

In retrospect, it is clear that the East Asian crisis in 1997–98 marked a watershed in Japan's engagement with its Asian neighbors. Before the crisis, Japan's presence as the second largest economy in the world was weighty enough to be taken seriously on any foreign policy front, if only the Japanese government could summon up the will based on public support to act and as long as its initiatives did not threaten its relations with the United States. As the history of the past few decades shows, Japan's actions on the international stage were largely constrained by its domestic politics and institutions as epitomized by the political stasis Japan experienced over the last two decades, as well as U.S. aims and strategy.

In the context of this political torpor and confronted with new challenges from its external environment, Japan has often opted for the path of least resistance. The Japan-U.S. alliance remained of paramount importance. Japan also opted for "shallow" rules with the WTO as the anchor of the international trade system without any intrusive regional arrangements. This was because Japan was confident that the productivity politics it pioneered would shape regional stability and prosperity anyway and that economic instrumentalities such as trade, investment, and aid would be effective enough to promote the network style market integration in the region.

Japan's Asia policy underwent significant changes, with the 1997–98 crisis as the turning point. To be sure, the United States remained hegemonic in the post-crisis years, casting a long shadow over the regional architecture. This was most evident in security, where Japan never seriously questioned the strategic importance of its alliance with the United States for Japan and the region. Deeply unhappy with the way in which the crisis was handled by the IMF and the United States, however, Japan opted for enhancing regional cooperation with the ASEAN+ processes as a framework, creating the mechanism to prevent the repeat of a liquidity crisis in the form of the Chiang Mai Initiative (so named by Miyazawa, then Japan's finance minister), and promoting regional trade liberalization through bilateral and multilateral FTAs and EPAs. Domestic resistance unfortunately has not allowed Japan's FTA/EPA initiatives to become as effective as they should as a foreign policy instrument. Economic cooperation policy thus remains as the most important foreign policy instrument in its engagement with Asia. It is now deployed to keep Asia open and to deepen ASEAN integration. This is best seen in Japan's economic cooperation with ASEAN new members like Cambodia, Laos, Myanmar, and Vietnam and in the development of the Greater Mekong Subregion (GMS). Japan is active in funding infrastructure development in mainland Southeast Asia not only because it is important for Japanese business to expand and deepen their production networks and supply chains there, but also because developing highways and power grids horizontally from Vietnam to Myanmar via Laos, Cambodia, and Thailand is instrumental in keeping the GMS open to the global and regional economy in light of China's attempt to build a hub-and-spokes system with Kunming as the center. But this does not deny that Japan's economic cooperation would be more effective if it were combined with Japan's trade policy, particularly EPAs, to expand Japanese imports from the region.

More importantly, Japan's strategy for strengthening the Japan-U.S. alliance in security and promoting East Asia regionalism in trade and finance was a balancing act whose stability was ultimately dependent on China. When Japan and the United States normalized their diplomatic relationships with China in the 1970s, it was assumed that integrating China into the global economy would spur China's economic development and a rise in Chinese standard of living, which would in turn temper Chinese nationalism and deepen China's engagement with the outside world in more accommodative and status quo–oriented terms. This remained the case as long as Deng Xiaoping's dictum of "hide and bide" formed the basis of China's foreign policy.

A rising China still beckons with all the economic opportunities it offers for neighboring states, industries, firms, and individuals. But China's military buildup has created insecurity among neighboring states. And China no longer hesitates to link its territorial and sovereignty issues with trade and investment issues to impose its position on its neighbors. Such actions on China's part have heightened the structural tension between the triangular trade system in which China occupies a crucial position and the U.S.-led hub-and-spokes regional security system, from which China is excluded. A stable and prosperous Asia founded on tamed nationalism, underpinned by a politics of productivity, and capable of some measure of autonomous action within the constraints of American hegemony had informed the post–Cold War Japanese vision. This vision, however, no longer holds.

Looking back, "Japan's decline" was in fact "Asia's rise." The rise of China was predictable, although no one foresaw how this rise would shape China's perception of itself and its place in the region and the world. Japan could have engaged Asia in a more effective way if it had been able to override its domestic political and institutional constraints, to address its wartime past without inviting right-wing nationalist backlash, and to combine economic cooperation with trade policy to promote regional economic growth built not on "Japan *and* Asia" but "Japan *in* Asia." However, with the exception of the Koizumi administration, government instability and political stasis in the wake of the bursting of the Japanese bubble could not overcome domestic resistance to craft a new set of foreign policy measures necessary for Japan, this time no longer as a great power, but as a major power, to engage Asia. Moreover, the ascension of China has changed the structure of Asian security, political alignment, trade, finance, and economic cooperation, in ways that pose new challenges.

We are still dealing with the effects of these lost decades and with Japan's unsuccessful attempt to come up with a long-term vision and the necessary policies to realize it. And yet, despite the lack of clarity regarding a long-term strategic vision, there remain certain imperatives that Japan as a major power can address. One is the question of political alignment with other powers to ensure the evolution of the regional order, especially in the areas of norm- and rule-making, while engaging China and managing the structural tension between the trade system and the security system. Second is the promotion of economic cooperation and trade liberalization as a way to restructure Japan's own domestic economy and a means to enable its middle-income neighbors to overcome the middle-income trap. Third is the promotion of ground-level regionalization by deepening and expanding transnational networks of businesses, NGOs, government officials, students, professionals, and ordinary people. These are not impossible dreams, but in order to realize them the Japanese public and government need to ask themselves some searching questions about the kind of Japan they want to create and be part of and how Japan can or should be located in this region and in the world.

Notes

1 I would like to thank Aizawa Nobuhiro for assisting with the research for this chapter and Caroline Sy Hau for her insightful comments and suggestions.
2 One of the best works that epitomized this vision in those heady days is Watanabe Toshio's *Ajia shin-chōryū: Nishi taiheiyo no dainamizumu to shakaishugi* [Asia's New Currents: West Pacific Dynamism and Socialism] (Tokyo: Chūō-Kōronsha, 1990).
3 Okazaki Hisahiko, *Atarashii ajia e no daisenryaku* [Grand Strategy on New Asia: Vision for Japan's Development] (Tokyo: Yomiuri Shimbunsha, 1993).

4 Steven Schlosstein, *Asia's New Little Dragons: The Dynamic Emergence of Indonesia, Thailand, and Malaysia* (Chicago: Contemporary Books, 1991), p. 22.

5 Ikeda Tadashi, *Cambojia wahei e no michi* [The Road to Peace in Cambodia] (Tokyo: Toshi Shuppan, 1996). See also Takashi Mikuriya and Takafusa Nakamura, eds., *Kikigaki Miyazawa Kiichi kaikoroku* [Interviews: Miyazawa Kiichi Memoirs] (Tokyo: Iwanami Shoten, 2005).

6 See *Oral History: Imagawa Yukio – Cambojia wahei to nihon gaikō* [Oral History: Imagawa Yukio, Cambodia Peace Process and Japan's Diplomacy] (Tokyo: National Graduate Institute for Policy Studies, 2005). Prime Minister Miyazawa decided to keep Japanese troops and civilian police in Cambodia when a Japanese police officer was killed in an ambush and the pressure mounted on the Japanese government to withdraw its personnel. Takashi Mikuriya and Takafusa Nakamura, *Kikigaki Miyazawa Kiichi kaikoroku.*

7 *"21-seiki Ajia-taiheiyō to nippon: Kaihosei no suishin to tayōsei no sonchō"* ["21st Century Asia Pacific and Japan: Promoting openness and respecting diversity"], December 25, 1992.

8 Yamakage Susumu, "Japan's National Security and Asia-Pacific's Regional Institutions in the Post-Cold War Era," in Peter J. Katzenstein and Takashi Shiraishi, eds., *Network Power: Japan and Asia* (Ithaca: Cornell University Press, 1997).

9 Ibid., pp. 297–98. See also Kitaoka Shin'ichi, *Nihonseiji no hōkai: Daisan no haisen o dō norikoeru ka* [The Collapse of Japanese Politics: How to Overcome the Third Defeat] (Tokyo: Chūō-Kōron Shinsha, 2012).

10 Yamakage, "Japan's National Security."

11 Shiraishi Takashi, "Japan and Southeast Asia," in Katzenstein and Shiraishi, *Network Power: Japan and Asia*, pp. 169–94.

12 Gary Hamilton, "Asian Business Networks in Transition: or, What Alan Greenspan Does Not Know about the Asian Business Crisis," in T.J. Pempel, ed., *The Politics of the Asian Economic Crisis* (Ithaca: Cornell University Press, 1999), p. 46.

13 Gregory W. Noble and John Ravenhill, *The Asian Financial Crisis and the Architecture of Global Finance* (Cambridge: Cambridge University Press, 2000), p. 32.

14 Sakakibara Eisuke, *Nihon to sekai ga furueta hi: Cyber shihonshugi no seiritsu* [The Day When Japan and the World Shook: The Emergence of Cyber Capitalism] (Tokyo: Chūō Kōron Shinsha, 2000).

15 Ginandjar Kartasasmita, *Managing Indonesia's Transformation: An Oral History* (Singapore: World Scientific, 2013).

16 Sakakibara, *Nihon to sekai ga furueta hi*, pp. 222–23.

17 David Shambaugh, *Power Shift: China and Asia's New Dynamics* (Berkeley: University of California Press, 2005), p. 1.

18 Shiraishi Takashi and Caroline S. Hau, "Only Yesterday: China, Japan and the Transformation of East Asia," in Zheng Yangwen, Hong Liu, and Michael Szonyi, eds., *The Cold War in Asia: the Battle for Hearts and Minds* (Leiden: Brill, 2010), pp. 25–38.

19 Carlyle A. Thayer, *Southeast Asia: Patterns of Security Cooperation* (Canberra: Australian Strategic Policy Institute: 2010), p. 31.

20 Ibid.

21 Ibid., p. 12.

12 Okinawa bases and the U.S.-Japan alliance

Sheila A. Smith

Introduction

The term "lost decades" is commonly used to describe an era in Japan of economic stagnation and chaotic political reform, but the phrase today also implies,
in addition, a loss of governance capacity in a nation that once led the Asia
Pacific. As Shiraishi Takashi argues in Chapter 11 on China and East Asia, Japan
was Asia's rising power, a model for developing and developed economies around
the globe – and this was a vision that seemed tenable until the late 1980s. In the
1990s, however, Japanese bureaucrats faced challenges as scandal and corruption were revealed in virtually every ministry. The political reforms in 1993 and
1994, described in detail by Machidori Satoshi in Chapter 8, resulted in kalei-
doscopic groupings and regroupings that seemed destined to confound Japan's
ability to govern. Other chapters in this book show that Japan's efforts to gain a
greater voice in world affairs were unsuccessful in foreign and security policy.
Michael Green and Igata Akira, in Chapter 9, show how Tokyo's response to the
Gulf War met with international criticism over its "checkbook diplomacy," while
Akiyama Nobumasa in Chapter 14 describes the ways in which Japan had failed
in its attempt to gain a seat on the UN Security Council. G. John Ikenberry, in
Chapter 15, takes a more optimistic view and posits that Japan took on a successful role as a "civilian power" – or a "stakeholder state," in his words – after World
War II; but this reputation seemed to be increasingly challenged as security trials
closer to home began to reveal the vulnerabilities in postwar security planning.
In the span of two decades, Japan seems to have fallen from grace as the world's
first and only "economic superpower" to an inward-looking and isolated regional
power incapable of strategic choice. Today, when Japanese look back at two lost
decades, they worry that their nation may be unable to find its way in an increasingly competitive world of geostrategic change.

   Like all symbolic representations, the vision of a Japan as lost overstates the
case. Today the political energy in Tokyo is much higher; the Liberal Democrats
have returned to power and Prime Minister Abe Shinzo presides over a party
chastened by time in opposition and determined to lead Japan forward. And yet
the problems of the past two decades ought not to be ignored. Many still remain.
Japan's government has recently set a priority on ending deflation and restoring

economic growth. In security policy making, there is a long list of reforms await-ing the Abe cabinet's attention. The world and the region continue to change, and Japan will need to develop greater capacity for strategic adjustment in the face of a rising China and the growing tensions in Northeast Asia. A look back at the policies that have confounded policymakers over the lost decades is imperative; no issue offers more lessons for policymakers than the realignment of U.S. and Japanese military forces in the aftermath of the Cold War.

Japan's challenge in coping with strategic adjustment is perhaps most conspic-uous in Okinawa. Alliance policymakers in Tokyo and Washington struggled to realign U.S. military forces in Japan in the aftermath of the Cold War. Roughly three-fourths of U.S. bases in Japan are concentrated on Okinawa; the bulk of these forces are Marines.[1] A shocking rape of a twelve-year-old schoolgirl in 1995 prompted an urgent policy review as Okinawans took to the streets in protest, calling for U.S. military forces to leave their island. A U.S.-Japan Special Action Committee on Okinawa (SACO) produced a comprehensive plan to address the Okinawa residents' complaints.[2] The centerpiece of this effort was the decision to close Futenma Marine Air Station, a large airfield located in the midst of Ginowan city in the south. Futenma could only be closed, however, if an alternative site within Okinawa was found, and this proved a crucial stumbling block for military planners. Eighteen years later, Futenma relocation continues to top the agenda of senior U.S. and Japanese officials.[3]

Resolving this longstanding problem has taken on a new urgency. Tensions erupted between Tokyo and Beijing over the Senkaku Islands in 2010, and even more seriously in 2012, highlighting Okinawa's place on the front line of Japan's southwestern defenses. Plans to move Japan's Self-Defense Force (SDF) to the southwest accelerated, and access to bases in Okinawa became necessary to cope with China's growing military interest in the waters and airspace around Japan.[4] China's expanding military presence, its dispatch of civil maritime patrols to the disputed islands, and its establishment of an "air-defense identification zone" raised the specter of a military clash between Japanese and Chinese forces in the East China Sea. These developments shook military planners in Washington and Tokyo.[5] For the first time, the two allies confronted the prospect of a direct use of force by another power against Japan.

The issue of Okinawa has thus become even more important to the way in which Tokyo adjusts to the changing strategic balance in Northeast Asia. In hind-sight, it is difficult to understand why Japanese policymakers became so paralyzed when confronted with Okinawa's grievances. If seen solely through the prism of the Futenma relocation problem, Japan's response to the end of the Cold War and to the emerging challenges in Northeast Asia seem hopelessly stalled. But this narrow focus misses a much more complex process of strategic adjustment in the alliance with Washington. An analysis of alliance military cooperation, including basing in Okinawa, reveals the impediments to change.

The United States and Japan have organized their alliance around a strate-gic bargain that assigns different roles to their national militaries. Throughout the Cold War the presence of U.S. forces on Japanese soil symbolized the U.S.

commitment to deter aggression against Japan, but that could be assumed would involve little direct threat to Japan; U.S. strategy focused on the role U.S. forces played beyond Japan's borders. The bilateral security treaty committed Japan to providing bases and facilities for the purpose of "peace and security in the Far East."[6] The conditions under which these forward-deployed forces would be used in combat were linked to the two flashpoints in Asia: the Korean peninsula and the Taiwan Straits. Even within Japan, few believed that these forces would actually be involved in defending Japan. Rather, the concern was that a conflict elsewhere in Asia would spill over to involve Japan. For critics within Japan, the U.S. military bases were a magnet for conflict rather than offering protection against aggression. For the Japanese government, the strategic bargain of providing bases for U.S. forces in exchange for Washington's extended deterrent in the nuclear era allowed Japan to limit its own military development.

Underlying the Futenma problem, therefore, have been larger alliance habits of cooperation that impeded a fresh look at military basing in Japan in the years since the Cold War ended. What are the determinants of the Japanese government's handling of the U.S. military presence in Japan, including the division of labor between U.S. and Japanese forces? Did the end of the Cold War alter that strategy? How does this compare to other relations among other Cold War allies and the situation in Europe? Have Japanese policymakers integrated basing policy with larger strategic goals in mind? To answer these questions, a closer examination of the premises of the U.S. military presence in Japan is needed.

The Cold War and the U.S. military in Japan

The Cold War's demise had quite different consequences for security cooperation arrangements in the Asia Pacific region to those in Europe. Like many other nations, the Japanese expected a "peace dividend" of lessened military tensions and an opportunity to build new regional dialogues on security. Japanese defense thinking in the early 1990s reflected this desire for regional security cooperation, and Japanese diplomats played a catalytic role in encouraging greater confidence building among Asian nations.[7] By 1994, the ASEAN Regional Forum emerged as the first Asian multilateral dialogue on security issues.[8]

The U.S.-Japan alliance, however, was not to be replaced. The rationale for continuing the U.S. troop presence was difficult to articulate initially, but what ultimately emerged was the idea that U.S. forces were necessary to ensure regional stability. North Korea's decision to pursue its nuclear and missile arsenal was an early indicator of new challenges for Japan. The 1996 Taiwan Straits crisis was a critical event that revealed yet another source of potential tension in Northeast Asia, and it reignited long dormant concerns about Chinese intentions in the East China Sea. U.S. military forces were seen as even more important as the global divide of East and West fell away.

A comparative look at the effort to realign U.S. forces after the Cold War reveals that not all the challenges of revamping the U.S.-Japan alliance can be attributed to domestic politics. Japan was only one of many sites across the globe where the

U.S. government sought to reduce and consolidate military bases in the 1990s. For the United States, cutting back forces had serious implications for communities that had organized jobs, land, and investment around the U.S. military presence. From this vantage point, the difficulties confronted by the United States and Japan over basing were no different. Nor were the unique circumstances of Okinawa the only challenge. In the wake of the Cold War, Tokyo policymakers faced a crossroads concerning their military relationship with the United States, an arrangement made manifest in the 1978 Japan Defense Cooperation Guidelines. This arrangement had created a formal division of labor between the two national militaries that would assign primary responsibility for territorial defense to the SDF and offensive strike capability to the United States. In short, Japan was responsible for defense while the United States was responsible for offense, and this premise had shaped military cooperation throughout the Cold War period.

These Cold War habits in the U.S.-Japan alliance proved difficult to break, and basing policy was no exception. Even as the United States sought to contend with a changing Northeast Asia in the years after the Cold War, the postwar aim of seeking greater SDF responsibility for Japan's defense continues to drive U.S. policymaking. Further, the driver of strategic adjustment in the U.S.-Japan alliance continues to be Washington's reassessment of its own strategic goals. Revising the U.S.-Japan defense cooperation guidelines followed as a mechanism for adjusting Japan's defense missions to contend with changes in U.S. planning goals. In the 1990s, however, Tokyo sought to slow the reduction of U.S. military presence in Asia as Washington redefined its global military goals, and only later, as tensions in the region challenged Japan's own defense, did Japan reorganize its own military to cope with this new security environment. Yet, a decade or more later, the lack of a politically sustainable strategy for organizing the U.S. military presence in Japan continues to plague the alliance.

The politics of basing in Japan

Localizing the impact of U.S. forces in Japan remains a Japanese government priority. Although thirteen prefectures technically host U.S. military bases, two carry the preponderant share of U.S. military deployments in Japan. Kanagawa Prefecture is home to the U.S. aircraft carrier George Washington at Yokosuka; Okinawa Prefecture is home to the U.S. Air Force's largest combat wing, the 18th Wing, at Kadena Air Base, and 18,000 combat troops in the III Marine Expeditionary Force, which are dispersed in bases throughout the island. For half a century, the politics that surround these bases in Japan created alliance management practices that sought to mitigate grievances but avoid overt discussion of the strategic rationale that required U.S. forces in Japan. These habits blinded policymakers to the need for a substantial transformation in the way that Tokyo and Washington thought about military cooperation in the alliance. Nowhere were those blinders more conspicuous than in the management of U.S. bases in Okinawa.

The existence of these U.S. bases in Okinawa has long been justified in terms of Japan's treaty obligations rather than Japan's defense. Under Article 6 of the

U.S.-Japan Security Treaty that was amended in 1960, the Japanese government provides bases to the U.S. military for "the peace and stability of the Far East." No clear rationale has been presented by Tokyo for the overarching scheme of basing U.S. forces in Japan or for the specific choices made when reorganizing U.S. forces. Moreover, there has been little attention to questions posed by citizens in Okinawa or elsewhere as to why U.S. and Japanese bases are organized as they are or what their relationship is to each other. The rationale for the bases thus seems solely a function of American rather than Japanese strategic needs.

The incident that provided a catalyst for change to this strategic inertia was the rape of a twelve-year-old Okinawan girl by three American soldiers in September 1995. This emotionally charged incident resulted in one of the largest local protests in Okinawa since the end of the occupation, with 85,000 participants. The island-wide protest demanding the removal of U.S. forces from Okinawa was not simply in reaction to the rape, but also reflected longstanding frustration with Tokyo. Governor of Okinawa Ota Masahide in 1995 refused to sign the rental permits required to sustain government access to base land. (Ultimately, the Japanese government took the governor to court and the Supreme Court forced him to conform to national land expropriation procedures.) Coincidentally, this was a time when the two governments were preparing a joint statement on the renewed role of the U.S.-Japan alliance after the end of the Cold War.

Available sources suggest that it was the U.S. government that first came up with the idea of returning Futenma base as a means to quell the anti-base movements.[9] A document sent by Okinawa to the central government placed the priorities it hoped to see resolved in the SACO process in three degrees of importance, but at this point Futenma was not even included in the list.[10] Prime Minister Hashimoto Ryutaro has admitted that he was reluctant to bring up the subject of Futenma in the February 1996 summit at Santa Monica, which was to be his very first meeting as prime minister with President Bill Clinton. With both the Ministry of Foreign Affairs and the Japan Defense Agency opposing any mention of the Futenma issue, Hashimoto remained unsure whether he should bring it up. During this meeting, it was Clinton who broached the subject of U.S. bases in Japan, and only then did Hashimoto, in cautious terms, mention the word "Futenma," for the first time laying the issue officially on the table. The Santa Monica meeting thus became the beginning of the long process of Futenma relocation that remains unresolved to this day.[11]

The exchanges at Santa Monica led to a secret negotiation process that ultimately became SACO, culminating in an agreement between the two governments to return the Futenma base within a five- to seven-year period. The responsibilities for negotiating the agreement were given to Tanaka Hitoshi deputy director-general of the North American Affairs Bureau, on the Japanese side, and Kurt M. Campbell, assistant secretary of state for East Asian and Pacific Affairs, on the U.S. side. Realizing the importance of the issue, Tanaka recalls Campbell half-jokingly stating that "I wouldn't be surprised if our bodies were found floating in the [Washington, DC] Tidal Basin tomorrow – this issue is that serious."[12] After a series of secret discussions, of which even the head of the Japan Defense Agency was kept in the dark, followed by sensational coverage by the media after the finalized details were leaked a day before the planned announcement, the agreement to return Futenma was born. It should be noted that, at this point, the exact site of the relocation had not yet been fixed.

Successive governors have continued to challenge Tokyo's plans for relocating Futenma to other locales in Okinawa. Both of Ota's successors as governor, Inamine Keiichi and Nakaima Hirokazu, were conservatives who supported compromise with Tokyo on the relocation effort, which would seem to belie the conventional wisdom that left-leaning politics in Naha, the capital of Okinawa, explain the policy stalemate. Rather, in recent years, it has been Tokyo's political realm that shaped outcomes on basing. Complicating the tensions between Okinawa and Tokyo was the rapid turnover in Japan's national leadership since the 1990s. Eleven prime ministers have come and gone since the 1995 crisis, and in election after election in Okinawa the fate of the Futenma Marine Air Station continues to mobilize gubernatorial and parliamentary candidates.[13]

A host of new political actors have populated the efforts to reduce the presence of U.S. forces in Okinawa.[14] While political parties may echo the conservative political divide of old, citizen activists and local politicians have a decidedly more contemporary purpose. The call for policy remedies to resolve the problems associated with hosting a large foreign military presence, rather than ideological conviction, drives most of the claims against the national government's handling of U.S. bases there. Citizen activists protesting for greater protections for women and the environment call for more stringent monitoring of the U.S. military bases. These citizen activists are not merely vocal actors without power – they have on numerous occasions had tangible influence in the base relocation debate. For instance, concerns that these activists would resort to physically blocking environmental assessment procedures or base construction played a large role in deciding the exact location and shape of the new runway at Camp Schwab in northeastern Okinawa.

Thus, complex party politics in Tokyo, as well as an active culture of citizen activism in Okinawa, have shaped Japanese deliberations over the relocation of Futenma. To be sure, the Futenma narrative is replete with drama and intrigue. There are villains and heroes, and rhetoric abounds. Defense and foreign ministers, indeed prime ministers and cabinet secretaries, have made their way to Naha to ask the people of Okinawa to accept their plans for the U.S. bases. However, few stay in office long enough to effectively address the problem.

The sheer number of changes made to the construction plan of the base at Henoko over the ten-year period following the SACO agreement demonstrates how the instability of the leadership of the central government helped result in the delayed, ineffective execution of the relocation plan. The plan started off as a removable offshore base plan proposed during the Hashimoto era, and it was then changed to a military-civilian joint-use airport plan that took nearly three years to finalize. This joint-use plan was then stalled for almost a year over the question of whether the local or central government was responsible for the payment of assessment procedures for the civilian-use part of the base. The central government caved in and expressed its will to pay for the assessment at the end of 2003. However, a CH-53 helicopter crash at Okinawa International University in August 2004 fueled a local anti-base movement. The process of further negotiation between the local and central government yielded even more plans: a land-based plan, the "L-shaped" plan, the "X-shaped" cross-landing strip plan, and finally the "V-shaped" plan on which both the Japan Defense Agency and the local government came to an agreement in April 2006.[15]

Some officials in Tokyo's security planning bureaucracy locate the problem in Okinawa; and others have accused Okinawan politicians of insincerity and even duplicity.[16] Former vice minister for defense, Moriya Takemasa, wrote a long treatise on the "real" back story of the Tokyo-Naha negotiations in which he laid particular blame on Governor Inamine Keiichi and others in Okinawa, who he thought were simply trying to push for more money from Tokyo. Bureaucrats in Washington and Tokyo bemoan the consequences, and in Okinawa the resentment of hosting a disproportionate share of U.S. forces on Japanese soil continues to fester.

The failure to close Futenma also became emblematic of broader consultative failings in the U.S.-Japan alliance. Blame was assigned to politicians and bureaucracies on both sides of the Pacific as confidence in alliance management practices eroded. In Washington, senior policymakers have at times seemed downright exasperated with what they characterize as lax Japanese political leadership, all the while convinced that there is only one viable solution. Japan's historic change of government in 2009 is often seen as the main point at which the U.S.-Japan effort to relocate this base was derailed and frustration in Washington peaked. Prime Minister Hatoyama Yukio resigned over the tensions that his plan for Futenma created with Washington.

U.S. policymakers, however, also had difficulties in deciding what to do about the U.S. Marines' presence in Okinawa. One Japanese expert, Morimoto Satoshi, who later went on to become Japan's defense minister in the final year of the Democratic Party of Japan (DPJ)'s rule, finds equal amounts of political twists in the saga that also have much to do with divisions within the U.S. government and across three U.S. administrations.[17] Each of these administrations has run up against the political difficulties of Okinawa. The first was the Clinton administration, in power when the 1995 rape occurred. Much energy went into formulating a comprehensive program for reducing the impact of the U.S. military on the island, and SACO was created to respond to the Okinawan resident complaints.[18] The decision to close Futenma was reached during the SACO discussions. Secretary William Perry and Deputy Assistant Secretary Kurt Campbell led this U.S. initiative, gaining support within the Pentagon for the first time to close one of the U.S. military's most important bases on Okinawa. However, even with all of the ambition to close Futenma, the plan to build an offshore structure, a plan crafted with the assistance of defense planners and industry in Tokyo, ultimately failed to gain local support in Nago City. Local industry in Okinawa was offered scant economic incentive in the highly ambitious, and commercially lucrative, plan.

In 2001, the Bush administration inherited the task of closing Futenma, but ultimately incorporated Okinawa basing in a broader realignment initiative for the

U.S.-Japan alliance. In the wake of the 9/11 attacks on the United States, the Bush administration began a broad strategic review of U.S. military strategy and began a Global Posture Review for U.S. forces. By the end of the Bush administration, a new plan for Okinawa was crafted and negotiated with Tokyo. Japan would move ahead with building a new runway on an existing base in northern Okinawa (Oura Bay), and the United States and Japan would develop facilities in Guam that would ultimately be a site for training for both the U.S. and Japanese militaries. It was this plan that the Obama Administration then took on when it came into office in 2009. Early in the administration, this deal was further cemented in the implementation agreement now referred to as the Guam Agreement in anticipation of Japan's Lower House elections and the likelihood of political change in Tokyo. For U.S. policymakers, the costs of these protracted deliberations over Futenma became a serious sticking point. Millions have been spent, and the budget constraints imposed by Congress on the plan to move forces to Guam have alerted legislators to the seemingly unsolvable problem of Futenma relocation.[19] For all three U.S. administrations, the policy was fundamentally the same – build a new runway for the Marines in Okinawa. For Tokyo policymakers, implementation of the relocation plan hinged on persuading Okinawa's political leaders to accept relocation of the Marines within the prefecture.

Okinawa was to remain the locale for the bulk of U.S. military facilities and Futenma was to be closed only if Okinawans accepted this new runway. Many other options were put forward, including consolidation on Kadena Air Base or use of runways on smaller, less populated offshore islands. The politics of these options seemed prohibitive, however, and the Japanese government held no public discussion of the alternatives. This was in stark contrast to the discussion of post–Cold War military reorganization in the United States and in other Cold War alliances. Over the decade after the Cold War ended, a broad restructuring of U.S. military forces had long been underway in the United States and by the era of the Bush Administration a similar process was unfolding in Europe.

A comparison with the U.S., Europe, and Asia

Japan was not the only country that struggled to consolidate and reorganize U.S. forces on its soil in the wake of the Cold War. Indeed, it took decades for the U.S. government to decide how to reorganize its military at home and across the world after the long term of Cold War competition. The promise of a "peace dividend" was widely heralded. Many initially welcomed the savings that were expected to accrue from downsizing the U.S. military, but the task of merging bases raised a complex array of questions. The local communities that hosted U.S. military facilities depended on federal spending and jobs. Moreover, defense production facilities had supported the Cold War military-industrial complex for nearly half a century. Finally, the strategy that would replace the broad Cold War configuration of U.S. military forces had yet to take shape. A post–Cold War world was not yet imagined in the immediate years after the dissolution of the former Soviet Union in 1991. Over the 1990s, therefore, U.S. attention focused first on cutting back its military forces at home, and it was not until 2004 that overseas bases became the locus of cuts and consolidation.

The political management of base closures was particularly difficult given the deep economic interests at stake. To avoid the pork-barrel politics that normally accompanied congressional decisions on defense and basing choices, the Base Realignment and Closure Commission (BRAC) was established to assess the Department of Defense's choices for base closures and consolidation.[20] Two rounds of base consolidation, first in 1991 and then in 1993, marked the initial post–Cold War realignment of U.S. forces at home. A decade later, in the wake of the 9/11 terrorist attacks on the United States, the Bush administration produced the first comprehensive attempt to review U.S. force posture for a new strategic era. The Global Posture Review was initiated in 2004 as a regular part of U.S. defense planning, and a new committee established specifically to consider consolidating U.S. bases abroad. The Overseas Basing Committee (OBC) was created to implement the Bush administration's new strategic vision as the president announced considerable cuts in U.S. forces in Europe.[21]

The European drawdown had a tremendous impact on host societies. U.S. forces in Europe went from 250,000 in 1988 to around 43,000 in 2013.[22] Eighty percent of U.S. forces in Europe were based in Germany. Furthermore, the unification of Germany in 1990 raised expectations within the country that a unified Germany would be free from the postwar burden of housing a foreign military. That sensitivity waned over time, however, as NATO developed new missions and purpose. A large part of the challenge for European hosts was the impact on their economy. In 1995, the Bonn International Center for Conversion (BICC) measured the impact on local economies across Germany. Overall, the impact in the period from 1991–95 was the hardest: tens of thousands lost their jobs, 92,000 acres of land was returned to commercial use, and there was a loss of roughly $3 billion in U.S. military spending.[23]

Domestic attitudes in Asia toward the U.S. military after the Cold War differed considerably from Europe, however, as U.S. forces had a far different history there. In both the Philippines and South Korea, democratization movements changed the domestic debate over U.S. bases. In the Philippines in particular, domestic political change led to a historic decision by the Philippine Senate not to renew the base agreement, and the U.S. military was asked to leave its oldest bases in Asia. Northeast Asia, however, posed different considerations, and concerns in Tokyo and Seoul over a possible U.S. military withdrawal from Asia were immediately communicated to Washington. Japanese and South Korean defenses relied on forward-deployed U.S. military forces. Furthermore, new worries arose quickly as North Korea announced its intention to become a nuclear power in 1993–94. In 1995, Assistant Secretary for Defense Joseph Nye published his rationale for maintaining U.S. forces in Asia to demonstrate "deep engagement" in sustaining the regional balance of power.[24] U.S. forces in Asia, unlike in other parts of the world, would remain at existing levels to deter new challenges to the region's stability. Within a year, China's threat to meet with a show of force any effort by Taiwan's new political party, the Democratic Progressive Party (DPP), to declare independence reignited tensions across the Taiwan Straits.

The protracted effort to transform U.S. bases at home and in Europe in the aftermath of the Cold War offers important insights into Japan's effort to manage its own strategic adjustment. Three factors offer a contrast from Japan. First, the strategic consequences of the end of the Cold War in Asia differed from Europe. The European response to the end of the Cold War was to celebrate the diminished threat posed by the former Soviet Union and the opportunity to work with Eastern European countries anxious for military cooperation with NATO. Reaching out to the newly independent Eastern European countries also provided an opportunity to build a "Partnership for Peace," and the military training and relationships that developed helped ensure a stronger sense of common identity in Germany and in nations formerly aligned with the Soviet Union.[25] Likewise, the UK found itself able to reduce considerably its own military and to reorganize its cooperation with those U.S. forces that remained there. By the time President Bush announced the cuts in U.S. deployments, NATO had transformed itself and host nation forces had assumed the bulk of military missions.

Second, the politics of military consolidation and base closures were anticipated in the U.S. effort to consolidate bases at home. The establishment of the BRAC signaled a new decision-making approach for the Defense Department and the Congress. Charged with evaluating the base closures and consolidations proposed by the Department of Defense, BRAC was asked to present a full plan to Congress and the executive branch for approval. No congressional committee or individual member would be allowed to pick and choose bases for retention; rather, the entire list was either approved or rejected. In the end, the BRAC approved four plans for U.S. military base closures, and 80 percent or more of the bases the DOD identified for transformation were completed.[26]

Third, military effectiveness and cost were equally important determinants in base consolidation. In the early post–Cold War planning for a drawdown of U.S. forces, cost-sharing agreements with allies in Europe, especially Germany, were a priority for Congress.[27] Both at home and in Europe new configurations for basing were evaluated for both operational and fiscal merit. Joint use of bases and the longer-term question of sustainability were both addressed in the BRAC effort. Joint use by different services offered both operational improvements and reduced costs for the Department of Defense. In Europe, U.S. military forces shared bases with host militaries, and in Germany the U.S. and German governments negotiated shared military use and civil-military co-location arrangements that satisfied both military requirements and access for civilian traffic.

There were other factors that complicated U.S. thinking about its military presence in Asia. Because U.S. Cold War defense treaties in Asia were bilateral, host nation politics were not driven by a collective vision of regional security but solely by their bilateral relationship with the United States. The domestic politics in Asia surrounding U.S. bases were quite different from those in Europe due to the historical legacy of colonization and occupation. In Japan, South Korea, and the Philippines, the presence of the U.S. military predated the full return of sovereignty, and this "compromised sovereignty" became the rallying cry of opposition to the host government as it managed the Cold War activities of U.S. forces.[28] Moreover, during the 1980s the U.S. military presence became a focal point for social action and popular movements as democratization pressures grew in the Philippines and South Korea. The Philippine Senate's decision not to renew the basing agreement with Washington in 1992 created ripples across the region about what this meant for other Asian allies. In Seoul, citizen calls for revising the terms of the U.S. military presence to reflect the changing nature of democratic governance in South Korea prompted the ROK government to request negotiations with the U.S. government to revise their Status of Forces Agreement (SOFA). The need for U.S. forces to defend South Korea, however, remained persuasive to most South Koreans.

Economic growth also shaped domestic responses to the U.S. bases in Asia. This was particularly obvious in Japan and South Korea where urbanization created severe pressures on bases in and around metropolitan Tokyo and Seoul. Land prices rose as economic growth took off and local municipalities sought greater commercial access to the mass real estate of bases such as Tachikawa and Yokota near Tokyo. Concentrating U.S. forces in the remote islands of Okinawa Prefecture meant that they were less of a target for domestic critics as well. Years later, Seoul faced similar urbanizing pressures on the Yongsan base. Yongsan had served as the Japanese headquarters during colonial rule, which added to the popular desire to see it returned to Korean ownership.[29]

Finally, postwar Asian militaries were far more dependent on the U.S. military for defense assistance during the Cold War, and only afterwards could the relationship with U.S. forces be reexamined. The American nuclear umbrella was assumed to deter nuclear coercion in Asia just as it was in Europe, but conventional capabilities in Asia were also far less developed in the years after World War II. The Imperial Japanese military was disbanded following the war, and Tokyo had to begin from scratch to rebuild a defensive force. Japan's SDF, redesigned for the purpose of "exclusive self-defense" under the postwar constitution, was not only dependent on U.S. defense assistance for rearmament but was designed to complement the U.S. military's offensive capability.

Military command structures for the alliances in Asia also differed. The United States and Japan had no joint command, and thus no integrated vision of how to respond to crises. Japan's national military was not allowed to plan for war or to plan for a transition to war until 2004, when new emergency laws were deliberated and adopted by parliament.[30] In South Korea, the UN Command provided the venue for U.S. and ROK military cooperation. U.S. commanders prepared to lead an allied response to any aggression against South Korea, but in 2007 President Roh Moo-Hyun initiated negotiations with the United States for the transfer of wartime command to ROK forces by 2012. President Barack Obama and President Lee Myung-Bak, however, agreed to delay that transfer of responsibility until 2015.[31] In the Philippine-U.S. alliance too, the Philippine military was the recipient of considerable defense assistance, both in training and in weapons sales, from the United States.

The slow pace of alliance transformation in Asia, therefore, was a function both of politics and of a different strategic setting. Whereas the United States and its European allies could readily agree on the need for a drawdown of U.S. forces, there was no similar consensus among Asian allies. The strategic environment was less compelling than during the Cold War but newer challenges in the region, the proliferation of missiles and nuclear technology from North Korea, and the rising military capabilities of China raised questions about how to adapt the Cold War alliances to the new security environment.

In Japan, other priorities took center stage. Economic reform after a decade of recession was imperative, yet growth remained illusory. Budget cuts across the government led to negative growth in Japan's defense spending. Political reform, triggered by dissension within the ruling Liberal Democratic Party, also altered domestic priorities. Tokyo's politicians were focused inward, competing for primacy in a new electoral landscape, with only minor interest in reconsidering the premises of Japan's postwar security architecture.

To be sure, there were some notable exceptions. In the early 1990s Ozawa Ichiro, one of the early proponents of reform, argued for "a new blueprint" to be implemented as Japan's future vision. This included both domestic and foreign policy reform.[32] Some of these early ideas would later inform the Prime Minister's Commission on Japan's Goals in the 21st Century (the Obuchi Commission) report in 2000, which G. John Ikenberry describes in Chapter 15, advocating for Japan to "play a constructive role in the international community" as "a global civilian power."[33] Koizumi Junichiro, when he came to power in 2001, advocated a rethinking of Japan's Constitution and its implications for his country's global responsibility. He also entertained the idea of an East Asian community, a vision that did not come to fruition as Japan failed to take concrete steps towards improving its relations with its neighbors. Later, Foreign Minister Aso Taro proposed the foreign policy goal of creating an "Arc of Freedom and Prosperity" throughout the Indo-Pacific, but this too produced little tangible benefits for Japan. Finally, the Democratic Party of Japan also flirted with the idea of a new national strategy and created a council responsible for its creation, but again nothing came of the effort. In short, the idea of creating a new strategic vision for Japan has had many proponents over the past two decades, but there has been little in the end to show for these various efforts. A rapid turnover in leaders, coupled with a certain degree of complacency about the changes underway in Japan's environment, made serious strategic reflection and a consistent effort to implement strategic goals impossible. The premise of U.S. support for Japan remained the framework within which Tokyo policymakers worked, and they looked to Washington for indicators of strategic adjustment for the alliance.

One of the glaring difficulties for both the Japanese and U.S. governments was the lack of cost controls on the Futenma relocation planning. The protracted difficulties in coming up with a good alternative for the U.S. Marines at Futenma were expensive. Cost projections put forward at various stages vastly underestimated the amount of money that would be spent. Multiple schemes generated new ideas, but also raised the costs. No ceilings were used to gauge the feasibility of any solutions and when broader defense budget cuts affected longer term military planning, first in Japan and then in the United States, the ballooning costs of the Guam relocation effort attracted the attention of both legislatures.

Alliance agreements had long placed a significant share of the fiscal burden for base consolidation on Japan. Past base consolidation in Japan had included a variety of government outlays. The Kanto Consolidation Plan that transformed bases in and around Tokyo in the 1970s had been costly, and Okinawa reversion incurred pricey expenses for the government of Japan, including the base land rentals, a lump sum compensatory payment to the United States for investments made there, and the associated costs of the transfer of U.S. forces from the main islands.[34] To date, the implementation of the recommendations of the SACO in the late 1990s has cost the Japanese government roughly 246 billion yen, including expenses for land returns, training improvement and relocation, noise reduction, and other projects.[35] The Japanese government continues to pay more than 8 billion yen annually for projects associated with SACO implementation.

The more recent agreement on relocating the U.S. Marines to Guam and the new plan for the Futenma relocation have also been an expensive project for the Japanese government.[36] In 2006, Japan's share of the Guam relocation costs was estimated at $6.09 billion of the total $10.27 billion.[37] Japan has already pledged almost $1 million in payments to the United States and spent another $433 million on military construction in Guam.[38] On Okinawa, a range of other costs associated with the effort to relocate Futenma since 2006 include 6.36 billion yen in costs for the environmental assessment, Futenma base land rental fees of 104.58 billion yen, and approximately 2.5 billion yen in other base community subsidies.[39] The cost of building the new runway has yet to be determined since the landfill permit has yet to be approved by the governor of Okinawa, but already the years of stalemate over consolidating bases in Okinawa continue to place a heavy burden on Japanese taxpayers.

Having slowly reduced U.S. bases around the country over the half century of alliance, Japan's political leaders were woefully unprepared to consider what the end of the Cold War meant for the infrastructure that sustained U.S.-Japan military cooperation. The small island of Okinawa had hosted the U.S. military for so long that Tokyo planners took it for granted that this quiet place far from Tokyo would always be the most expedient political solution to the U.S. military presence. After the Cold War ended, however, this became the Achilles heel of Japan's alliance policy. Maintaining two national militaries on Japanese soil also became increasingly costly. Yet there was little effort to consider how to rationalize the aggregate costs of basing.

The SDF and Japan's strategic adjustment

Japan's own military has been largely absent from the debate over U.S. basing in Japan, especially in Okinawa. The Senkaku Islands dispute between Japan and China changed that. For the first time, the U.S.-Japan alliance faced the possibility that Japan would need to use force before the United States would. During the Cold War, and even afterwards, the scenario for the SDF to engage militarily depended in large part on a contingency elsewhere spreading to involve Japan. Defending the country in the context of a broader conflict had long been the basic premise and alliance planning for a defense-of-Japan scenario. There was little direct threat to Japan independent of a scenario that involved the United States military elsewhere. A Korean contingency or perhaps an emergency across the Taiwan Straits meant that U.S. bases in Japan would be important, and thus how Japanese forces might support U.S. capabilities in such a situation became the focus of post–Cold War planning. Rear-area support rather than direct engagement alongside U.S. forces was the assumed role for Japan's SDF.

Japan's approach to housing U.S. forward-deployed forces had long been seen primarily as a treaty commitment. In practical terms, it was a problem for civilian bureaucrats in the Ministry of Foreign Affairs and the Ministry of Defense with direct responsibility for SOFA and basing administration. Japan's military was not directly engaged in the deliberations for two reasons. First, the establishment of civilian control in the postwar era was largely a practice of isolating the new SDF; it took decades for Japan's civilian bureaucrats in the Defense Agency (later the Ministry of Defense) to feel comfortable in sharing defense planning with the SDF. It was only after the Cold War ended that Japan's postwar military became formally integrated into the Ministry of Defense planning processes.

The second factor was that it took time for Tokyo to develop its own approach to the strategic shifts in Northeast Asia. From 1995 to 2005, Japan's defense planners largely responded to U.S. assessments and adjustments of its force posture. To be sure, the alliance was developing its own deterrent response, but the decision making that guided Japan's military did not necessarily emerge from this process.[40]

In the mid-1990s, a review of the U.S.-Japan Defense Cooperation Guidelines attempted to clarify roles and missions in the context of the new threats emanating from North Korea and the rise of Chinese military capability in the region. Yet this review failed to capture the larger question of how Japan's military would cope with this new unpredictability. Instead it focused on drawing Japan into a broader regional framework and loosening restrictions on the SDF's ability to work with U.S. forces in "areas surrounding Japan." The Cold War security cooperation between Japan and the United States had stopped short of planning to fight a war and focused instead on exercises and studies premised on a peacetime status.[41] Japan's gaps in its own contingency planning were largely to blame. In 2004, the long-awaited parliamentary approval of the law governing how Japan would organize itself in case of armed conflict was passed. The same year, the first real post–Cold War rethinking of the Japanese military's goals and mission was announced in the 2004 National Defense Program Outline.

The perception of a more dangerous security environment in Northeast Asia prompted considerable revision of U.S.-Japan alliance priorities, but very little in the way of reforming the political management of realignment within Japan. Two rounds of alliance consultations in 2005 guided alliance priorities. In February "new alliance strategic goals" were announced, and in October a study of force realignments followed. In May 2006 this study presented the realignment plan, the "United States-Japan Roadmap for Realignment Implementation."[42] The 2006 realignment plan was a comprehensive adjustment in the military missions identified as high priorities for the U.S.-Japan alliance, but it was also another look at how to consolidate bases in Okinawa. Futenma remained open, although operations there had been cut back considerably.

Realignment proceeded relatively smoothly in other parts of Japan, and the air force and navy adjustments seemed easier to manage politically. For the air and ground missions, there was little resistance to basing reform plans. Counterterrorism cooperation between the U.S. Army and the Central Readiness Forces (CRF) prompted the co-location of forces at Camp Zama, in Kanagawa Prefecture; in March 2013, about three hundred CRF soldiers moved to join the U.S. Army Japan and I Corps (Forward).[43] The development of ballistic missile defense (BMD) capabilities did not require significant changes in U.S. basing, but it did mandate the introduction of new Japanese capabilities, including PAC-III defenses and AEGIS ships, which moved the two militaries in the direction of greater interoperability. Command and control for BMD required some adjustment in Japanese law, but the tracking functions necessary for the United States and Japan were already integrated. New research and development (R&D) efforts for BMD technology also improved interoperability between the two militaries. Overall, the Defense Policy Review Initiative (DPRI) process added to the effectiveness of U.S.-Japan military efforts to respond to the new types of security challenges emanating from North Korea.[44]

The integration of SDF and U.S. military missions was easier for the services that had a direct role in Japan's defense.[45] The mission for the U.S. Marines was long seen as preparing for a contingency beyond Japan. After the Cold War ended, the U.S. Marines were needed in case of threats on the Korean peninsula; later, the role of the U.S. Marines focused on regional disaster relief, including the Philippines and even as far as Aceh, at the northern end of Sumatra, during the 2004 Indian Ocean tsunami. When the SACO plan suggested a reduction in the use of Futenma, Tokyo and Washington decided to relocate the Marine's fixed wing aircraft and only keep helicopters in Okinawa. Iwakuni Marine Corps Air Station in Yamaguchi Prefecture was designated as the home to the KC-130 aircraft.[46] A new offshore airfield was to be constructed there and met with far less political resistance than expected. Yamaguchi was a far more conservative political arena and home to well-known LDP politicians who were long supportive of the U.S. military presence in Japan. Yet, even in Yamaguchi there were new political costs for local leaders as citizen groups organized in opposition to the plan. For some missions, the reorganization of U.S. forces did not directly impinge upon Japan's own defense priorities.

By 2010, new thinking that guided Japan's military planning emerged with an emphasis on greater flexibility and readiness to meet the growing likelihood of a regional contingency. North Korea's provocations against the South, including the sinking of the South Korean frigate Cheonan and later shelling of Yeonpyeong Island, brought home the real risk of conflict that continued to emanate from the Korean peninsula. Missile and nuclear proliferation remained a concern to Tokyo, and by 2012 Japan had invested $1.3 billion in missile defense and had successfully tested its ability to respond effectively to a possible missile attack.[47]

A new defense scenario, the Senkaku Islands dispute, emerged suddenly to further motivate military planning. Even as the final details of the 2010 defense plan were being deliberated, the tensions between Beijing and Tokyo over a Chinese fishing trawler near the disputed islands confirmed the need for greater attention to the island defense mission. Japan's many islands in its southwestern region created a difficult mission for the SDF, but China's growing interest in using waters in and around Okinawa prompted Japan to redeploy its military to the south. The SDF was now tasked with developing a cohesive "island defense" strategy, and all three services – ground, air, and maritime – were needed to cope with China's growing presence in Japan's maritime region.

These two new mission priorities prompted greater integration with U.S. forces in Japan. From the start, ballistic missile defense depended on close coordination between the two naval forces. The Japanese purchase of AEGIS destroyers and the R&D on developing ship-borne capabilities ensured seamless operational cooperation. The 2011 Great East Japan Earthquake provided an unexpected opportunity to consider how to integrate operations in a crisis. Establishing integrated communication and command capabilities, as well as considering for the first time the overarching division of labor in the case of a broader combat operation, were the lessons learned from Operation Tomodachi.[48] U.S. Navy ships offered a base for SDF units sent into the Tohoku region; U.S. military transport and eventually mission support for the SDF's search and rescue and then relief operations were clear demonstrations that the two militaries could work together effectively in a crisis. The role of the U.S. Marines in helping to restore the Sendai Airport in the aftermath of the 2011 earthquake was well documented, as was the continuing role of the Marines in assisting the SDF in regional search and rescue, clean-up, and in the urgent effort to manage the meltdowns at the Fukushima Daiichi nuclear power plant. A year later the value to Japan of the U.S. Marine Corps – and the need to continue to deploy them in Japan's southwestern islands – was amply demonstrated when tensions rose precipitously with China over the Senkaku Islands. China's growing maritime reach had worried Japanese security planners, but when tensions between Tokyo and Beijing over the disputed islands in the East China Sea flared in 2010 and again in 2012, it became far more obvious to the Japanese public why cooperation with the U.S. Marines might provide a direct benefit for Japan's defense.

Bases on Okinawa also became a priority for the SDF. With air and naval bases on the main island of Okinawa, Japan's Ground and Air Self-Defense Force needed a bigger presence on Miyako and Ishigaki, islands geographically closest to the Senkaku group, to manage the growing pressures in the waters and airspace above the disputed islands. With Beijing's growing military and coast guard presence in and around the Senkaku Islands placing new pressures on Japan's defenses, Okinawa now assumed a much more conspicuous place in national military goals. As the U.S. Marines and Ground Self-Defense Force ramped up their amphibious landing exercises in anticipation of a possible Chinese attempt at a takeover, the rationale for military bases on Okinawa changed from the abstract notion of regional security to providing back up for Japan's own defense needs.

New strategic habits for the U.S.-Japan alliance

The lingering problem of relocating Futenma Air Station in Okinawa symbolizes the confusion and indecisiveness that characterized Japanese politics over the past two lost decades. There were numerous attempts to find an alternative site for the U.S. Marine Corps, but to date Okinawa's political leaders have not been convinced of the need to build a new runway inside their prefecture. Attributing this to a problem with Japan's governance suggests either that there was little effort to solve the problem or that implementation of a decision was ineffectual. Clearly there was no lack of effort to find a compromise that satisfied local residents. However, an inability to persuade Okinawa's leaders to accept the base plagued the effort to find an alternative basing option for the U.S. Marines. Multiple ideas were explored, and significant resources invested, in the effort to find a replacement facility. But the political strategy of offering compensation and fiscal incentives simply failed to gain local acceptance.

A more important question, perhaps, is how the United States and Japan could allow the Futenma issue to dominate the alliance agenda at such a critical turning point in the Asia Pacific geopolitical environment. Frustrations grew to the point that the alliance seemed to be in jeopardy. The arrival in 2009 of a new, inexperienced political party, the DPJ, that had little background in security policy revealed just how much Japan had relied on its bureaucrats to manage the alliance. Politicians had not been critical actors in devising strategy; rather, they were expected to galvanize local support for plans that came out of U.S.-Japan consultations. But the arrival of the DPJ cannot explain the decade or more of problems that plagued basing in Okinawa. The LDP had repeatedly suffered similar setbacks in the previous decade. The easy blame assigned to individual politicians, such as successive governors of Okinawa and the DPJ's Hatoyama, offers solace to some in the policy community and deflects criticism from others.

Seeing the problem simply in terms of Tokyo's internecine political struggles misses the larger challenge for the alliance as it ignores the broader structural changes that ought to have been deliberated by military planners. Seeing it simply as an ideological struggle distorts the facts, and misses much of the policy relief required in Okinawa. In fact, much of the difficulty over closing Futenma can be attributed to the inability of Washington and Tokyo to see beyond how the military division of labor developed over the decades of Cold War and the U.S.-Japan alliance. Moreover, the end of the Cold War did not lessen defense pressures on Japan; rather, as events in Northeast Asia unfolded, the region became ever more difficult for Japanese security planners to manage. A nuclear crisis on the Korean peninsula in 1993–94 and renewed military tensions across the Taiwan Straits in 1996 prompted the two allies to review their defense cooperation. Washington encouraged Tokyo to play a larger role in responding to these longstanding flashpoints in Northeast Asia, but Tokyo urged Washington not to lessen its commitment to defend its allies as the security environment deteriorated. The United States seemed focused elsewhere, however, once the September 11, 2001 terrorist attacks reoriented American perceptions of its national security priorities. The recent U.S. rhetoric to "pivot" or "rebalance" toward Asia is a sign that its focus is once again back in Asia, which provides Japan and the United States an opportune moment to rethink the old alliance habits of cooperation.

Today, an entirely different contingency and a much more dynamic strategic context motivate U.S.-Japan alliance discussions on Okinawa. Rather than the U.S. Marines, it is Japan's military that would issue the first response to a challenge from China over the disputed Senkaku Islands. U.S. planners continued to prescribe alliance initiatives that suited Washington's strategic goals without relating them directly to Japanese defense missions. Japanese planners continued to meld their own defense goals within a rationale for U.S.-Japan military cooperation, without a direct explanation of how their defense needs may differ from U.S. strategic goals. China's pressure on Japan over the island dispute was a rude awakening and revealed how little thought had gone into a scenario where Japanese forces would need American military assistance in defending their country. Tokyo now needs to articulate a strategic vision that integrates U.S. forces in Japan into Japan's own contingency plans.

Finally, those who manage the alliance in Tokyo and Washington have been unable to acknowledge that they have failed on Futenma. In Tokyo, to admit that the idea of relocating within Okinawa was mistaken meant different things for each of the parties. For the LDP, it would mean failure to defend the alliance; for the DPJ, it did in fact prove to be political suicide. In Washington, the protracted effort to relocate Futenma had engaged alliance managers for a good part of their career; but there was little understanding at the higher levels of government about why the problem was so intractable. Most U.S. policymakers simply assume the bilateral treaty entitles the U.S. Marines to a replacement base. No deadlines were set, no budgetary boundaries were created, and no indicators of success or failure were discussed in advance. Futenma relocation was taken as a given rather than planned.

This case study of the Okinawa bases suggests a broader thesis about Japanese capacity for strategic adjustment. Japan's ability to adjust is largely dependent on a division of labor between Washington and Tokyo that is no longer adequate for Japan's defense needs. In this division of labor, forward-deployed U.S. forces provide the offensive strike capability necessary to complement Japan's own defenses. For much of the Cold War, this formula worked, as there was little real threat to Japan itself. U.S. forces could concentrate on missions elsewhere as the SDF developed greater capability for territorial defense. Today, however, such a premise no longer holds. U.S. and Japanese militaries must be deeply integrated in the complex missions required to ensure Japan's security and the stability of Northeast Asia.

The strategic bargain forged with Japan half a century ago gave Washington the lead role in formulating strategy for the alliance. No one wanted to openly question the mechanics of U.S.-Japan military cooperation because of this dependence on the U.S. presence. Now, few in Japan want to openly question the premises that underlie the U.S.-Japan strategic bargain, especially when confronted by a rising Chinese military role in the region. Thus, the old habits of alliance management have proven remarkably resilient. As the political pressures in Japan grew and as regional security challenges multiplied, Japanese policymakers were even less willing to innovate. The long delay in closing Futenma created deep frustrations, and the alliance seemed precariously close to a breakdown. Policymakers stuck with what they knew rather than considering new options. Even worse, the task of relocating the U.S. Marines and closing Futenma, originally designed to ease the burden on Okinawa's residents, came to be seen as a strategic imperative for the alliance rather than a means to an end. At a time when a broader menu of options for considering how U.S. and Japanese military forces could cooperate was urgently needed, diversifying basing options would have been a wise choice. There were plenty of options from the U.S. and European experiences to draw from, and yet Japanese policymakers seemed reluctant to advocate for either an alternative location for the Marines or a different kind of basing arrangement.

Conclusion

The stalled effort to relocate Futenma Marine Air Station is often seen as the best example of the impact of Japan's lost decades. Yet why this particular policy seems such a compelling piece of evidence to substantiate the "lost decades" narrative is unclear. The frustration with repeated failed efforts to find a compromise between the residents of Okinawa and the alliance policymakers in Washington is amply clear. But does this really have much to do with the "lost decades" and its imputed impact on Japanese governance?

Alliance reform was the central task in the post–Cold War era, and Japanese decision making seemed to lag behind Washington's concerns about the trajectory of North Korean and Chinese military development. Three fundamental conclusions can be drawn about what the "lost decades" meant for Japanese decision making on the alliance. The first is that opportunities for change were lost, and this implies that they were irrecoverable. The second is that Japanese decision makers either had no capacity or no drive for reforming Japanese security planning. While this is undoubtedly true, it is important to consider where the energy for security reforms was expected, and who exactly failed to demonstrate leadership. Finally, this narrative assumes that Japanese decision making is shaped solely by, and focuses only on, Japan's problems. In fact, the security alliance is not driven solely by Tokyo, or indeed by Washington.

In the case of the Okinawa bases, all three of these conclusions have some resonance, but ultimately, they prove to be an incomplete explanation for the seventeen years of strained effort to forge compromise.

To fully appreciate the multiple causes of the protracted struggle over Futenma, the analytical lens needs to be wider. If we take a step back from the conventional wisdom about politics in Tokyo and instead look at the debate over Northeast Asian security, then there is a different set of causal links to consider. With 20/20 hindsight, it seems easy to look back at certain moments and link their trajectory as if what followed was amply apparent. Quite often, however, it was not – at the time. For example, there was no agreement over the import of strategic changes in

Northeast Asia in either the Japanese or U.S. governments for much of the 1990s. Granted there were a series of events that "shocked" policymakers, but there was considerable debate over each event and its implications for the alliance. With the fall of the Berlin Wall, it took the United States and Europe over a decade to interpret how that would change their military cooperation. Similarly, faced with the 1993 North Korean announcement of its intent to withdraw from the Nuclear Nonproliferation Treaty and the 1996 Taiwan Straits crisis, it took U.S. and Japanese policymakers until 2005 to articulate a common strategic vision for the post–Cold War era. Yet the truly important consequence was not the dismantling of the military force postures of the United States and Japan, but rather their strengthening. The end of the Cold War thus brought different consequences to Northeast Asia than those it brought to Europe.

Second, in Washington, the preferred strategy for coping with the changes in Northeast Asia was not to rely solely on the military instrument, but to include a strong diplomatic component. It took time for Washington and Tokyo to fully understand, for example, when and how extended deterrence would be affected by North Korea. Moreover, the threat to Japan was geographically closer, and thus demanded independent action from the alliance. Japanese analysts identified the growing threat of Pyongyang's missile proliferation far earlier than did U.S. analysts. Washington was much more focused on nuclear proliferation. Each country focused on the threat most imminent for their country, and when Prime Minister Koizumi came into office, he acted on Japan's security perceptions by visiting North Korea to negotiate a freeze on their missile production. But the most important conclusion by both Washington and Tokyo was that diplomacy – regionally organized – was the best tool for persuading North Korea to abandon its nuclear and missile ambitions. The Six Party Talks ultimately were not successful, but there was a consensus that a collective negotiated effort was required.

Finally, while there are many who look back and see Japanese complacency, the reality is that Japan's strategic planners fully understood the implications of the changes underway in their security environment. But their prescription was not always the same as that of Washington's planners. Japanese planners also interpreted China's growing military modernization somewhat differently. Part of that had to do with geography, and when Chinese maritime activities around Japan grew steadily in the early 2000s, a shift in Japanese force posture, as well as in SDF missions, emerged. The southwestern region was now Japan's primary military concern. The convergence with U.S. forces in Okinawa would not be seen, however, until the Senkaku Islands dispute ushered in a partnership in amphibious capability between the U.S. Marines and the CRF; this too changed alliance priorities. Yet Japanese planners had long worried about the Chinese nuclear capability, as well as Washington's willingness to continue to maintain sufficient strategic superiority to deter Beijing from coercive use of that arsenal.

Today, there is more latitude in Japan's domestic politics for considering future security choices. China's defense budget nearly doubled from 1990 to 2000, then quadrupled from 2000 to 2010.[49] China has increased its naval, air, and missile capabilities in an effort to deny access to U.S. forces in the first island chain off its coastline.[50] The People's Liberation Army Navy now operates beyond this first island chain, exiting through the straits and between the islands of Okinawa, far closer to Guam.[51] Ultimately, the Chinese navy will operate farther out into the Western Pacific, and already has increased its expertise in blue-water operations through participation in the Gulf of Aden antipiracy effort. The announcement of a Chinese Air Defense Identification Zone (ADIZ) in the East China Sea also suggests that the People's Liberation Army Air Force will continue to expand its range of operations, with an aim to challenge air superiority in and around Japanese airspace. The U.S.'s ability to defend Japan will be affected by these changes in Chinese capabilities. Many Japanese policymakers are more intent on responding to the challenges China poses to Japan's interests, and thus are more open to a change in Japan's strategy towards Beijing. Ironically, Japan may have fewer options today than it had a decade ago for confronting a rising China.

Changes are underway within Japan also. Today, there is a far greater popular receptivity to Japan's Self-Defense Force, long viewed with some suspicion in postwar Japan. Popular appreciation for the SDF after the Great East Japan Earthquake and the nuclear disaster at Fukushima emerged as their disaster response demonstrated their service to the country. Nearly all (97.7 percent) of the public held favorable views of these relief efforts, and their work with U.S. forces in Operation Tomodachi was also praised. This rise in trust in Japan's postwar military, combined with rising Japanese concerns about their regional environment, may allow for a faster pace of Japanese defense reform.

Nonetheless, as in the past lost decades, the question will be how much change is required. Does Japan need a wholesale revision of its postwar security strategy? Or will adjustments in its strategic cooperation with the United States suffice? Japan's ingrained preference for incrementalism may be part of the problem, and the lesson of the lost decades is that the bureaucratic tendency for adjustment rather than redesign dominated. These were not only decades of economic stagnation, but also decades of incomplete and uncharted political change that created confusion among Japan's political elites and uncertainty among the Japanese public. Maintaining local support for bases, both SDF and U.S. military, requires both incremental adjustments and political capital. For larger tasks such as relocating a large U.S. airfield, political capital is in far higher demand. Few Japanese prime ministers were willing to expend it in Okinawa. Hashimoto Ryutaro was the exception rather than the rule, and his willingness to concentrate his energies so fully on Okinawa is often attributed to his desire to help improve the quality of life in the prefecture rather than his strategic vision for the alliance. Koizumi by contrast was interested in making the necessary adjustments for U.S. and Japanese forces, but he was also interested in using his political capital for economic restructuring and other alliance priorities. Base policy is hard – and highly political – work.

Seeing the alliance, and its ability for strategic adjustment, as all about Japan will lead to a rather imbalanced understanding of what motivates moments of serious policy change. Today, it may be the United States that is struggling to adjust. The United States spent the last decade or more fighting two wars – one in Iraq and one in Afghanistan – rather than focusing on Northeast Asia. Even as the

Obama Administration sought to pivot to Asia, its attention has been repeatedly drawn to other regions with new demands.

The alliance between Tokyo and Washington will continue to be pulled and pushed by a multiplicity of factors. Japan's lost decades limited the scope (and the fiscal resources) necessary to concentrate on a wholesale rethinking of its postwar strategy, including Tokyo's reliance on Washington as a strategic partner. Beijing's challenge to Japanese sovereignty over the Senkaku Islands has refocused Tokyo's attention. What remains is the difficult question of how Japan's long-term security can best be assured. Once that question is answered, the role of the alliance in assuring that security can be addressed. Then, and only then, will Tokyo be able to address head-on how to base U.S. forces in Japan in the most effective and politically sustainable manner.

Notes

1   There are 47,300 Americans in Okinawa as a result of the U.S. military presence there. Of those, 25,843 are service members; most of the others are dependents of service members. 2,000 are civilian employees of the U.S. military. The Marines claim the largest share, with 23,583 service members, civilians, and dependents. Of these, 15,365 are military personnel. The Air Force has a total of 14,605 personnel associated with their presence on Okinawa, with 6,772 military personnel. The Navy comes in third with a total of 5,384, of which 2,159 are military personnel. Finally, the Army claims 3,728 with only 1,547 military personnel. Annual data is available online via the website of the Okinawa Prefectural Government, http://www.pref.okinawa.lg.jp/site/chijiko/kichitai/documents/h25–2_2.pdf.

2   The proposed reduction in the impact of U.S. forces on Okinawa by the Special Action Committee on Okinawa were announced on December 2, 1996, and included closing live-fire exercises, returning base land, and restricting the off-base access by U.S. Marines. See Ministry of Foreign Affairs, Japan, "The SACO Final Report," December 2, 1996, http://www.mofa.go.jp/region/n-america/us/security/96saco1.html.

3   On December 3, 2013, Vice President Joe Biden reiterated in a press conference alongside Prime Minister Abe Shinzō in Tokyo that "the United States is determined to implement our roadmap to relocate the base for Futenma as quickly as possible." The White House, "Remarks to the Press by Vice President Joe Biden and Prime Minister Shinzō Abe of Japan," December 3, 2013, http://www.whitehouse.gov/the-press-office/2013/12/03/remarks-press-vice-president-joe-biden-and-prime-minister-shinzo-abe-jap.

4   See for example China's announcement that it would establish an Air Defense Identification Zone (ADIZ) over the East China Sea. Ministry of National Defense, People's Republic of China, "Announcement of the Aircraft Identification Rules for the East China Sea Air Defense Identification Zone of the P.R.C.," November 23, 2013, http://eng.mod.gov.cn/Press/2013–11/23/content_4476143.htm. The United States and its allies are also concerned with China's military strategy of developing anti-access area-denial (A2AD) capabilities. For more information on the U.S. vision for how its forces will respond to emerging A2AD challenges, see U.S. Department of Defense, "Joint Operational Access Concept (JOAC)," January 17, 2012, http://www.dcfcnsc.gov/pubs/pdfs/JOAC_Jan%202012_Signed.pdf.

5   Sheila A. Smith, "A Sino-Japanese Clash in the East China Sea," *Contingency Planning Memorandum*, Council on Foreign Relations, No. 18 (April 2013); International Crisis Group, "Dangerous Waters: China-Japan Relations on the Rocks," *Asia Report No. 245*, April 8, 2013; and Paul J. Smith, "The Senkaku/Diaoyu Island Controversy: A Crisis Postponed," *Naval War College Review* 66, no. 2 (Spring 2013).

6 United States and Japan, "Japan-US Security Treaty," January 19, 1960, available via Japan's Ministry of Foreign Affairs website, http://www.mofa.go.jp/region/n-america/us/q&a/ref/1.html.

7 Advisory Group on Defense Issues, "The Modality of Security and Defense Capability of Japan: The Outlook for the 21st Century (Higuchi Report)," August 12, 1994, accessed via the "World and Japan" Database Project, Institute of Oriental Culture, University of Tokyo, http://www.ioc.u-tokyo.ac.jp/~worldjpn/documents/texts/JPSC/19940812.O1E.html. For the U.S. response to the report, see Patrick M. Cronin and Michael J. Green, "Redefining the US-Japan Alliance: Tokyo's National Defense Program," Institute for National Strategic Studies, National Defense University, No. 31 (November 1994).

8 Foreign Minister Nakayama Tarō had strongly advocated for Japan to support ASEAN-based architecture during the ASEAN Post-Ministerial Conference held on July, 1991. Paul Midford, "Japan's Leadership Role in East Asian Security Multilateralism: The Nakayama Proposal and the Logic of Reassurance," *Pacific Review* 13, no. 3 (2000), pp. 367–97.

9 Details remain vague. See Morimoto Satoshi, *Futenma no nazo: Kichi henkan mondai meisō 15-nen no subete* [The Mysterious Twists in the U.S. Marine Corps Air Station Futenma Relocation Plan] (Tokyo: Kairyūsha, 2010), pp. 20–21.

10 Ibid., pp. 42–43.

11 For the description of the summit in Hashimoto's own words, see Iokibe Makoto and Miyagi Taizō, *Hashimoto Ryūtarō gaikō kaikoroku* [Hashimoto Ryūtarō's Memoir on Foreign Policy] (Tokyo: Iwanami Shoten, 2013), pp. 63–67. For a comprehensive account of the Santa Monica Summit that covers both Japan and the U.S. internal dynamics, see Yōichi Funabashi, *Alliance Adrift* (New York: Council of Foreign Relations, 1999), pp. 14–22. For other memoirs by related personnel, see Orita Masaki, *Gaikō shōgen roku: Wangan sensō, futenma mondai, iraku sensō* [Memoir of a diplomat: The Gulf War, Futenma, and Iraq War] (Tokyo: Iwanami Shoten, 2013), pp. 194–97.

12 Tanaka Hitoshi, *Gaikō no chikara* [The Power of Diplomacy] (Tokyo: Nihon Keizai Shinbun, 2009), p. 78.

13 The eleven prime ministers are Murayama Tomiichi, Hashimoto Ryutarō, Obuchi Keizō, Mori Yoshiro, Koizumi Junichirō, Abe Shinzō, Fukuda Yasuo, Aso Tarō, Hatoyama Yukio, Kan Naoto, and Noda Yoshihiko. Prime Minister Abe Shinzō returned to power in December 2012 to yet again contend with the closure of the Futenma airbase. In Okinawa, there have been three governors, Ōta Masahide, Inamine Keiichi, and Nakaima Hirokazu, and four mayors of Nago City, the site identified as the best replacement location: Higa Tetsuya, Kishimoto Tateo, Shimabukuro Yoshikazu, and Inamine Keiichi. Tokyo's politics have thus been far more volatile than Okinawa's.

14 This is true also of citizen responses to U.S. bases elsewhere in Asia. See Sheila A. Smith, *Shifting Terrain: The Domestic Politics of the US Military Presence in Asia*, East-West Center Special Reports, No. 8 (Honolulu: East-West Center, 2006).

15 For a detailed account of this negotiation process, see Moriya Takemasa, *"Futenma" kōshō hiroku* [The "Futenma" Chronicle: The Negotiations behind the Scenes] (Tokyo: Shinchōsha, 2010).

16 Ibid.

17 See Morimoto, *Futenma no nazo*, pp. 3–7.

18 See Sheila A. Smith, "Challenging National Authority: Okinawa Prefecture and the US Military Bases," in Sheila A. Smith, ed., *Local Voices, National Issues* (Ann Arbor: University of Michigan Press, 2000), pp. 75–114; Kent E. Calder, *Embattled Garrisons: Comparative Base Politics and American Globalism* (Princeton: Princeton University Press, 2008); Gabe Masa'aki, *Sengo nichibei kankei to anzen hoshō* [Postwar Japan-U.S. Relations and Security] (Tokyo: Yoshikawa Kōbunkan, 2007), Funabashi Yōichi, *Alliance Adrift* (Washington, DC: Council on Foreign Relations Press, 1999),

and Chalmers Johnson, ed., *Okinawa: Cold War Island* (Cardiff, CA: Japan Policy Research Institute, 1999).

19 U.S. Government Accountability Office, "Military Buildup on Guam: Costs and Challenges in Meeting Construction Timelines," June 27, 2011, http://www.gao.gov/new. items/d11459r.pdf.

20 A study published in *Public Affairs Quarterly (PAQ)* in 1997 reviewed this premise and the BRAC outcomes and found that the pattern of influences in fact remained the same in policy decisions made by independent commissions and those made by regular Congressional processes. But the factor that mattered most was the number of members from a state on key House (not Senate) defense-related committees, especially the three key committees of Armed Services, Appropriations, and Budget. See "The Politics of Military Base Closings: A New Theory of Influence," *PAQ* (Summer 1997), pp. 176–208. A full description of the process of the Base Closings and Realignment Commission was described in the 1993 memo prepared by the Commission staff; see "The Defense Base Closing and Realignment Commission: The Process," Washington, DC.

21 Secretary of Defense Donald Rumsfeld announced this new review of U.S. global forces in September 2004. U.S. Department of Defense, "Rumsfeld Says Future Calls for 'More Agile, Efficient Force,'" September 23, 2004, www.defense.gov/home/ articles/2004.09/a0923046.html. In 2004, President Bush announced 80,000 military personnel and 100,000 family members; and a year later, the Overseas Basing Commission announced plans for consolidating bases and returning land to the European nations that hosted the U.S. military during the Cold War. The Overseas Basing Commission carried out its review of U.S. basing requirements on the foundation for "global reposturing" found in the 2004 Department of Defense Integrated Global Presence and Basing Strategy (IGPBS), and spent one year deliberating on the priorities for consolidating and closing U.S. bases abroad. Its conclusions are found in Commission on Review of the Overseas Military Facility Structure of the United States (Overseas Basing Commission), "Report to the President and the Congress," August 15, 2005, http:// govinfo.library.unt.edu/osbc/documents/OBC%20Final%20Report%20August%20 15%202005.pdf.

22 Data compiled from U.S. Department of Defense, Defense Manpower Data Center, "Military Personnel Statistics," accessed November 2013, https://www.dmdc.osd.mil/ appj/dwp/reports.do?category=reports&subCat=milActDutReg.

23 The bulk of U.S. forces were concentrated in four German states: Rhineland-Palatinate, Baden-Württemberg, Hesse, and Bavaria. Keith B. Cunningham and Andreas Klemmer, "Restructuring the US Military Bases in Germany: Scope, Impacts and Opportunities," Report 4, June 1995, http://www.bicc.de/publications/publicationpage/publication/ restructuring-the-us-military-bases-in-germany-scope-impacts-and-opportunities-224/.

24 Nye advocated that 100,000 U.S. forces should remain in Asia. U.S. Department of Defense, Office of International Security Affairs, "United States Security Strategy for the East Asia-Pacific Region," February 1995.

25 According to the NATO website, "The Partnership for Peace is a program of practical bilateral cooperation between individual Euro-Atlantic partner countries and NATO. It allows partners to build up an individual relationship with NATO, choosing their own priorities for cooperation." For more information, see NATO, "The Partnership for Peace Programme," http://www.nato.int/cps/ar/SID-91A898D5–7584DA15/natolive/ topics_50349.htm.

26 BRAC Commission, "2005 Defense Base Closure and Realignment Commission," 2005, http://www.brac.gov/docs/2005CommissionProcessBriefing.pdf.

27 See for example an early U.S. Administration effort to persuade Congress that burden-sharing with allies would play an important role in U.S. military drawdown. U.S. Government Accountability Office, "US Military Presence in Europe: Issues Related to the Drawdown," Testimony of Joseph E. Kelley, Director in Charge of International Affairs,

National Security and International Affairs Division of the General Accounting Office before the Subcommittee on Readiness, Committee on Armed Services, U.S. House of Representatives, April 27, 1993, http://www.gao.gov/products/T-NSIAD-93-3.

28 Smith, *Shifting Terrain*.

29 The return of Yongsan to Korean ownership was part of a broad consolidation plan for U.S. forces in Korea. Agreed upon on October 26, 2004, the return has since been delayed until 2016 to accommodate the construction of new facilities in other parts of South Korea and urban development plans for the returned land in Seoul. Ad Hoc Subcommittee for the Yongsan Relocation Plan, "Memorandum of Agreement between the Government of the Republic of Korea and the Government of the United States of America Regarding the Agreed Recommendation for Implementation of the Agreement between the Republic of Korea and the United States of America on the Relocation of United States Forces from the Seoul Metropolitan Area," October 26, 2004, http://www.state.gov/documents/organization/95894.pdf.

30 According to the Ministry of Defense, three laws related to responding to armed attacks on Japan and other emergency situations, including the Armed Attack Situation Response Law, were enacted in 2003. Furthermore, seven laws including the Law Concerning the Measures for Protection of the Civilian Population in Armed Attack Situations (Civil Protection Law) were enacted in 2004. Ministry of Defense, "Framework for Responses to Armed Attack Situation and Other Situations," *Defense of Japan 2006*, Section 3, 2006, p. 125, http://www.mod.go.jp/e/publ/w_paper/pdf/2006/2–3–1.pdf.

31 Obama and Lee, at a meeting in June 2010, agreed to delay operational control (OPCON) transfer to 2015. The White House, "Remarks by President Obama and President Lee Myung-bak of the Republic of Korea After Bilateral Meeting," June 26, 2010, http://www.whitehouse.gov/the-press-office/remarks-president-obama-and-president-lee-myung-bak-republic-korea-after-bilateral-/. However, in October 2013, ROK Defense Minister Kim Kwan-jin expressed reservations about taking over OPCON control by 2015. "South Korean Defense Chief Says 2015 OPCON Transfer 'Inappropriate,'" *Global Post*, October 8, 2013, http://www.globalpost.com/dispatch/news/yonhap-news-agency/131008/s-korean-defense-chief-says-2015-opcon-transfer-inappropri-1.

32 Ozawa Ichirō, *Blueprint for a New Japan: The Rethinking of a Nation* (Tokyo: Kōdansha International, 1994); Iijima Isao, *Koizumi kantei hiroku* [Secret Notes of the Koizumi Cabinet] (*Nikkei Shimbunsha*, 2006); and Kurashige Atsurō, *Koizumi seiken 1980 nichi* [1,980 Days of the Koizumi Administration], Two-Part Volume (Tokyo: Kōgen, 2013).

33 The Prime Minister's Commission on Japan's Goals in the 21st Century, *The Frontier Within: Individual Empowerment and Better Governance in the New Millennium*, chap. 6, pp. 10, 21, http://www.kantei.go.jp/jp/21century/report/pdfs/8chap6.pdf.

34 For an interesting account of Prime Minister Satō Eisaku's evolving negotiations on Okinawa reversion, see the diary of his political secretary, *Kusuda Minoru, Kusuda Minoru Nikki – Satō Eisaku sōri shūseki hishokan 2,000 nichi* [Diary of Kusuda Minoru: 2,000 Days of the Executive Secretary to Prime Minister Satō Eisaku] (Tokyo: Chūō Kōron Shinsha, 2001).

35 The SACO-related costs are compiled from the annual defense white paper, *Defense of Japan*, from 1997 to 2012. The breakdown of the costs for 2000–2006 can be found in Ministry of Defense, Japan, "*Kyū bōei shisetsu chō kōhyō shiryō hokan shōko peji*" ["Website for the Archives of Disclosed Materials from Former Defense Facilities Administration Agency"]; the costs for 2007–2009 in "*Bōei kankeihi*" ["Defense Related Costs"]; and the costs for 2010–2013 in "*Zainichi beigun kankei keihi (Heisei 22–25 nendo)*" ["Expenses Related to USFJ (FY2010–2013)"]. I am grateful to Igata Akira for his research assistance in compiling these figures.

36 The costs associated with Futenma relocation are not presented in one source, but rather dispersed throughout Japanese bureaucracies responsible for implementation.

This may not be an exhaustive list of expenses associated with Futenma relocation, but it includes the major expenses: Japanese government cost-sharing for the relocation of U.S. Marines to Guam, environmental assessments related to Futenma relocation, base land rental fees, maintenance fees for public facilities around Futenma, noise insulation for housing in base communities (Ginowan City), and a grant for Nago City related to realignment. I am grateful to Igata Akira for his research assistance in compiling these figures.

37 After the Joint Statement in April 2012, this was recalibrated so that the total cost would only be $8.6 billion, with Japan contributing $3.1 billion. See Shirley A. Kan, "Guam: US Defense Deployments," *Congressional Research Service Report*, November 15, 2013, http://www.fas.org/sgp/crs/row/RS22570.pdf. For early planning on relocation, see Ministry of Foreign Affairs, Japan, "Agreement between the Government of Japan and the Government of the United States of America Concerning the Implementation of the Relocation of III Marine Expeditionary Force Personnel and their Dependents from Okinawa to Guam," February 17, 2009, http://www.mofa.go.jp/region/n-amer ica/us/security/agree0902.pdf. The most recent accounting of Japanese expenditures can be found at the Ministry of Finance 2009 breakdown of defense expenditures at Ministry of Finance, Japan, "*Bōei kankeihi ni tsuite*" ["Summary of Defense-Related Costs"], April 2009, http://www.mof.go.jp/public_relations/finance/f2104c.pdf.

38 Pledges were made in notes exchanged in July 2009 (between Japanese Foreign Minister Nakasone and Deputy Chief of Mission, U.S. Embassy, James Zumwalt), September 2010 (between Japanese Foreign Minister Okada and U.S. Ambassador Roos), and March 2013 (between Foreign Minister Kishida and Ambassador Roos). Military construction on Guam is from the Ministry of Defense budget, and an accounting of that spending can be found at Ministry of Defense, Japan, "*Zaioki beikaiheitai no guamu isetsu ni tsuite*" ["Summary of the Relocation of U.S. Marines in Okinawa to Guam"], October 4, 2013, http://www.mod.go.jp/j/approach/zaibeigun/saihen/iten_guam/pdf/gaiyo_131004.pdf.

39 "*Futenma isetsu no asesu sakuseihi 63 okuen okinawa bōeikyokushō akasu*" ["Okinawa Ministry of Defense Bureau Reveals Futenma Relocation Environmental Assessment Costs to Be 6.3 Billion Yen"], *Nikkei Shimbun*, December 21, 2012. Okinawa Prefectural Government, *Okinawa no beigun kichi oyobi jieitai kichi* [Okinawa's U.S. Bases and SDF Bases] (Tōkei Shiryōshū, March 2013), pp. 58–59. These expenditures include maintenance fees for buildings in base communities (Futenma), noise insulation work (in and around Futenma), and a 2008 realignment grant of 1.38 billion yen for Nago City. Statistics for 1997–2001 for the maintenance fees and noise insulation can be found on the Military Affairs page of the Okinawa Prefectural Government website, at "*Kuni no kichi saihen taisaku to sono jisseki*" ["Countermeasures for Areas Surrounding Bases and Results"], accessed November 2013, http://www.pref.okinawa. jp/kititaisaku/DP-04.pdf. Grants for those municipalities that would face an increased burden as a result of realignment were introduced in 2007, but Nago City's application was rejected. Nago City applied in 2009 and 2010 but was also rejected. See "*Saihen kōfukin, Nago-shi shikyū miokuri – bōeishō ga hōshin*" ["Issuance of Realignment Subsidy to Nago City Deferred: Ministry of Defense States Its Policies"], *Ryūkyū Shimpō*, December 24, 2010. The 2008 grant was included in the Ministry of Defense accounting of that year's realignment costs at Ministry of Defense, Japan, "*Heisei 20-nendo saihen kōfukin ni tsuite*" ["Summary of Realignment Costs, Fiscal Year 2008"], 2008, http://www.mod.go.jp/j/press/news/2008/11/14b.pdf.

40 A comprehensive look at the U.S.-Japan alliance during this time can be found in Michael J. Green and Patrick M. Cronin, *The US-Japan Alliance: Past, Present and Future* (New York: Council on Foreign Relations Press, 1999).

41 In fact, the first effort to define the military roles and missions for the SDF and U.S. military forces came in 1976 as Washington sought to reduce its military presence in Asia. This resulted in the creation of U.S.-Japan Defense Cooperation Guidelines.

U.S.-Japan Security Consultative Committee, "Guidelines for US-Japan Defense Cooperation," November 27, 1978, http://www.fas.org/news/japan/sisin1e.htm.

42 U.S.-Japan Security Consultative Committee, "United States-Japan Roadmap for Realignment Implementation," May 1, 2006, available at http://www.mofa.go.jp/region/n-america/us/security/scc/doc0605.html.

43 See "Hundreds of Japanese Troops to Join U.S. Soldiers at Camp Zama," *Stars and Stripes*, February 28, 2013, http://www.stripes.com/news/pacific/hundreds-of-japanese-troops-to-join-us-soldiers-at-camp-zama-1.210022.

44 According to the U.S. Department of State, "Japan provides bases as well as financial and material support to US forward-deployed forces, which are essential for maintaining stability in the region. Over the past decade the alliance has been strengthened through revised defense guidelines, which expand Japan's noncombatant role in a regional contingency, the renewal of the agreement on host nation support of US forces stationed in Japan, and an ongoing process called the Defense Policy Review Initiative (DPRI). The DPRI redefines roles, missions, and capabilities of alliance forces and outlines key realignment and transformation initiatives, including reducing the number of US troops stationed in Okinawa, enhancing interoperability and communication between the two countries' respective commands, and broadening cooperation in the area of ballistic missile defense." U.S. Department of State, Bureau of East Asian and Pacific Affairs, "US Relations with Japan," October 24, 2012, http://www.state.gov/r/pa/ei/bgn/4142.htm.

45 The U.S. Navy and Air Force had longstanding relationships of cooperation with their counterparts in the Self-Defense Force, and they had shared basing facilities in major naval ports of Yokosuka and Sasebo and air bases such as Yokota and Misawa. The Marines, however, had not operated jointly with a SDF service, and indeed had little need for integrated operations given their mission and their own organizational priorities. For some missions, the reorganization of U.S. forces did not directly impinge upon Japan's own defense priorities. The debate over whether the Marines were really necessary for Japan's defenses had shadowed the debate over the Futenma relocation project.

46 "The base population at Iwakuni is scheduled to double to approximately 10,000 residents by 2014, when Iwakuni receives a squadron of KC-130 aircraft and Carrier Air Wing 5 relocates from Naval Air Facility Atsugi west of Tokyo." Quoted from Matthew M. Burke, "Marine Base Construction Brings Headaches to Iwakuni Residents," *Stars and Stripes*, August 8, 2012, http://www.stripes.com/news/pacific/japan/marine-base-construction-brings-headaches-to-iwakuni-residents-1.185103.

47 North Korean missile tests in 2006 and again in 2009 gave Tokyo the opportunity to test its new BMD response procedures outlined in the 2005 law. The law, passed in July 2005, was an amendment to the Self-Defense Force Law, and gave the defense minister (with approval from the prime minister) to ability to order the destruction of incoming ballistic missiles. Ministry of Defense, "Section 2: Effective Responses to New Threats and Diverse Contingencies," *Defense of Japan 2007* (2007), p. 221.

48 On April 11, 2011, the Center for Strategic and International Studies (CSIS) formed a task force of prominent Americans to examine ways the United States and Japan can partner on recovery and reconstruction from the March 11 earthquake and tsunami. The task force was chaired by Jim McNerney, chairman, president, and CEO of the Boeing Company. For more information, see CSIS, "Partnership for Recovery and a Stronger Future: Task Force on US-Japan Cooperation after 3/11," accessed November 2013, http://csis.org/program/partnership-recovery-and-stronger-future-task-force-us-japan-cooperation-after-311.

49 The SIPRI Military Expenditure Database. http://milexdata.sipri.org/.

50 National Institute of Defense Studies, Japan. *NIDS China Security Report 2011* (Tokyo: Urban Connections, 2012), p. 10.

51 Ibid., pp. 11–12.

13 Japanese historical memory

Togo Kazuhiko

Introduction

Japan's defeat in World War II was catastrophic for Japan in a great many respects. In all its history, Japan had never before been defeated by a foreign power. The surrender represented not only a physical defeat but also a collapse of an entire system of values, one that people had believed to be right and that had grown and developed from roughly the middle of the nineteenth century, with the Meiji Restoration in 1868 and evolution thereafter. But in the postwar years Japan drew a line with its past. Japan's separation from World War II started with the acceptance of new policies brought in by the occupation forces. Gradually Japan came to grips with the new values with which it was to rebuild itself: peace, democracy, economic reconstruction, and a continuation of the imperial tradition.

This chapter analyzes the situation from the early 1990s, which marked the end of the Cold War and the end of the Showa Era, to the present, and explores why and how the issue of how to remember and acknowledge the wartime past, which I call the "historical memory" issue, remains so unresolved in Japan. My main focus lies in the area of Japan's domestic logic and in particular in the internal power balance that prevented Japan from achieving a nationwide consensus. In addition, I touch upon how China's and Korea's positions have affected this issue and continue to impede the three countries from reaching reconciliation. For my argument, I use three case studies related to reconciliation: the visit of Emperor Akihito to China in 1992, an extremely important event for reconciliation with China but one which failed to produce a decisive impact; the issue of the comfort women on which the Japanese government took decisive action in the Kono Statement of 1993 and which led to the establishment of the Asian Women's Fund in 1995, but on which there remains no reconciliation with Korea; and finally, Prime Minister Koizumi Junichiro's visits to the Yasukuni Shrine and efforts and ideas that have emerged since then to resolve the issue of mourning the war dead and to reconcile this desire with the pain that Japan caused to Asian countries.

The last two decades of government in Japan have witnessed a total of 15 prime ministers. In the seventeen years from 1989 to 2006, there were nine prime ministers, starting with Kaifu Toshiki in 1989 and ending with Koizumi Junichiro in 2006. In the eight years from 2006 to the present, Japan has seen six prime ministers head seven cabinets of one-year duration, with Abe Shinzo holding office twice.

The emperor's visit to China in 1992: Background of the visit

Diplomatic relations between Japan and China were reestablished in 1972, and 1992 marked the twentieth anniversary of this reestablishment of relations. Very clearly there was a mutual desire in the governments of both countries to capitalize on this anniversary. It was thought that an ideal way to celebrate would be an imperial visit, and plans were made.

Broadly speaking, relations between Japan and China continued to evolve during the twenty years that followed reestablishment of diplomatic relations, and the evolution can be divided into three stages. During the first stage, from 1972 until 1978, China was still under Mao Zedong and Zhou Enlai, and the two governments were busy opening embassies and concluding agreements on aviation, maritime transport, trade, and fisheries. Zhou and Mao both died in 1976 and, after the initial turmoil, power shifted to Deng Xiaoping. Deng's policy of "Reform and Opening" was adopted in 1978 as China's new major policy direction. Meanwhile, in view of these changes in Japan, Prime Minister Fukuda Takeo, one of the best and brightest of the Ministry of Finance, was making every effort to conclude the Treaty of Peace and Friendship, and he succeeded in doing so in August 1978.

The second stage, from 1978 until 1989, was characterized by large amounts of official development assistance (ODA) from Japan and more intense economic relations. These moves started with private sector linkages in February 1978 but were followed by some confusion on the Chinese side, which was at yet unfamiliar with market economies. To save this situation and to set a course for stable economic cooperation, Prime Minister Ohira Masayoshi, who succeeded Prime Minister Fukuda in December 1978, decided to deliver massive ODA in December 1979.[1] These advances in economic cooperation, combined with exchanges of people and information, continued relatively unhampered even when two issues related to historical memory surfaced. The first was a textbook controversy, which erupted in June 1982 when a Japanese newspaper reported that the word "aggression" had been altered to "advance" in relation to Japan's military incursion in China as described in Japanese school textbooks. Reports of this news resulted in widespread student unrest in China and Korea, but the tension was overcome by Cabinet General Secretary Miyazawa Kiichi's statement that in future, when screening textbooks, Asian people's feelings would be much more taken into account.[2] The next issue was Prime Minister Nakasone Yasuhiro's visit to the Yasukuni Shrine on August 15, 1985. Nakasone had organized an advisory group to look into matters of constitutional infringement and many other aspects, but his visit to the Shrine that year drew massive criticism in China; and Hu Yaobang, the then leader and the number-one trustee of Deng Xiaoping, was severely criticized in China because of his Japan-friendly stance. Out of consideration for the sensitive nature of domestic politics in China, Nakasone withheld further visits to Yasukuni from 1986 on and the matter simmered down.

The contradictions in China's domestic policies resulted in the Tiananmen Square Incident of June 4, 1989. The third stage in my schema is marked by an unusually assertive policy on the part of Japan, which joined with the international community in the condemnation of China's violations of human rights. However, the tone of Japan's criticism was comparatively subdued, and the same moderate attitude was seen in its policy stance. At the Paris G7 Summit in July 1989, Prime Minister Uno Sosuke championed efforts not to isolate China, and as the result of the Japanese position, in the Declaration on China issued after the Summit the following passage was included in the third and final paragraph: "We look to the Chinese authorities to create conditions which will avoid their isolation and provide for a return to co-operation based upon the resumption of movement toward political and economic reform, and openness."[3] The Declaration met with a positive response from China. Li Peng, the premier, later expressed praise and gratitude to Miyazaki Isamu, a renowned Japanese economist, in the very same month, for Japan's moderation.[4]

Realizing the emperor's visit

Both Japan and China had endeavored to develop sound, mutually beneficial and cooperative relations for nearly twenty years after they established diplomatic relations. But the two countries faced fundamental political difficulties: the historical memory issues quieted down after Nakasone's visit and appeared to have stopped altogether after the Tiananmen Incident. However, there was still no guarantee that the residual indignation of the Chinese people with regard to the historical memory issue would not once again bring its influence to bear in the context of major political flare-ups. It was felt that Japan's readiness to acknowledge a Chinese way of development, even given China's repressive attitude to human rights as shown in and after the Tiananmen Square Incident, could provide a unique opportunity for creating more stable relations. If the two countries capitalized on their efforts and acted in a joint spirit, the emperor's visit might well serve as a means to overcome a mutual distrust over interpretations of the past.

The Chinese government had in fact divined the strategic opportunity to strengthen bilateral ties that would be presented by an imperial visit, even before the Tiananmen Incident. In April 1989, when Premier Li Peng visited Japan, he extended an invitation to the emperor. After Tiananmen, the invitation was repeatedly made at key diplomatic exchanges such as Foreign Minister Watanabe Michio's visit to Beijing in January 1992, when Chinese Foreign Minister Qian Qichen indicated for the first time that the visit might be implemented that very year, the twentieth anniversary of reestablishing diplomatic ties.[5] President Jiang Zeming, in his first visit to Japan after Tiananmen in April 1992, reiterated the invitation.[6] By the time the LDP decided to support, or at least not to oppose the visit, at the end of July 1992, Chinese leaders had already proffered nine official invitations.[7]

In contrast, Japanese Prime Minister Miyazawa went through a slow and careful process of deliberation before accepting the invitation. Miyazawa's strategy was twofold: he wanted to "make this visit a breakthrough occasion for enhanced cooperation between Japan and China, which are the two major countries in Asia," and he wanted to "bring [. . .] closure to the historical memory issue." As newspapers of the time reported, he had two criteria: that the Emperor "shall not be misused for certain political objectives"; and that "there be overall support by the Japanese people for the visit."[8] Chinese leaders repeatedly assured their Japanese counterparts that they were not going to "make difficulties for visiting foreign leaders."[9] Such flexibility actually made Miyazawa's position more problematic he now had to grapple with the domestic politics surrounding the issue. Japanese nationalist conservative political forces objected on the grounds that the emperor would be misused in the domestic struggle between the left and right in China; that the emperor would be forced to make an apology about Japan's past; and the political environment that surrounded Japan and China, such as China filing objections to Japan's ownership of the Senkaku Islands or objections to Japan's participation in United Nations peacekeeping operations, were not conducive for an imperial visit.[10] The Ministry of Foreign Affairs apparently shared similar views to those of Prime Minister Miyazawa, and were engaged in quiet domestic consensus-building exercises that culminated on July 29 when Miyazawa succeeded in gaining basic agreements from the five LDP top leaders. In the end, there was little particularly strenuous opposition from the LDP party.[11]

Once minimal consent was achieved, the final critical issue became what kind of wording the emperor was going to use concerning his thoughts on World War II. The key section of what the emperor announced at the state dinner, held on October 23, 1992, reads as follows: "During the lengthy history between our two nations, there was an unfortunate period when Japan inflicted great pain and suffering on the Chinese people. This feels me with deep sorrow."[12] The first part, concerning the "unfortunate period when great pain and suffering was inflicted," was almost identical in its wording to the statement that the emperor expressed to President Roh Tae Woo of Korea when he visited Japan in May 1990. The wording of the latter expression drew on what Emperor Hirohito stated in his visit to the United States in October 1975: "that unfortunate war over which I have deep sorrow."[13]

After the dinner, at the press conference, many a question was asked as to whether the phrase "deep sorrow" contained the idea of an "apology."[14] There was no official response regarding the emperor's statement from the Chinese side, but according to the Japanese press, there was criticism that the word "sorrow" did not mean "apology" and a general feeling that the statement had been welcomed by the party but not by the people. Nevertheless, the general consensus of the Japanese media was that the visit had been a success and that the emperor and empress had no doubt left a favorable impression on the Chinese. The warmth was shared by Chinese officials who accompanied the imperial couple during their visits, as seen in some television broadcasts.[15]

However, as we now know, relations with China did not continue at the level hoped for at this time. Just three years later, in 1995, on the fiftieth commemoration of the end of World War II, President Jiang Zemin's government instructed all Chinese schools to make exhibitions to commemorate the Nanjing massacre.

Reconciliation was clearly far from achieved. Nevertheless, the spirit of reconciliation as embodied by the imperial visit was kept alive as an important pointer in the latter part of the 1990s under Prime Minister Hashimoto Ryutaro and Obuchi Keizo. With the advent of Koizumi Junichiro and his Yasukuni visits, however, Japan-China relations witnessed a reversal.

Japan's limitations

Why was it that an imperial visit did not help Japan achieve its fundamental objective to move toward reconciliation? Was the Japanese decision to send the emperor to China in October 1992 premature? Was Miyazawa's judgment correct when he took this step forward toward reconciliation? It is not easy to make a retrospective evaluation. However, in considering the grounds on which Miyazawa made his decision, it is worth bearing in mind the larger process of détente with China and the international atmosphere in the wake of the Cold War when every country, including Japan, tried to bring closure to the past and take initiatives toward the future.

The larger question we need to ask is whether Japan did all it could to render this visit a key moment for reconciliation. The fact that the emperor's visit did not bring about a reconciliation of any lasting depth surely means that the actions taken in preparation by the Japanese government were not sufficient. When West German Chancellor Willy Brandt knelt down in 1970 in front of the memorial to the victims of the Warsaw Ghetto, the image went around the world and left an indelible impression of a sincere German apology. If the emperor had visited Nanjing and knelt down in front of its memorial, what would the effect of this have been? Even if he had not knelt down on a visit to Nanjing (or the Marco Polo Bridge), perhaps if he had made a deep bow, the impression of an apology would have been given. In 1978, when Deng Xiaoping visited Japan to exchange ratification of the Treaty of Peace and Friendship, it is said that Emperor Hirohito told him: "All the suffering which was caused to the Chinese people is my responsibility."[16] Could the emperor not have said something of this nature during his visit to China in 1992, something impromptu, daring, even, and from the heart, which would have moved the spirit of Chinese people for many years to come? Lastly, even if this sort of remark could not be hoped for, could the emperor not have pronounced a decisive message of apology that went beyond his personal feelings of sorrow and so cleared the air once and for all?

These are complicated, intricate questions, which need to be considered in the light of postwar Japan's constitutional system, and indeed the political situation. The present-day imperial system, prescribed in Article One of the Constitution, designates the emperor as a "symbol of state." The postwar Constitution deliberately revised the role of the emperor as it was prescribed under the Meiji Constitution, where "The Empire of Japan shall be reigned over and governed by a line of Emperors unbroken for ages eternal (Article one)" and "The Emperor is the head of the Empire, combining in Himself the rights of sovereignty, and exercises them, according to the provisions of the present Constitution (Article four)."[17] Although in practice the system worked as a form of European-style constitutional monarchy (where monarchs preside but act in accordance with decisions taken by the government and are thus immune from responsibility), the Meiji Constitution left room for the emperor's direct involvement to make substantive political decisions.[18] The new Constitution, in contrast, unambiguously declared that the emperor does not possess any power to make political decisions and remains solely as a symbol of state. Acts of apology and compensation are therefore important political decisions that by their very nature *are impossible* to be asked of the emperor.

The political situation surrounding the 1992 imperial visit also shows the limits within which the Miyazawa government could act. The visit was not keenly supported by LDP political circles, and their position was clearly not to let the emperor express any major apology. Their reasoning, in part, appears to have stemmed from their adherence to the postwar constitutional principles. But other factors included their conviction, with regard to China, that there had already been sufficient apology as expressed at the time of normalization of relations in 1972 in the Joint Communiqué statement: "The Japanese side is keenly conscious of the responsibility for the serious damage that Japan caused in the past to the Chinese people through war, and deeply reproaches itself."[19] Nothing in the record shows that Miyazawa was cognizant that more was needed other than the emperor's "words" to express "deep sorrow" to make the visit in 1992 a critical turning point for reconciliation. If Miyazawa had this understanding, would he and his government have orchestrated more decisive action for the emperor to take, despite the constitutional limitations and strong domestic opposition? This is a very complex set of questions to unravel.

But in retrospect, a quick comparison of what Japan managed to achieve on the occasion of the imperial visit to the Netherlands in 2000 objectively demonstrates another possible approach. In 1999 when the imperial visit was in the planning stages, there was a clear recognition within both the Dutch and the Japanese governments that concrete action for a more precise apology was needed to make the imperial visit a success. The Obuchi government took on that responsibility, and after thorough negotiations from the end of 1999 Obuchi issued a historic statement of apology to Dutch Prime Minister Wim Kok during his Tokyo visit in February 2000. In other words, in accordance with the present-day Japanese Constitution, the government took responsibility for the apology. The emperor made a symbolic apology with the deep bow that he made when presenting a wreath to the memorial of the Dutch war dead. At the state dinner, representatives of war victims were invited to have direct contact and personal talks with the emperor, from which they reportedly gained quite positive impressions. The emperor's speech was confined to statements of his personal feeling but the overall visit became a turning point for Japanese-Dutch reconciliation.[20]

China's limitations

The contrast with the Dutch case brings to light another critical question: What did the Chinese government hope for by wooing the emperor to visit China? The

Chinese government's official position is unambiguous and can be summarized in Jiang Zemin's statement made in front of the Japanese press corps in Beijing on April 1 before his visit to Tokyo: "The purpose of our invitation to the emperor to visit China is to deepen friendship between Japan and China. I firmly believe that the emperor's visit to China will further enhance the development of Sino-Japan relations."[21] As a general statement, this looks fine. But what were the real motives? In short, for sure, the Chinese leadership wanted to have a successful visit to foster a better environment for China's international standing. But this seems to have been the extent of it. There is no evidence from records of the process of the preparations to suggest that this visit was to be a decisive occasion for reconciliation, with requests or suggestions from the Chinese side regarding what would be minimally necessary to heal the wounds of those who had suffered and thence move forward. Once again, comparison with the 1999–2000 Dutch negotiations, in which the Dutch negotiator knew exactly the kind of wording needed from Prime Minister Obuchi to console the victims and indeed insisted that these phrases should be used, provides a very different perspective to the Sino-Japanese negotiations.[22]

Retrospectively, we see that the Chinese government's position on historical memory was by then pivoted on its post-Tiananmen stance. Deng was determined not to permit freedom of political thinking that would endanger the foundation of the legitimacy of the Chinese Communist Party's rule. The most "reform-oriented" segment of the Chinese political movement, the students, had to be put under proper control. Chinese "patriotic education" is said to have been launched in 1993, and it goes without saying that the nation that caused the greatest harm to China in its modern period was Japan. It was necessary to teach about the evil that had been initiated by Japan and the fight against it that had given legitimacy to the PRC. Gil Rozman describes this situation: "The Chinese narrative against Japan's rise was firmly in place in the beginning of the 1990s, centered on its moral unworthiness even if other reasons undoubtedly played their part. Ignoring the nature of Japan's development from 1945 through the 1980s, the narrative identified it [i.e., Japan] as deeply steeped in its past and lacking the moral quality of other states that had the right to become a military or even political great power."[23]

Had the Miyazawa government and the political right in Japan been farsighted enough to grasp this situation before China had requested an imperial visit, the prime minister might himself have taken an upper hand and made a much clearer and more decisive gesture for reconciliation *before* the visit, which would have altered the status quo. Even if the emperor might not have considered it appropriate to visit Nanjing, Miyazawa might perhaps have gone there himself and made an announcement similar to the Murayama statement given three years later. Such a move might have taken the sting out of Chinese patriotic education. A clear rationale for not imbuing the Chinese children with patriotic fervor would have been demonstrated by Japan, or at least the patriotic education that China engaged in might have been less fervently antagonistic toward Japan.

Unfortunately, this is not what happened; such thinking simply did not characterize the way in which people in Japanese political circles approached the outside world. The imperial visit to China in 1992 proved to be one positive step in the long history of Japan-China relations, but in the end it was unable to overcome decisively the historical divide between the two countries.

The Asian Women's Fund, 1995–2002

Opinions vary concerning the establishment of the Asian Women's Fund (AWF) in 1995, after the Kono Statement of 1993 and its failure in Korea. Perhaps the most authentic documentation so far comes from the AWF website which the Fund formulated in March 2007 after the closure of its activities.[24] This source should not be considered completely authoritative but nevertheless offers an invaluable primary testimony regarding how and why the Fund was created, what it tried to achieve in Korea, and how its endeavor failed to gain support.

The existence of comfort women in the wartime Japanese army was not a secret. It was common knowledge to all soldiers who went to the front and was described openly in novels and reports from the front. No information is available that it was not so in Korea as well, during colonization. After Japan's defeat, however, the story of comfort women in Korea was such that people knew about it but preferred not to discuss it, and the issue was not raised during the 1965 negotiations of the South Korea-Japan normalization agreements.

Toward the end of the 1980s and particularly after the end of the Cold War, during the critical wave of Krean democratization, the issue first surfaced in bilateral talks. The first prominent article in Korea was published in January 1990 by Yun Chung-Ok in the *Hankyoreh Newspaper*. The issue attracted greater attention later in a report emanating from a Japanese House of Councilors' (Upper House) Budget Committee hearing on June 6, 1990, which said "it appears that the wartime comfort women were hired by private entrepreneurs," seemingly as if to deny any government involvement or responsibility. On October 17, 1990, thirty-seven women's organizations in Korea issued a declaration criticizing the Japanese government's statement denying its responsibility and requesting that the Japanese government acknowledge, apologize, investigate, commemorate, compensate, and educate the public on this issue. These demands were widely reported in Japan around the end of the 1990. By the summer of 1991, Ms. Kim Hak-Sun had come forward in Seoul to demand that Japan take responsibility when she lodged an international lawsuit in December of that year.

On January 10, 1992, on the eve of Prime Minister Miyazawa's visit to Korea, Yoshimi Yoshiaki, a Chuo University professor, announced that documents existed that proved the involvement of the Japanese military in the comfort women system. On January 16, Prime Minister Miyazawa during his visit to Korea apologized for the suffering that these women experienced and promised a thorough inquiry.[25] The results of the first inquiry were released on July 6, 1992, with a statement from Chief Cabinet Secretary Kato Koichi. The results of a second inquiry, which included sixteen interviews of former Korean comfort women, were released on August 4, 1993, with a statement from the Chief Cabinet Secretary Kono Yohei. The essence of the Kono Statement was that the government accepted responsibility for having run the facility, acknowledged that many women had had to serve against their will, apologized for the pain caused, and promised to remember through research and education, pledging that similar actions would not be repeated.[26]

Once the statement had been made, vigorous debate continued for some time on how to express the government's apology and remorse. This debate took place during a time of dynamic change in the Japanese political structure: the Miyazawa government was replaced by a coalition of eight parties, headed by Prime Minister Hosokawa Morihiro in August 1993, a development that ended the LDP monopoly on power. But this non-LDP system lasted only for eight months and in June 1994 an extraordinary coalition of the LDP, the Japan Socialist Party (JSP), and Sakigake, a reformist-oriented party, was formed, with Murayama Tomiichi from the JSP as Prime Minister and an overwhelming majority of cabinet members from the LDP. On August 15, 1995, Prime Minister Murayama issued a statement looking ahead to the fiftieth anniversary of the end of the war, expressing his "profound, sincere remorse and apologies" with regard to the comfort women issue, and stating his desire to find "an appropriate way which enables a wide participation" of Japanese people in order to share such feelings of apology and remorse."[27] Following up on the Prime Minister's statement, the three ruling parties launched a project to deal with the comfort women issue.

The AWF English website explains that views ranged in that debate carried out by the three-parties project: on the one hand, some argued that Japan could not offer compensation to individuals because reparation issues, material restitution, and the right to claim wartime compensation had already been dealt with by signed international treaties. In the case of Korea, with the Treaty on Property and Claim and Economic Cooperation signed on June 22, 1965, Japan agreed to provide South Korea with economic assistance in the form of US $300 million in grant aid and US $200 million in loans. In Article 2–1 of the Treaty, Korea agreed that "issues on claims between the two peoples are resolved completely and finally."[28] On the other hand, there were those who strongly objected and said that Japan should pay compensation to individuals. This disagreement subsided due to the need for a quick resolution, and a compromise solution emerged to calculate individual compensation as moral compensation still payable after the legal settlement made nearly thirty years ago.

On December 7, 1994, the first report on the comfort women issue was released. It stated that "to acknowledge moral responsibility for the comfort women issue, Japan would establish a Fund in cooperation with the people of Japan, and promote projects expressing atonement to the former comfort women." The AWF website explains that the Japanese government set aside a budget of 480 million yen (roughly US $4.8 million) to subsidize the Fund's expenses in 1995. On June 14, 1995, Chief Cabinet Secretary Igarashi Kozo explained what "cooperation with the people of Japan" meant: the Fund would call for donations from Japanese society to atone for the comfort women, but some medical and welfare projects to serve comfort women would be funded by the government, and the basic sum of atonement to comfort women would be limited to two million yen (roughly

US \$20,000) per individual. Igarashi's statement also ensured that at the time of its implementation, the government would express sincere remorse and apology to each woman.

Implementing the Asian Women's Fund in Korea

Initially, it appears that the Korean government was favorably disposed toward the establishment of the AWF. However, this later changed to disinclination due to the vigorous campaign mounted against it by one nongovernmental organization that supported the victims, the Korean Council for the Women Drafted for Military Sexual Slavery by Japan, or *Chongdaehyop*. As the AWF website explains, at the heart of the Korean Council's campaign were calls for the Japanese government to acknowledge "legal responsibility," apologize, pay compensation, and punish those responsible.

Former comfort women varied considerably in their attitudes and responses to the Fund. Some criticized the Fund and repudiated it, others were dissatisfied that a private funding source was involved, but still wanted to accept the projected benefits. Those who publicly stated that they intended to accept benefits were then criticized and they faced great social pressure to abandon their decisions. Some of these women then reluctantly issued further statements repudiating the AWF.

In this somewhat complicated context, the AWF decided to aim to implement its atonement project in Korea regarding those persons whom the government authenticated as having served as "comfort women" (207 women as of November 2002). In August 1996, a Team for Dialogue visited Korea, met with about a dozen or so former comfort women, and explained the Fund's goals. In December 1996, Ms. Kimiko Kaneda (a pseudonym) announced that she appreciated the Fund's efforts and intended to accept its benefits. Soon after that, another six women announced that they too would accept benefits. On January 11, 1997, representing the Fund, Director Kanehira Teruko offered seven victims a letter of apology from incumbent Prime Minister Hashimoto Ryutaro at a hotel in Seoul. After the ceremony Ms. Kanehira presented her credentials and explained the details regarding the project, but she met with severe media criticism and protests by the Korean Council. Strong pressure against the seven victims who had received Fund benefits quickly mounted in Korea together with a growing storm against those who took the Fund's money. This was an unbearable situation for the AWF. In response, the Fund temporarily suspended services in Korea, but in the interim a campaign by the Korean Council grew to collect private donations to persuade women to refuse AWF's project benefits. The Korean donations were used to provide former comfort women with a fixed amount of assistance money to the exclusion of the seven who had originally accepted compensation from the Fund.

After some difficult reflection, on January 6, 1998, the Asian Women's Fund placed advertisements in four newspapers in Korea and announced that it was resuming its projects. Very quickly the Fund received word from some victims that they wished to receive benefits and Japan resumed the project. Kim Dae-Jung became President of the Republic of Korea in March 1998 and in May the new administration decided that although it would not demand state reparations from the Japanese government, the Korean government would pay 31.5 million won (at the time, about 3.1 million Japanese yen [roughly US $31,000]), plus an additional 4.18 million won [roughly US $4,180] from capital collected by the Korean Council to each former comfort woman who refused AWF benefits. The Korean government paid this sum to 142 former comfort women, but did not pay it to eleven – the seven who had previously accepted Japanese benefits in the early stages, and four others who did not sign the written oath because they had accepted Japanese Fund benefits.

In June 1998, the AWF sent a letter signed by Fund President Hara Bunbei to the President of South Korea. The letter stated the belief that atonement money from Japan and living expense subsidies from the Republic of Korea were different in nature and requested that the South Korean government acknowledge to citizens that it should be possible to accept both. However, the South Korean government did not change its position. Realizing that there was no future, the Fund decided to halt these activities at the beginning of 1999 and reorient its objectives to group medical care. At the same time, the Fund decided to issue payments to victims who had already begun the application process. However, it became clear that the Fund would be unable to obtain the cooperation of the Korean side, even with these new objectives, so the Fund suspended all projects in Korea in July 1999. Under these circumstances, the January 10, 2002, deadline for applying to the project for benefits drew nearer to a close, and in the end the Fund eventually terminated all of its projects in the Republic of Korea on May 1, 2002. As the AWF English website explains, those who had accepted Fund project benefits sent their thanks. One message said, "I never thought that during our [sic] lifetime I would receive apologies from the Prime Minister and money. I know they express the feelings of good will of the Japanese people. Thank you very much."

The AWF website contained the following message on its concluding page: "Asian Women's Fund projects were concluded in the Republic of Korea without obtaining the full understanding of activist groups or the Government there. Even so, many more victims than we had first predicted agreed to accept the Prime Minister's letter of apology and benefits from the Fund's atonement projects, and for this we are grateful."[29]

Japan's limitations

The long process of Japan's acknowledgement of responsibility, apology, and atonement on the Korean comfort women issue, including the 1993 Kono Statement and all the activities of the Asian Women's Fund, demonstrated sincere and genuine efforts toward reconciliation. The best of the Japanese left-of-center liberal intellectuals supported this Asian Women's Fund and spent much of their personal time, money, and energy to realize its goals. With all countries where the AWF extended its work some sort of political reconciliation was achieved, even if it was not perfect.

Nevertheless, it is useful to compare the case concerning the Korean comfort women with the case of the Dutch comfort women in the Netherlands and the compensation paid to them. In the former colonial Dutch community in Indonesia, there was undeniable evidence of using young women as comfort women for the Japanese military; but after the hard work and good will on both sides, seventy-nine Dutch women received money from the Fund and a prime minister's letter of apology. In Korea, however, where a similar or much greater amount of energy was spent in crafting apologies, the activities of the Fund did not bear satisfactory results. The fundamental objection from the Korean activists working at the *Chongdaehyop*, the Korean Council, was that Japan had not accepted its "legal responsibility."

There are two aspects to the legal responsibility argument. The first aspect is the use of people's donations and the rejection of using government budgetary money for atonement. The Japanese government considered that the official money could not be used because it could be construed that Japan was thereby accepting the legal responsibility of which it had been absolved once and for all by the 1965 agreement. Was this legal interpretation really apposite and necessary? Had the budgetary money been used for atonement, would this have meant that the Japanese government had gone back on itself and that all legal claims were revived? This is an issue to which only international lawyers can respond. However, perhaps the reason was political as well. The legal stance of the Ministry of Foreign Affairs (MOFA) has to be understood against an increase in court cases in Japan waged by former comfort women who appealed for compensation and apologies. MOFA presumably did not want to take any action that would undermine its established position on legal responsibility. If the money had come from the budget, and the Korean Council had agreed to accept the AWF's atonement money, this legalistic caution on the part of MOFA would have been a high price to pay for ultimate failure.

The second aspect was the interpretation taken by MOFA that all legal issues were settled completely by the 1965 agreement. This position is central to Japanese government thinking. If the Korean Council's position was precisely to take aim at and oppose this Japanese stance, regardless of the issue of the use of budgetary money, there would be very little hope of convergence between the two sides. Given this limitation, all efforts conducted by the AWF are commendable but unfortunately noteworthy mostly for lack of success.

But in fact the limitations that these issues placed on AWF activities might hold the key for new possibilities of a breakthrough on this issue. The April 2007 verdict of the Supreme Court of Japan ruled that all claims related to war, either by governments or by individuals, are not sustained as the result of the international treaties that Japan has concluded with all countries to settle issues on the war and prewar situations. This legally secured position may open a new path for Japan to act more actively and proactively, that is to say using budgetary money, and taking more account of moral grounds, to resolve the outstanding differences between the two countries on the issues of atonement and reparation.[30]

Korea's limitations

At the same time, however, Korea's position was far from unified. The original request in October 1990 by the Korean women's organization was to get Japan to acknowledge, apologize, investigate, commemorate, compensate, and educate the public. Their actions did not include demands for legal responsibility, which only became a pillar of the request by the Korean Council after the AWF scheme was established in June 1995. There were clearly former comfort women who were willing to accept apologies and the atonement money presented by the AWF. On June 20, 2014, the Study Team on Details Leading to the Drafting of the Kono Statement published its report in which it revealed that altogether 61 Korean comfort women each received "atonement money" of 2 million yen, government contributions from medical and welfare projects of 3 million yen, and a signed letter of apology from the incumbent prime minister.[31]

The Korean Council may indeed have had reason to insist that the Japanese government acknowledge its legal responsibility. But questions remain as to how appropriate it was for this body to place the former comfort women who accepted the AWF's atonement money and apology under social pressure and discrimination, for the purposes of their own objectives; indeed, on the moral grounds they had to exclude women from the benefits which the Korean government was prepared to grant. It is highly questionable whether the members of this body prioritized the restoration of honor and equilibrium to the lives of the women who had suffered or the achievement of their own political objectives by forcing Japan to accept legal responsibility. The monomaniacal thirst for self-centered justice that the Council showed became a truly insurmountable stumbling block, on which South Korea will have to reflect for many decades in the future.

In concluding my analysis on the Asian Women's Fund, it may be useful to introduce voices from within Korea, equally critical of the activities of the Korean Council. Professor Park Yuha published a seminal book in Japan, *Toward Reconciliation*, in 2006, in which she makes an extensive analysis on the textbook issue, the comfort women issue, Yasukuni Shrine, and Dokdo Island.[32] At the beginning of the chapter on comfort women, Park strongly rebukes the comfort women's system, which infringed gender rights, and she makes quite clear her conviction of the absolute necessity of pursuing the Japanese government's responsibility, even if there is lack of evidence that the Japanese military and officials forcefully kidnapped these women.[33] However, she then acknowledges that the efforts of the AWF were the best possible action that could realistically have been taken by the Japanese government in 1995 and represented the best intentions of Japanese liberals. She then turns to a criticism of the Korean Council. She first analyzes the unwillingness of this body to accept these Japanese initiatives as a "total lack of knowledge and inability to understand the other side, the Japanese government, while waging cases against it."[34] She is unsparing in her criticism of the self-righteous attitude of the Korean Council, stating that "to rebuke those who accepted the AWF's atonement is to humiliate once more those who went through the most painful experience, to exceed the sphere of their rightful activities, and to suffocate and control the minds of those who suffered most."[35] She even goes so far as to state that some measure of responsibility must be shared by Korean society – the parents and relatives of the women and the officials of the time – who either knowingly or through deception sent these girls to the front.[36] Park may not be the most popular scholar in Korea, but she gains deep respect among some Japanese concerned with Japan-Korea relations, including myself.

The Yasukuni controversy under Koizumi, 2001–06

I now turn to one of the most complicated and vexing issues in postwar Japan, the issue of the Yasukuni Shrine.

The Yasukuni Shrine is a Shinto shrine, founded by the Meiji emperor and built to commemorate individuals who fought and died for imperial Japan after the Meiji Restoration. Over the ensuing years, its purposes have expanded and it now enshrines the spirits of over two-and-a-half million soldiers, the majority of whom died during World War II.

During the initial stages of the U.S. occupation of Japan, an American directive issued in December 1945 established the general occupation policy with regard to Shinto. The order banned state Shinto, which had has served as the base of the ideology of imperial expansion, but allowed the continuation of ordinary Shinto as a religious faith free from government intervention. Yasukuni was therefore permitted to continue as an ordinary Shinto shrine with a shared recognition that its function was to serve as a locus to mourn the war dead.

There was an additional complication in that, as an extension of a generally recognized consensus that war criminals found guilty at international tribunals were not criminalized under Japanese domestic law, all war criminals who were sentenced to death or who had died in detention could eventually be enshrined in Yasukuni. And so it was that the fourteen Class A war criminals found guilty at the Tokyo trial (seven were sentenced to death and seven had died in detention) were enshrined in 1978.

In 1985, Prime Minister Nakasone, aiming to close all issues lingering from World War II, attempted to inaugurate a system of prime ministerial mourning. However, in light of the indignation in China that this aroused and the damage that his visits might incur to relations with President Hu Jintao, Nakasone decided not to repeat any shrine visits after 1986. After that, with the one exception of Prime Minister Miyazawa's incognito visit in 1992 and another one in 1996 by Prime Minister Hashimoto (to which China protested strongly), for a time all prime ministers refrained from further visits to the Yasukuni Shrine.

Then in 2001 Koizumi Junichiro was elected as prime minister and in the election campaign he announced his commitment to visit Yasukuni on August 15, the date that Emperor Hirohito announced Japan's unconditional surrender in 1945. It is a most important day of commemoration in Japan. Despite the feverish criticism that this evoked in China and the suspension of bilateral Japan-China visits, Koizumi continued to visit Yasukuni once a year, although it was in fact on a day other than August 15. He made his visit on August 15 only in 2006.

Was there no alternative?

Koizumi made his first visit to the Yasukuni Shrine on August 13, 2001. The visit triggered strong protests from the Chinese government, but this did nothing to prevent Koizumi's one-day visit to China on October 8. Koizumi visited the Marco Polo Bridge and its adjacent memorial hall, which commemorates the war of resistance against Japan. He lunched with Premier Zhu Rongji and held meetings with President Jiang Zemin. MOFA issued an evaluation that "personal relations based on trust between Prime Minister Koizumi and Chinese leaders were created, and the visit will serve to improve Japan-China relations. The two sides confirmed that they would cooperate at the forthcoming Shanghai APEC and ASEAN+3 meetings."[37]

After Koizumi's trip to China, however, it was clear that the problems surrounding the Yasukuni Shrine remained unresolved. A group of people who seriously desired to be able officially to mourn the fallen in Japan, and who were concerned that they might never be able to do so freely, sincerely, and without controversy, gathered to consider establishing a facility where everyone could mourn and pray without hesitation. Immediately following Koizumi's visit to China, on December 14, 2001, a Consultative Group was established under Cabinet General Secretary Fukuda Yasuo, with the objective of "considering the establishment of a commemorative facility to mourn the dead and pray for peace." Ten prominent intellectuals gathered, chaired by Imai Takashi, president of the Japan New Steel Company. Altogether, the group held ten meetings, and at the last meeting, on December 24, 2002, they adopted their final report.[38]

The gist of the report was as follows: First, the group had concluded that it would establish a permanent nonreligious state facility to mourn and pray for peace. Second, Japan had been reborn as a peaceful state under the postwar Constitution and peace was a national interest to be pursued. Third, in assuring Japan's activities for peace making, there was a need to consider past wars in which Japan had been engaged. Fourth, the group proposed to create a facility to mourn all those who had died in wars in which Japan took part, military and civilian, Japanese and foreign all-inclusive, where everyone could "gather without hesitation." Fifth, the facility would be nonreligious and ahistorical, so that people of all religions and of any historical worldview could come and mourn. Sixth, the facility would be built on the prerequisite of "co-existing with other countries," and cognizant of the fact that neighboring countries are watching carefully how Japan behaves in international society. And seventh, the facility would be compatible and would coexist with Yasukuni Shrine, which aims to "honor specific individual spirits."

However, when the work of the consultative body started, Nishimura Shingo, a conservative deputy within the LDP, filed some Official Questionnaires to the Cabinet. He suggested that the wording of "gather without hesitation" was unclear; that the issue of for whom the facility was going to be built needed to be discussed further, attending to the question of whether it would be for Japanese or foreigners alike; and that there were specific issues remaining with regard to Yasukuni, which he highlighted.[39] The greatest opposition against the establishment of a nonreligious memorial site came from Yasukuni supporters who took a highly antagonistic position on two accounts: that any dilution of Yasukuni weakened the best part of Japan's tradition, and that, whatever the logic, the idea of a neutral memorial site merely served the interests of China.[40] There was a less nationalistic line that argued that the creation of a religiously neutral memorial and the preservation of Yasukuni in reality duplicated, or possibly split, locations for mourning; for the sake of preserving national unity, it would be more useful to reform Yasukuni in a way that would be acceptable to Japanese and foreigners alike, particularly because for some families Yasukuni was the only place to come together in the memory of deceased soldiers. This is also my view.[41] After the report by the Consultative Group was finalized in December 2002, however, and as anti-China feelings mounted in Japan and Koizumi's yearly visits continued, support for the Group's report waned in the media and in political circles.

What took its place were increasingly vocal ideas for reforming Yasukuni, emanating from Yasukuni supporters. The key idea from this quarter was to "de-shrine" the fourteen Class A war criminals. However, this idea met with opposition by Yasukuni priests on the grounds that their theology did not allow for any "division" of the spirits once they have been enshrined. For many Yasukuni supporters, however, this "theology" was, and remains, far from satisfactory. First, there was one major problem in the fact that from 1978 onwards, after the enshrinement of Class A war criminals, neither Emperor Hirohito nor his successor Emperor Akihito had paid a visit to Yasukuni Shrine: they in fact ceased visiting it entirely. If the argument is that the value of Yasukuni resides in its memorializing those who died for their country – and in World War II, they died for a Japan that had the emperor at its very center – it is difficult indeed to explain away imperial neglect. On July 20, 2006, the *Nihon Keizai Shimbun* reported that former Grand Chamberlain Tomita Tomohiko had a memo from Emperor Hirohito in which he recorded his displeasure regarding the enshrinement of Class A war criminals.[42]

Second, there is a feeling of discomfort and displeasure among the families of the soldiers enshrined at Yasukuni, that those who commanded others to die and those who had no option other than to follow those commands, are treated in exactly the same way at the Shrine. This feeling persists to this day. On August 17, 2008, the president of the War Bereaved Families Association, Koga Makoto, stated during a TV Asahi program that "we do not consider that the explanation for enshrining Class A war criminals is satisfactory; nor do we understand the Yasukuni theology that 'de-shrining' them is impossible. The War Bereaved Families Association should have a thorough discussion on this issue and find its own way."[43]

Third, the Class A war criminals who were enshrined in the Yasukuni Shrine were chosen from a list sent to the Shrine by the Japanese government. There is no escaping the fact that the government is at least half responsible for the enshrinement of these people. However, when this issue came under international scrutiny, on April 20, 2007, in response to Tsujimoto Kiyomi's Official Questionnaires to the Cabinet, the Abe government gave the wholly false response that: "the decision to enshrine Class A war criminals was made entirely by the Yasukuni Shrine and the government was not involved." This false claim that the government had no say whatsoever, and the obvious hypocrisy in this stance, discredited the government's position entirely.[44]

It is worth noting that the issues of China and Sino-Japanese relations played little role in all of these debates. Within Japan, the issues of emperor, soldier-versus-commander, and government responsibility were the real crux. The proposal for de-shrining did not require international consideration; or rather, given the intensely nationalistic character of some of Yasukuni supporters, it would have been counterproductive to bring the China factor into the argument. But the policy of de-shrining clearly addresses a key aspect of China's concern. There was no question that the proposals regarding de-shrining Class A war criminals had to be advanced discreetly, in view of the difficulties that might be created by any critical interference from China. But discussions of both the nonreligious state facility proposed by the Fukuda Consultative Group in 2002 and the many ideas for reforming the Yasukuni Shrine to make it acceptable inside Japan waned in the latter part of the 2000s. After Koizumi's visit to Yasukuni on August 15, 2006, the media's interest gradually dissipated and, despite everything, Japan-China relations began to stabilize under Prime Minister Abe Shinzo.

Japan's limitations

Koizumi's yearly visits to Yasukuni, and his apparent fixation on these visits, were a diplomatic disaster for Japan in terms of sustaining trustworthy relations with China. And yet ironically each yearly visit and the rising tension that resulted had the side effect of directing more attention than ever before to the issue of mourning the fallen. The result was that two serious ideas emerged from this maelstrom to find a national consensus. But why did both of them fade by the end of the 2000s? One simple but probably correct answer was that a consensus was too difficult to achieve. Fukuda's group clearly met opposition from activists who were determined to do anything, within the boundaries of legally accepted norms, to crush any ideas that would weaken or dishonor Yasukuni. Political power to convince staunch Yasukuni supporters was evidently too costly for any liberal prime minister after Koizumi. On the other hand, Yasukuni reformers had to overcome contemporary Yasukuni priests' views. Yasukuni doctrinal experts were not very vocal in the latter half of the 2000s, but it was also evident that they were not prepared to simply bow down to the challenge, and that if stronger pressure were applied they could have easily gathered themselves around activist political forces to protect their convictions. For both sides, it became politically too costly to tackle reform of the Yasukuni Shrine when, at least on the surface, the situation looked calm. Japan remains adrift on this extremely difficult issue.

Given this deadlock, I would argue that there is still a need to dig deeper into the root causes of the problem. If the verdicts reached at the Tokyo Trial dissatisfies both right and left of the Japanese political spectrum, then Japan itself should make a judgment on how to identify, remember, and mourn those who were responsible. The 1995 Murayama Statement appears to be the only official pronouncement of historical recognition, but it had to be made through a cabinet decision. And ironically, it also begs the question: If wrongdoing was done, who should be held responsible? The Statement goes so far as to make an admission that Japan was responsible, but this in itself does not cover the commander-soldier locus of responsibility. If there is truth in the idea that responsibility should be shared between commanders and soldiers, the Class A war criminals enshrined in Yasukuni are only a few of the responsible people, those at the very top, against whom there was verifiable evidence. But what if we do not accept the criteria used at the Tokyo Trial? What, then, would constitute the correct criteria? Is there a way to develop a position based on the recognition that Japan as a nation was responsible? This is the problem that lies behind the issue of the Yasukuni Class A war criminals' enshrinement.[45] Of course, for those who do not accept the Murayama Statement as based on a national consensus, this problem is entirely without merit.

Furthermore, Japan's position vis-à-vis China was limited by the fact that from 1972 onwards, when the two countries had normalized relations, Japanese leaders appear to have acquiesced to the Chinese view that Japanese military leaders were the common enemy of the Japanese and Chinese people. (This is a subject that I will examine in the following section). Starting from Prime Minister Tanaka Kakuei and Foreign Minister Ohira Masayoshi, who led the Japanese delegation in 1972, no Japanese political leader has ever told the Chinese side that the reality might be somewhat more open to question. The previous delineation of responsibility for war as having been shared by a small number of Japanese militarist leaders and leaving ordinary soldiers beyond blame was highly expedient in the postwar period and served to stabilize an economically shattered and psychologically devastated world in Asia, as well as in Europe. In the case of Japan and China, from 1972, Japanese leaders were tacitly acquiescent about this delineation and they profited from the resulting stabilization of Japan-China bilateral relations. This acquiescence in turn allowed Chinese leaders to expect that Japanese leaders would not challenge the fragile structure based on refraining from delving into issues of responsibility any further. Thus, China also created a narrative, not without foundation, that visits by prime ministers to Yasukuni were totally unacceptable for the reason that such visits would challenge the basis of this mutually accepted (or default) recognition.[46]

Given the rise of China and the inability of politicians on both sides to find any meeting ground on which to clarify the root causes of the Yasukuni Shrine problem, the only realistic policy is for Japanese leaders to place a moratorium on further prime ministerial visits until a solution can be found and implemented. This is the policy that I proposed in June 2006 and that has indeed been implemented by all Japanese prime ministers who succeeded Koizumi from 2006 onwards. Until, that is, December 26, 2013, when Prime Minister Abe Shinzo made his sudden visit to the shrine.

China's limitations

The Chinese point of view concerning the Yasukuni Shrine is relatively simple. The structure of political governance in China does not allow for the divergence of views that exist in Japan, but more importantly, the logic with which the Chinese Communist Party structures itself is consistent and clear. First, Japan has caused enormous pain and suffering to the Chinese people in its war of aggression, starting in 1931 with the Manchurian Incident. Second, notwithstanding this fact, Premier Zhou Enlai adopted the line in 1972, when the two countries normalized relations, that the Japanese people had been the victims of their military leaders, in the same way as the Chinese people had, making the case for unity and friendship to be offered to the Japanese people. This view was transmitted unambiguously to the Japanese side. This delineation then begged the wholly understandable question, the implied answer to which provides the third element to the stance of the Chinese government: Who were these Japanese militarists who harmed the Chinese and Japanese people? Only one group of people has been identified as such internationally – the Class A war criminals who are enshrined in Yasukuni Shrine. The Chinese view was thus that, at least, the Japanese government should have the decency not to honor them.

At time of writing, it is politically advantageous for China to preserve the Zhou Enlai thesis outlined above, and the Chinese government restrains any lines of argument that may stand outside that framework, at least in public or formal discussion.

Conclusion

The lost decades idea that forms the basis of our discussions in this book very clearly connects to the question of why Japan cannot achieve reconciliation with China and Korea. What do we learn from the three case studies I have outlined? I will attempt to answer this query by posing three further questions for examination.

First of all, looking at these three case studies, we may ask: Did the Japanese have the intention to reconcile with China and Korea? Broadly speaking, I would say yes, though this intention varied in strength. Without a doubt there have been genuine intentions toward reconciliation coming from Japan's side. On the comfort women issue, with the AWF plan, and all the efforts that emerged from the Miyazawa cabinet to the Murayama cabinet from 1992 to 1995, we see undeniable good will, sincerity, and a determination to apologize and to make atonement to those who suffered as the result of past Japan's misdeeds. This wish accompanied by actual steps taken can be seen in the establishment of the AWF and the long years of endeavor for its implementation in Korea. Regarding the emperor's visit to China, the Miyazawa cabinet also cannot be doubted, as it genuinely wished to bring political closure to Japan's unfortunate past with China. Even on the Yasukuni issue, among the religiously neutral supporters, but also among the Yasukuni reformers with their goal of de-shrining the Class A war criminals, there were honest efforts to do something to pull Japan-China relations out from the difficulties caused by Koizumi's yearly visits and to take major steps toward reconciliation.

Second, did those wishes for reconciliation meet Korean and Chinese needs? Clearly they did not. Yasukuni is the most obvious case because neither the proposal to construct a religiously neutral facility, nor the de-shrining of Class A war criminals, was actually implemented. It was quite clear that Japan was not satisfying China's requests not to mourn the Class A war criminals at Yasu-kuni. Regarding the emperor's visit to China, Miyazawa might have been led up the wrong path by the misguided approach of the Chinese leadership that a "successful visit" in itself would suffice to bring about a new era of reconcili-ation. To that extent, the Chinese share a certain responsibility in that they did not strive for a genuine visit for the purpose of reconciliation, which might have produced enduring results. On the comfort women activities of the AWF, as the AWF itself acknowledges, the failure to produce reconciliation with South Korea impeded the process. But the AWF did achieve genuine reconciliation with a siz-able number of Korean comfort women, who remain incognito due to Korean social pressure. History will judge the responsibility of the Korean Council for its insistence on Japan's acceptance of legal responsibility. Thus, though the degree of responsibility for failure to produce lasting reconciliation varies, it is evident that reconciliation was not fully achieved in any of these arenas.

Third, even if one side were to blame, either wholly or mostly, in these failures, if reconciliation with Asia is indeed important to Japan (whether from the liberal, or moral, point of view or from a realist, pragmatic point of view), why did Japan not take more effective measures? As these case studies show, there was genuine good will and hope for reconciliation in the Japanese camps. It is possible that the answer might come down to certain structural reasons and to the action (or inaction) of responsible individuals. During the imperial visit to China, there were strong political and constitutional considerations that restricted the emperor's behavior. But there is no gainsaying the fact that Japanese leaders at this period also entirely failed to foresee or apprehend the sheer depth of China's indignation or the possibility of historical memory issues rising again to the forefront of bilat-eral negotiations. The present-day impasse concerning the Senkaku Islands offers the same challenge to Japanese leaders even as they attempt to grasp the depth and complexity of China's decision-making processes.

On the issue of comfort women, opinions shared by a majority of Japanese leaders that legal issues had been resolved by treaties became the founding posi-tion for the establishment of the AWF. On that basis, the efforts made by Japa-nese people wishing to make amends during the decade from 1992 to 2002 were commendable. But were the people involved in the founding of the AWF in the end too legalistic in not allowing the use of national budgetary money for atone-ment? There is still the possibility of utilizing budgetary money based on moral considerations as a renewed basis for reconciliation, if there is sufficient politi-cal will. But the present issue of the Korean court's new decisions on prewar enforced labor may ignite new legal debates that will be even harder to resolve in the future. The issue of legality might still become a key factor in Japan-Korea historical issues.

On the Yasukuni visits, the structural rigidity that emerged from the complete split inside Japan on how to mourn the war dead has perhaps made it impossible to find an alternative to the present impasse. It is my view therefore that trying to resolve this issue with prime ministerial visits just exacerbates domestic contra-dictions and international tensions. Prime Minister Abe's visit on December 26, 2013, has resulted in just such controversies inside Japan and in international forums. Yasukuni supporters around Abe who desire visits at all costs may be happy, but many Japanese opinion leaders doubt that such visits resolve any prob-lems inside Japan and they certainly do nothing for Japan's international standing at a time when Japan particularly needs improved relations with all countries, par-ticularly China and the United States. It is difficult to comprehend the immediate impact and long-term implications of Abe's visit in December 2013.

The broader picture of Japan's international standing, particularly in Asia, is well described by Shiraishi Takashi in Chapter 11. Suffice it to say that Japan's initial bright hopes of leading other countries in Asia have had to secede to an implicit acknowledgment of Japan's relative decline and the relative rise of all other Asian countries over the two lost decades. Strategically, too, the naïve or optimistic expectation that the economic rise of China would turn that country into a peacefully integrated regional partner for Japan shattered, particularly after the 2008 Lehman shock. In short, the overall situation for Japan seems to be one of increasing resignation concerning China's forceful rise. There is the possibility that Abe might gain wider attention and support, given the apparent success of "Abenomics" and Japan's "active pacifism." Regrettably, his visit to Yasukuni in December 2013 did nothing but revive old controversies.

Notes

1 Kazuhiko Togo, *Japan's Foreign Policy 1945–2009: The Quest for a Proactive Policy*, (Leiden: Brill, 2010), pp. 138–39.
2 Ibid., pp. 141–43.
3 Tanaka Akihiko, *Nichū kankei 1945–1990* [Japan-China Relations 1945–1990] (Tokyo: University of Tokyo Press, 1991), p. 178.
4 Ibid., pp. 178–84.
5 *Yomiuri shimbun*, January 5, 1992.
6 Ibid., April 7, 1992.
7 Ibid., July 30, 1992.
8 Ibid., May 24, 1992.
9 Ibid., July 30, 1992.
10 Ibid., May 24, 1992.
11 Ibid., July 30, 1992.
12 Ibid., October 24, 1992, translation by the author.
13 Ibid.
14 Ibid.
15 Ibid.
16 Personal communication to the author on September 16, 2013, by Sugimoto Takashi, professor at Kyoto University, translator of Ezra Vogel's biography of Deng Xiaoping.
17 http://history.hanover.edu/texts/1889con.html, accessed January 4, 2014
18 It is generally understood that Emperor Hirohito took a personal decision to crush the military coup of the February 26, 1936, incident and regretted it; he also made the deci-sion to surrender in August 1945, but only when requested by Prime Minister Suzuki Kantarō.
19 http://www.ioc.u-tokyo.ac.jp/~worldjpn/documents/texts/docs/19720929.D1E.html

20 Togo, *Japan's Foreign Policy*, pp. 282–85.
21 *Yomiuri*, April 2, 1992.
22 Togo, *Japan's Foreign Policy*, pp. 282–85.
23 Gilbert Rozman, *Chinese Strategic Thought toward Asia* (New York: Palgrave Macmillan, 2010), p. 162.
24 http://www.awf.or.jp/e-preface.htm
25 *Yomiuri*, January 16, 1992.
26 http://www.mofa.go.jp/policy/women/fund/state9308.html
27 *Asahi Shimbun*, August 15, 1994 (evening edition).
28 http://www.ioc.u-tokyo.ac.jp/~worldjpn/documents/texts/JPKR/19650622.T9J.html
29 http://www.awf.or.jp/e3/korea.html
30 Tōgo Kazuhiko, *Rekishito gaiko: Yasukuni, ajia, tokyo saiban* [History and Foreign Policy: Yasukuni, Asia, Tokyo Trial] (Tokyo: Kodansha, 2008), pp. 99–102.
31 http://www.mofa.go.jp/files/000042173.pdf, pp. 20–21.
32 Park Yuha, *Wakainotameni: Kyokasho, ianfu, yasukuni, dokutou* [Toward Reconciliation: Textbook, Comfort Women, Yasukuni, and Dokto] (Tokyo: Heibonsha, 2006)
33 Ibid., pp. 61–65.
34 Ibid., p. 82.
35 Ibid., pp. 78–79.
36 Ibid., pp. 85–92.
37 http://www.mofa.go.jp/mofaj/kaidan/s_koi/china0110/gh.html
38 http://www.kantei.go.jp/jp/singi/tuitou/kettei/021224houkoku.html
39 http://www.shugiin.go.jp/itdb_shitsumon.nsf/html/shitsumon/a154070.htm
40 http://www.max.hi-ho.ne.jp/m-shinomiya/ron/2003/ron001.htm; http://seisaku.sblo.jp/article/3620921.html
41 Tōgo, *Rekishito Gaiko*, pp. 31–32.
42 Ibid., p. 45.
43 Ibid.
44 Ibid., p. 310.
45 Tōgo Kazuhiko, *Rekishininnshikio toinaosu: Yasukuni, ianfu, ryodomondai* [Requestioning Historical Recognition: Yasukuni, Comfort Women, Territorial Problems] (Tokyo, Kadokawa One Theme 21, 2013), pp. 106–48.
46 I first dealt with the need to face China's views squarely in a blog in 2005: *Yamatono Hitono iken* [A View from a Person of Yamato], July 18, 2005, Number 17; http://jinyamato2005.no-blog.jp/1/2005/07/index.html

14 Japan's failed bid for a permanent seat on the UN Security Council

Akiyama Nobumasa

After the end of the Cold War in the late 1980s, as the international security environment underwent rapid change, Japan sought a new role and identity for itself. The nation's economy had become the second largest in the world, with a significant impact on the global economy. It was natural for Japan to search for a leading position in international politics and security as well.

One of the ways in which it sought to increase its diplomatic presence was to gain a permanent seat on the United Nations Security Council. Japan sought to do this along with reforming the structure of the UN, at the same time as strengthening the U.S.-Japan alliance. The campaign for a permanent seat on the UN Security Council (UNSC) was Japan's first major attempt to diplomatically reconfigure the institutional alignment of the postwar international world order.

The United Nations embodies the democratic ideals and norms of the international community formed at the end of World War II. As such, it institutionalized the distribution of power and the reality of international politics along lines laid out by the major powers. It will be remembered that Japan once held the position of a great power in the Council of the prewar League of Nations before it withdrew in 1933. As a country that had been defeated in World War II, Japan came to view reform of the UN as a kind of responsibility and destiny, and a permanent seat at the UN Security Council was the ultimate goal. More precisely, the permanent seat was not a reward for being a "good loser." Japan wanted to step forward to a new status, beyond that of a good loser, and a permanent seat was seen as the symbol of this achievement. Japan had adapted itself to the new order established at the end of the war and performed well within the set framework. By accomplishing a reform of the UN and gaining a seat in the Security Council, the hope was to create a feeling of having wiped the slate clean of any negative legacy left after World War II, including the bitter taste of defeat. The change that Japan had brought to the UN would signify to the world that Japan was genuinely reintegrated into the postwar global governance system and was now a legitimate major power.[1]

Unfortunately, the efforts made in pursuit of a permanent membership on the Security Council of the United Nations coincided with an era when Japan began to experience significant political and economic challenges both at home and abroad – the so-called lost decades. After the burst of its economic bubble Japan had great difficulty in escaping the ensuing recession, which consequently lasted many years. At the same time, due to the emergence of new economic powers such as China, Japan's influence in the international economy began to decline. These challenges eroded Japan's strategic position in the international community. In the end, by the early twenty-first century it became clear that Japanese economic power was no longer what it once was. Japan had to face two challenges, namely regaining a position of legitimate international power and consolidating, as well as managing, its slow economic decline.

The first Gulf War (1990–1991) made it clear that the previously economics-based posture of Japan's foreign policy, characterized by the Yoshida Doctrine, was no longer viable to maintain the respect of and exert influence in the inter-national community. Ironically, the end of the Cold War and the start of the Gulf War provided critical wake-up calls for redefining Japan's security policy and its previous approach to international politics. Japan found itself at a critical juncture: it needed a new national strategy that could respond to the new realities of the international security environment.

In the two decades after the first Gulf War, the question of how to respond to the emergence of a new international order, and adjust foreign policy strategy and domestic institutional foundations to structural changes in that order, continued as a *basso continuo* for Japan. The requirements of this strategic adjustment to the changing international environment are twofold: to redefine strategic goals to fit into new geopolitical realities and to make policy resources and tools available to the government itself, which has been under certain institutional constraints.

The campaign for permanent membership on the UN Security Council can be seen as part of a larger effort at strategic adjustment in two ways. First, it was part of an effort to establish a strategic platform for Japan's foreign policy, to gain esteem for Japan, and to strengthen international collaboration. In the 1990s it was natural for Japan to seek such esteem, which was seen as critical in the early twenty-first century. With the rise of emerging economies in the 1990s and Japan's relative decline, reform of the UN became perceived as even more key as a way to keep Japan's voice heard. Japan wanted both to adapt itself to the changing distribution of power in international politics and to reconfigure the structural base, the UN decision-making mechanism, to gain a portal to exert influence.

Second, a robust foreign policy and the ability to mobilize political and economic resources for perceived objectives require strong domestic foundations and a national consensus on strategic goals. A new national strategy to adapt to a new security environment required a new national narrative, or identity, for Japan's post–Cold War era. Campaigning for a permanent seat was seen as the best way to seek out and build this new national strategic narrative. Such a narrative might also provide the impetus for reconfiguring domestic institutions, which would then serve to mobilize political and economic resources.

This chapter seeks to review Japan's diplomatic campaign for a permanent seat on the UN Security Council during the 1990s and 2000s as a case study of Japan's "strategic adjustment" to a changing international security environment and to find a way to effectively exert its influence in international politics.

Japan's postwar foreign policy: The Yoshida Doctrine

Japan's return to the international community after World War II was made possible because it accepted settlements associated with the San Francisco Peace Treaty. Accepting norms, rules, and institutional arrangements based on this new international system was part of the tradeoff. Japan chose to be a "good loser" and was determined to find success in the liberal democratic international order.

After accession to the United Nations in December 1956, Japan continued to make clear that its UN-centered diplomacy was one of three pillars on which it based its diplomacy. The other two pillars were Japan's position as a "member of Asia" and "cooperation with liberal democracies."[2] These three pillars were not in fact of equal value. In the midst of the Cold War, Japan's foreign policy agendas, including UN diplomacy, were naturally melded into the U.S.-Japan alliance (or "cooperation with liberal democracies"). Thanks to the U.S. commitment to the alliance, the Japanese did not need to think about the military dimension of its commitment to international peace.

During the tense Cold War era, the role of the United Nations in international peace and security dimensions was limited. Economic and social development of the Third World became a central issue, toward which UN activities were heavily inclined. Japan's contribution to the UN therefore naturally centered on this field. Japan was able to focus on its economic growth and to allocate foreign policy resources including official development assistance (ODA) to strengthen ties with Asia.

Japan's foreign policy was oriented toward establishing strong economic links with Asian countries, and could thus be described as "economistic," or economy driven. Starting with de facto reparations for World War II, the vast majority of Japan's economic assistance in the early postwar period was directed to Asian countries, and Japanese businesses also expanded their activities in Asian markets, which were also stimulated by Japan's economic cooperation. Japan was often criticized for buying influence with its ODA. However, its contributions to the development and stability of many Asian countries cannot be denied.

As the economy grew, however, Japan was criticized for its limited foreign policy goals and relatively low profile in international peace and security arrangements. As the world's second largest economy, which to some in Japan gave it the right to aspire to loftier goals, Japan became more aware of increasing demand from the international community to commit to its share of responsibility and to contribute to the maintenance of the international order (although many people in Japan also did not recognize this). "International responsibility" and "international contribution" were conceived of within the context of Japan's role in its alliance with the United States or in multilateral (i.e., UN) programs such as development, humanitarian assistance, and the environment.

Responding to the growing demand for more international contribution, Prime Minister Nakasone Yasuhiro, a popular and long-serving prime minister in the late 1980s, tried to transform Japan's politics and foreign policy into that of a major economic, political, and military power by advocating moving beyond the framework of postwar politics. His aims included an attempt to depart from the Yoshida Doctrine toward a more proactive commitment to international politics and security, as well as restructuring foreign policy platforms including revising the Constitution, which, unfortunately, did not succeed.

The Yoshida Doctrine had been an appropriate national strategy to adapt to postwar international exigencies, in an environment where various institutional arrangements for economy, peace, and security, as well as power distribution, were already set. Japan's foreign policy was not based on the idea of it playing a part in "governing the international order." That was the province of the United States, which was competing with its Cold War foes. The end of the Cold War and consequent changes in the international environment made Japan aware of the limits of this previous era of adaptive foreign policy.

Lessons from the Gulf War

The Gulf War (August 1990–February 1991) was a critical turning point in the history of Japan's postwar foreign policy. It forced Japan, as the greatest beneficiary of the postwar liberal international economic order, to reconsider its approach to international contribution. Lessons learned in the response and aftermath to the Gulf War shaped Japan's discourse on UN reform in the early stages.

The experiences of the Gulf War had a profound impact on Japan's diplomatic community in two ways. First, in the Gulf War Japan's approach, which at first limited itself to a conventional economistic foreign policy framework, did not meet the expectations of the rest of the international community. Japan's response to the war was initially criticized as "too little, too late." Japan in fact made the greatest financial contribution to the operation of multilateral forces, totaling US $13 billion, so it was certainly not too little. However, it became clear that the financial contribution alone was not sufficient to gain public credit. As is well known, when the Kuwaiti government took out a "thank you" advertisement in the *Washington Post* after the Gulf War and did not name Japan as a country that helped to liberate Kuwait, Japanese political circles were crestfallen.[3] This omission clearly demonstrated the limits of Japan's economistic foreign policy. When more than 200 Japanese nationals were taken hostage in Iraq, Japan started to view the Gulf War as a direct outgrowth of the inadequacy and blind spots of its own national security policy.[4]

In other words, Japan's contribution to the resolution of the Gulf War crisis was mainly interpreted within the narrow confines of alliance management: it was seen as having been made only in response to U.S. demands and through the prism of the U.S.-Japan relationship, or else out of self-serving reasons such as the need to secure oil and gas imports from the Middle East, rather than out of the necessity to secure stability in the region.[5] Critical voices from the United States concerning Japan's initially tardy response wondered whether the Japanese government had intentionally delayed as a means of manipulative move. Many in the diplomatic community argued that such limits, along with the absence of a consensus at home concerning the role that Japan should play, rendered the government unable to respond effectively to the situation, whether in contributing to the restoration of peace in the Gulf or employing crisis management plans to rescue Japanese nationals stranded in Iraq.

At the same time, the utilization of the UN to legitimize the actions of the multilateral forces led by the United States during and after the Gulf War, along with the rise of UN peacekeeping operations, reminded the Japanese of the growing importance of "multilateralism" in international security. This idea had remained submerged under the severely bipolar international system that had existed during the Cold War. Consequently, two different approaches to the idea of contribution to international security arose in Japan: the multilateral approach to peace cooperation attained through the auspices of the UN and the bilateral security cooperation with the United States. Both of these came under the rubric of international contribution.

It was also realized that without access to informal consultations with Security Council members (or among permanent members), Japan would not get full participation rights or a full say in decision making at the UN or regarding actual operations on the ground.[6] According to Ambassador Hatano Yoshio, it was because Japan did not sit on the UN Security Council that it had such difficulty gaining up-to-date information about the situation, which hindered appropriate and timely decision making. This experience roused Hatano to the urgency of being more intimately involved in the Security Council.[7]

The lessons of the Gulf War led the nation to strengthen its commitment to the UN in two ways. Japan increased its level of participation in UN activities such as peacekeeping operations, fiscal and administrative reforms, and advocating the concept of human security as symbolized by the establishment of the United Nations Trust Fund for Human Security in 1999.[8] At the same time, Japanese foreign policymakers began to consider reform of the UN system, and in particular the Security Council, with the aim of getting Japan more involved. Japan's increased involvement in the UN would accommodate its desire to augment its political influence in international security even under existing domestic institutional constraints; that is to say, overcoming such constraints through the use of UN mechanisms would allow Japan to participate more fully in peace activities. If Japan could reform the UN and gain a permanent seat on the Security Council, this might then become a justification for changing domestic legal constraints against activities related to peace and security.

UN reforms in the 1990s

In the post–Cold War environment, the UN faced conundrums produced by three major changes that had taken place in its composition and raison d'être.

First, whereas in 1945 there had been fifty-one member nations, in 2013 there were 193. This meant that the disposition of its members was not equitably reflected in the membership of the Security Council, certainly not the permanent membership. There was mounting pressure for reform to make the UN more democratic and accountable, as well as to expand participation in decision-making processes. The institutional reform of the Security Council can be understood as a greater project to adjust the UN to meet the new realities of power distribution and to the emerging agenda of the growing international community.

Second, the nature of threats to international peace and security that the UN Security Council needed to address had taken on more complex, protean forms. Asymmetrical, low-intensity civil wars, a proliferation of weapons of mass destruction, and so-called nontraditional security challenges had escalated. A reconceptualization of these threats has triggered a rising awareness of the issue of "human security," an area of concern that combines protection of people, peacekeeping, economic security, and sustainable development that Japan had been actively promoting.

Third, the actions that the United Nations required of its member countries now tended to be ones that stemmed security challenges, quelling the recurrence of conflicts, stopping the proliferation of weapons of mass destruction, and curbing terrorism. The prioritization of these objectives, along with nonmilitary measures for stabilizing war-torn communities, are highly suited to Japan's foreign policy orientation, given its legal and institutional constraints at that time.

Japan's UN diplomacy has also become more and more driven by the motive of projecting its capability and power in international politics. While Japan's willingness to contribute to the international community had increased, a consciousness of the mismatch of its economic power with the influence that it might exert in such areas also grew. Japan's aspiration for a permanent position in the UN Security Council seemed reasonable, given that Japan was the second-largest economy and its financial contribution to the UN was larger than all of those received from the permanent members on the Security Council put together, with the exception of that from the United States.

First steps

As mounting institutional stresses grew, the UN moved toward reform. In December 1992, the General Assembly adopted a resolution, which was cosponsored by forty member states, including Japan, to formally launch discussion on reform in the General Assembly and the Security Council. In December 1993, the General Assembly adopted a resolution, deciding to set up an Open-Ended Working Group (OPWG) under the General Assembly to consider "all aspects of the question of increase in the membership of the Security Council, and other matters related to the Security Council."[9] The year 1993 saw activities related to the Council peak with ninety-three council resolutions and eighty-eight statements; that year also saw a huge rise in the demand for peacekeepers (78,500 "blue berets," sometimes also known as "blue helmets"), a fivefold increase over the previous two years. In 1993, the Security Council passed more Chapter VII resolutions than in its first forty-four years, and it cast only a single veto in the three years before 1993.[10] In a sense, the United Nations Security Council received more global attention than ever before. It also faced higher expectations in its expanded role in maintaining peace and security.[11]

Within the Japanese foreign policy establishment, Japan's lack of influence in international affairs, despite being the second largest economy in the world, worried MOFA's UN policy division. In 1992 Watanabe Michio, Japan's foreign minister for the first time as a Japanese representative at the United Nations General Assembly, expressed an interest in seeking a permanent seat on the Security Council. He stated the need for a serious discussion concerning the composition of the UN organization, including its functions and the composition of the Security Council.[12] This was the first official reference to albeit a somewhat indirect one, Japan's interest in permanent membership on the Security Council.

Also in 1992, Prime Minister Miyazawa Kiichi stated Japan's wish at the General Assembly. Prime Minister Hosokawa Morihiro, who succeeded Miyazawa, mentioned in a 1993 UN speech the need for UN reform and announced that Japan was willing to offer constructive participation in such discussions and was ready to play a larger role in a reformed UN. Despite his remarks, Hosokawa was personally not interested in a permanent seat on the Security Council. He was keen on contributing to international society in other ways, such as development assistance or environmental protection.[13] The phrase that Hosokawa used, "to play more of a role in a reformed UN," was seen as a step back from the government's former position. In contrast to Miyazawa's desire "to play more of a role in the Security Council," Hosokawa sounded cautious about Japan's willingness to be a permanent member.

In the meantime, Japanese politics in the early 1990s was in serious turmoil, hijacked by political scandals and reforms. It so happened that when the debate over UN reform arose, in Japan the 1955 political system was collapsing and a power transition was proceeding. In this transitional era, political leaders and managers (including Ozawa Ichiro, who was the engine behind the collapse of the LDP-dominant political system) were preoccupied with managing their fragile coalitions. There was also very weak political leadership at this time and little attention could be given to foreign policy issues, with the result that foreign policy largely reflected the views of individual leaders.[14]

Prime Minister Hosokawa's stance on the issue of a permanent seat for Japan was cautious, and he left matters related to UN reform to Tanaka Shusei, special assistant to the prime minister. Tanaka was rather dubious about MOFA's explanation concerning the necessity of campaigning for a permanent seat and he insisted that Japan should not be overambitious. He believed that if Japan were to gain permanent membership it should only be after having been nominated by other nations. He was also somewhat skeptical that Japan could play a role as a permanent member as stipulated in the UN Charter. He was particularly concerned that because the Japanese Constitution did not allow the government to exercise the right of collective self-defense, it would be not able to participate in the Military Staff Committee, which commanded UN Forces.[15]

In general, Prime Minister Hosokawa stayed close to Tanaka's conservative view.[16] Tanaka handled the drafting of Hosokawa's speech at the United Nations General Assembly. A heated discussion over the issue of Security Council membership arose between Tanaka and MOFA during the lead-up, and Tanaka in fact asked

MOFA to revise the text of the speech more than twenty times.[17] This friction was symbolic of the gap of between political leaders and MOFA. Owada Hisashi later said that when he met Prime Minister Hosokawa before departing for a new post as Japanese ambassador to the UN in 1994, he sensed that the prime minister was not so keen on pursuing permanent membership.[18] Hosokawa was in fact much more focused on domestic issues, including political reforms and economic policy such as tax reform. He believed that it would be almost impossible to achieve reform of the UN, which was necessary to allow Japan to get a permanent seat in the Security Council. Hosokawa wanted to use his time on other foreign policy matters, including improving relations with China and South Korea.[19]

Murayama Tomiichi succeeded Hata Tsutomu as prime minister in 1994, with an administration that was an alliance of the Socialist Party, the LDP, and the Sakigake Party. This coalition government likewise took a careful approach toward the issue of gaining a permanent seat on the Security Council. Foreign Minister Kono Yohei, a member of the LDP, had to consult with other members of the Cabinet for his speech at the United Nations on September 27, 1994. The Sakigake Party and several Socialist members of the Cabinet were concerned that Japan would be required to offer a stronger military commitment to UN activities, and so Kono had to convince them by emphasizing that Japan's commitment would be made under the existing constitutional framework.[20] In a "Note of Agreement regarding the Contents that should be Included in the Foreign Minister's Speech at the United Nations" in September 1994, a foreign affairs coordination meeting of the three coalition parties included the following items: it should be made clear that Japan could not participate in any military action accompanying the use of force, on the basis of the principles laid down in Japan's Constitution and, upon obtaining the approval of many countries and a national consensus, Japan would make every effort to fulfill its responsibilities in the Security Council.[21] The very existence of a Note of Agreement on the foreign minister's speech at the UN suggests that there was no consensus within the coalition government on Japan's prospective proactive role. Quite clearly, at this time, in the early 1990s, Japanese leaders were simply not ready to craft a campaign strategy.

In the discourse in Japan over the issue of permanent membership in the Security Council, the greatest discord centered on the question of whether permanent membership would entail a requirement of greater military contribution. This question was linked with the revision of Article 9 in the Japanese Constitution. There were reports in the media that high-ranking U.S. officials had stated that some change in the renunciation of the right to collective self-defense in the Constitution would be a prerequisite for Japan's pursuit of permanent membership on the Security Council.[22] On the other hand, the Japanese commitment to the alliance was sometimes seen as one and the same thing as international contribution through the United Nations, and vice versa.

Opponents of UN Security Council permanent membership claimed that proponents had a hidden agenda to use the UN as leverage for their ultimate objective, which was revision of the Japanese Constitution, the remilitarization of Japan, and a change in Japan's alliance with the United States. The official position of the Japanese government in the 1990s was to deny any direct connection between permanent membership on the Security Council and the revision of the Japanese Constitution, as well as any military contribution. In October 1994, Foreign Minister Kono Yohei was asked in the Diet about the relationship between permanent membership of the Security Council and Japan's Constitution. He replied that the Japanese government's interpretation was that since there was no distinction between permanent members on the Security Council and other members of the United Nations in their obligation under the Charter of the United Nations, including military obligation, Japan could make a contribution within its own constitutional framework. The UN Charter did not stipulate additional obligations for being a new permanent member of the Security Council and thus there was no need to harbor reservations about legal obligations under the Charter.[23]

The government also pointed to Article 47 of the UN Charter, which stipulates the role of the Military Staff Committee, a body that exists to "advise and assist the Security Council" on "military requirements." The Article states that "the Military Staff Committee shall consist of Chiefs of Staff of the permanent members of the Security Council" and "shall be responsible under the Security Council for the strategic direction of any armed forces placed at the disposal of the Security Council." It was the Japanese government's assessment that the words "strategic direction" could be interpreted loosely and did not necessarily mean directly holding command and control over armed forces on the ground.

The division in the government on Article 9 and the highly ideological framework in which the issue of UN reform was placed, involving not only issues to do with the UN itself but also, if not principally, issues of the Japanese Constitution and the U.S.-Japan alliance framework, did not help in the creation of a visionary narrative of the post–Cold War international order. Instead, the issue of UN reform was consistently seen in terms of the narrow domestic political context.

The Razali Plan

Meanwhile in the mid-1990s discussions were raised in the UN concerning reform plans for the Security Council, but with little mutual consensus forthcoming. In 1997, Malaysian Ambassador to the UN Razali Ismail, who was chairman of the General Assembly and the OPWG at the time, unveiled a two-step plan for reform, which became known as the Razali Plan.[24] The plan called for the enlargement of the Security Council from fifteen to twenty-four members, with the addition of five permanent and four nonpermanent members. The five new permanent members of the Security Council would comprise two new members from the "industrialized nations" and one member each elected from the developing states of Africa, Asia, and Latin America and the Caribbean. The four new nonpermanent members of the Security Council would comprise members elected from the African states, Asian states, Eastern European states, and one each from either the Latin American or the Caribbean states.

Opposition to this plan centered on a movement called "Uniting for Consensus," nicknamed the "Coffee Club," which originally included Italy, Pakistan, Egypt, and Mexico, but eventually up to fifty nations. This group aimed to counter the bids for permanent seats by G4 countries, namely Brazil, Germany, India, and Japan. It opposed the increase of permanent members on the Security Council and argued instead for an increase in nonpermanent seats, elected on a rotational basis by the General Assembly. The thesis behind this stance was that the increase in permanent seats would only accentuate the disparity and imbalance in privileges in member states.

U.S. Ambassador to the UN Bill Richardson expressed opposition to the idea of expanding the membership of the Security Council from fifteen to twenty-four, saying there was no flexibility above and beyond twenty to twenty-one seats on a reformed Council. This would permit expansion of the Council by one-third, with up to five new permanent members, while supporting Germany and Japan as potential permanent members of the Security Council.[25] However, he welcomed the stage-by-stage procedure outlined in the Razali Plan. That process included the adoption by the General Assembly of two resolutions under different voting requirements: first, a resolution for deciding the size of the enlarged Security Council, and second, after a decent period of consultation, a resolution for the election of new permanent members. It seems that the United States, along with other permanent members, was less concerned with the geographical balance or imbalance of the Security Council and more concerned that the Council remain manageable and efficient and not become unwieldy.[26]

The Razali Plan also faced opposition from the Non-Aligned Movement (NAM), a groups of states in the UN that is not formally aligned with any power bloc. The proposal in the Razali Plan that a few member states who were in NAM might be raised to become permanent members of the Security Council was seen as potentially undermining its unity and reducing political leverage with potential effects on political status for candidates in NAM. Ministers for foreign affairs of NAM states met in New Delhi in April and New York in September 1997 to discuss how NAM should respond to the Razali Plan. In keeping with its previous critical stance on power structures and power dynamics in the UN, NAM opted for rejection, calling for, if anything, greater increases in membership and increases in particular in the nonpermanent category; it also called for a curtailment of the Security Council's veto, with a view to its elimination. As a first step, the group argued that an amendment should be made so that the Security Council's veto power only applied to actions under Chapter VII of the UN Charter.[27]

In the end, the Razali Plan was not submitted to the General Assembly. The recommendation from the working group did not mention specific countries, but presented ideas on the expansion of both permanent and nonpermanent memberships on the Security Council and no veto power for new permanent members.

After the Razali Plan, few specific reform plans were submitted but little progress was made with UN reform. Nevertheless, Japan continued trying to lay the groundwork for reform. Japan initially sought reform based on the Razali Plan, in cooperation with the United States, the United Kingdom, France, and Germany (P3+2). But this framework of coalition invited more suspicion and resentment than sympathy and support. Ultimately, Japan abandoned the framework and shifted to an "omni-directional" campaign for boosting political momentum toward the UN Millennium Summit in the autumn of 2000.[28]

A major obstacle for moving reform forward was the gap between the United States and reform advocates, including Japan, concerning the size of the Security Council. As long as regional and equitable representation remained a criterion for expansion of the Security Council, the United States did not change its position on the number of members. Japanese Ambassador to the UN Satoh Yukio worked to persuade the United States to accept a number larger than twenty-one. He repeatedly held bilateral discussions with his counterpart in the United States, Ambassador Richard Holbrooke, on the size of an expanded Security Council. In April 2000, the United States officially changed its position, stating that it was prepared to consider an increase in membership up to a number slightly higher than twenty-one.[29] At the same time, Japan and the United States worked together to try to resolve the issue of the formula for financial contribution to the United Nations – the top priority on the U.S. side.

According to Ambassador Satoh, by the Millennium Summit, 155 member states, more than two-thirds of all member states, supported the idea of expanding *both* permanent and nonpermanent members of the Security Council.[30] If Ambassador Satoh's account is accurate, it would seem there was indeed a moment when a resolution for Security Council reform could have been passed at the General Assembly in the late 1990s or early 2000s.

The formation of the G4

In the 1990s, one important development in UN reform was the formation of the G4 interest group. The G4 consisted of the four nations of Japan, Germany, India, and Brazil. Japan and Germany were the second and third largest financial contributors to the UN, Brazil was the largest country in terms of geographical area, and India was the second largest in terms of population. All of them were strong permanent membership aspirants, and they mutually supported one another's bids for permanent member seats. These countries frequently held meetings at the ambassadorial level in New York.

On September 21, 2004, Brazil's President Luiz Inácio Lula da Silva, Germany's Vice-Chancellor and Minister for Foreign Affairs Joschka Fischer, India's Prime Minister Dr. Manmohan Singh, and Japan's Prime Minister Koizumi Junichiro met in New York to discuss UN reform. Upgrading their meeting from the UN ambassadorial level to state leader level gave the G4 significant political importance.

In the spring of 2005, the G4's strategy was to seek adoption of the framework resolution at a General Assembly in September 2005. In March 2005, the G4 convened a conference to advocate its position on UN reform and gathered 131 countries. The following month, Uniting for Consensus (UfC) held a conference to gain support for its position on the reform and 119 countries attended. High attendance at both meetings suggested that many countries were interested in both positions and were in a sense "hedging."

The G4 strategy was to create a fait accompli situation where there was no choice but for the United States and other permanent members, which were luke-warm to the reform, to support or accede to the resolution. The Japanese representative, Ambassador Oshima Kenzo, made it clear in his General Assembly speech on April 7, 2005, that with the expansion of the Security Council in both permanent and nonpermanent categories "developing countries should be represented better in an expanded Security Council, including with permanent seats."[31] Behind this statement was an assessment that the bloc support of Africa, which had fifty-three votes, would be essential to passing a framework resolution at the General Assembly. In the same statement, Oshima also mentioned the possibility of holding a vote, rather than trying to gain a consensus, on the early adoption of a reform plan. As Oshima remarked, the Secretary General "states that, although consensus would be preferable, if we are unable to reach consensus 'this must not become an excuse for postponing action.'" "History," he added, "tells us that important steps forward are rarely made through consensus but through bold decisions. It should be recalled that the decision to expand the membership in the nonpermanent category in 1963 was made by vote."[32]

Within this divide in the UN, the G4 considered bringing its draft resolution to a vote. The idea was that although a consensus would be preferable, the lack of consensus should not become an excuse for inaction – and a vote would bring about progress. In fact, when the UN Charter was amended to increase nonpermanent members of the Security Council in 1963, only one permanent member voted for a General Assembly resolution for the amendment, two opposed, and the rest abstained. But this amendment eventually passed, which meant that even those states that opposed the amendment were unable to prevent this amendment in the face of the overwhelming majority support at the General Assembly.

Responses by major stakeholders

In the process of the G4 campaign for a framework resolution, despite extensive diplomatic demarches vis-à-vis Asian countries, Japan was able to secure only three cosponsors from Asia: Afghanistan, Bhutan, and the Maldives. Indonesia, another possible aspirant for a permanent seat at the Security Council, expressed its opposition to the G4 proposal. Facing strong pressure from China to oppose Japan's permanent membership, many Asian countries faced a dilemma of choosing either Japan or China, a situation that many Asian countries wished to avoid. Therefore, many Asian countries took a position that they would vote for Japan to be a permanent member on the Security Council, but they would not cosponsor the resolution. There was much disappointment in Japan that despite Japan's long-term, extensive economic cooperation in Asia throughout the postwar period, these efforts had been unable to bear fruit in the face of a rising China.[33]

Another factor was Africa, and in particular the African Union (AU). To pass a resolution at the General Assembly required the bloc support of Africa, but the Union failed to agree on which two countries from Africa should be nominated as candidates for permanent members of the Security Council. Like NAM, the

AU chose to prioritize unity over progress in the reforms of the United Nations. The Japanese government's approach to the AU was to respect their decision as a bloc. Although Japan extensively endeavored to gain the support of the AU, it had waited for the Union to draw its own conclusion on the representatives to the Security Council, supporting G4's framework resolution.[34] Ultimately, the AU failed to reach an internal consensus.

Germany's prediction was that the G4 resolution would be able to gain twenty to thirty votes from Africa.[35] Japan could have approached individual African states to gain these votes instead of looking for bloc support by the Union. However, Japan did not do so for two reasons. First, other estimates calculated that the number would not be sufficient to reach two-thirds of the General Assembly. Second, MOFA considered that it was critical to obtain bloc support from Africa to avoid China exercising its veto vote. If Japan and Africa partnered, China could not oppose. Eventually, MOFA did not pursue an option to put the framework resolution to a vote at the General Assembly. MOFA was afraid that if it were voted down, it would be even more difficult to put forward a new resolution for the Security Council reform in the future.

On July 3, the AU decided not to support the G4 proposal but to submit its own resolution bill, which included a demand for two permanent seats from Africa with full veto power.

In addition to the divide of the AU, another fatal problem that G4's framework resolution faced was that it failed to consolidate support from UNSC permanent members, in particular the United States. On July 6 the G4 resolution bill was submitted to the General Assembly, without coordination with the AU. It met opposition from the United States and China, along with other states.

For Japan, it was essential to gain the support of the United States for Japan's permanent seat on the Security Council. The United States had been supportive, in principle, of Japan's permanent membership as early as the 1970s, although this was mostly lip service. At the same time, given that U.S. interests were to improve the efficiency and effectiveness of the UN, any increase in the number of states participating in critical decision making would be largely contradictory to a U.S. game plan. As Prime Minister Koizumi stated, an important concept in Japan's foreign policy was the balance between the Japan-U.S. alliance and international cooperation (helping the United States shape its commitment to forming international solidarity). Such a statement emphasized the strong alliance at the same time as allowing for working within the G4.[36] During this time, the Japanese and U.S. governments held extensive consultations on the issue of UN reform, including frequent telephone conversations between Foreign Minister Machimura Nobutaka and Secretary of State Condoleezza Rice.

On July 12, 2005, Professor Shirin Tahir-Kheli, American ambassador and senior advisor to Secretary of State Condoleezza Rice and senior director for democracy, human rights, and international operations at the National Security Council, made a speech at the UN in which she clearly stated that the United States opposed G4's framework draft resolution, along with other proposals. She pointed out that criteria for permanent membership should be based on the capability to contribute to international peace and security, and geographical representation and balance should be realized in the General Assembly. She then urged member states to oppose the resolution when it was put to a vote.[37] It was clear that the United States did not support the G4 plan that Japan advocated.[38]

Due to these signification divisions, the General Assembly gave up adoption of the G4 resolution on August 20 and the bill was abandoned on September 13. Not long after, Japan and the G4 also had to abort the option of passing a framework resolution at the General Assembly.

The essence of the game: Managing politics over power and legitimacy

Regardless of the affinity between the direction of UN reform and the rationales behind Japan's claim, the bid for a permanent membership in the UN Security Council posed an extremely difficult challenge to Japan in management of its relations with major powers – in particular the United States and China. The increase of permanent members on the Security Council would mean a major overhaul of the status quo power distribution in international relations. It was natural for it to face major resistance from those who would not benefit and even suffer a relative loss of power. The existing permanent members (P5) saw little benefit in expanding the number of seats on the Security Council. It would only dilute their own power in international politics and undermine the effectiveness and responsiveness of the UN in taking actions for international peace and security.

Japan's greatest strategic choice was to form the G4, a campaign alliance with Germany, India, and Brazil for UNSC permanent membership, established in September 2004. This was a rational option for Japan, given that the logic of legitimizing and advocating Security Council reform was to correct the imbalance of regional representation and to adapt the organization to the realities of the post–Cold War era. Democratization and legitimate equitable representation became the most important concepts in the movement for this reform of the United Nations. But a critical problem in G4 strategy was the absence of a vision concerning how to engage status quo stakeholders, namely existing permanent members, in particular the United States and China.

Japan-U.S. relations within UN diplomacy have not always been smooth. During the Cold War, a national debate over Japan's foreign and security policy was ideologically divided between a pro– and anti–U.S.-Japan alliance. Despite this friction, there was a general consensus about the Yoshida Doctrine and UN diplomacy was merged into this doctrine. During the 1980s and 1990s, Japan increased its financial commitments to UN agencies as a part of its international contribution with an eye toward two objectives. One was a quest for power and influence in the international community; as its economy grew, Japan sought more influence in the wider world. The other was burden sharing within the U.S.-Japan alliance. Article I of the Japan-U.S. Security Treaty stipulates joint efforts to strengthen the United Nations so that "its mission of maintaining international peace and security may be discharged more effectively."[39]

During the 2000s, Japan's UN diplomacy was placed in a dilemma, torn between its alliance with the United States, which had unilateralist tendencies, and UN-centered multilateralism. This challenge tied into Japan's new vision of the post–Cold War international order. According to Takeuchi Yukio, vice minister for foreign affairs from 2002 to 2005, there were two important concerns with regard to Japan's formulation of the post–Cold War order. One was how Japan should manage its economic retreat while maintaining and even strengthening its influence in international politics. The second was how to keep the United States, the sole superpower, engaged in multilateral coordination, particularly the United Nations. In the spring of 2003, Japan joined the United Kingdom in persuading the United States to go through the UN in taking its military action against Iraq.[40] Prime Minister Koizumi emphasized the importance of consistency in the U.S.-Japan alliance and multilateral cooperation.[41] Japan also suggested to the United States that it would be important to frame the issue of Iraq as a confrontation between Iraq and the rest of the international community, not merely between Saddam Hussein and George W. Bush.[42] However, the U.S. move was contested in the UN not only by Russia and the NAM countries, but also by European countries such as France and Germany.

In the meantime, the difference in opinion between Japan and the United States over the issue of reform of the Security Council was never filled. The United States did not want expansion of the Council, which it saw as posing a threat to the Council's effectiveness and limiting U.S. power. This was why the United States did not support the G4 as a group. It was particularly opposed to Germany's inclusion. The United States had been rankled by the opposition of France and Germany to UN authorization for use of force against Iraq when it was suspected of possessing weapons of mass destruction. Japan failed to convince the United States on the indispensability of Japan's inclusion on the Security Council and that the G4 campaign would not harm U.S. interests.

Diplomatic rivalry with China was also one of drivers behind the campaign. In MOFA there was a strong view that irrespective of China's remarkable rise in economic power, Japan deserved to be a new permanent member because of its substantial financial contribution to the UN system. Meanwhile, gaining equal status with China in the UN system would be symbolic of the full recovery from the Japan's legacy of defeat in the war and an acknowledgement of Japan's legitimate position in the postwar world.

Despite rivalry with China, it was critical for Japan that China would not block the reform. But Japan's approach to that mandate was ineffective, because Japan's actions disengaged China. Japan sought bloc support from the AU so that China could not oppose a resolution since it was supported by Africa.

At the same time, however, Koizumi's numerous visits to the Yasukuni Shrine in the early 2000s triggered anger, or at least offered a plausible excuse for such, on the Chinese mainland. Subsequently, Beijing intensified diplomatic counter-operations against Japan's campaign for permanent membership. Special envoys dispatched by the Japanese government to various parts of the world faced China's strong campaign against Japan. Koizumi was informed by MOFA that his visits to the Yasukuni Shrine antagonized the Chinese and that this was making it difficult to pursue the support of China in Japan's efforts at UN reform. However, Koizumi insisted that he wanted to do both things – continue his visits to the shrine and to drive forward a campaign for a permanent Security Council seat.[43] Some MOFA officials viewed Koizumi's assessment rather skeptically and were puzzled and frustrated by his contradictory behavior.[44]

The conundrum: Why did Japan do what it did?

Investigating Japan's quest for a permanent UN Security Council seat, and the concomitant quest for a strategic security adjustment, can proceed along two lines of questioning. First, what were the reasons for the diplomatic failure – why did Japan not succeed in gaining permanent membership on the Security Council? The issues that come into play here are the appropriateness of the strategy used in the campaign, domestic political dynamics, and external environmental factors.

Second, what significance did diplomatic campaigning for a permanent seat on the UN Security Council have on Japan's postwar foreign policy ideology? What adjustments did Japan try to make to its national strategy in a changing international environment? To what extent was such strategic adjustment successful in shaping a national narrative for Japan in the post–Cold War world? What did Japan lose or gain by committing itself to the campaign for a permanent seat?

The campaign strategy

As the UN reform agenda matured, and especially from the 1990s onwards, diplomatic campaigns by various countries wanting reform became a critical factor. During the campaign in the 2000s, when the Security Council reform became a realistic agenda, Japan faced some important choices in campaign strategy.

The first question was whether it was a good choice for Japan to have partnered with three other major aspirants for permanent membership – Germany, India, and Brazil (G4) – to promote the campaign for UN Security Council reform. This partnership scheme had pros and cons. The G4 members united their voices for Security Council reform, making it more perhaps more relevant to the international community. However, the G4 also attracted opposition. Rivals of the G4 members banded together as United for Consensus and intensified their campaign against a G4 proposal. Japan thus attracted potential unwanted opposition in its partnership with G4 members.

The second important question was why Japan tried to commit to an omnidirectional approach to push through the G4 framework resolution, which was based on Model A, adopted at the General Assembly, to gain approval from permanent members of the Security Council. The proactive support by the United States, a permanent member of the Security Council and the closest ally of Japan, should have been a key to the success of the campaign. But in the mid-2000s Japan placed higher priority on increasing support for the General Assembly to induce more U.S. support. Why did Japan (have to) choose that strategy?

Domestic politics: Seeking a national narrative
for Japan's new role

A robust foreign policy rests on a strong domestic foundation. When any government tries to step in a new direction in international politics, a firm domestic political consensus is essential. The domestic political foundation consists of three elements: robust public support, or a national consensus or a national narrative on foreign policy or strategy widely shared across various sectors of the society, which shapes the identity of the country; commitment from political leaders; and policy machinery that enables policymakers to mobilize resources and implement the policy.

In the new era after the Cold War, Japan needed a new national narrative across a diverse political spectrum to provide a common sense of direction for the whole country and to locate its position in the changing international community.[45] During the 1980s and 1990s when Japan grew itself into the second-largest economy in the world, major sources of Japan's influence in the international community were economic measures such as trade (or export), finance, and official development assistance. Under the Yoshida Doctrine Japan had enjoyed a relatively light burden in helping to maintain international peace and security, relying on the U.S.-Japan alliance and focused on its own economic development. But Japan now sought a new foreign and security policy posture in the post–Cold War era, in an attempt to move beyond the conventional Yoshida Doctrine.

It must be noted that, as an important element that shaped the discourse over international aspiration, the underlying hidden agenda in the political dynamics over "international contribution" was whether or not the government could transcend the conventional interpretation of Article 9 in Japan's postwar Constitution. Article 9 stipulates the nation's commitment to the nonuse of forces to resolve international conflict, and thus puts constraints on Japan's participation in international security activities involving armed forces. The twin issues of national identity in the post–Cold War era and constitutional revision in building (or failing to build) a national consensus for the Security Council permanent seat are intimately linked. The extent to which this linkage affected Japan's campaign and created a political cleavage over Japan's international contribution remains a question.

Intertwined with the discourse over a new narrative for a national strategy was the domestic political environment. Coincidentally, the quest for a new international position with a larger international footprint developed in parallel with major political changes at home. Japanese politics in the 1990s ran through a very unstable period after the end of the so-called 1955 political system, in which the Liberal Democratic Party (LDP) had dominated government since 1955, with frequent changes in party alignments. With fragile political foundations foreign policy agendas were often overlooked, and prioritization of more urgent, domestic political issues such as electoral reform or tax issues took precedence.

Ironically, during another important period for the campaign, namely the first half of the 2000s, an unusually strong political leader, Prime Minister Koizumi Junichiro, led Japan. Koizumi's foreign policy orientation was always based on a strong U.S.-Japan alliance. Koizumi's posture toward reform of the UN Security Council was ambiguous, or even contradictory: although he supported the campaign for Security Council permanent membership and played a role in establishing the G4 group, certain moves that he made went against the spirit of such campaigns. These include his controversial visits to Yasukuni Shrine, which he made in full knowledge that they would irritate and outrage China. The effect of Koizumi's leadership on the campaign for Security Council membership remains a question.

Environment defines the game

Despite efforts to produce a sound strategy, a question remains if external environmental factors beyond Japan's control were decisive in shaping how the UN reform agenda was devised and how the stage was set for Japan's campaign.

In UN reform, an increase in the number of member states brought forth the issue of equitable representation as a central concept behind any reform. Currently, the United Nations has more than 190 member states, but it only numbered fifty-one at its nascency in 1945. As many former colonies become independent in Asia and Africa, the Non-Aligned Movement (NAM) became an important and powerful group of member states, especially in the General Assembly. Such a power shift also affected political dynamics by increasing the number of stakeholders in any potential UN reform. The African continent, with fifty-three members (at that time), also developed into a key constituency in debates on UN reform. As such, these groups were important for Japan to woo, in terms of gaining support for its position, as well as engaging it as potential running mates for the reform campaign. How the African Union responded became a decisive factor in UN reform.

The rise of emerging powers also constituted another challenge for Japan's campaign. A drastic shift of global power distribution took place from the 1990s to the 2000s. Naturally, these changes affected the environment surrounding Japan's campaign for a permanent seat at the Security Council. BRIC (Brazil, Russia, India, and China) nations lead the world in economic growth. Many also saw them as rising powers in the future, which would alter the nexus of international power centers. The countries were critical players that Japan could no longer ignore. India and Brazil were running mates, while China and Russia were status quo stakeholders in politics concerning the UN. In particular the role of China, a rival regional power, was fundamental.

The emergence of these environmental factors shaped the modality of the diplomatic game of UN reform. The issue of how Japan responded to these factors in shaping its objectives and strategy was crucial.

Conclusion: Searching for a new national narrative of foreign policy

Japan's quest for permanent membership in the Security Council in the 1990s and 2000s and its ultimate failure demonstrated that such a huge diplomatic project required a well-coordinated effort that married good strategy, political leadership, and public support, as well as skillful management of conflicting foreign policy objectives so that they could all line up in the same direction. A favorable international environment was also necessary. At least one or several of these elements were missing at various times in Japan's campaigns, which prevented Japan from achieving success.

In the early 1990s, while the issue of UN reform came to attract more attention in the international community, ideas on UN reform were frequently floated but few well-formulated plans developed into concrete programs or projects. Security Council reform became a buzzword, but only actually took concrete shape in the late 1990s in the form of the Razali Plan.

Japan's emphasis on economy could have helped it to form stronger relationships with other countries in the postwar era. But the project of Security Council reform was beyond the scope of bilateral relations within the international system. Reform might have brought fundamental structural changes to the postwar institutional arrangements in the international community, which embodied and consolidated power distribution. This would require a strategy to envision the post-reform international order and the state's capability (or skills) to get other countries to accept such changes.

Japan's weak political position in the 1990s prioritized domestic policy issues and maintaining political coalitions. Within fairly turbulent domestic political circumstances and fragile coalition governments, it was difficult for Japan to build a consensus or national narrative for a new vision of the post–Cold War world order and Japan's position in it. The need to overcome a lack of agreement over the issue of Article 9 of the Constitution and to establish a strong domestic foundation for mobilizing political and economic capital for that purpose meant that the campaign never coalesced.

Japan's inability to make wise strategic choices at this critical juncture of a potentially shifting international security environment left many issues unaddressed at the leadership level. Leaders left the national narrative of a new foreign policy untested and underdeveloped in public discourse. Japan was not ready to take a leading role in the international arena to shape the agenda of UN reform in the 1990s.

However, even if there had been a better campaign strategy, it is unlikely that the Japanese campaign for permanent membership on the Security Council during the 2000s would have been successful. It was logical and probably inevitable that Japan become one of the members of the G4 group and also that it respect the interests of Africa, due to the fact that the idea of equitable representation had become a major legitimization factor for UN reform, in particular of the Security Council. As the African Union became more aware of its possible representation on the Security Council, Japan became less autonomous in its choice of campaign strategy. The trade-off between equitable representation and effectiveness as principles of the UN reform placed Japan in a huge dilemma. Japan needed to engage both the United States and developing countries, in particular Africa, as a bloc. But for the former, the main objective was maintaining the Security Council as it was, for effectiveness. For the latter, it was greater equity in the institution.

Michael J. Green and Igata Akira (Chapter 9) and Sheila Smith (Chapter 12) show how Japan's security policy has been one of gradually adapting to a changing security environment in the context of the U.S.-Japan alliance – which has been characterized as "reluctant realism."[46] Japan's strategic changes were consistently reactive, piecemeal adaptations to the international environment.

In this sense, Japan's attempt at reform of the Security Council was unusually and uncharacteristically proactive. Japan was lending its energies to transform one of the fundamental frameworks of the postwar international political system. It was Japan's first diplomatic attempt to shape and lead the global agenda. Such a grand project required a multidimensional approach that would mobilize domestic and international assets in an integrated fashion. It was also important that different elements of diplomatic policies toward China, the United States, and Asia should be fully coordinated and synchronized. A sense of national consensus on the direction of foreign policy under a solid leadership was needed. However, in the 1990s and 2000s Japanese political leaders and foreign policy circles were incapable of establishing this cohesive strategic vision. Although Koizumi was in some ways a very strong leader, his leadership was not visionary enough to take Japanese society toward a consensus on the role that Japan should take in the world.

Japan lost two important things in its failed campaign for UN Security Council membership. One was a chance to acquire a new foreign policy style with strong domestic leadership, ready to engage in power politics at the structural level of the international community and moving beyond its usual passive strategic adjustment or adaptation. The other was actual vision. The campaign for a permanent seat might have provided an opportunity to build a national consensus for a policy to follow the Yoshida Doctrine, previously formulated to offer a "catch-up" style national strategy to match the international order during the Cold War era. In the end, what Japan was left with were even more critical and difficult challenges in the following decades to retain its international influence within a more complex international strategic environment.

Notes

1 It should be clear that though this view was widely shared in foreign policy circles in Tokyo, it was never explicitly laid down as a policy goal. Author's interview with Ambassador Satoh Yukio (permanent representative of Japan to the UN 1998–2002, and Ambassador of Japan to the Netherlands, 1994–96), October 15, 2013.
2 MOFA, *Diplomatic Bluebook 1957*, September, 1957, http://www.mofa.go.jp/mofaj/gaiko/bluebook/1957/s32-contents.htm.
3 Author interviews with former MOFA officials, who wish to remain anonymous.
4 Shinyo Takahiro, "*Nihon no gaiko kiko to tai-kokuren seisaku*" ["Japan's foreign policy institutions and policy toward the UN"], *Kokusai Mondai* 1994, pp. 34–52.
5 Ibid., p. 35.
6 Author interview with Ambassador Hatano Yoshio, September 20, 2013. Ambassador Hatano was a permanent representative to the UN from 1990 to 1994.
7 Interview with Hatano.
8 The first dispatch of Japan's Self Defense Forces to a UN peacekeeping operation was for UNTAC in 1992. For Japan's activities during the 1990s, refer to Reinhard Drifte, "Japan and Security Council Reform: Multilateralism at a Turning Point?" *Asia-Pacific*

Law and Policy Journal 14 (2000), and Reinhard Drifte, *Japan's Quest for a Permanent Security Council Seat: A Matter of Pride or Justice?* (London: Palgrave Macmillan, 2000).

9 United Nations General Assembly, "Question of equitable representation on and increase in the membership of the Security Council," A/RES/48/26, December 3, 1993, http://www.un.org/documents/ga/res/48/a48r026.htm.

10 These statistics are drawn mainly from the website of the Global Policy Forum, http://www.globalpolicy.org/security/data/index.htm.

11 The UN also experienced setbacks in its PKO with failures in the Balkans and Somalia.

12 Watanabe Michio, "Statement by Foreign Minister Michio Watanabe at the 47th Session of the General Assembly of the United Nations," MOFA, September 22, 1992, http://www.mofa.go.jp/mofaj/gaiko/bluebook/1992/h04-shiryou-2.htm#b9.

13 Author interview with former Prime Minister Hosokawa Morihiro, November 6, 2013.

14 Interview with Hosokawa, and author interview with Kono Yohei, October 28, 2013.

15 Interview with Hosokawa.

16 Hosokawa Morihiro, *Naishoroku*, *Nihon Keizai Shimbun*, 2010, p. 41.

17 Interview with Hosokawa.

18 Owada Hisashi *"Nanko suru anpori-kaikaku"* ["Security Council Reform in Hardship"], in Akashi Yasusi, et al., eds., *Nihon to kokuren no 50 nen* [50 Years of Japan and the UN] (Tokyo: Minerva Shobo, 2008), pp. 226–27.

19 Interview with Hosokawa.

20 Interview with Kono.

21 The Nippon Foundation Library, "Timeline of Japan's move towards appealing for United Nations Security Council permanent membership," *Mainichi Shimbun*, September 28, 1994, https://nippon.zaidan.info/seikabutsu/2003/01297/contents/229.htm.

22 Mainichi Daily News, "Armitage Says War-Renouncing Constitution Blocking Japan-US Alliance," *Mainichi Daily News*, July 22, 2004; Kyodo News, "Japan Must Examine Article 9 in Quest for UNSC Seat: Powell," *Kyodo News*, August 12, 2004.

23 Kono Yohei's answer to a question, *Dai 131 kai Shuugi-in Yosan-iinkai, kaigiroku 2gou* [Minutes Vol. 2 of the Budget Committee of the House of Representatives 13th Session], October 12, 1994, http://kokkai.ndl.go.jp/cgi-bin/KENSAKU/swk_dispdoc.cgi?SESSION=5134&SAVED_RID=2&PAGE=0&POS=0&TOTAL=0&SRV_ID=7&DOC_ID=3236&DPAGE=1&DTOTAL=14&DPOS=9&SORT_DIR=1&SORT_TYPE=0&MODE=1&DMY=7836.

24 Paper by the Chairman of the Open-Ended Working Group on the Question of Equitable Representation on and Increase in the Membership of the Security Council and Other Matters Related to the Security Council, 20 March 1997.

25 Bill Richardson, "Statement on Security Council Reform to the Open-Ended Working Group of the General Assembly on Security Council Reform," July 17, 1997, http://www.globalpolicy.org/security-council/security-council-reform/32891.html?itemid=915.

26 Ibid.

27 Dimitris Bourantonis, *The History and Politics of UN Security Council Reform* (London: Routledge, 2005), p. 68.

28 Satoh Yukio, *"Nihon wa jonin-rijikoku iri dekiru-ka"* ["Can Japan Be a Permanent Member of the Security Council?"], *Gaiko Forumu*, 2001 no. 3, p. 21.

29 Ibid., p. 22.

30 Ibid., p. 23.

31 Statement by H.E. Mr. Oshima Kenzo, Permanent Representative of Japan at the Plenary Meeting of the General Assembly on the Report of the Secretary-General, "The Time is Ripe for Action," April 7, 2005, http://www.un.emb-japan.go.jp/statements/oshima050407.html.

32 Ibid.

33 Yamada Muru, "UN Reform: G4 Resolution Faces Harsh Reality, Attracts Only Three Asian Nations," *Mainichi Shimbun*, July 8, 2005.

34 In early summer of 2005, Foreign Minister Machimura Nobutaka attended meetings of AU three times in three weeks. Author interview with Machimura Nobutaka, November 5, 2013.

35 Author interview with a MOFA official, November 27, 2013.

36 Some interviewees mentioned Koizumi's "change of mind" before summer 2004. He became more enthusiastic about the idea of pursuit of a permanent membership through G4. Two interviewees talked of Koizumi's "*baransu kankaku*" ["sense of balance"] in their personal accounts.

37 U.S. Ambassador Shirin Tahir-Kheli, Senior Advisor to the Secretary of State for UN Reform, On UN Reform, United Nations General Assembly, July 12, 2005, http://www.globalpolicy.org/component/content/article/200-reform/41376.html.

38 Interview with an anonymous MOFA staff, November 27, 2013. Ultimately, ratification by the U.S. Senate was critical if the government aimed to support the expansion of the Security Council and the resolution was adopted at the General Assembly. In the mid-2000s, MOFA viewed such a ratification process in the Senate as extremely difficult given the strong skepticism among conservative U.S. Senators against the United Nations, due to the difficulty that the United States had experienced in legitimizing its invasion of Iraq in 2003.

39 "Treaty of Mutual Cooperation and Security Between Japan and the United States of America," http://www.mofa.go.jp/region/n-america/us/q&a/ref/1.html.

40 Author interview with Takeuchi Yukio, October 25, 2013.

41 Ibid.

42 Ibid. Takeuchi was told by his counterparts in the U.S. Department of State that Japan-U.S. strategic dialogue on August 27, 2002, was the turning point of the United States getting back to the UN for seeking an endorsement by the Security Council.

43 Interview with Machimura.

44 Interviews with former MOFA officials.

45 Mr. Y, *A National Strategic Narrative* (Woodrow Wilson Center, 2011).

46 Michael J. Green, *Japan's Reluctant Realism: Foreign Policy Challenges in an Era of Uncertain Power* (London: Palgrave Macmillan, 2001).

15 The stakeholder state

Ideology and values in Japan's search for a post–Cold War global role

G. John Ikenberry[1]

Introduction

In the modern era, Japan has been a country in search of a vision of itself and its role in global affairs. It rose up in the twentieth century to become one of the world's great powers, yet struggled to find its voice in that position. In this search, Japan has periodically reinvented itself. In the late nineteenth century, the country shed its old political traditions and acquired the trappings of a modern state: it was to be a peer of the European great powers. In the decades spanning the turn of the century, Japan turned itself into a military great power and pursued empire: it fought wars with China and Russia, invaded neighboring countries, and built an imperial order across East Asia. After World War II, Japan reinvented itself again as a "civilian" great power: democratic, internationalist, and tied to the United States. In this most recent phase Japan emerged on the global stage as a "stakeholder" state, working within a regional and world system whose terms were largely set by the United States and the other Western powers.

As the Cold War ended, Japan was riding high within this liberal global system. Japan had transformed itself into a vanguard industrial economy. It had joined the major global institutions. Together with Western Europe and the United States it became a "trilateral" partner in providing leadership and managing the democratic capitalist world. It enjoyed the prestige of a well-respected great power. But in the last decade, that is to say the first decade of the twenty-first century, this success and status appear to have waned. China has passed Japan in economic size and Japan's influence on the global stage has weakened relative to its capacities and earlier decades of prominence.

What led Japan to make these strategic choices in the post–World War II era? And what are the ideas and values around which Japan has shaped its regional and global identity? As Japan's position in the regional and global system has shifted in the post–Cold War era, what ideas and values has Japan embraced as it adapted to changes at home and abroad? How successful has Japan been in its struggle to define itself and its global role? Did Japan have a "lost decade" in its efforts to define its postwar great power role and identity? Were there opportunities that Japan missed to renew or redefine its postwar "great power" identity and global role?

My argument is that Japan has pursued a quite consistent and mostly successful grand strategy over the decades. In this regard my conclusion might coincide with part of Michael J. Green and Igata Akira's research, in Chapter 9, that Japan was able to gain knowledge and learn from its foreign policy mistakes over the last decades. Japan fashioned itself as a "stakeholder" state in the postwar global system. It pursued a grand strategy that was built around a "civilian" conception of itself as a great power and "liberal internationalist" ideas about world order. Japan's political identity, indeed its constitutional system, have been profoundly linked – even fused – to the U.S.-Japan security alliance and the American global hegemonic order. Over the decades Japan has embedded itself within this global order – and this has had paradoxical effects. It has given Japan a platform upon which to project ideas and authority. It has allowed Japan to be a global player. Yet this order has also meant that Japan is constrained in its foreign policy autonomy and limited in its room to maneuver. Japan has relinquished its geopolitical freedom in return for the benefits that flow from its stakeholder commitments. For the most part this trade-off has been seen in Japan to generate more benefits than costs. But in recent decades, with global power shifts and Japan's own changing economic fortunes, these merits and demerits continue to be debated. Indeed, at various moments since the end of the Cold War, Japan has experimented with new messages and new roles, although it has tended to come back to its long-standing postwar civilian/liberal internationalist identity.

Japan has made tough choices about how to position itself in the regional and global system. It has chosen to travel along a pathway defined by regional power realities and liberal internationalist opportunities. Alternative grand strategies – such as, at the extremes, militarized nationalism or pacifist isolationism – are less attractive or sustainable. Japan has also debated the advantages of pivoting away from the United States toward Asia, positioning itself as a regional leader. But again, the costs and dangers of this alternative strategy – including the fraught problem of managing relations with China within a regional context, as Shiraishi Takashi explains in Chapter 11 – have reduced its appeal. Today, Japan is a core member of the capitalist democratic world. Did it miss an opportunity to reinvent itself during the post–Cold War decades when its fortunes were changing? Can it – or should it – reinvent itself again?

In this paper, I look first at the post–World War II setting of Japanese foreign policy, which is dominated by the Cold War and the American-led liberal international order. I analyze Japan's postwar choices within this order, focusing on the logic and character of stakeholder grand strategy. In the next section, I examine Japan's postwar ascendancy, the debates and choices that shaped Japan's evolving regional and global orientation, and the successes and limitations of this orientation. In the third section, I look at Japan's struggles after the end of the Cold War to update and/or move beyond its stakeholder grand strategy. In the conclusion, I consider Japan's choices today. Alternatives to a stakeholder grand strategy do exist, including a radical move to a more "normal" great power role in East Asia. But there are risks and dangers that come with these alternative grand strategies. These issues are taken up by Shiraishi Takashi in Chapter 11 and Michael J.

Green and Igata Akira in Chapter 9, as well as Sheila Smith in her discussion of Japan's defensive posture connected to Okinawa and the Senkaku Islands dispute in Chapter 12. Looking to the future, Japan should not abandon but rather update and upgrade its stakeholder grand strategy, searching for ways to build, reform, and help lead a twenty-first-century liberal international order.

American hegemony, liberal order, and strategic choices

One of the marvels of twentieth-century world politics is how quickly and thoroughly Japan was integrated into and rose up within the postwar American-led order. The United States and Japan had been deadly enemies locked in a savage war. War began with Japan's surprise attack on Pearl Harbor and ended with the horrific spectacle of American atomic bombs falling on Hiroshima and Nagasaki. Yet by the 1950s, these two countries were cooperating and working to build a regional and global economic and security order. What were the circumstances that allowed this geopolitical reconciliation and collaboration to develop? To ask this question is to inquire into the setting in which Japan has found itself down through the decades, illuminating its grand strategic choices.

The most salient feature of Japan's postwar setting was the United States. The United States brought the war to Japan and ended it with unconditional surrender and occupation. But this was only part of a larger world historical upheaval that gave the United States unprecedented opportunities to shape the postwar order. Europe, which had been the geopolitical center of world power for centuries, was now in ruins. The United States had actually gained in economic and military power as the war went on, and it emerged in a commanding position. It was now truly a global power with its forces spread across the Asian and European theaters. The weakness of the old Western great powers created vacuums of authority with crumbling empires, drawing the United States and the Soviet Union into competition and conflict.

In the shadow of the Cold War, the United States built a sprawling international order, organized around trade openness, alliances, client states, multilateral institutions, and democratic solidarity. American grand strategy was driven by the view that the viability of the United States as a great power depended on a global order that was open, friendly, and stable. The order would need to be open so that the United States would have access to markets and resources in all regions of the world. The arrangement would need to be friendly in that the major states in these various regions would need to be pro-Western – or at least not threatening to dominate these regions as hostile hegemonic powers. Arguably, America's most basic grand strategic goal since World War II has been to prevent Eurasia from being dominated by a hostile hegemonic power. Despite shifts in other costs and benefits, this goal probably remains the ultimate rationale for the maintenance of a United States security commitment to East Asia. The order would also need to be stable so that it could last for the indefinite future. An open, liberal international order served American interests, and the United States had the power and opportunity to build such as order. Even at a moment when the Cold War gathered force the grand strategic interest in building such an order was appreciated. U.S. National Security Council Paper Number 68, issued in 1950 during the presidency of Harry S. Truman, laid out a doctrine of containment – but it also articulated a rationale for building a positive international order. The United States needs, it said, to "build a healthy international community," which "we would probably do even if there was no international threat." The United States needs a "world environment in which the American system can survive and flourish."[2]

This American-led world system embodied a revolution in the relationships between the democratic-capitalist states. It was a vision of international order in which Western Europe, Japan, and the United States would be tied together in new forms of economic, political, and security partnerships. The security of each was to be tied to the security of all. Permanent multilateral institutions were created to manage their growing economic interdependence. The European community was founded and regional institutions were put in place that tied Germany and France together, putting to an end generations of war and insecurity on the continent. The United States stood at the center of this liberal hegemonic order. It provided security and open markets to a "free world" order of partners, clients, and allies. Alliance institutions and an array of formal and informal intergovernmental institutions provided this liberal hegemonic order with mechanisms and channels for consultation and collaboration. As the Cold War threatened the world, a new type of international order – binding together the advanced capitalist-democratic world – took shape.

For Japan, this emerging U.S.-led liberal international order created both opportunities and constraints. It provided opportunities in the sense that it was a postwar order that contained invitations and incentives to rebuild and reintegrate into the advanced industrial world. Japan would not be contained and boxed in. There was geopolitical "space" for it to grow and project influence. It was not a simple balance-of-power order, and so Japan would not need to rely simply on military power to reestablish itself as a great power. The liberal hegemonic order was built on bargains and reciprocal deals enabling Japan to bargain and negotiate at least some of the terms of its relations with the United States. At the same time, the order that the United States sought to build also created constraints on Japan. It would need to operate under an American security umbrella. There would be limits on its ability to pursue an independent foreign policy. It would tie itself to the United States and integrate into the liberal international order. It would support the leadership by the United States of the larger order, and in return, it would gain the benefits that such as order offered those participating within it.

It is in this sense that we can talk about a "stakeholder" grand strategy. It is a strategy in which a secondary or weaker state ties itself to and supports the existing order – in this case, a liberal international order. The U.S.-led liberal order has a complex array of rules, institutions, and grand bargains. It is a political order not unlike domestic political orders in which participating states join and play by the rules. In its idealized form, it is a sort of "political community." To be a member of this political community, a state accepts obligations and commitments. Participating states also expect other participating states to act accordingly as well. A

stakeholder state within such an order agrees to integrate into and operate according to these rules and mutually agreed-upon expectations.[3] It joins, it supports,
and it integrates. In the American postwar liberal international order, this means
that the nation embraces the open and loosely rule-based system of rules and institutions. It allies itself with the United States. It accepts the basic bargains of this
order, namely that the United States will provide security for Japan and, in return,
Japan will support the United States and the wider system that it leads.

As grand strategy, a stakeholder orientation can be contrasted with other strategic postures. The two major alternatives are either a strategy of independence, or
a strategy of resistance and counterbalancing.[4] For postwar Japan an independent
grand strategy would entail building its own self-reliant military capabilities and
refusing alliance ties with other great powers. This strategy would entail "normalizing" itself after occupation and gathering back its legal and political rights
of sovereign independence. The other strategy would be a balancing strategy of
building alliance ties with neighboring East Asian states with the objective of
creating a counterweight to American power. Japan would either lead a coalition
of East Asian states or it would join one led by another great power. As we will
see, Japanese political leaders and strategic thinkers have debated both of these
alternative grand strategic postures in the postwar decades. But each one comes
with its own costs and risks. A grand strategy of a "normal" great power – with
independent military capabilities – would entail financial costs and the risks of
triggering security competition with other neighboring states, not least China and
South Korea. A grand strategy of counterbalance would require willing and able
allies, and East Asia simply has not offered itself these opportunities to Japan.
Nonetheless, these grand strategic alternatives do illuminate the range of strategic
options for Japan as it entered the postwar era.

Japan's postwar ascendancy and stakeholder strategy

The early postwar era was a historical moment when Japan did once again reinvent
itself. Japan had limited options in the immediate aftermath of war, but over the
course of the next sixty years it turned necessity into a virtue. It articulated a grand
strategy of liberal internationalism and strategic partnership with the United States.
Along the way, it fashioned a political identity as a new type of great power – a
civilian great power. Japan would be great again, but in new ways. State power
would be redefined. It would be manifested not in military capabilities but by economic growth and social advancement, in some of the ways described by Andrew
Gordon in Chapter 5, and Peter Drysdale and Shiro Armstrong in Chapter 10. Ultimately, imperialism would give way to liberal internationalism. Leaders articulated a vision of Japan as a stakeholder and good global citizen. Japan championed
antinuclearism, nonproliferation, and the United Nations. The horrific experience
of the two atom bombs dropped on Japanese soil in August 1945 gave this agenda
moral force. Japan's foreign ministry states: "As the only country to have experienced the devastation of nuclear weapons and a responsible non-nuclear-weapon
State, Japan has the moral responsibility to take concrete steps to realize a world

without nuclear weapons."[5] Since the late 1960s, Japan has committed itself to the Three Non-Nuclear Principles of nonpossession, nonproliferation, and nonintroduction into Japanese territory of nuclear weapons. Moreover, the country has been actively engaged beyond its borders in nuclear disarmament and nonproliferation, as well as in conventional arms control and disarmament, primarily through the UN framework. Japan also stipulated that it would trade, advance, and promote enlightened internationalist values. As Yoichi Funabashi observes, "In the postwar era Japan's image as a small, strategically naked and economically fragile island nation gradually changed as it became a respected member of the world community. Japan's inclusion in 1975 as a founding member of the Group of Seven (G-7) leading industrialized nations helped transform the Japanese public's perception of its own country. A decade later Japan's self-image as an economic power was supplanted by the image of Japan as an economic superpower, as Japan suddenly found itself the world's largest creditor nation."[6] All of this would be possible within a security framework organized around an alliance with the United States within the context of a wider American-led global order.

For its part, the United States emerged after 1945 as a global superpower and sought to integrate Japan into its evolving global Cold War order. Efforts during the American occupation to promote democracy and eliminate concentrated financial and industrial conglomerates gave way in the late 1940s to more immediate imperatives of fostering growth and political stability. With the defeat of the Chinese Nationalists and establishment of the Communist-led People's Republic of China in 1949, America's postwar grand strategy in East Asia increasingly was centered on the growth and integration of Japan in the wider non-Communist regional economy. In the 1950s, the United States and Japan also began to forge a security alliance, signing a security treaty in 1951. The Treaty on Mutual Cooperation and Security, signed in 1960, established the United States as Japan's security patron. Japan's Constitution forbade it from maintaining "land, sea, and air forces" and renounced "the threat or use of force as a means of settling international disputes."[7] The treaty also established the legal terms for an ongoing American military presence. During the 1950s and 1960s, the United States also took steps to "pull" Japan's trade and economic ties into the Western world economy. In the mid-1950s, Japan gained membership status in the General Agreement on Tariffs and Trade (GATT). In these various ways, a framework was established for Japan's economic, political, and security ties to the wider world.

Within Japan, debates about the country's role and identity ranged widely from right to left, from the reestablishment of Japan as a "normal" country to pacifist idealism. Out of these debates and political struggles, the so-called Yoshida Doctrine emerged that established the major terms of Japan's roles and relationships for over half a century. The major pillars of the Yoshida Doctrine were threefold. The first pillar was the "Peace Constitution": Japan would constitutionally limit its ability to become a traditional military great power; the Self-Defense Forces would protect the homeland but Japan would not allow the country to project military force and engage in collective security. The second pillar was the U.S.-Japan alliance: Japan would turn the provision for its security over to the United

States. The third pillar was the liberal internationalist agenda: Japan would regain authority and status as a major power through economic growth and the embrace of UN-centered diplomacy and global liberal ideals.

The Yoshida consensus provided the terms for several generations of Japanese leaders to define and redefine Japan's identity and regional and global roles. As Richard Samuels argues, "Yoshida's mainstream successors expelled the ultrana-tionalists, pacified the revisionists, and watched as the pacifists revised their own positions. The Left learned to live with the alliance and the Right with Article 9. Security policy would now aim to enhance autonomy but would center on trade and international cooperation. A new consensus would be achieved around a Japan that would be a 'non-nuclear, lightly armed, economic superpower.'"[8] Michael J. Green characterizes the Yoshida Doctrine as a "strategic settlement," one that was not so much a consensus as a compromise situated in between anticommunists seeking rearmament and pacifists denouncing all use of force.[9]

As Japan's economy and international standing grew, domestic debates about the Yoshida Doctrine periodically emerged. Conservatives sought to revise the Constitution and build independent military capabilities. The Left challenged the alliance, demonstrating in large-scale protests against renewing the alliance treaty in the 1960s and 1970s. Yet these debates about Japan's grand strategy tended to end with a reaffirmation of the Yoshida settlement. As Michael J Green notes, "with each challenge to the Yoshida doctrine . . . the result was always a further institutionalization of Yoshida's view."[10]

Indeed, this Yoshida consensus embodied the ideas for a postwar Japanese grand strategy that has lasted for decades – and it has proved remarkably success-ful. It provided a framework that allowed Japan to emerge as a leading state in the Cold War and post–Cold War global system. The strategy paid dividends to Japan in three areas. First, by tying itself to the United States, Japan was able to become secure without remilitarizing. This in turn made a revived postwar Japan more welcome in East Asia. The alliance had a double effect. It allowed Japan to feel secure without fully rebuilding its military, and it provided an institutionalized guarantee to the region that Japan would not break out and become an autono-mous militarized great power. In effect, the United States played the role for Japan that France played for Germany. As Germany did with France, Japan bound itself to the United States and charted a "civilian" path back to great power status. Indeed, the alliance was even more important to Japan because unlike Germany's situation in Western Europe with NATO and the EC, regional institutions did not exist in East Asia to help bind Japan to its neighbors. China has in quiet ways acknowledged the usefulness of the U.S.-Japan alliance in stabilizing geopoliti-cal rivalry in East Asia.[11] This can be seen as early as the Nixon administration's diplomatic overture to China. Significantly, China did not insist on any modifica-tions of the U.S. alliance with Japan as a precondition for rapprochement. On the contrary, the alliance may well have been seen in China as a check on Japanese military resurgence.

Second, Japan was able to gain authority and standing in the international sys-tem through rapid growth and economic advancement rather than geopolitical mastery in East Asia. This was the core of Japan's new postwar great power identity. The American security guarantee and Japanese postwar economic growth were linked. As Akira Iriye argues, "given America's commitment to the status quo, and to its willingness to use military force to uphold the regional balance of power, countries such as Japan, Taiwan, and South Korea were able to spend much less than they otherwise have done on defense, and so to divert more and more of their resources to economic development and growth."[12] Japan would become a regional and global leader in trade and economic affairs. The rapid economic rebirth and transformation of Japan reinforced the appeal of this identity. Between 1955 and 1975, Japan quintupled the size of its economy. It went from 5 percent of the American GNP in the late 1940s to over 60 percent by the early 1990s, an extraordinary economic ascent. Japan's brand of capitalism provided a model for the advanced industrial world and the smaller Asian Tigers that were also beginning to trade and grow. The countries of East Asia were a flock of "flying geese," and Japan was in the front leading the way. Japan became the first Asian country to join the ranks of the advanced industrial world. It was democratic, capitalist, and increasingly integrated into the top tier of the world system.

Third, based on this new civilian great power identity, Japan began to project its own global agenda. Japan became a major provider of official development assistance (ODA) in Asia and across the wider developing world. It was a central supporter of the United Nations. It was a key voice against the spread of nuclear weapons. It articulated various sorts of ideas about "human security" and "comprehensive security." It was in the vanguard of advanced energy and environmental technology. In effect, Japan found its own voice in the area of international security, emphasizing global solutions and multilateral cooperation.[13] Through its ODA program, Japan has given high priority to global issues such as global warming and other environmental problems, infectious diseases, population, food, energy, natural disasters, terrorism, drugs, and internationally organized crime. In terms of environmental issues, Japan cooperates with other states on global warming and adaptation to the adverse effects of climate change; pollution control through measures on air pollution, water contamination, and waste management; and conservation of the natural environment by means such as the management of nature reserves, conservation and management of forests, measures against desertification, and natural resource management. Japan has provided "support to developing countries by making use of its experience and know-how in overcoming environmental problems and its scientific technology in combating complex environmental problems." In particular, it has supported other countries in disasters such as earthquakes and tsunamis by "utilizing its own experiences, technology and human resources in which it has international comparative advantage."[14]

In all these ways, Japan pioneered its own distinct identity as a civilian great power. It would not be a military power but it would be deeply internationalist. Its authority and role in the regional and global system would be tied less to military capabilities and more to its role as an example of a new type of advanced society. The alliance system and the wider American-led liberal international order provided a platform and multilateral venues for Japan to project its ideas and authority. Along the way, Japan turned itself into the premier stakeholder state. It joined the IMF and World Bank in 1952, the United Nations in 1956, the GATT trade system in 1956, the OECD in 1966, and the so-called G-7 system in 1976. Japan was decidedly not a revisionist state – it was not offering ideas and values that were subversive of the existing global system. It was a supporter, and increasingly it shared various economic burdens of upholding and managing this political-economic order. Japan joined the system, supported America's leadership role within it, and, in return, it gained voice and authority as a close ally and senior partner.

Japan's postwar identity was further burnished by domestic accomplishments. The education system was democratized, even though criticism later followed as Kariya Takehiko explains in Chapter 6. The society became one where the overwhelming majority of its citizens saw themselves as members of the middle class, although that has also been tested during the lost decades as Andrew Gordon shows in Chapter 5. Regardless, political stability prevailed. Hard work became a sort of national motto. Together with its fast-growing economy, these successes allowed Japan to gain international respect and prestige. In the early decades, this was symbolized by Tokyo's hosting of the 1964 Olympic Games – the first Asian country to do so. Japan's cultural identity remains very distinct – and decidedly non-Western. But the long trajectory that Japan has followed is one of upward movement and steady integration into the existing international system. Japan was the first and most successful stakeholder state in the American-led era of global order.

Searching for a post–Cold War strategic vision

The end of the Cold War provided a sort of crescendo for Japan's stakeholder identity – as it did for the wider American-led international order. Japan and Germany were the twin "junior partners" in a democratic capitalist world system that had overcome all the major ideological and geopolitical challengers to it. Yet, beginning in the 1990s, and certainly by the time of the Asian financial crisis in 1997–98, Japan's position in the global system began to become more unsettled.

The leading edge of this new period of challenge and uncertainty was, of course, creeping and chronic slow economic growth – or, in the view of some, outright stagnation. An emblem of this new sense of drift and uncertainty was the cover of the *Economist* in February 2002, which was emblazoned with the words "The Sadness of Japan." The article in question talked about the failure of reform and the growing sense that reform itself was not possible or capable of actually addressing deep and long-term structural problems. The message was that "Japan is in a slow, so far genteel decline."[15] Apart from an anemic economy and stalled reform, Japan also began to grapple with its postwar grand strategy. Japan's position in the global system was intimately tied to its economic accomplishments, but these were now fading into the past. In the meantime, China's economy was now booming and its prominence in the region was also on the rise.

In the background, other longer-term problems had emerged to unsettle Japan's postwar consensus and stakeholder identity. By the mid-1980s, Japan had become a global economic heavyweight, and this raised questions in Japan and within the international community about Japan's global responsibilities. It was drawn into international conflicts and controversies that previously it could avoid. A focus on economic expansion and stakeholder diplomacy became increasingly debated – and even untenable. Funabashi identifies three sources of this growing strategic impasse in the mid-1980s: "First, the scale of the Japanese economy and its overseas penetration caused repercussions that forced Japan to respond politically as well. The voluntary restrictions on automobile exports to the United States throughout the 1980s were one such example. Second, Japan's creditor status compelled it to endorse many international programs with strategic implications: Latin American debt relief, East European recovery, Middle East peacekeeping, and the changing the nature of its economic diplomacy. At the same time, louder criticism of Japan's 'checkbook diplomacy' was also likely to be heard. Finally, Japan increasingly acquired and developed military relevant technology, transforming the nation's strategic significance. Japan's long standing nonmilitary strategy was based on its status as 'have not' in terms of indigenous military resources."[16]

For some observers, Japan's stakeholder identity was increasingly manifest as "free riding." Japan was caught in between two shifting currents. On the one hand, it had become a global economic power and pressures were mounting to "step up to the plate" and more actively involve itself in addressing global challenges, including security challenges. On the other hand, Japan's halcyon days of rapid economic growth were ending, creating worries and uncertainties about its economic and foreign policy capabilities.

As a result, in the years after the end of the Cold War, a contested discourse emerged in Japan over grand strategy. For some, Japan really did not have a grand strategy at all – indeed, it had a "strategy allergy." It was not capable of strategy and diplomacy at the high table of world politics. In the United States as well, to many the vision of Japan as a pioneering civilian great power with an internationalist agenda had faded. Japan was "adrift" and "reactive." Japan's identity as a great power was faint and ambiguous at best. At least in the post–Cold War period, Japan's politicians and diplomats were merely singing along to "karaoke diplomacy" where the tunes and lyrics were written by the United States.[17] Others continued to see strategy and purpose in Japan's foreign policy, describing it variously as "quiet diplomacy," "leading from behind," and "indirect leadership."[18]

The terms of the domestic debate on Japanese grand strategy were altered by the end of the Cold War. On the one hand, the Left in Japan virtually disappeared – and with this there was a decline in the calls articulating a vision of a pacifist and neutral Japan. On the other hand, conservative opinions favoring a more "normal" Japan grew louder. The rise of security challenges from China and North Korea and the relative decline of the United States since the 1990s have served to reinforce and give more prominence to this conservative agenda.[19]

As Richard Samuels argues, there are at least three visions of a more "normal" Japan: globalist, realist, and revisionist. Globalists seek a more normal military capability which would be put at the service of an internationalist agenda, supporting, for example, United Nations peacekeeping operations (PKOs).[20] Realists favor a more capable military but one that remains firmly allied with the United States: Japan and the United States would build a more equal and traditional alliance partnership. These realists recognize the need for Japan to deal with its history problems that Togo Kazuhiko explores in Chapter 13, and to establish stable diplomatic relations with its neighbors. Revisionists also seek to reestablish Japan as a "normal" great power but, as Samuels notes, they are "less apologetic about the past and more willing to pander to those who feel nostalgia for it."[21] All these advocates are eager to see Japan build a more capable military and they see constitutional reform as an essential step in a return to a more traditional grand strategy.[22]

These political figures seeking a "normal" Japan have pursued various policy agendas. They have been leading voices in Japan favoring a permanent seat on the United Nations Security Council. Japan signaled its interest in a seat as early as the 1990s following the Gulf War, and it made a bid again in 2005, which ultimately failed. Akiyama Nobumasa outlines the history behind this episode in Chapter 14. Prime Minister Koizumi Junichiro and later Prime Minister Abe Shinzo have pushed for revision of the Constitution, dispatched troops abroad in areas of active combat operations (Iraq and the Indian Ocean), elevated the defense agency into a ministry, and built up a de facto self-defense military capability.[23]

But the end of the Cold War also prompted others to reaffirm Japan's global orientation as a "civilian" great power. Various Japanese thinkers articulated this view. As Christopher Hughes notes, "the most faithful proponent of the concept of global civilian power has been Funabashi Yoichi. Funabashi acknowledges the need for Japan to support UN PKOs and maintaining the U.S.-Japan Security alliance, but sees the alliance purely as a stop-gap measure to allow Japan to build a post–Cold War UN-centered regional security system." Funabashi adds that "Japan should act as a new type of global civilian great power and that its economic power resources are tailor-made to deal with the post–Cold War, low-intensity security problems of environmental destruction, refugee crises, environmental damage, economic dislocation, and proliferation of weapons of mass destruction."[24] The argument made by Funabashi and others is that the emerging post–Cold War global system was even more suited to a Japanese civilian grand strategy than in the past.

Other Japanese thinkers, such as Soeya Yoshihide, have advanced the idea of Japan as a "middle power." In this view, Japan should see itself as one of a group of middle powers, including, most prominently, Germany, Australia, and Canada. Along with these states, Japan should pursue a liberal internationalist strategy, promoting trade and multilateral cooperation.[25] This is a version of the "stakeholder" grand strategy. Japan would reaffirm its commitment to an open and loosely rule-based international order. It would collaborate with other middle powers to create global public goods. It would seek to bring security conflicts – within Asia and in other regions – into the United Nations and other multilateral forums.

It is in the context of this debate that Japanese leaders have offered visions of Japan's post–Cold War grand strategy and great power identity. The most critical question after the Cold War was the status of the U.S.-Japan alliance. This question was addressed most explicitly in the mid-1990s when President Clinton and Japanese Prime Minister Hashimoto Ryutaro reaffirmed the security alliance and redefined it for the post–Cold War era. The alliance was now to be seen as a public good for the region. The alliance played a key role in maintaining peace and stability and helped dampen security dilemma-driven conflicts that might emerge with shifting regional power. The alliance was also a reflection of values that the United States and Japan shared – freedom, democracy, and human rights. The United States itself reaffirmed its commitment to Japan and to its "deep engagement" in the region.[26] These sorts of American and Japanese post–Cold War affirmations of security partnership and shared values reflect the various and profound ways in which the alliance is seen by both countries as critical to national security and a cornerstone of regional order.

But Japanese leaders have also sought ways to reestablish Japanese authority and influence in the region. The alliance with Washington ties Japan's hands. The search has continued over the last two decades for new ways for Japan to "use its hands" and shape its position in the region and beyond. Three initiatives are emblematic of these efforts – undertaken by Prime Ministers Obuchi Keizo and Koizumi and Foreign Minister Aso Taro. These leaders sought in different ways to offer a new vision of Japan's regional and global role, focusing respectively on domestic reform and societal transformation, East Asian regionalism, and values leadership.

In the late 1990s Prime Minister Obuchi came to office seeking to shape Japan into a nation of "wealth and virtue." He saw a pressing need for Japan to undertake a "third reform" – if the Meiji Restoration and the post–World War II rebuilding project were the earlier society-wide efforts to reshape the socioeconomic foundations of the country. Obuchi died in office and his agenda was never fully realized. But he did articulate an ambitious "Agenda for the Year 2000" that envisaged fairly significant domestic social and economic transformations. Japan would seek to become a more knowledge-based and information-intensive economy. The social security and education systems would be upgraded to allow Japan to enter a new phase of advanced industrial development. Backing these ideas, the prime minister established the so-called Obuchi Commission, whose mandate it was to offer sweeping proposals for the reinvigoration of Japan. The findings did offer ambitious ideas, including making English a mandatory second language and a relaxation of immigration laws. A vision of a very different Japan was embedded in the Commission Report and in the grand rhetoric of the prime minister. Japan would be a more open, pluralistic, high-tech, knowledge-based society, deeply integrated into the global system, positioned at its vanguard.

In the early 2000s, Prime Minister Koizumi came forward with a vision of Japanese leadership organized around the building of an East Asian community. An important moment came in a January 2002 speech that the prime minister delivered in Singapore, proposing the establishment of just such a community. Koizumi said that the building of this community would start with Japan and ASEAN and also include China, South Korea, Australia, and New Zealand. Koizumi was seeking to do several things with this initiative. One was to style Japanese leadership around an agenda for regional cooperation. This was where Japan could establish its independent voice in regional affairs. Another aspect of Koizumi's agenda was almost certainly aimed at China, which was grappling with its own vision of a regional community. Koizumi's inclusion of Australia and New Zealand was also aimed at tying East Asian regionalism to universal values, including economic openness and the rule of law, which would ensure that regionalism in East Asia would be enmeshed within the wider American-led liberal international order.

Koizumi's idea of an East Asian community echoed in various ways the efforts of earlier Japanese leaders to periodically offer a vision of a Japanese-led regional order. The stumbling block was always Japan's relationship with China. As early as the beginning of the 1970s, Japan found itself concerned about a regional alternative or supplement to the bilateral American security relationship. The "Nixon shock" – that is, the dramatic announcement by President Nixon on July 15, 1971, that Henry Kissinger had undertaken a secret mission to Beijing – unsettled American relations with Japan. Soon after that, Japanese leaders began to pursue their own engagement of China. Five months after President Nixon made his historic visit to China, Japanese Prime Minister Tanaka Kakuei also visited China. The Japanese leader offered regrets for wartime atrocities committed against the Chinese and reaffirmed Japanese commitments to peace and friendly relations. This approach to China did give Japan a moment of flexibility to think about alternative strategic visions. But it was not pursued to its logical conclusion and it was not tied to an explicit agenda for regional cooperation. Japanese ideas about Asian regionalism came and went. Prime Minister Ohira Masayoshi, who held office from 1978 to 1980, offered a proposal for a "Pacific Basin Concept" focused on regional economic cooperation. As Akira Iriye notes, "the idea was significant because it went beyond the framework of the bilateral security alliance with the United States as the key to the country's foreign affairs."[27] Japan had become the leading regional economic power and had begun to extend development assistance to countries in Southeast Asia as well as China. Regional trade was expanding, so again the conditions for Japanese regional leadership were growing. Somewhat earlier, Prime Minister Fukuda Takeo visited Southeast Asia and articulated the so-called Fukuda Doctrine, which called for "heart-to-heart diplomacy" across the region so as to overcome psychological, cultural, and intellectual barriers to cooperation. Japan was beginning to dazzle the world with its economic performance. China was still in the early stages of reform, looking to Japan and the other East Asia "tigers" as models of the developmental state. This was Japan's best moment for pivoting to an Asian regionalism strategy. But again, Japanese leaders did not take systematic steps to turn these ideas into the centerpiece of its grand strategy. The rapprochement with China never fully crystallized – and alternatives to the security alliance with the United States were more speculative than real. This inability to translate desire into action is also demonstrated in the foreign trade investment arenas as well, described by Drysdale and Armstrong in Chapter 10.

Finally, in 2006, Foreign Minister Aso put forward the vision of an "Arc of Freedom and Prosperity" in East Asia. This was an explicit effort at establishing "values diplomacy" for Japan. Aso admitted, "[W]hen it comes to freedom or democracy, or human rights or the rule of law, there is not a single country on the planet that can claim perfection."[28] Nonetheless, he argued, Japan "deserves to be considered as one of the true veteran players out there on the field." Aso said that Japan should no longer hesitate to state its values or seek to build close ties in the region with other democracies. In effect, Japan was being urged to step forward with a more explicit and activist set of values for its foreign policy. After all, democracy and the rule of law had spread across Asia in the last half-century, with many countries in Northeast and Southeast Asia making political transitions in this direction. The idea was for Japan to be the regional champion – and therefore leader – within this expanding values community. Obviously, this sort of diplomacy had invidious implications for China. A "values" foreign policy would elevate Japan's position in the region, allowing Japan to position itself on the moral high ground even if its economy was losing out to China.

Each of these efforts to articulate a new or updated vision of Japan within the wider regional and global order fell short. The Obuchi vision never really came to fruition. Koizumi's vision of Japan as the leader of an emerging regional community also never gained much traction. The region has taken steps to build new institutions, including the Asian Summit. But Japan is not at the center of these undertakings. The values diplomacy of Aso was criticized by various countries, most obviously China, that saw it as a crude effort to isolate China from the rest of the region. At each turn, Japan has tended to retreat back to its longer-term postwar strategy as an alliance partner and stakeholder state.

The reasons for the failure of these efforts illuminate Japan's central grand strategic dilemma. The Obuchi Commission initiative offered a vision of far-reaching domestic reform: Japan would become a truly open and thoroughly liberal society. It proposed a fairly radical recasting of Japan's social and cultural traditions. Much like past Japanese efforts to reinvent Japan, the goal was to become more like the West to gain more independence from the West, in this case the United States. But the agenda failed in the face of weak political leadership and entrenched social and cultural institutions. The Koizumi initiative for building Japanese leadership around an agenda of regional integration and community building also fell short of its promise. In part, this was because Japan itself is no longer the leading great power in East Asia. Its relative position has been declining in the face of a rising China. This imbalance makes a bid for regional leadership more difficult. But this is the dilemma. If Japan were to acquire more power – that is, if it were to become a more normal great power – it would risk backlash from its neighbors. The Aso efforts at "values diplomacy" was perhaps more promising. It offered Japan a way to assert leadership in promoting widely shared principles and norms of political life. The initiative did not so much fail as it simply was not sustained or integrated into a wider Japanese grand strategic vision. And, indeed, this is precisely Japan's ongoing strategic challenge.

Stepping back, Japan has not had a "lost decade" in foreign policy. But it has found itself in a grand strategic debate over the last two decades that has not yet yielded a clear and coherent vision. The choice before Japan seems to be between two rival visions. One is the realist vision of Japan slowly becoming a "normal" great power. In the view of some, the problem with Japan is that it has not recognized and acted upon this choice soon or fast enough. Japan's reluctant realism needs to be turned into exuberant realism. It needs to tackle head-on constitutional reform and the normalization of itself as a militarily capable great power. In the view of advocates, this grand strategy will address multiple challenges. It will allow Japan to respond to shifting power relations in Asia, generated by the rise of China. It will also allow Japan to become less dependent on the United States, creating opportunities for a more independent foreign policy. Japan does not need to renounce its alliance with the United States to gain these dividends from a more normal grand strategic identity and role.

The other vision is a liberal internationalist vision where Japan continues to articulate a special role for itself in world politics. It embraces its stakeholder identity. It remains a civilian great power – or, at least, it updates and builds upon its civilian great power legacy as it moves into the future. In this view, the problem with Japan is that it has only weakly and episodically expressed a clear liberal internationalist vision. In the 1990s and onward, Japan missed opportunities to speak loudly and with conviction about its civilian great power agenda. This agenda might include, for example, stronger leadership within the United Nations, including ideas for reform of the Security Council. It might suggest getting more involved in the G-20 and enunciating ideas about global governance challenges more generally. It might involve an agenda for East Asian regional cooperation, including financial and monetary relations. Japan had some ideas in the wake of the 1997–98 Asian financial crisis, but it failed to move forward with them after it was rebuffed by the United States. It might involve tackling head-on the "history issues" dealt with by Togo Kazuhiko in Chapter 13 that have weakened Japan's position in the region for more than half a century. Finally, it might involve outlining an ambitious agenda for regional arms control and disarmament. Japan has embodied many of the ideas and principles that inform these various proposals. If Japan sought to renew and redouble its commitment to a civilian great power role, it would need to equip itself with ideas and proposals of this sort.

Conclusion: Pathways, opportunities, constraints

Japan's postwar grand strategy has been shaped by both constraints and opportunities. Japan has labored under the heavy burden of history. The idea of reestablishing itself as a normal great power has some appeal for nationalist-oriented Japanese, but it comes with massive costs and dangers. The idea of Japan as a sort of Switzerland of Asia – a pacific, nonallied, neutral country – has also had its appeal for some world-weary Japanese. The actual course chosen by Japan has been a middle-ground grand strategy, organized around the Peace Constitution, alliance with the United States, and liberal internationalism. Japan turned itself into a civilian great power and managed a stakeholder identity for itself. It is a grand strategy that began as a necessity but was turned into a virtue.

Japan has had two types of grand strategy debates. One type might be called "existential" debates. These are debates where Japanese leaders and political parties open up the big questions about Japan's national security and alliance position. They are debates about the radical repositioning of Japan – revising the Constitution, overturning Article 9, normalizing the country, building a full-scale military, acquiring atomic weapons, ending the alliance, and so forth. The question of the alliance has tended to be at the heart of these debates because this is where Japan abdicated so much of its autonomy. The rise of China may make the U.S.-Japan alliance more valuable and worth keeping, but uncertainties about America's staying power in Asia makes it more problematic. Japan's contentious relations with China make the vision of an autonomous Japan positioned between Washington and Beijing seem quite fanciful. Growing nationalism keeps these existential debates alive – and indeed domestic politics in Japan may be increasingly friendly to these ideas – but the costs and risks of normalization and security autonomy are very real and not going away.

The deeply embedded problem for these nationalist and normalization visions is the failure of Japan to put the history issues to rest. It is very difficult to see Japan as an autonomous great power with traditional military capabilities – that is, a Japan with an independent power base in East Asia – without a resolution of the historical grievances and antagonisms from the imperial and World War II era. Looking back, the lost opportunity to settle the history issues might have been in the early 1990s when Japan was at the high tide of its economic growth and international prestige. China was still then in a weaker position. Somehow, Japanese leaders might have found a way to settle these issues, doing so from a position of strength. Today, growing nationalism in Japan interacts with worries about Japanese geopolitical decline to make gestures of historical reconciliation very difficult.

The other kind of grand strategy debate in Japan is about incremental shifts in ideology and diplomatic agendas. Here the question is: How can Japan increase its stature and influence on the regional and global stage? This is not a debate about whether to break out of the postwar framework of the alliance with America. It is about how to use the existing platform of alliance and governance institutions to project new ideas and influence. No doubt, there are ways that Japan can step forward to provide new ideas and leadership.

One place that Japan might take inspiration is South Korea. South Korea has found ways to elevate its influence in the global system through its vision of Global Korea. Under the past presidency of Lee Myung-bak, Korea ushered forward a wide variety of initiatives to support and underwrite global governance. Seoul hosted the G-20 Leaders Summit in 2010 and the Nuclear Security Summit in 2012. It has built bridges with the developing world, pushing forward programs for sustainable development and clean energy. South Korea is stepping forward on the global stage as a rising stakeholder state. This is, of course, precisely what Japan did in the past – and it continues to be Japan's best strategic option. The central problem with the major alternative to this strategy – the vision of a "normal" Japan with a major military buildup – is that it risks triggering a regional backlash. Doing so invites a regional arms race and the exacerbation of regional antipathy emerging from unresolved historical memory controversies.

Prime Minister Abe hinted at a renewed Japanese effort at stakeholder diplomacy in the major speech that he gave during his February 2013 visit to Washington. Abe said that Japan's foreign policy mission must be built around three tasks. The first is to remain "a leading promoter of rules." By rules, he meant rules "for trade, investment, intellectual properties, labor, environment, and the like." The second task was for Japan to continue to be a "guardian of global commons, like maritime commons, open enough to benefit everyone." And the third task was for Japan to work even more closely with the "U.S., Korea, Australia and other like-minded democracies throughout the region."[29] These three tasks are at the core of the liberal internationalist agenda. By wrapping up Japan's identity and role as a regional and global leader in these liberal internationalist tasks, Abe is arguing – as past Japanese leaders have repeatedly done – that Japan's best path forward is as a stakeholder state.

Notes

1 I thank Adam Liff and Darren Lim for helpful comments on this paper.
2 NSC-68 as published in Ernest May, ed., *American Cold War Strategy: Interpreting NSC-68* (New York: St. Martin's Press, 1993), p. 40.
3 This is what Robert Zoellick was referring to when he used the term "responsible stakeholder" to describe a vision of Chinese integration and supportive participation in the existing international system. See Robert Zoellick, "Whither China: From Membership to Responsibility?" Remarks, National Committee on the United States and China, New York City, September 21, 2005.
4 For surveys of grand strategies that range from balancing to bandwagoning, see Randall Schweller, "Bandwagoning for Profit: Bringing the Revisionist State Back In," *International Security* 19, no. 1 (Summer 1994), pp. 72–107.
5 "Japan's Contribution to International Peace and Security," http://www.mofa.go.jp/policy/un/sc/contribution.html.
6 Funabashi, Yoichi, "Japan and the New World Order," *Foreign Affairs* (Winter 1991/92), p. 61.
7 Article 9 of the Constitution enshrines this restriction. "Aspiring sincerely to an international peace based on justice and order, the Japanese people forever renounce war as a sovereign right of the nation and the threat or use of force as a means of settling disputes. In order to accomplish the aim of the preceding paragraph, land, sea, and air forces, as well as other war potential, will never be maintained. The right of belligerency of the state will not be recognized."
8 Richard J. Samuels, *Securing Japan: Tokyo's Grand Strategy and the Future of East Asia* (Ithaca: Cornell University Press, 2007), p. 35.
9 Michael J. Green, *Japan's Reluctant Realism: Foreign Policy Challenges in an Era of Uncertain Power* (New York: Palgrave Macmillan, 2001), p. 11.
10 Ibid., p. 13.
11 Thomas J. Christensen, "China, the U.S.-Japan Alliance, and the Security Dilemma in East Asia," *International Security* 23, no. 4 (Spring 1999), pp. 49–80.
12 Akira Iriye, *Across the Pacific: An Inner History of American-East Asia Relations.* rev. ed. (Chicago: Imprint Publications, Inc., 1992), p. 336.
13 In the 1960s, Cabinet resolutions gave voice to this civilian great power identity, limiting defense spending to one percent of GNP and establishing the three nonnuclear principles (Japan will not produce, import, or sell nuclear weapons).

14 "Japan's Medium-Term Policy on ODA," http://www.mofa.go.jp/policy/oda/sector/environment/action.html.

15 "The Sadness of Japan," *Economist*, February 14, 2002.

16 Yoichi Funabashi, "Japan and the New World Order," *Foreign Affairs* (2001/2002), pp. 61–62.

17 Takashi Inoguchi and Purnendra Jain, eds., *Japanese Politics: Beyond Karaoke Diplomacy* (New York: St. Martin's Press, 1997). In 1988, Kent Calder depicted Japan as a "reactive state," with a foreign economic policy that was shaped by responses to foreign pressure and not from the strategic calculations of domestic actors. See Kent Calder, "Japanese Foreign Economic Policy Formation: Explaining the Reactive State," *World Politics* 40, no. 4 (1988), pp. 517–41.

18 Akitoshi Miyashita and Yoichiro Sato, eds., *Japanese Foreign Policy in Asia and the Pacific: Domestic Interests, American Pressure, and Regional Integration* (New York: Palgrave Macmillan, 2001).

19 Narushige Michishita and Richard Samuels, "Hugging and Hedging: Japanese Grand Strategy in the Twenty-First Century," in Henry R. Nau and Deepa Ollapally, eds., *Worldviews of Aspiring Powers: Domestic Foreign Policy Debates in China, India, Iran, Japan and Russia* (Oxford: Oxford University Press, 2012), p. 156. For a recent discussion, see Martin Fackler, "Japan Shifts From Pacifism as Anxiety in Region Rises," *New York Times*, April 1, 2013.

20 Ichiro Ozawa, *Blueprint for a New Japan* (Tokyo: Kodansha International, 1994).

21 Samuels, *Securing Japan*, 125.

22 Michael Green sees these various schools of thought favoring a "normal" Japan as a "reluctant realism" with a shared belief that "Japan must take more proactive steps to defend its position in the international society and that these steps can no longer be defined by the U.S.-Japan alliance or by facile assumptions about economic interdependence alone, even as alliance and economics remain at the core of Japan's world role." Green, *Japan's Reluctant Realism*, p. 32.

23 Michishita and Samuels, "Hugging and Hedging," p. 156.

24 Christopher W. Hughes, *Japan's Economic Power and Security: Japan and North Korea* (New York: Routledge, 2002), p. 32.

25 Yoshihide Soeya, "A 'Normal' Middle Power: Interpreting Changes in Japanese Security Policy in the 1990s and After," in Yoshihide Soeya et al., eds., *Japan as a "Normal Country"?: A Country in Search of Its Place in the World* (Toronto: University of Toronto Press, 2011), and Yoshihide Soeya, "U.S. and East Asian Security Under the Obama Presidency: A Japanese Perspective," *Asian Economic Policy Review* 4, no. 4 (2009), pp. 292–307.

26 Joseph Nye, "East Asian Security: The Case for Deep Engagement," *Foreign Affairs* (July/August 1995).

27 Akira Iriye, *Across the Pacific*," p. 372.

28 Taro Aso, "Arc of Freedom and Prosperity: Japan's Expanding Diplomatic Horizons." Speech at the Occasion of the Japan Institute of International Affairs Seminar, November 30, 2006.

29 Shinzo Abe, *Japan is Back*. Policy Speech at the Center for Strategic and International Studies, Washington, DC, February 22, 2013.

Conclusion

Something has been "lost" from our future

Funabashi Yoichi

Five features of Japan's "lost decades"

Japan's "lost decades" have many characterized, but the main factors are the following five features. The first (and perhaps most striking) is the speed of the economic decline witnessed and the dramatic contrast this made with the earlier era of high economic growth and global prowess. Why did this trigger runaway deflation? As in the proverb, "The higher the mountain, the greater the descent," the bubble economy of the 1980s rose to such extreme heights that the subsequent burst was equally astonishing. The value of the loss of stocks and real estate brought about by the bursting of the bubble was 2.9 times larger than the 1989 GDP. This loss was even greater than the drop in asset value after the 1929 Black Thursday stock market crash that led to the Great Depression in America.[1]

Another indication of the decline is the rapidly declining population. If Japan continues with its current population policy and the fertility rate remains in free-fall, it is estimated that by 2050 Japan's population could drop to around 100 million, nullifying the postwar population growth.[2] Japan's postwar growth was largely sustained by an expanding population. Indeed, until 1972 the Japanese government advocated the position that Japan was overpopulated. It is only from 1992 that we start to see this theory being revised, with the use of the word *sho-shika* (decline in the number of children) in the White Paper on National Life-style.[3] However, the policy responses lagged behind the tremendous rapidity of the decline in population.

The contrast between the lost decades and the preceding era is particularly stark in the area of public finance, that is to say Japan's soaring public deficit. A "demographic bonus" greatly supported postwar Japan's economic growth but, conversely, since the 1990s a "demographic onus" has exacerbated Japan's financial plight.

The second feature of Japan's lost decades is its prolonged duration – coupled with remarkable, if not paradoxical, social stability. Opinions differ on the start of Japan's lost decades. Some say it started in 1989, with the end of the Showa era and death of Emperor Hirohito, others say it began with the start of the Heisei era when Emperor Akihito took the throne, while just as many credit the end of the Cold War. Even more theorists point to 1990 when the bubble economy

burst, others 1992, when the economic situation worsened – and some equally
underscore the situation in 1995 as the cause, when the working-age population of
Japan peaked. Regardless, at least two of these lost decades have already passed.
Compared to the ten years of Japan "As Number One," referring to when Ezra
F. Vogel published his seminal work "Japan as Number One" in 1979, the lost
decades were twice as long.[4] Nonetheless, throughout its lost decades Japanese
society has remained stable. As Kuttner, Iwaisako, and Posen state in Chapter 2,
Japan's crisis is most distinctive in that it is "not catastrophic." Analysts point out
that such an experience ought to be keenly noted. Indeed, Japan's preservation
of economic viability and national security, despite more than twenty years of
deflation, is something of a marvel. As was evident from the stoicism shown by
the victims of the March 2011 northeast Japan earthquake and tsunami, Japanese
society is resilient in the face of adversity. Nevertheless, Japan's stability was
financed by its massive public debt and underpinned by passivism and financial conservatism. The system was characterized both by a closed market and by
risk-averse investors and savers. This high level of savings, in some ways, saved
Japan from a deeper disaster. Andrew Gordon points out that one of the aims of
Japan's social security system (specifically its income policy) was to prevent the
elderly from falling into poverty. As Gordon says, "income policies across the
lost decades have ameliorated what would have been a far more dramatic rise in
economic inequality." However, in any case it is also certain that Japan is running
out of time.

The third feature is that the lost decades were in fact an era marked by
reform – or at least attempts at reform. It was a time of considerable political
instability, and with the single exception of the Koizumi administration, governments were short-lived. As Machidori Satoshi underscores: "From the first half
of the 1990s through the early 2000s, reforms in the political system took place
on a scale comparable to those of the Meiji era of modern state building and the
period of postwar reconstruction." Underlying the attempts to reform was the
understanding that politics had to change to match the shifting international and
economic environments, and indeed Japan's own socioeconomic structure. The
lost decades are peculiar not for a deficiency of reforms, but ironically for their
plethora of reforms whose goals never achieved their desired conclusion. Successive governments made numerous attempts to reform – for example, reform of the
Lower House electoral system, other government administration reforms (including a radical overhaul of the prime minister's office and the Cabinet), and political
decentralization. However, many of the reforms were implemented too late and
ended up achieving very little. In Japanese society, where consensus is often the
lowest common denominator, reforms had to be reached through a process of
compromise, and consequently, such efforts never moved beyond halfway measures. Even as reforms were advanced, they were frequently subjected to modifications, which meant that they were watered down and stripped of long-lasting
value. Machidori describes Japan's decision-making process as one of "plural
immobility": excessive expectations toward strong leadership which, however,
ultimately depends on stakeholders with excessive veto power. In this closed

circuit, when reforms appeared to be stymied, leaders simply replaced them with another round of reforms, without attempting to critically review why previous reforms had failed.

As Kariya Takehiko illuminates in Chapter 6, numerous reforms were proposed in support of "relaxed education," a new form of teaching that was supposed to allow children room to grow. However, when this new policy appeared ineffective, teachers' performances were called into question and more reforms were then formulated, including the institution of a system of teaching license renewals and teacher evaluations. The resulting chain of cookie-cutter reforms ended up undermining the morale of teachers and workers in education, weakening their credibility in society.

This pattern suggests that the concept of the lost decades requires an understanding in particular of the reforms that were "lost" at this time. The failure of the Democratic Party of Japan (DPJ) government, whose original aim and purpose following its landmark accession to power in 2009, had been to carry out a complete overhaul of Japan's governance. This change only sharpened the perception that chances to make such reforms were being lost. During this period politics was overwhelming unstable, as was made painfully evident by the succession of short-lived administrations. The nineteen-year period between 1992 and 2011 saw as many as fourteen governments in Japan. The ineffectiveness of governmental institutions at this time parallels that of the fourteen governments between the Manchurian Incident in 1931 and Japan's defeat in 1945 at the end of World War II.

The short-lived governments of the lost decades emerged out of a series of political crises that beset Japan – just as the short-lived governments in the years leading to the Fifteen Years War arose out of the turbulent political times marked by the stifling of party politics, militarism, and an aggressive foreign policy. One of these obstacles was the phenomenon of a divided Diet, where the Lower House and the Upper House are controlled by different political parties. Over the course of the lost decades, it was only during the Koizumi administration that a ruling coalition of parties maintained control over both Houses. This lack of unity during most administrations made it difficult to attain resolutions on Diet matters. (Conversely, the control that the Koizumi administration managed to retain over both Houses added considerably to its effectiveness and to its endurance – it lasted five-and-a-half years.)

When the party in power suffered defeat – in both general and local elections, for example – senior officials were held responsible, with the result that administrations ended prematurely. Another factor behind the short-lived nature of Japanese governments has probably been the depletion of "political lubricants," along with worsening public finances due to low economic growth and the pressure of national debt. Under public financial constraints, all administrations found it difficult to hammer out bold policy measures oriented at fiscal readjustments. Such policies were basically unpopular, which meant a fall in Cabinet approval ratings.

The fourth feature of the lost decades pitted a stagnant Japan against two particularly vibrant and rising neighbors: China and South Korea. The rise of these two nations seems to have caught Japan off-guard, both politically and psychologically. Regional policy cooperation with China faltered and what we saw instead was the rise of diplomatic friction.

China constitutes a huge challenge for Japan and indeed other countries in the twenty-first century. To many Japanese, China's rise cuts a stark contrast to Japan's decline during the lost decades – and at the same time it is one of the causes of the lost decades. In 2007, China replaced the United States as Japan's largest trading partner, and in 2010, Japan lost its position as the second-largest economy in the world to China. This shook Japanese people's perception of the Asian regional order. To many Japanese, "Japan as Number One" in the world sounded too good to be true, but "Japan as Number One in Asia" had been taken for granted for more than a century. During the lost decades however, the concept of "Japan as Number One" was shaken to its core.

For the first time, Japanese shipbuilding, steel, electronics, and mobile phone industries faced intense competition from Chinese and South Korean rivals. The fact that Japan no longer had the edge is evidenced in Interbrand's Best Global Brands Ranking, in the relative positions of Sony and Samsung. When Interbrand began this ranking system in 2000, Sony ranked eighteenth and Samsung forty-third. Just five years later, in 2005, Sony ranked twenty-eighth and Samsung ranked twentieth. The latest rankings from 2013 show a complete turnaround with Samsung as high as eighth, while Sony has dropped to forty-sixth place.[5] Japanese firms in many sectors lost global market shares to their Chinese and South Korean counterparts. In the Japan-South Korea-China trade triangle, Japan "lost" South Korea to China. In 1992, China accounted for a mere 3 percent of South Korea's exports, while Japan accounted for 15 percent, second only to the United States at nearly 24 percent. Compare this to 2010, when China had firmly established itself as South Korea's number one trading partner, accounting for 25 percent of its exports. In the same year both the United States and Japan fell to 10 percent and 6 percent respectively.[6] Notably, South Korea emerged as an "FTA power" after forging many FTA agreements one after another, such as KORUS, EU-South Korea FTA (effectuated in 2011) and U.S.-South Korea FTA (effectuated in 2012), and it is now aiming to conclude the South Korea-China FTA. These series of movements in the first decade of the twenty-first century left Japan behind. FTA contracting countries account for 33.9 percent of South Korea's total trade in comparison with Japan, which stands at a mere 18.6 percent, nearly half that of South Korea.[7]

Nevertheless, initiatives were taken to create a new era for the Japan-China relationship, including the imperial visit to China in 1992, the first time such an event had taken place, and the visit to Japan by President Jiang Zemin in 1998, the first visit to Japan by a Chinese head of state. Prime Minister Obuchi Keizo assembled an advisory panel, the Council on Japan's Goals in the Twenty-First Century, to develop Japan's national goals for the future. This advisory panel presented the prime minister with a vision for Japan-China and Japan-Korea relations beyond mere diplomacy to include deeper regional cooperation. Both the Chinese and Korean governments warmly welcomed this initiative.

During the premiership of Koizumi Junichiro, however, Sino-Japanese relations and Korean-Japanese relations took a sudden turn for the worse. Symbolic of this malaise was Japan's failure to secure a seat as a permanent member of the UN Security Council in the face of China's strident opposition. A diplomat who was at the center of Japan's campaign recalls Japan's "inconsistent diplomacy" at that time, but also noted "while we made many mistakes ourselves, the opposition by China dealt us a mortal blow."[8] Prime Minister Koizumi's visits to the Yasukuni Shrine presented China with a decisive pretext to block Japan's accession to permanent membership on the UN Security Council. Following the 2010 and 2012 clashes between Japan and China over the Senkaku Islands, the idea of coexistence and cooperation between the two countries seems to remain far out of reach.

In a poll taken in 2013, 90 percent of the people in both China and Japan stated that they regarded the other as an "unfriendly nation."[9] Sino-Japanese relations appear to have gone back to square one. In December 2007, Japan ended the ODA it had begun in 1979 under the administration of Prime Minister Ohira Masayoshi in the form of yen loans. Such aid to China had been seen at the time as being in Japan's interest, in the hope that with it "China [would] progress toward a more open, stable society and take on greater responsibilities as a member of the international community." The Japanese government initiated its ODA policy to assure "that international cooperation becomes the heart of China's 'modernization' policies."[10] Japan's total yen loans to China amounted to more than US $28.2 billion (3.1 trillion yen is roughly 28.2 billion dollars at the 2014 exchange rate).[11] This massive aid greatly helped with the construction of much infrastructure in China, but Beijing has consistently avoided publicizing these efforts, with the result that the Chinese people are largely ignorant of the extent of it, as well as its important political significance as a symbol of Japan-China friendship.

From the Japanese perspective, China's attitude toward Japan changed saliently following the Beijing Olympics and the Lehman shock in 2008. In other words, Japan is beginning to question whether Beijing has started viewing its economic mutual interdependence as a sign of Japan's weakness and dependency on China, rather than as a source of bilateral stability. In fact, in the first decade of the twenty-first century, the ratio of Japan's exports to China rapidly grew from around 6 percent to nearly 20 percent, while the ratio of China's exports to Japan sharply dropped from roughly 17 percent to just over 7 percent.[12] When the Senkaku Islands conflict sparked in September 2010, the Chinese government banned rare earth exports to Japan, and during the same flare-up in September 2012, the Chinese government tolerated rioting crowds who attacked Japanese businesses. As demonstrated in these cases related to territorial disputes, China no longer seems hesitant to use its mutual economic interdependence with Japan as a weapon of foreign policy.

From the perspective of Japanese diplomacy, the loss of a stable vision regarding the Japan-China relationship may have been the largest loss of the lost decades.

The fifth feature of the lost decades is the effect that the Showa era (1926–89, the reign of Emperor Hirohito) continues to exert over the people of Japan – even though nearly a quarter of a century has passed since the start of the new Heisei era (Emperor Akihito's reign). The wartime Emperor Hirohito and his long reign, which began long before the war and continued for many decades beyond it, still casts a shadow on Japan. The trauma of the prewar years continues to have an effect on various aspects of society, for example, on demographic policy. During World War II, governmental policies encouraged women to have as many children as possible for the sake of the nation. In contemporary Japan, in sort of a reaction against this wartime policy, a strong antipathy toward government interference in the private lives of citizens remains. This aversion makes it difficult for the government to formulate policy to deal squarely with the issue of Japan's declining population. Distrust toward government on this matter was vividly demonstrated by the public reaction to the Minister of Health, Labor and Welfare, Yanagisawa Hakuo in 2007, when he made an inappropriate statement in an address at a local LDP politician's meeting in Shimane prefecture that "women are birth-giving machines."[13] He was subsequently dismissed from office.

At the same time, however, there is also an abiding nostalgia toward the postwar period, in particular the years associated with Japan's economic miracle. From 2000 to 2005, NHK aired a weekly documentary series titled *Project X: Challengers*, which celebrated the success of people, companies, and products associated with Japan's high-growth period, and focused in particular on exceptionally dedicated salarymen. The 2005 film that grew out of that series, directed by Yamazaki Takashi, *Always – Sunset on Third Street*, abounds with the can-do spirit of the 1960s and 70s. Prime Minister Abe Shinzo has singled out this movie for praise and has "Liked" it on his Facebook page. Such postwar nostalgia pales in significance when compared with the negative legacy of Japan's past – the weighty historical issues and the fresh memory of Japan's former relations with South Korea and China. The historical issue has been further complicated by China's rise to great power status, South Korea's democratization, and the ensuing heightened nationalism in both countries. Nonetheless, Japan has made various attempts at reconciliation, including the 1995 Prime Minister's Statement by Murayama Tomiichi, and the 1998 Japan-Republic of Korea Joint Declaration under Prime Minister Obuchi Keizo. With these initiatives, Japan formally acknowledged its prewar aggression, apologized, and pledged to learn the lessons of that experience.

The 1995 Prime Minister's Statement constituted a major step forward toward forging a fundamental framework for reconciliation with Japan's Asian neighbors. As Togo Kazuhiko notes in Chapter 13, this initiative aimed at "closure" once and for all of the entire issue of historical memory. However, in a clumsy attempt to assuage the nationalistic furor that it unleashed in Japan, Prime Minister Koizumi then paid several visits to the Yasukuni Shrine – and this resulted in a furious outbreak of anti-Japanese protests in China. All the moves toward reconciliation that had been initiated during the 1990s, including the 1992 visit to China by Emperor Akihito, the mid-1990s establishment of the Asian Women's Fund for the provision of relief and support to Korean "comfort women," as well as the proposal to build an alternative official memorial to the Yasukuni Shrine, ultimately ended in failure. No political closure was reached at all.

Why were the decades lost?

One cause of the lost decades was surely the postponement of issues of primary importance and of loss-cutting policies. Politicians and bureaucratic organizations alike delayed unpopular policies, as well as policies that entailed high political and administrative costs. This "political procrastination" was very pronounced throughout the first ten years of the lost decades due to the weak political leadership and the ostrich-like approach of bureaucrats. At the heart of this inaction was risk aversion.[14] Such delays were most egregious in monetary and fiscal policies: the refusal to deal decisively with the disposal of nonperforming loans (NPL), for example, from 1991 to 1997. In the summer of 1992, Minister of Finance Miyazawa Kiichi attempted to liquidate the NPLs of the housing finance companies (known as *jusen*, the Japanese equivalent of U.S. savings-and-loan associations). The Ministry of Finance (MoF) refused to allow this move because it acted only on its traditional assumption that the partner bank would take full responsibility.

The risk-averse behavior of the bureaucracy and the lack of political leadership lay at the heart of this. In such cases the first instinctive response of the MoF was to "manage the problem without costs to the national treasury." (As an aside, we should note that this is the same reason why the Ministry of Finance did not apply the clause in article number three of the Atomic Energy Damage Compensation Law – an exemption clause in case of a "catastrophic natural disaster" – when the Tokyo Electric Power Company's Fukushima Daiichi nuclear disaster occurred in 2011. Even though severe nuclear plant accidents inevitably turned into a national disaster, the bureaucracy refused to foresee the risk, and Tokyo Electric Power Company accepted unlimited liability.)

However, for nearly five years the government and the Liberal Democratic Party refused to solve the problem through the injection of public funds over fears of a public backlash. At that time, Japanese people were deeply resentful of the political and bureaucratic corruption, particularly in relation to dealings with the agricultural bank, collusion within the financial system (such as commercial banks), and monetary authorities. The serious financial crisis of November 1997 drove the government into a corner and forced it to use public funds, but the timid injection made the situation even worse. In the spring of 1998, concerns over the stability of Japan's financial system escalated once more and in the autumn the Long-Term Credit Bank of Japan went bankrupt. In the end, the scale of public funds injected in the country's coffers jumped from 10 trillion yen to 30 trillion yen (including 20 trillion as government guaranteed), then to 60 trillion yen, and finally to 70 trillion yen in December 1999.[15]

Such delays of "loss-cutting policies" led to the huge expansion of the debt held by financial institutions, which contributed to the 1997 financial crisis. The crisis exacerbated deflation, and reduced consumption, as well as general tax intakes. The first half of Japan's lost decades was the result of a cascade effect of forfeitures due to the tardy attention to NPL disposal. Monetary policy failure brought fiscal policy failures. Such procrastination politics also left a deep imprint on politicians' inability to tackle the demographic problems head-on. Possible remedies included putting a halt to the rise of medical expenses, taking measures to raise Japan's fertility rate, and easing the pressures on women in the labor force. Despite the pressing need for such policies, the government and the LDP shied away from pushing such measures through out of political consideration to elderly voters. As Seike Atsushi shows in Chapter 1, medical reform was another major "lost issue."

Another cause of the lost decades was that policymakers could not seem to hammer out a national strategy that overcame suboptimal solutions in favor of overall national interests. The essence here too is the absence of political leadership. In other words, there was a lack of will and ability to set clear prioritized policies and pursue these goals effectively. The absence of a well-coordinated macroeconomic policy that harmonized monetary and fiscal policies is the clearest example of this. As Kuttner, Iwasaiko, and Posen point out, the Bank of Japan (BoJ) and Ministry of Finance "viewed each other as rivals and threats, rather than as entities that could constructively coordinate policies." The BoJ, which was responsible for price stabilization, was particularly criticized for not fulfilling its obligation. Before becoming the BoJ governor, Kuroda Haruhiko pointed out that throughout the first half of the 1990s monetary easing lagged behind fiscal expansionism, which spurred yen revaluation and in turn "provoked a vicious cycle of disinflation or deflation. This has persisted until today and is the main factor behind persistent deflationary spirals."[16] In 1997, the government decided to raise the consumption tax from 3 percent to 5 percent. However, this had the effect of cooling domestic demand, which added to the decreased demand due to the Asian economic crisis. The monetary policy of the government in fact stumbled three times: it stumbled on "overkill" in the early 1990s; on arguments in favor of "good deflation," which caused yen appreciation in the second half of the 1990s; and on the rushed termination of zero-interest rates.

Kuttner, Iwasaiko, and Posen criticize the MoF's overestimation of the recovery of internal demand and its bad decision to hike the consumption tax in 1997. They posit that the Ministry should have at least waited for one additional year. Clearly, politicians, who should primarily aim at optimal solutions, bear a great deal of the responsibility regarding absences of cooperative consistency in their monetary and fiscal policy for their utter negligence. The Ministry of Finance and Bank of Japan were able to take these decisions because they were not held accountable by politicians to the Japanese public.

An example of the gap between suboptimal and optimal solutions could be seen in Japanese firms' cost-cutting policies, characterized by an increase of nonregular employees and the progressive commodification of the young and female labor force. As Andrew Gordon points out, this institutionalized a new inequality. Large numbers of young people were forced to become nonregular workers, joining female workers who had always overwhelmingly participated in the work force as nonregular workers and became further bound to this secondary role. From the short-term perspective of individual corporations, adjusting to the sluggish growth and the rapid progress of IT and globalization through expanding nonregular employment was a rational response. However, from the long-term perspective of national strength it represented a major forfeit and "lost opportunity" as it deprived the youth of job training, career paths, and a desire to take risks.

Another factor in the lost decades was the albatross of vested interests. This tendency for insider groups and cozy collusions to form, which cling to the status quo, resist change, and seek to preserve their rent-seeking activities, is exemplified by excessive profits. In Chapter 3, Kobayashi Keiichiro qualifies these as, "negative externalities . . . stemming from 'insider decision making.'" Whether these groups were agricultural cooperatives (as in the savings-and-loan problem) or the medical establishment, they consistently stood in the way of structural reform and/ or market liberalization and affected other sectors with similar negative economic externalities. Consequently, technological and business innovations were slow to take root.

The fact that a culture of such insiders could exist is, in small part, due to the sense of exceptionalism that pervades many institutions in Japan. Such exceptionalism is sometimes dubbed the "Galapagos syndrome" and involves the view that developments that take place in Japan are somehow special, unique, and should be judged accordingly. The concept of the Galapagos syndrome was originally used as a metaphor to explain how the Japanese mobile phone industry developed, becoming highly specialized only to fail later. The view that Japan is particularly unique and different from the rest of the world, and has its own unique value system, tends to lead to a resistance to globalization and the need to meet any global standards. It is a negative and wholly inward-looking stance.

Companies that were affected by the Galapagos syndrome were able, with the superior technical skills of which they were so proud, to develop sophisticated, highly specialized products that were, however, only suitable to Japan's domestic market; they had no interest in attracting overseas markets. This blind spot exists because Japanese firms are reluctant to venture into coalition building with strategic alliances, a common practice among foreign firms. This is also closely tied to the problem of Japan losing its innovativeness of the 1970s and 1980s. As one of Japan's leading global business leaders, the Chairman of Takeda Pharmaceuticals and Chairman of the Japan Association of Corporate Executives, Hasegawa Yasuchika, states that in Japan "We continue to excel at developing and manufacturing the parts that go into machines and devices, but we miss the larger opportunities that developing new product concepts would bring. In other words, we are too focused on partial optimization and therefore miss out on radical innovation."[17] Japanese companies have holed themselves up and have gone from "Made in Japan" to "Made inside Japan." The combination of this Galapagos syndrome and vested interests gives rise to the "village" mentality that remains impervious to change and the outside world, detailed by Kitazawa Koichi in Chapter 7 on Japan's nuclear industry and the Fukushima power plant accident. These issues formed part of the reasons behind the development of the prevalent myth of absolute safety.

A further factor in the lost decades was that both the government and the private sector fell prey to Japan's "success" in the past. Japanese companies clung to business practices that had been developed during the era of high growth, in seeming disregard of the new environment which was characterized by globalization, new information technologies, and the challenge posed by rising economies in other countries. It is a mistake to think that the practices of the so-called Japanese management system were somehow traditionally Japanese. Such practices had in fact been developed relatively recently during the postwar period. As Toyama Kazuhiko discusses in Chapter 4, the Japanese management system was simply a rationalistic system based on the mechanism of Japanese companies, which were very functional under the particular environment of the high-growth period.

At the end of the era of high growth, this system was outdated and Japan needed to ditch it. But nostalgia for the previous "successful experience" meant that Japanese companies latched onto their conventional systems – with the result that opportunities for innovation and thus continued growth were lost. This phenomenon was particularly true of the electric appliance industry. Sony, for example, had acquired a solid standing and market share in the music and music player business: it strongly opposed the digitization of music because it feared this would have adverse effects on the company's record sales. Apple's former CEO Steve Jobs said that Sony became immobilized due to fear of the "cannibalism phenomenon." He argued that "if you don't cannibalize yourself, someone else will."[18] In fact, however, Ibuka Masaru, the cofounder of Sony, would often tell in-house engineers to "make Sony's hit products obsolete!" in the fear that otherwise they would just sit back on their laurels, content with the status quo.[19] It is possible that we should understand this phenomenon as arising out of the difference between the particular kind of catch-up capitalism that Japan adopted and American entrepreneurial capitalism.[20] Connected to this, we need to point out that the deeper structuring of deflation dampened risk-taking entrepreneurship. Deflation weakened corporate appetites for investment, as well as the offering of risk money in financial markets. It impeded income redistribution, which would have developed with inflation and shrank growth and employment in the service sector. Most importantly, however, it fostered a timid, pessimistic attitude.

Another factor was that even though there was widespread pessimism, evident already in surveys taken in the early 2000s, neither private citizens nor government officials truly grasped the depth or scale of the impending crisis. We might say that the period was characterized by a "pessimism that had no sense of crisis." In December 2002, a Pew Research Center global public opinion survey showed that 27 percent of Japanese respondents thought that "the prospects for the next five years were bleak" (which was considerably more than the respondents of South Korean and Chinese respondents, of whom only 9 percent and 8 percent had this view).[21] Nevertheless, 43 percent of Japanese respondents considered that "there was nothing in particular to worry them." This last figure was considerably higher than most other countries. In other words, quite a few people were pessimistic, but the general state of affairs in Japan was considered to be satisfactory.[22]

This divided mindset only contributed to Japan's gradual and gentle decline. At the same time, this period also saw the growth of a rather emotional skepticism toward growth and toward "GDP-ism." There were serious arguments questioning the validity of raising the GDP in view of the implications of global warming, for example. Nevertheless, such arguments did not give rise to any serious consideration of the effects of a "growth-less age" on intragenerational fairness, pensions, public debt, or democracy. And of course there was scant analysis of the political factors that stifled growth.

Japan's responses to the problem of its demography were typical of its "sense-of-crisis-less pessimism." First, Japan experienced the 1.57 shock of 1990, after which the fertility rate continued to drop throughout the following decade. Yet, despite the fact that everyone voiced concern over the declining birthrate and the shrinking working-age population, a sense of crisis never characterized public debates. In the early 1990s, a private think tank projected that the number of births for the year 2000 would drop to 1.1 million, but the Ministry of Health, Labor and Welfare continued to predict that the future birthrate would recover.[23] In 2002, the Minister of Health, Labor and Welfare, Sakaguchi Chikara, went on record as saying that "if fertility rates keep declining, the Japanese people will go extinct," but no strong government stance was adopted in support of this warning.[24] As a senior official from the Ministry later pointed out: "Over this period, Japanese policymakers treated the demographic problem as a parenting problem. Even if they raised the issue, there were no prospects for a solution, and so politicians shunned the issue altogether."[25]

Throughout the lost decades, never once did the demographic problem become an electoral issue. Experts on demographics reiterated the statistics and possible scenarios that would result from any further population decline. Yet, no major policy debate on the population problem developed. Nor has there ever been an open and frank discussion on immigration. The lack of a sense of crisis paralleled the overall absence of public discussion and public debate.

During the lost decades, Japan searched for the source of the malaise and tried to make adjustments. However, for the most part these were for suboptimal solutions aimed at particular problems – with no integration at all into an overarching optimal solution. The huge discrepancy between such suboptimal and overall optimal solutions is perhaps the most disturbing of all the factors mentioned so far. This absence arose due to lackluster political leadership and Japan's consequent inability to consolidate a new vision to succeed the previous one, which had dominated the years after the war and the Cold War – whose chief aim had been "catching up with and surpassing the West." The gap between suboptimal and overall optimal solutions was most clear in the time frames of policies pursued. Pursuit of suboptimal solutions focused on the "immediate" problem with scant attention given to future-oriented overall optimal solutions.

The question of paying off public debt – which will fall unfairly and extremely heavily on the younger generations – to cover pensions, medical care and nursing, and other expenses of the elderly, remains an issue of great importance. Moral values that were once taken for granted in Japan, such as consideration of others before oneself, and an appreciation of the value of "delayed gratification," have clearly been lost in the lost decades.

Beyond the lost decades, and beyond Japan

Throughout the lost decades, calls for "a third opening of Japan" were continuously launched. Ozawa Ichiro, Hosokawa Morihiro, Obuchi Keizo, Hatoyama Yukio, Kan Naoto – all of these prime ministers called for a "third opening." Political leaders loudly argued that it was time once again to "open up" the country to the wider world, following the examples of the Meiji Restoration and the postwar years, and to rebuild Japan in line with the new era. The basic idea underlying such calls was to "end Japan's catch-up with the West."[26] According to Kariya Takehiko, this belief was the zeitgeist that took hold as new educational ideals arose in the 1980s, when the Japanese economy reached its apex. At the same time, such concepts also concealed and implied a strong sense of Japanese exceptionalism.

However, arguments for ending Japan's catch-up with the West were ineffective prescriptions for the new problems that had emerged – the widening educational gap, for example, which reflected expanding household income inequality, and indeed the decline in educational quality. These solutions were also ineffective for the new challenges posed by the post–Cold War globalized world that centered mainly on the United States and the European Union and to deal with the rise of China and South Korea, which rode the wave of globalization so successfully. In the lost decades Japan faced issues that were much larger and more entrenched than they had ever been before. It was impossible to deal these issues by resorting to ideas of Japanese particularism or with the help of any shock cures.

Japan has no option but to continue to pursue reforms in the face of the demographic decline, the ageing population, the bottoming economic growth, expanding social security expenses, and the worsening public debt. Reforms are still necessary in a plethora of areas – healthcare and social security, agriculture, local government, education (particularly in high schools and universities), and the Diet.

These years will also most likely be years of rising taxes. There is every likelihood that the public will develop a heightened sensitivity to politics due to the burden of taxes and social security benefits and that they will call all the more vociferously for more reforms. At the same time, the friction between the government and the people will increase. Such conflict may actually be a welcome catalyst for the revitalization of Japan. Ohira Masayoshi, prime minister of Japan in the late 1970s, who sought a "post-catch-up" vision for Japan, once said the following: "People who obediently and submissively follow the government's lead can accomplish very little. It is only the people who are dissatisfied with, and resist the government that will truly experience hardship with the government, and will be able to shape the next era."[27]

Perhaps it is this kind of tension between the government and the people, and indeed within the government itself, that is needed to shape the era that will succeed the lost decades. If this is the case, it is essential that we have a correct understanding of the lessons of the lost decades so that we can work toward forging a better mutual understanding between the government and the people. However, a few issues and dangers need to be noted.

First, the people's distrust of the government has increased significantly during the lost decades. The mounting resentment was especially marked on two occasions: the Kobe earthquake in 1995 and the Fukushima nuclear accident in 2011. In addition, recent tax hikes have added to the public's distrust of politics. The reconstruction of trust between the people and the government is essential.

Next, through the tax hikes and the public's sharpened political awareness, there is a high likelihood that this will give rise to the spread of nationalism and populism. To vent popular political pressure from those dissatisfied with fiscal policies, among others, political parties have started to adopt slogans elevating national prestige – already in the early twenty-first century we have seen a marked escalation in identity and symbol-based politics to appeal to the people's sense of belonging. We can see examples of this with the prime minister's visits to Yasukuni Shrine as well as "values diplomacy," such as the proposed "arc of freedom and prosperity."

It is essential for Japan to break away from the spiral of entrenched growth-less deflation. Deflation fosters self-centeredness, as people become ever more preoccupied with their share of a shrinking economic pie. Such an environment favors populism and the "politics of envy."[28] For all these reasons, measures to guarantee stable employment for younger people and technical training and regular employment of nonregular workers must be quickly improved. Growth needs to be promoted and efforts made for the employment of the younger generation. If Japan fails in this regard, the social stability that was preserved despite everything during the lost decades will eventually crumble into nothing. As economic historian Niall Ferguson has warned, an "economic stationary state" may have "dangerously dynamic political consequences."[29] These results include public debt pressure, a widening economic gap, and prolongation of deflationary spirals, problems shared by many mature Western democracies. In Japan, too, it is impossible to deny that the lost decades may have sown the seeds for politically dangerous forces for all that they have been marked by a risk-adverse, long-term deflation, inward-looking, and socially alienating lifestyle. We have to learn the appropriate lessons from Japan's lost decades, in addition to promoting intergenerational understanding. Slogans like "Take Japan Back!" in fact have little practical use.

As has been noted, the term "lost decades" refers to an era in which many things were lost – but in some cases things that were outdated and needed to be replaced. In the words of Toyama Kazuhiko, in many instances "more should have been lost." During this era, the government preserved companies even though they had lost their competitiveness simply because they wielded political influence. This maintenance of the status quo and protection of vested interests resulted in the preservation of zombie companies, which impeded the entry of new challengers. Aside from web-based businesses, throughout the lost decades there were only a small number of innovative companies in the financial, agricultural, medical, labor, and education sectors. This politically prevented the withdrawal of marginal enterprises, and as a result stagnated industry turnover. Hanging on to things when they are unnecessary can lead to lost opportunities. At the same time, some things should be protected and there are things that should have been more carefully retained.

It is worth noting that Japan consistently ranks high in the annual Country Ratings Poll of the BBC World Service. In the 2011–12 poll, it ranked as the most popular country, and in the 2012–13 poll it was the fourth most popular country. Further, more than 90 percent of respondents in an opinion poll on Japan in six ASEAN countries responded that Japan is a "trustworthy friend."[30]

Clearly, Japan still retains many of its most precious assets – in the image it has in many countries, for example. This should lead us to another important question, which is what Japan did *not* lose during this period of time. Rather than focusing solely on Japan's "losses" we should assess the losses in question and the perceptions and opportunities that surrounded them, as well as what was involved in the losses. Some caution also needs to be exercised regarding the passive nuances that can sometimes inhere in the use of the word "lost." It can sometimes be used in a way that implies that the Japanese are simply victims of a situation, and that the situation is someone else's fault. It is easy, perhaps, to fall prey to the mindset that globalization and China are the "Pandora's box" responsible for Japan's woes. However, that is not the case. Japan is an agent – Japan is responsible for its own losses. The country's delayed adaptation to the international environment and its weaknesses in international competition in terms of industrial bases, workforce, businesses entrepreneurship, and globalization – none of these things were forced on Japan by any external actor. The results have all stemmed from Japan's own domestic situation and are of Japan's own making. Politicians who say simply that they want try to return to an era before the lost decades risk lapsing into the politics of nostalgia. There is a danger of using as models certain schemes and practices that were effective only for no-longer-existing environments, making them shibboleths. It is only when we can view the lost decades as the result of the choices that Japan took, rather than simply in terms of things that malfunctioned or were taken away, that the lost decades will be seen for what they are, and freed from myth.

The ultimate outcome of Japan's lost decades is of immense importance for the entire world – and I do not speak here only of the successes, or failures, of Abe's economic policies. The resolution of Japan's lost decades, and of Japan writ large, carries profound historical implications for the country's role as a force for enduring stability on the global stage, especially in the Asia-Pacific geopolitical context. One worst-case scenario would be if Japan were to default on its sovereign debt, which would then inflict a catastrophic shock on world financial markets. Such an event would bring major destabilization in the global and regional arenas. Even if Japan manages to avoid such a catastrophe, it is clear that any more of the lost decade syndrome will place the world economy and the global geopolitical balance in danger.

If, however, Japan breaks away from its lost decades and stops the cycle repeating itself, it will provide an indispensable point of reference for countries such as those in Western Europe, and even China, that now confront similar challenges. In other words, the lessons of Japan's lost decades are lessons for the whole world to learn. This is especially true in view of Japan's deep and mutual interdependence with other nations and the deeply held basic principles and ideas that it shares with the rest of the world.

Notes

1   Martin Wolf, "Unreformed, But Japan is Back," *Financial Times*, March 7, 2006.
2   National Institute of Population and Social Security Research, *Nihon no shōrai suikei jinkō: 2011–2060. Sankō suikei: 2061–2110* [Population Projections for Japan: 2011–2060. Auxiliary Projections 2061–2110], January 2012, http://www.ipss.go.jp/syoushika/tohkei/newest04/gh2401.pdf.
3   Sato Ryuzaburo, *Nihon no chō shōshika* [The Rapid Decline in the Number of Children], National Institute of Population and Social Security Research, June 2008, pp. 10–24, http://www.ipss.go.jp/syoushika/bunken/data/pdf/18811202.pdf.
4   See Ezra F. Vogel, *Japan as Number One: Lessons for America* (Cambridge, MA: Harvard University Press, 1979).
5   Interbrand, *2013 Best Global Brands Report*, http://www.interbrand.com/best-global-brands/.
6   See Korea, Rep. "Country Profile," export data for the years 1992 and 2010 at *World Bank Data: World Integrated Trade Solution*, http://wits.worldbank.org/.
7   Mizuho Research Institute, *"Kankoku no FTA senryaku: FTA wo sekkyoku suishin dekiru yōin to nihon he no shisa"* ["South Korea's FTA Strategy: The Factors behind Being Able to Actively Promote FTA and the Implications for Japan"], in *Mizuho Sōkenronshū*, Issue 2, 2012, http://www.mizuho-ri.co.jp/publication/research/pdf/argument/mron1210–2.pdf.
8   From the transcript of the author's interview with a former Japanese diplomat (December 27, 2013).
9   The Genron NPO, *The 9th Japan-China Public Opinion Poll* (August 12, 2013), http://www.genron-npo.net/en/issues/archives/4962.html#1.
10 " *'Kindaika no seika kitai' Ohira shushō, kōryū mo kyōchō, pekin de kōen"* ["Anticipating the results of modernization: Prime Minister Ohira also emphasizes bilateral exchange in his speech in Beijing"], *Asahi Shimbun*, December 7, 1979, evening edition.
11 Ministry of Foreign Affairs of Japan, *Overview of Official Development Assistance (ODA) to China*, June 2005, http://www.mofa.go.jp/policy/oda/region/e_asia/china/.
12 See Japan and China "Country Profiles," export data for the years 2000 and 2010 at *World Bank Data: World Integrated Trade Solution*, http://wits.worldbank.org/.
13 *"Josei wa 'Umu kikai, souchi': Matsue shi de Yanagisawa rōshou"* ["Women Are 'Child-Bearing Machines,' States Minister of Health, Labor and Welfare, Yanagisawa, in Matsue City"], *Kyodo News*, January 27, 2007, http://www.47news.jp/CN/200701/CN2007012701000324.html.
14 Zbigniew Brzenzinski, who resided in Japan after the period of the Nixon shock, examined the "indecisiveness in Japanese politics" in his book, *The Fragile Blossom Crisis and Change in Japan*. He describes the "dominant pattern in the Japanese mentality. It has a tendency to sidestep as far as possible any kind of confrontation. This, in turn, leads to the tendency to retain the existing stability with the least amount of modification and sacrifice of a thoroughgoing solution. As a result of this predilection for abrupt change after considerable gestation, Japanese society can be said to be characterized by a kind of metastability, that is to say, a stability that appears to be extremely solid until all of a sudden a highly destabilizing chain reaction is set in motion by an unexpected input." Zbigniew Brzezinski, *The Fragile Blossom: Crisis and Change in Japan* (New York: Harper & Row, 1972), p. 16.
15 Nihon Keizai Shimbun Editorial Committee, *Kenshō baburu: Hani naki ayamachi* [Examining the Bubble: Unintended Mistakes] (Tokyo: Nihon Keizai Shinbun, 2000), pp. 18–20.
16 Haruhiko Kuroda, *Zaisei kinyū seisaku no seikō to shippai: Gekidō suru nihon keizai*, [Success and Failure of Fiscal and Monetary Policy: The Turbulent Japanese Economy] (Tokyo: Nihon Hyōronsha, 2005), pp. 100, 109.

17 Yasuchika Hasegawa, "Toward a Lasting Recovery," in McKinsey and Co., eds., *Reimaging Japan: The Quest for a Future that Works* (San Francisco: VIZ Media, 2011), p. 49.

18 Walter Isaacson, *Steve Jobs* (New York: Simon & Schuster, 2011), p. 408.

19 From the transcript of the author's interview with Morio Minoru (September 26, 2013).

20 Glenn Hubbard and Tim Kane, *Balance the Economics of Great Powers from Ancient Rome to Modern America* (New York: Simon & Schuster, 2013), p. 171. Hubbard and Kane point out that "catch-up capitalism" enabled the likes of Japan, China, and South Korea to come just short of "entrepreneurial capitalism" without being able to surpass it. They conclude that, "The Japan supermodel proved that there is a successful way to develop from any level of poverty up to 80% of the frontier (the level of U.S. GDP per capita)."

21 Pew Research Center, "Global Publics View Their Lives," in *What the World Thinks in 2002*, Pew Global Attitudes Project, December 4, 2002, chap. 1, http://www.pew global.org/2002/12/04/chapter-1-global-publics-view-their-lives/.

22 According to the "National Livelihood Survey," by Japan's Cabinet Office, the "life satisfaction" of Japanese youth in their twenties remained as high as around 70 percent throughout the lost decades. This figure stands out when compared with that of the preceding decades or with other generations. Japanese sociologist, Furuichi Yoshinori, examined this phenomena and concluded that these "happy youth" lead a lifestyle focused on the joys of the "here and now." Nevertheless, 67 percent of the "happy youth" said that they "had concerns over the future." Furuichi Yoshinori, *Zetsubō no kuni no kofuku na wakamono tachi* [The Happy Youth of a Desperate Country] (Tokyo: Kodansha, 2011), pp. 98–102, 110.

23 *Mirai yosoku kenkyūjo* [Future Forecast Institute], *Shussei sū ijō teika no eikyō to taisaku*, [The Unusual Decline in the Number of Births: Consequences and Measures] (Tokyo: Mirai yosoku kenkyūjo, 1990). Masuda Masanobu, "*Naze shōshika taisaku ga kōka wo hakki shinai no ka: niizu ni soku shita sōgōteki na seisaku no tenkai he*" ["Why Measures to Deal with the Decline in the Number of Children Hasn't Been Effective: Towards a Comprehensive Set of Policies That Match the Needs"], in *Meiji Yasuda Institute of Life and Wellness Quarterly* 18, no. 2, pp. 33–34, http://www.myilw.co.jp/life/publication/quartly/pdf/70_02.pdf#search='%E5%8E.

24 "*Shōshika taisaku wo shiji: shushō, kōrōshō ni 9 gatsu medo chūkan hōkoku*" ["Prime Minister Koizumi Calls for the Ministry of Labor, Health and Welfare to Submit a Midterm Report on Countermeasures to the Decline in Birth Rate by September"], *Nikkei Shimbun*, May 21, 2002, evening edition.

25 From the transcript of the author's interview with a senior official from the Ministry of Health, Labor and Welfare, October 7, 2013.

26 After World War II, Ohira Masayoshi understood better than anyone else the limitations of "catching up with the West," and thus attempted to find "a higher purpose." In an article published in January 1970, Ohira stated that "Now entering into the 1970s, Japan is finally about to end its catch-up stage," but "both the policymakers and the people are failing to take hold of new creative values." Hattori Ryūji, *Ohira Masayoshi: Rinen to gaikō* [Ohira Masayoshi: Ideals and Diplomacy] (Iwanami Shoten, 2014), pp. 95–96.

27 "What should be done with the overly latent Japan," Fumio Fukunaga, Ohira Masayoshi: "*Sengo hoshu*" *to ha nanika* [The Thoughts and Behavior of the "Postwar Conservatives"] (Tokyo: Chūō koron shinsha, 2008), p. 276.

28 Benjamin Friedman, *The Moral Consequences of Economic Growth* (New York: Knopf, 2005), p. 182.

29 Niall Ferguson, *The Great Degeneration: How Institutions Decay and Economies Die*, (London: Allen Lane, 2012), p. 20.

30 Japan Ministry of Foreign Affairs, *Opinion Poll on Japan in Six ASEAN Countries*, May 2008, http://www.mofa.go.jp/announce/announce/2008/5/1179528_1010.html.

Index